MOUNTAIN,
CANYON,
and
BACKCOUNTRY
FLYING

MOUNTAIN, CANYON, *and* BACKCOUNTRY FLYING

AMY L. HOOVER *and* R.K. "DICK" WILLIAMS

AVIATION SUPPLIES & ACADEMICS
NEWCASTLE, WASHINGTON

Mountain, Canyon, and Backcountry Flying
by Amy L. Hoover and R.K. "Dick" Williams

Aviation Supplies & Academics, Inc.
7005 132nd Place SE
Newcastle, Washington 98059-3153
asa@asa2fly.com | asa2fly.com

See ASA's website at www.asa2fly.com/reader/mountain for the Reader Resources page containing additional information and updates relating to this book.

ASA-MOUNTAIN
ISBN 978-1-61954-741-4

Printed in the United States of America

2023   2022   2021   2020   2019   9   8   7   6   5   4   3   2

Cover photos: *Front:* Todd Huffman/Pipeline Digital Media, LLC. *Back:* Patrick Williams

Library of Congress Cataloging-in-Publication Data:

Names: Hoover, Amy, author. | Williams, Dick (Richard K.), author.
Title: Mountain, canyon, and backcountry flying / Amy L. Hoover and R.K. "Dick" Williams.
Description: Newcastle, WA : Aviation Supplies & Academics, Inc., [2019] | Includes
    bibliographical references and index.
Identifiers: LCCN 2018059487| ISBN 9781619547414 (trade pbk. : alk. paper) | ISBN 1619547414
    (trade pbk. : alk. paper)
Subjects: LCSH: Mountain flying. | Bush flying. | Airplanes—Piloting.
Classification: LCC TL711.M68 H665 2019 | DDC 629.132/52—dc23
LC record available at https://lccn.loc.gov/2018059487

CONTENTS

Dedication   viii

Foreword   x

Acknowledgments   xii

About the Authors   xiv

Introduction   xvi

SECTION I: Preparation and Planning   **1**

Chapter 1: The Pilot and the Airplane   **3**

Practicing for Mountain, Canyon, and Backcountry Flight   4

The Airplane   11

Preflight and Post-Flight Inspections   22

Accident Scenario   25

Review Questions and Exercises   26

Chapter 2: Mountain and Canyon Meteorology   **29**

Preflight Weather Knowledge   31

Global Circulation and Pressure Patterns   32

Mountain Winds   33

Cloud Types and Weather Systems   36

Fog   37

Haze and Smoke   39

Small-Scale Local Weather Phenomena   40

Accident Scenario   54

Review Questions and Exercises   56

Chapter 3: Flight Planning and Navigation   **59**

VFR Charts   60

Basic Navigation   64

Route Selection   66

Global Positioning System (GPS) Navigation   70

Automatic Dependent Surveillance Radar—Broadcast   74

Dispatching and Flight Following   75

Accident Scenario   78

Review Questions and Exercises   80

SECTION II: Operations   **83**

Chapter 4: En Route   **85**

Altimeter Settings   86

Visual Illusions   86

Crossing Ridges   88

Terrain Flying   90

Flying in Canyons   92

Turning Safely   94

Emergency Turn 102
Low-Level Maneuvering 104
Climbs and Descents 112
Accident Scenario 113
Review Questions and Exercises 116

Chapter 5: Approach and Landing **117**
Before You Go 120
Flying a Stabilized Approach 120
Airport Environment 136
Go-Arounds and Abort Planning 141
The Airstrip 147
Landing with Wind 152
Sloped Airstrips 158
Wind versus Slope 169
Touchdown and Rollout 170
Taxi and Ground Operations 171
Accident Scenario 173
Review Questions and Exercises 176

Chapter 6: Takeoff and Departure **177**
Takeoff 178
Departure 183
Taking Off with Wind 188
Sloped Airstrips 192
Wind versus Slope 197
Accident Scenario 198
Review Questions and Exercises 202

Chapter 7: Cold Weather and Ski Flying **203**
Guest Author Michael Vivion 204
Why Ski Flying? 204
Weather 205
The Ski-Equipped Airplane 207
The Skis 209
Other Equipment 217
Factors Affecting Ski Flying 219
Ski Operations 224
Glacier Flying with Paul Claus 230
Rocky Mountain Ski Flying with Mike Dorris 234
Summary 238
Accident Scenarios 238
Review Questions and Exercises 240

SECTION III: Aircraft and Human Performance   **241**

**Chapter 8: How to Lighten Up: Density Altitude, Loading
    and Aircraft Performance**   **243**
What is Density Altitude?   244
Aircraft Performance   247
Power versus Density Altitude   249
Power Loading and Weight Reduction   250
Takeoff Performance   252
Climb Performance   255
Landing Performance   262
Leaning the Mixture   263
Accident Scenario   265
Review Questions and Exercises   268

**Chapter 9: Risk Management for Mountain
    and Canyon Flight**   **271**
Physiological Effects of Altitude   272
Human Factors   274
Backcountry Flight Safety and Etiquette with
    Jeanne MacPherson   281
Emergencies   284
Precautionary Landings   290
Forced Landings   291
Post-Crash Survival   294
Survival Vest   295
Survival Kits   296
Accident Analysis—Amy Hoover's Story   300
Review Questions and Exercises   324

Appendix A: Axioms, Rules, and Suggestions   **325**

Appendix B: Answers to Review Questions   **331**

Appendix C: Glossary of Terms   **337**

Appendix D: References Cited   **355**

Index   **365**

DEDICATION

This book is dedicated to one of our personal heroes, the late James Larkin. Jim's love for flying started as a young lad in 1927 when he got a ride with a passing barnstormer. He served as a U.S. Army Air Corps pilot during World War II, including time in the Himalayas as a Curtiss C-46 pilot flying "The Hump" over western China and Burma, and ferrying Lockheed P-38 Lightnings and other aircraft to South America and all over the world. After the war, Jim flew the Idaho backcountry for Johnson Flying Service and later formed his own company, Larkin Air. Jim used his Cunningham Hall PT-6F freighter to haul supplies, deliver mail and medical supplies, support backcountry ranches, and launch rescue operations for downed pilots, logging thousands of hours on wheels and skis in all kinds of conditions. He was a Designated Pilot Examiner for the venerable Ford Trimotor.

As an airline transport pilot (ATP) rated in more than two-dozen fixed-wing types as well as helicopters, Jim's 67 years of flight experience made him one of the most experienced backcountry pilots of all time. He flew for the U.S. Forest Service and still holds the all-time longevity record (31 years) as a card-carrying smokejumper pilot. Jim later served as Director of Region 4 of Air Operations for the National Interagency Fire Center in Boise, Idaho. Even after retirement, Jim continued to fly the backcountry and could often be spotted helping carry supplies and people into

James Larkin with his Waco UPF-7. *(Photo courtesy Bev Larkin)*

ranches or giving flight instruction to aspiring mountain pilots. Some of our favorite memories of Jim include his time flying Harrah's Middle Fork Lodge de Havilland Twin Otter with Dick Williams and his time as the premier flight instructor for Amy Hoover's mountain and canyon flying school in McCall, Idaho.

Jim received numerous awards, including 2 Million Miles of Non-Accident Safe Flying; the Wright Brothers Master Pilot Award; FAA Safe Pilot Award; and induction into the Idaho Aviation Hall of Fame. Jim flew until the age of 84, shortly before his passing.

With all his vast experience, Jim could usually be seen attending aviation seminars and workshops, saying there is always more to learn. Our friend Jim was a master storyteller, and memories of his escapades live on through the vast knowledge, experience, and advice he gave about flying and life in general. A generous, humble, and thoughtful man, Jim's attitude and sense of humor have been a source of constant inspiration, as is his memory.

The de Havilland Twin Otter Jim Larkin flew with author Dick Williams. *(Photo by R.K. "Dick" Williams)*

FOREWORD

A confession: I love books. Several thousand of them rest on shelves throughout my home. Being intimately familiar with nearly all of them, I feel as if they are my children. At least that explains why I occasionally point to one and say, "Who's your daddy?" That's why I felt as if I had just adopted the brightest student on campus when I received a copy of Dr. Amy Hoover and R.K. "Dick" Williams's book, *Mountain, Canyon, and Backcountry Flying*.

In my opinion, all pilots should own a copy of this wonderful book, especially if they intend to fly anywhere beyond the borders of Florida. Think about it: If the highest terrain in the state is 345 feet MSL, you don't need to know about mountains, only molehills. Unfortunately, more than a few flatlander pilots have run their ships aground on craggy mountain slopes while unintentionally installing authentic, life-size, pine cone air fresheners in their cockpits. This should be a warning to any pilot who believes that a subscription to *Field & Stream* is sufficient education to set off on a flying adventure into the backcountry. It's not.

The honest truth is that the steepness of the terrain often reveals the shallowness of one's backcountry flying knowledge. While it's who you know that determines your success in business, it's what you know that ensures your safety in the mountains. Safety, however, shouldn't be the only reason to inspire deeper and practical knowledge in this area. The fact is that you won't have that much fun during your backcountry flying adventure unless you know how to behave properly in, near, and around that terrain. Herein lies the great value of *Mountain, Canyon, and Backcountry Flying*.

Packed with more general and specific knowledge than I've seen in most educational books, this volume can rightly be called the babushka doll of practical ideas on backcountry flying: It's like one practical idea reveals another useful tool, tip, and technique. Within these pages, you'll find valuable information on backcountry pre-flighting, flight planning, navigation, terrain-specific meteorology, emergency operations, approaches, landings, departures, and much more. Without a doubt, it will be the recognized source for backcountry operations for years to come.

There were two things, however, that took this book over the top for me. First, I love axioms and rules of thumb. Despite being general in nature, they are concentrated bits of wisdom that help train our intuition and confirm our performance calculations. For example, one of Amy's Axioms (which are sprinkled throughout the book) is: *If the rocks and trees are your enemies, keep them close!* While your untrained intuition might suggest staying as far away from the terrain as possible, certain situations require snuggling up to the side of a mountain or canyon. While it's not possible to mention all the fantastic rules in this book, rest assured you won't be opposed to using these rules of thumb.

Then there is the other feature that allows this volume to pack a punch beyond the weight class of most educational books. I'm speaking of its many educational, entertaining, and sometimes "eyebrow-raising" first-hand stories about backcountry flying. What a wonderful treasure this is for any pilot who wants to identify the physical risks and psychological traps of mountain and canyon operations. Read even a few of Amy's and Dick's sidebar stories—some personal, some about others, some by others—and you'll profit as if you were flying an airplane with a slow-running Hobbs meter. Go? No go? Commit? Abort? Fail to plan properly? Didn't see that coming? These are just a few of the many themes covered by these educational stories.

Pilots with a thirst for practical adventure and a soft spot for the esthetics of mountains and canyons will find immense pleasure in backcountry flying. But— flyer beware! You can do this safely only when the contours of your knowledge match the contours of the terrain. To obtain that knowledge, you need experience, and this is what Dr. Amy Hoover and R.K. "Dick" Williams bring to the table in *Mountain, Canyon, and Backcountry Flying*. Both of them have thousands of hours of flying in backcountry terrain that is so far back, you can almost see it coming around the other side. Feel confident in knowing that by studying this book and adding it to your collection, you'll have the tools to help you fly safer should you venture beyond the flatland.

Rod Machado
San Clemente, California
2018

ACKNOWLEDGMENTS

To plan and write a book can be a precarious and time-consuming venture. 〝〞

Richard H. Holm, Jr. [1]

We would like to thank all the dedicated mountain pilots and flight instructors around the world who are doing their part to improve awareness and promote flight safety in this specialized type of flying.

Nothing is created in a vacuum, and this book would not have been possible without the help, input, insight, and thoughtful contributions from many others.

Several experts contributed to the book through personal interviews and stories. A short introduction is provided here, and more detailed biographical information is located in the section or chapter where each person's primary contributions and stories occur.

- **Paul Claus** is an Alaska native and renowned glacier pilot whose life has been devoted to aviation. He owns the Ultima Thule Lodge (www.ultimathulelodge.com) with his wife and family and has a commercial flying operation with a dozen airplanes that provide access for skiers, climbers, outdoorsmen, as well as rescue operations on glaciers of the Alaska ranges.

- **Mike Dorris** was born and raised in central Idaho. He followed in his father's footsteps flying the backcountry, and he has more than 23,000 hours delivering the U.S. Mail, supporting backcountry ranches, and transporting hunters, rafters, and other users into the Frank Church Wilderness and other areas in the Idaho backcountry. He owns Sawtooth Flying Service (www.sawtoothflyingservice.com).

- **Ron Hanks** served as a U.S. Naval Aviator. He is an ATP with a Ph.D. in Aviation Administration and is retired from the positions of National Aviation Manager for the U.S. Bureau of Land Management in Washington, D.C., and Chief of Aviation Operations for the U.S. Forest Service in Boise, Idaho. He flies fixed-wing aircraft, gliders, and helicopters. Ron is the director of the aviation program at Treasure Valley Community College (www.tvcc.cc/cte) in Ontario, Oregon.

- **Jeanne MacPherson** is a retired Chief of Safety and Education for Montana Department of Transportation Aeronautics Division and a Master CFI who teaches mountain flying and emergency maneuvers training in Helena, Montana. She owns and operates Mountain Air Dance flight school (mountainairdancellc.com).

- **John Reed** has been flying as a commercial pilot for forty years. He has approximately 18,000 hours, half of them flying float planes in Southeast Alaska and the other half on wheels in the Idaho backcountry and Pacific

---

1 Holm, Richard H. Jr. (2012). *Bound for the Backcountry*. McCall, ID: Cold Mountain Press

Northwest. He served as Chief Pilot for several air taxi companies in both locations. His passion will always be safely flying in the mountains and continuing to learn new things with students and fellow aviators.

- **Lenny Skunberg** has owned and operated Lenny's Airmotive, a Certified 14 CFR Part 145 Repair Station in Salmon, Idaho, for 38 years. He is a past recipient of the FAA National Maintenance Technician of the Year Award, and he has extensive experience and expertise maintaining airplanes used for backcountry operations.

- **Michael Stockhill** is retired from many vocations, including test pilot in experimental airplanes, aviation magazine editor, airmail pilot, FAA Inspector, FBO owner, NTSB Investigator, and A&P mechanic with Inspection Authorization. He now flies gliders and splits his time between Montana and Arizona.

- **Michael Vivion** spent more than 30 years flying for the U.S. Fish and Wildlife Service as a wildlife biologist/airplane pilot in Alaska and has extensive experience operating on skis in the Alaska interior. Retired from teaching at a university flight program, Michael travels the country giving seminars on backcountry and short takeoff and landing (STOL) flying.

We also thank the following people for reviewing and critiquing all or parts of the book:

Patricia Bening, MSA, aviation safety officer; Cathy Busha, J.D., aviation law professor; Rebecca Cozad, ATP, airline pilot and Alaska glacier pilot; Andrea Dugan, M.A., retired; Rod Machado, MA, ATP, aviation author, humorist, and guru; Sherry Knight Rossiter, Ph.D., ATP, CFI, helicopter and airplane pilot, college instructor; Rich Stowell, B.S. and MCFI (the "Spin Doctor"), National Flight Instructor of the Year (2006); and USAF call sign "Man Bear," a major airline pilot, glider pilot, Super Cub owner, and F22 instructor pilot.

These individuals contributed photography, concept drawings, and other input for this book:

Josi Barinaga; David Berger, M.D.; kimberly millen brown, artist; Mike Chapman, Flying Brokers (flyingbrokers.com); Grayson Davey, Alaska Paracord (alaskaparacord.com); George Dorris, G&S Aviation (gsaviation.com); Katie Dorris, pilot; Larry Driskell, U.S. Air Force (ret.); Karl Geisler, Ph.D., economics professor; Andrew George, pilot; Bob Hannah, Northwest Backcountry Aircraft (northwestbackcountryaircraft.com); Galen Hanselman, QEI Publishing (flyidaho. com); Richard H. Holm Jr., aviation author; Brian Hoover, engineer; Todd Huffman, Pipeline Digital Media (pdmtv.com); Jim Inkster, pilot; Jim Juza, pilot; George Kounis, Pilot Getaways (pilotgetaways.com); Kasey Lindsay, Northwest Backcountry Aircraft (northwestbackcountryaircraft.com); Christine Mortine, DPE; Graeme Prankerd, Kiwi; Dave Shallow, pilot; Cliff Smart, FAA; Brad Thornberg, pilot; Fred Williams, Adventure Flying (advflying.com); Patrick Williams, pilot.

ABOUT THE AUTHORS

(Photo by kimberly millen brown)

Dr. Amy L. Hoover

Amy Hoover's journey into mountain and canyon flying started in the early 1980s when her work as a geologist and whitewater river guide entailed flights into the remote river canyons in central Idaho. She has been hooked ever since. Hoover obtained her private pilot license in 1989 in Salmon, Idaho. The following year, she bought a 1947 Cessna 120, which she flew from Idaho to Florida and back, stopping over to obtain her instrument/commercial and flight instructor certificates. In 1992 she landed a job as a commercial backcountry air taxi pilot and taught mountain flying seminars for the FAA. She received the Amelia Earhart Memorial Scholarship from the International 99s in 1994, which she used to complete her multi-engine commercial rating. Hoover combined her love of flying with that of teaching and began work as a full-time flight instructor in 1995. She is one of three original co-founders of McCall Mountain/Canyon Flying Seminars in McCall, Idaho, where she spent four years developing the curriculum and creating the company's training materials. Realizing her desire to reach out to a broader spectrum in aviation training, Hoover took the position as Director of Aviation at Mt. Hood Community College in Oregon before joining the faculty at Central Washington University (CWU), where she currently teaches. At CWU, she served eight years as Aviation Department Chair and achieved rank of Full Professor in 2012.

Hoover has B.S. and M.S. degrees in geology and a Ph.D. in education. She has published approximately 25 articles in technical and aviation journals and magazines, including *Pilot Getaways* and *Power Cruising*, and more than a dozen scholarly publications and book chapters on aviation human factors and research methods, including papers for the *International Journal of Aviation Psychology*, *Collegiate Aviation Review*, and *International Journal of Applied Aviation Studies (IJAAS)*. Hoover served as a reviewer and contributing editor for *IJAAS* and is a reviewer for the *Journal of Aviation and Education Research (JAER)*. She has given more than 100 presentations on mountain and canyon flying to various organizations and forums throughout the United States. Hoover has been nominated by students for "Who's Who in America's Teachers" every year for the past 18 years, and she is a past recipient of the National Residence Hall Association Outstanding Faculty Award. In 2011, she was selected for the "President's Faculty of the Year" Award at Central Washington University. She was awarded the Marquis Who's Who "Albert Nelson Lifetime Achievement Award" in 2018.

Hoover has approximately 7,000 flight hours, more than two-thirds of which were flying and teaching in the Idaho backcountry. She has given 1,000 hours of instruction in flight simulators. Hoover founded and operates Canyon Flying (canyonflying.com), a company specializing in tailwheel and backcountry flying in Idaho and the Northwest. She owns a 2011 American Champion 8GCBC Scout and can be found somewhere in the backcountry in the summers.

R.K. "Dick" Williams

(Photo by Josi Barinaga)

R.K. "Dick" Williams received a B.A. in psychology from the University of California, Berkeley, in 1972. He earned the Aviation Safety Certificate from the University of Southern California's Institute of Safety and Systems Management, Human Factors emphasis, in 1997. He was also given the United States Department of Agriculture Award for Significant Contribution to Aviation Safety in 1995.

As a licensed pilot since 1972, Williams holds all fixed wing and instructor certificates, several turboprop and jet type ratings, and has flown more than 18,300 hours as an instructor, charter, government, and corporate pilot. He was an FAA Designated Pilot Examiner for 10 years, and an FAA Safety Counselor. Williams started one of the first mountain flying schools in Idaho in 1985 and has more than 8,000 hours flying and instructing in mountain and canyon terrain.

He is the author of *The Mountains to Canyons Flying Manual* (1986), *Aged in Saltwater* (2014), and *Notes from the Cockpit: A Mountain Pilot's Perspective* (2015). His video *Mountain Flying with Dick Williams* was produced in 1996. He was the safety editor for the Super Cub Pilot's Association Newsletter and wrote 44 columns between 1986 and 1992. Williams has given presentations at numerous aviation seminars, expositions, and flight instructor refresher courses around the region.

Williams is retired and lives in Salmon, Idaho. He flies his Super Cub for fun and enjoys river rafting and exploring the nearby mountains. As a sailor, he adventured in the South Pacific for 10 months in the early 1970s, and he still enjoys sailing in the Pacific and Caribbean Oceans as well as Lake Michigan.

INTRODUCTION

What is Mountain, Canyon, and Backcountry Flying?

For more than a century, pilots have been lured into and intrigued by the challenges of flight in the highest mountains and the deepest canyons on every continent. Mountain, canyon, and backcountry flying allows them to get off the beaten path and enjoy the outdoors. It opens up a whole new world of recreation, including activities such as airplane camping, hiking, fishing, and staying at guest lodges or bush camps in areas where there may not be roads or easy access either by land or water.

From the Australian Outback to the European Alps, from the high Andean deserts to the African bush, from canyons in the western United States to the Alaskan tundra, pilots will encounter varied topography, weather, heat, cold, wind, high density altitudes, and reduced aircraft performance. The challenges presented by those possibly harsh environments are numerous and diverse. Flying there often entails operations at high altitude over relatively inaccessible terrain and necessitates the proper mindset, discipline, and procedures to operate efficiently and safely in a challenging and sometimes unforgiving environment.

This specialized type of flying can be hazardous to a relative newcomer with only a few hundred hours as well as to a seasoned pilot with thousands of hours of flight time, depending on their training and willingness to apply various well-tested principles. Words are no substitute for actual experience. However, the observations, recommendations, and guidelines in this book represent many years and thousands of hours of experience that have been passed along by those who have "been there" themselves, who love aviation, and who are committed to safety. Hopefully, they will help promote best flying practices. This book is not about off-airport operations or extreme bush flying; it is meant to help all pilots develop skills to aviate off the beaten path in areas where there are established airstrips.

The authors and contributors all have experience flying and teaching mountain, canyon, backcountry, and bush flying, primarily in the western United States and Alaska. Examples and scenarios draw from lessons learned in those geographic regions with the hope that you will be able to use the insights for similar operations anywhere around the world. This work references and cites expertise from the literature, including books, articles, and public documents spanning decades of practice and research, to give readers additional information for further study.

How to Use This Book

This book's focus is to provide information to assist owners and pilots of fixed-wing **general aviation (GA)** aircraft who intend to fly into mountain, canyon and backcountry regions. Whether considering a route over high mountain terrain or planning for takeoff and landing at unimproved airstrips, pilots will find the content and techniques presented in this book useful. Mountain and backcountry flight instructors, as well as college and university professors, can use the text to supplement their classroom and flight instruction. Organizations that conduct mountain flying seminars may find it helpful to augment their curricula.

Key terms indicated in **bold text** are defined in Appendix C (Glossary). Questions and exercises at the end of each chapter are designed to enhance understanding and help pilots apply the material to their own flying. If used to supplement a college or university course, a seminar or workshop, ground school, or flight instruction, the end-of-chapter questions and exercises can help evaluate student progress. The text is organized into three sections, each with chapters relevant to a specific subject or application. Key concepts may appear in more than one section or chapter to frame them in context and emphasize their importance.

Section I is about planning and preparing for flights in mountain and canyon terrain. Chapter 1 addresses how to prepare the airplane and the pilot. Although information is applicable to many types of GA operations, it specifically addresses aircraft inspection and maintenance items relevant to operating on unimproved airstrips. It also introduces specific techniques to help prepare for backcountry flying. Chapter 2 delves into meteorological phenomena unique to mountains and canyon environments. Chapter 3 explores flight planning and navigation in mountainous terrain and in canyons.

Section II is primarily about operating in remote areas and on unimproved airstrips. Individual chapters are delineated with respect to specific types of operation, including enroute operations (Chapter 4), approach and landing (Chapter 5), and takeoff and departure (Chapter 6). Chapter 7 includes contributions from guest authors who have expertise in winter and ski flying in the Alaska bush, glacier flying, and flying in high Rocky Mountain terrain.

Section III pertains specifically to performance, both aircraft and human. Chapter 8 discusses density altitude and aircraft loading as they relate to performance. It includes some theory for readers who want to explore the mathematical as well as practical considerations. It also provides suggestions for common sense solutions to reductions in performance. Chapter 9 introduces risk management, human factors, backcountry etiquette, planning for emergencies, and post-crash survival strategies.

Although the most cohesive reading experience will be to study each section in sequence, the book was designed so that individual chapters and sections could stand alone. Content is cross-referenced throughout the text to help readers relate different subject areas to one another, which instructors should find helpful should they choose to rearrange the order in which they teach subject areas.

Resources such as links to websites, videos, pdf documents, and online training courses are provided on the Reader Resources webpage for this book at www.asa2fly.com/reader/mountain.

References and Citations

The material in this book is based mainly on the authors' and contributors' personal experience, enhanced by references from the literature relevant to each topic. Citation style follows that recommended by the *Harvard System of Referencing* (6th edition) and the *Publication Manual of the American Psychological Association* (6th edition). The author–date method is used throughout to make it easy for the reader to find the book, paper, or other work without having to search through footnotes. In-text citations are placed in parentheses and the corresponding references are provided in Appendix D at the end of the book, divided by chapter. Examples of the two citation formats are as follows:

1. Hoover and Williams (2019) found that pilots who flew around the backcountry for many years developed a variety of ways to be safe and have fun.

2. Pilots can use specialized skills to ensure their mountain flying experience is enjoyable and safe (Hoover & Williams, 2019).

Applying Rules of Thumb to Performance Estimates

Merriam-Webster Dictionary (2018) defines a *rule of thumb* as "a general principle regarded as roughly correct but not intended to be scientifically accurate." According to Wikipedia,[1]

> The English phrase *rule of thumb* refers to a principle with broad application that is not intended to be strictly accurate or reliable for every situation. It refers to an easily learned and easily applied procedure or standard, based on practical experience rather than theory. This usage of the phrase can be traced back to the seventeenth century.

The rules of thumb in this book are cited from various government publications and individual authors. The intention is to inspire a critical thinking process rather than a strict adherence to numbers and calculations. They are not meant to replace the aircraft manufacturer's operating procedures nor actual experience. Hopefully they will help readers explore their own practices in more depth and have fun.

---

[1] Rule of Thumb. (n.d.). In *Wikipedia*. Retrieved January 8, 2019, from https://en.wikipedia.org/wiki/Rule_of_thumb

The Literature

Learning a new skill involves much thought, study, and practice. Sometimes years' worth. During the process of writing this book, we recognized that our own practices were influenced through collaboration and sharing information with other pilots, from advice given by mentors and "old hands," and through careful and thoughtful study of books, manuals, and other resources. We are grateful to other authors who have contributed to the body of literature in the past, and we have cited their expertise in context with the intent of bringing their work forward. We believe this provides a richness and depth that enhances our own experience and gives the reader a broader scope from which to reflect and learn.

Some of the works cited are from prominent authors in the field, and others are from more obscure books. Listed below are several references we believe provide sound advice, techniques, and insight into mountain, backcountry, and bush flying. Full citations are provided in the references in Appendix D, and the authors are credited for their contributions throughout the text.

- *Guide to Bush Flying,* **by F.E. Potts** (1993), is a seminal work that gives excellent advice and in-depth descriptions of bush flying techniques, weather, aircraft operations, and mountain flying concepts.
- *Flying the Mountains,* **by Fletcher Anderson** (2003), has good descriptions of mountain weather phenomena as well as other mountain flying tips.
- *Mountain Flying,* **by Doug Geeting and Steve Woerner** (1988), provides a solid introduction to the basics of mountain flying.
- *Mountain Flying Bible Revised,* **by Sparky Imeson** (2005), is the latest version of his books that have been long-standing sources of information and tips on mountain flying for many years.
- *Survival Flying: Bush flying tales and techniques as flown and taught in Alaska,* **by C. J. Baldwin** (2010), is full of great stories as well as excellent advice on bush flying techniques.
- *Fly the Wild and Stay Alive,* **by Hal Terry** (2000), has many excellent insights into bush flying and backcountry flying, as well as some great stories from his experiences in the Alaskan bush.

SECTION I

Preparation and Planning

(Photo courtesy Andrew George, Idaho Aviation Association)

1

THE PILOT
and
THE AIRPLANE

Mountain, canyon, and backcountry flying can lead to fun and exciting adventures. Whether you plan to spend the weekend at a mountain resort, camp at an airstrip on a remote lake, or venture into the canyons for some hiking and fishing, you can take measures to enhance the safety and enjoyment of both you and your passengers. Before heading over mountain ranges, through canyons, or over large expanses of desert, tundra, or other inhospitable terrain, it is important to ensure that both you and your aircraft components and systems are operating properly and safely. Careful preflight planning, consideration of pilot currency and skill level, and a thorough inspection of the aircraft are essential. Preparing the aircraft, pilot, and passengers is the best insurance toward making a flight memorable for the right reasons.

There are many online resources for mountain flying, such as courses and publications provided by the Aircraft Owners and Pilots Association, the New Zealand Civil Aviation Authority, the Federal Aviation Administration, and Transport Canada (see links for these and other resources at www.asa2fly.com/reader/mountain). Hire a qualified flight instructor to help you work on your skills when planning to fly in a new area or a new flight regime, such as mountain and canyon backcountry operations. Guidance from a professional pilot or instructor familiar with the terrain and nuances of wind and weather patterns for the area in which you plan to operate is invaluable.

Evaluate your total flight time, type of experience, and time in make and model of aircraft you intend to use. Straight-and-level flight time, especially in large turbojet aircraft, does not transfer to the mountain and canyon or backcountry environment. Takeoff and landing practice, proficiency maneuvers, and preparing for emergencies is much more useful. Glider experience is helpful, especially ridge soaring; glider time will help you understand updrafts and downdrafts as well as other elements unique to mountain and canyon flying. Chapter 9 explores personal attitude and experience in more detail. This chapter describes several maneuvers to help prepare you for safe flight into the mountains and canyons.

Practicing for Mountain, Canyon, and Backcountry Flight

Canyon flying can be intimidating to "flatland" pilots, as they must maneuver in a confined space, close to terrain, and often with no discernable horizon or familiar visual cues. Pilots new to this can easily become disoriented and lose situational awareness, especially if their attention is focused on the aircraft instruments and not the visual environment outside the cockpit. Proximity to terrain can also add

---

[1] McCollough, David (2015). *The Wright Brothers*. New York, NY: Simon & Schuster.

an extra layer of stress, which may decrease **situational awareness** (SA) and cause errors such as tunnel vision, fixation, and loss of control. It is critical to be able to fly your airplane based solely on visual cues during turns, climbs, descents, and approaches, backed up by quick checks of the appropriate instruments. As long-time, highly experienced mountain pilot Carol Jarvis stated, "The ability to fly by feel, so the wings are your fingertips, the wheels are your feet, and the approach to stall is a whisper in your brain instead of a mechanical shout, is so old and fundamental...it is an ability that every pilot needs, whether or not he ever ventures into the hills" (Parfit, 1977).

A key element to canyon flying is slowing down to give your airplane more room and time to maneuver; turn radius decreases as the airplane slows and you can operate more safely in a confined space. Slowing down also allows for shallower banks to avoid overstressing the airplane. (Chapter 4 explores maneuvering, canyon turns, and emergency turns.)

Maneuvers

You can prepare for mountain and canyon flying by practicing maneuvers that enhance precise aircraft control. Be proficient in all phases of **slow flight**. Practice with different configurations and weight and load distributions and at different airspeeds. You should be able to use different flap (and gear, if applicable) settings and execute climbs, descents, and turns with precision, accuracy, and coordination. Try to make pitch and power changes, and transitions between different speed and flap/gear configurations, as smoothly as possible. It may help to go with an experienced mountain/canyon pilot or flight instructor who can help you determine power settings, flap settings, and indicated airspeeds in different configurations at various weight and **center of gravity** (CG) positions to help you become intimately familiar with the airplane.

A good exercise is to load your airplane to the weight and CG positions you plan to use, and practice flying at **density altitudes** (DA) similar to what you anticipate encountering. Consult the airplane owner's manual or operating handbook for appropriate speeds at different weight or flap and gear settings. Fly at different speeds, including **maneuvering speed** (V_A), **maximum flap extended speed** (V_{FE}), **maximum gear extended speed** (V_{LE}), and **minimum controllable airspeed** (MCA). Although there is normally no reason to operate at MCA, practicing will give you an idea of "aircraft feel" and control responsiveness. Reduce power to idle at MCA and observe the amount of pitch down required to transition to best glide speed.

Load your airplane as light as possible to maximize performance (see Chapter 8). Remember that maneuvering speed decreases at lighter weight. Flying too fast in turbulence or maneuvering abruptly can overstress the airplane, so know the correct V_A for your operating weight. Machado (2017) gives the following rule of thumb to easily calculate V_A at your airplane's current weight:

Stowell (2007) noted that "for airplanes certificated since 1993, the standards have made a clear distinction between the design maneuvering speed (V_A) and the placarded operating maneuvering speed (V_O)." Stowell presents a more in-depth discussion of the relationship between V_O and V_A, and notes that for airplanes which list both, choose the slower of the two speeds for maneuvering and turbulence (Stowell, 2007).

Perform climbs and descents in straight flight, while turning, and in various configurations. Note the power required and whether there is sufficient power at the DA to execute each maneuver. If there is not enough power available due to high DA, a heavy airplane might be able to climb during straight flight, but not while turning. You may need to add power (if available) to maintain altitude. Or you may need to descend (i.e., sacrifice altitude) to maintain airspeed while

R.K.'s
Rule

Practice, practice, practice!

turning. Excessively steep banks come with increased stall speeds, so medium-bank turns are recommended for most maneuvers (see Chapter 4). Learn the precise control pressures required to roll into and out of turns while level, climbing, and descending, and remain coordinated. Be able to do all maneuvers with outside visual cues as your primary reference.

A great maneuver to help you develop a feel for aircraft control characteristics and inputs is the **"Dutch roll" coordination exercise**. Proper execution requires manipulating aileron, rudder, and elevator throughout the maneuver to keep the longitudinal axis of the airplane aligned with a fixed point. This maneuver will help develop a feel for the correct amount of rudder to compensate for adverse yaw caused by the ailerons when rolling into or out of a turn. It is essentially a "wing wag" around the longitudinal axis of the airplane. Visually align a spot on your windscreen to a point on the horizon and roll from level flight to 30–40 degrees of bank in one direction, reverse to roll 30–40 degrees in the other direction, then reverse again back to level flight, keeping aligned with the horizon point. Perform the Dutch roll coordination exercise at different airspeeds and configurations to improve your feel for the flight control characteristics and to develop more precise inputs.

Done correctly, the nose stays "on point" as the longitudinal axis of the airplane remains aligned with a point on the horizon (Figure 1-1A). If the nose of the airplane traces a "U" shape (Figure 1-1B), coordination needs improvement.

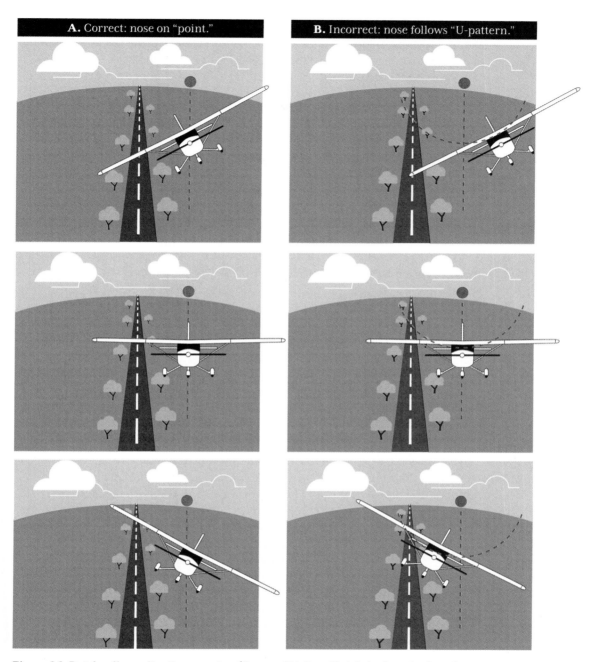

Figure 1-1. Dutch roll coordination exercise. *(Courtesy Rich Stowell's Aviation Learning Center)*

Ground reference maneuvers, such as S-turns, turns around a point, and eights on pylons, are important skills for mountain and canyon flying. If you want to observe an object on the ground, know how to do it correctly (see Chapter 4). Take an experienced instructor with you and do it at different altitudes, with and without wind.

Be able to consistently land within 50 feet of a designated spot on the runway for both **short-field** and **soft-field** operations. Practice **maximum performance takeoffs** at the weight and CG position you plan to use, preferably at a similar altitude as your planned destination. See Chapters 5 and 6 for more detailed discussions of maximum performance takeoff and landing techniques.

Mountain and canyon approaches are made with power on (see Chapter 5), so it is important to prepare for an **emergency landing** by practicing **power-off glides** to land on a pre-determined spot. As with other exercises, do these at different weight and CG positions so you know what to expect.

Airspeeds and Power Settings

One of the most important aircraft control items is to know your airplane's required power settings at different weights, CG positions, and density altitudes at different airspeeds and configurations.

Knowing target power settings will help you set the airplane up confidently and efficiently without having to guess. That will free up your time and mental resources during periods of high workload, such as when maneuvering in canyons. Following is an exercise to help determine appropriate target power settings and airspeeds. This is a good exercise to do for every airplane you fly and each time you check out in a new airplane type.

Load your airplane to the weight and CG you intend for your flights. You can vary the weight and CG and note differences at heavier and lighter weights, various forward or rearward CG positions, and different altitudes and temperatures. Table 1-1 shows values determined empirically for a Cessna 182P at three different weight and CG combinations at a given DA. You can use this as an example to make a template for your airplane. Have your instructor or passenger record numbers so you can concentrate on flying the airplane.

Start by setting up the airplane for level cruise flight and record the indicated altitude, temperature, power setting, and indicated airspeed.

After the airplane has stabilized, slow to V_A in the clean configuration (flaps and gear at cruise settings) and record the power required to establish V_A for your given weight and CG configuration. Also note the **pitch attitude** of the airplane for straight-and-level flight and turns. Make medium-bank turns at V_A to determine whether the power setting is sufficient to maintain altitude or more power is needed for turning. This will provide you with target power settings and give an idea of how the pitch attitude of the airplane should look when you need to slow to V_A for turbulence or to maneuver in a confined area.

Table 1-1. Power required at three different weight/CG combinations for a Cessna 182P at various airspeeds and configurations. (Numbers were recorded empirically during flight tests and should not be used as a reference for other airplanes. V_{CANYON} is described in the following section.)

Example only—not intended for actual use.

Indicated Altitude 8,000 ft 16°C		Weight 2,950 lbs CG 40"	
	IAS	Power	Flaps
Cruise	129	21"/2,350 RPM	0
V_A	109	19"/2,350 RPM	0
V_{FE}	95	16"/2,350 RPM	0
V_{CANYON}	80	17"/2,400 RPM	20

Indicated Altitude 8,000 ft 16°C		Weight 2,750 lbs CG 40"	
	IAS	Power	Flaps
Cruise	131	20"/2,350 RPM	0
V_A	104	19"/2,350 RPM	0
V_{FE}	95	16"/2,350 RPM	0
V_{CANYON}	80	16"/2,400 RPM	20

Indicated Altitude 8,000 ft 16°C		Weight 2,550 lbs CG 41"	
	IAS	Power	Flaps
Cruise	134	20"/2,350 RPM	0
V_A	101	18"/2,350 RPM	0
V_{FE}	95	13"/2,350 RPM	0
V_{CANYON}	80	14"/2,400 RPM	20

The power required for a given airspeed in level flight depends on aircraft weight and CG position, with more power required as the airplane gets heavier and the CG moves forward. Without enough power to maintain both altitude and airspeed while turning, you will have to balance between the two. Either accept a slower airspeed to hold altitude or decrease the pitch attitude to descend and maintain airspeed. If the trade-off causes excessive airspeed loss (e.g., approaching stall speed), then accepting a loss of altitude during turns will be your only recourse.

For a V_A higher than V_{FE}, slow to V_{FE} and record the power required for level flight, both straight and in turns. If V_A is below V_{FE}, proceed to the next step.

Once you have slowed to V_{FE}, apply partial flaps. Start with either the manufacturer's recommended takeoff flap setting or approximately half the full-flap setting for your airplane; both will be close to the maximum lift-to-drag ratio for the wing. You can experiment with different partial flap settings. Generally, any setting between 10–20 degrees works for most **general aviation** (GA) aircraft.

With partial flaps, set the power to maintain altitude and allow the airplane to slow. As the airplane stabilizes, note the **indicated airspeed** (IAS) and make some turns to determine how much power is required to maintain altitude, just as you did while maneuvering at V_A. After the airplane stabilizes, record the power setting and airspeed required to maintain altitude while flying and turning with that flap setting.

The partial flap speed and power setting are important bits of information, since you can target them as you enter and maneuver in a confined area, such as a canyon. For example, slowing down and configuring the airplane before you enter the traffic pattern at a canyon airstrip will give you more time. You can use that time to circle and assess the environment and plan your approach, departure, and emergency options without having to divide your attention trying to also slow down and set up the airplane. Many pilots refer to this speed as "**canyon speed**" and use it any time there is a need to slow down and maneuver. It is designated here as V_{CANYON}.

An important caveat is to know the limit load factor with flaps down. Limits for normal category airplanes with flaps up is from –1.52 to +3.8 G, and for utility category airplanes, they range from –1.76 to +4.4 G. However, with flaps deployed, the limit load factor for many airplanes decreases dramatically. The positive load limit with flaps down for a Cessna model 182S is decreased to +2.0G, and the airplane could exceed that with a 60-degree bank or during straight-and-level flight with light to moderate turbulence. In turbulence, it is best to keep the flaps up for more than medium-bank turns.

There is an additional step and set of data to compile for airplanes with retractable landing gear. Depending on the manufacturer's recommendations and the speed at which you can extend the gear (V_{LE}), you can determine power settings at V_A, V_{FE}, and V_{CANYON} with landing gear retracted and with gear extended.

In addition to determining power settings at a selected DA for V_A or V_{CANYON} speeds, transition to maximum available power and record whether a climb is possible, and at what rate, for each airspeed. You may not have enough excess power to climb at those speeds, or you may have only a marginal climb rate at best.

The point of the exercise is for you to become more familiar with the handling characteristics and performance of your airplane so you can make sound decisions with respect to what the airplane, and you, can do. Additional exercises are described in Chapter 4 (canyon turns) and Chapter 5 (approaches and landings) to help you determine the power settings, airspeeds, and configuration for maneuvering and flying a stabilized approach to landing. Ultimately, you should be able to control your airplane by outside visual reference with only quick glances at the instruments to verify your flight attitude and airspeed.

Aircraft Loading

The key to loading your airplane is to keep it as light as possible. The following section discusses fuel planning, which should be a primary concern with respect to aircraft loading. It may be better to carry lighter loads and make more than one trip than to load the airplane to maximum weight (see Chapter 8).

Note differences in the way the airplane handles and performs while maneuvering at different weights and CG positions. At a given weight, you can position the CG for the type of performance you want to achieve. The airplane should always be loaded within the CG limits. A forward CG increases longitudinal stability, but also increases the stall speed. Since the wing must be flown at a higher angle of attack to compensate for greater tail-down force with a forward CG, it creates more induced drag. The higher stall speed means your approaches and departures will need to be flown at a higher IAS.

Loaded with an aft CG, the airplane will be less stable (more maneuverable) longitudinally, and the stall speed will be lower, allowing for slower approach speeds and better climb performance. However, stall recovery will be more difficult due to decreased elevator authority.

The next section gives tips on what to look for and how you can maximize safety and performance by ensuring that the airplane you fly is mechanically sound as well as by providing preflight items for mountain and canyon flight.

Get rid at the outset of the idea that the airplane is only an air-going sort of automobile. It isn't. It may sound like one and smell like one, and it may have been interior decorated to look like one; but the difference is—it goes on wings. 99

Wolfgang Langewiesche [2]

The Airplane

General aviation aircraft come in all shapes and sizes. Deciding what kind of airplane to use on unimproved airstrips, or whether your airplane has the capability to operate in the mountain and canyon backcountry environment, is your primary concern. Some airplanes, such as the Piper Super Cub, Britten-Norman Islander, de Havilland Beaver and Otter, Pilatus Porter, and larger single-engine Cessnas have been used successfully for decades to haul loads into and out of remote areas. Also common

---

[2] Langewiesche, Wolfgang (1944). *Stick and Rudder, An Explanation of the Art of Flying.* New York, McGraw Hill.

are American Champion airplanes, the Aviat Husky, Maules, and others. Many experimental aircraft are now specifically targeted toward the mountain, canyon, and backcountry environment.

Tricycle-gear airplanes, such as the Cessna 182, Cessna TU206, de Havilland Twin Otter, and Britten-Norman Islander, perform well at high DA and on unimproved, short airstrips. Conventional gear airplanes are well-suited to operations at unimproved airstrips because they generally have more propeller clearance and the ability to maneuver in a tighter space on the ground, but there are more ground loop accidents involving tailwheel aircraft than tricycle-gear aircraft. Some retractable-gear aircraft, such as the Beech Bonanza, may have strong enough landing gear to withstand rough airstrips, but others, such as the Cessna 210, might not be as durable. Ultimately, it is a personal choice. Know your aircraft limitations and fly accordingly, particularly regarding weight and DA. Use the proper equipment for the planned mission. Low-performance aircraft may be severely limited with respect to airstrip length, obstructions, gross weight, temperature, and wind.

R.K.'s
Rule

Use the right equipment.

Short takeoff and landing (STOL) kits can enhance airplane performance with features such as **leading-edge cuffs**, **gap seals**, **stall fences**, **canards**, and **drooping ailerons and/or wingtips**. These features alter the wing's camber, chord, or surface area and increase takeoff, climb, and stall performance. STOL modifications by Robertson, Sportsman, Peterson, Horton, and the Katmai conversion are some of the most common. De Havilland airplanes have various built-in STOL designs depending on the model. These include single and double slotted flaps (some full span), ailerons that droop with flap deflection, and flaperons. Increased weight, control heaviness, and lack of aileron effectiveness in crosswind conditions are some of the reported negative side effects of the various STOL kits. Choosing which system will be most effective or have the best feel on your airplane will be personal preference. Test fly various STOL modifications before making an investment. As pointed out by Vivion (2000) "The most effective STOL kit is not installed by a mechanic. The single most important factor contributing to the safe operation of an aircraft in the short field environment is the skill and knowledge of the pilot, not the number of gadgets attached to the airplane."

Vortex generators (VGs) are perhaps the most popular, economic, and widespread STOL modification for GA airplanes. VGs are small plates strategically placed on the wing, stabilizer, or control surfaces that change boundary layer airflow, causing it to be more turbulent. A turbulent boundary layer increases the energy of the airflow and delays flow separation from the wing or other airfoil surface. Aero-Service (2010) outlined the benefits of VGs:

- Easy to install
- Relatively inexpensive compared to other STOL components
- Lower stall speed
- Make it possible to fly at slower speeds and higher angles of attack
- Gentler stall characteristics
- Increased stability and more control effectiveness at slow speeds
- Shorter takeoff roll
- Higher rate of climb

Boundary Layer Research (BLR) and Micro AeroDynamics are the two main manufacturers of VGs. Both offer VGs on the upper wing surface, but they have different tail configurations (Figure 1-2), making the choice one of personal preference.

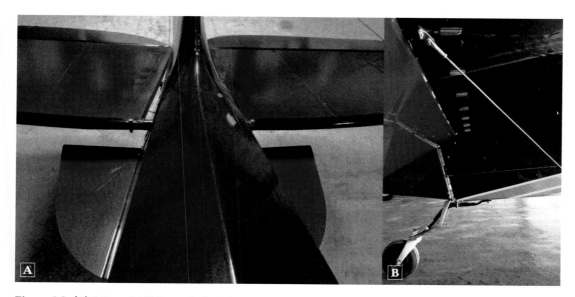

Figure 1-2. (A) A Piper PA18 Super Cub with a strake in front of the horizontal stabilizer (BLR). *(Photo by R.K. Williams)* **(B)** An American Champion Scout has VGs on the underside of the stabilizer (Micro AeroDynamics). *(Photo by Amy Hoover)*

Unimproved airstrips made of gravel, dirt, and turf subject your airplane to a lot more vibration than paved runways. Parts can rattle loose, screws can come out, and components can crack or rupture. Regardless of the type of airplane you fly, you can best prepare with a thorough check of your aircraft systems and components, preventive maintenance, and adding some extra items to your normal aircraft preflight checklist.

The following information within this chapter incorporates maintenance knowledge from interviews with Maintenance Inspector Lenny Skunberg, of Lenny's Airmotive, a Certified 14 CFR Part 145 Repair Station in Salmon, Idaho. Skunberg established his business in 1980 and was awarded the Federal Aviation Administration National Maintenance Technician of the Year Award in 1987. He holds Inspector Authorization and is a certified Cessna technician. Skunberg has extensive experience maintaining and repairing backcountry-operated aircraft as well as helicopter, radial engine, fabric, and complex aircraft.

Fuel Planning and Fuel Management

Planning your fuel load is critical for remote area operations. You must have an accurate way to measure fuel. The older, mechanical or electric fuel gauges can be inaccurate and legally are only required to be accurate when the tanks are empty. Aircraft owners should consider investing in an electronic fuel flow computer, such as the ones from JP Instruments or Electronics International. Calibrated correctly, fuel flow instruments are highly accurate and give real-time information for fuel consumption, fuel used, and fuel remaining. Such instruments require manual input of fuel quantity, so there is a chance for error. Add a check and verification of the fuel meter to your preflight checklist to ensure the fuel quantity is entered correctly.

You may not be able to fly with full fuel at high DA, especially with long range tanks, because the aircraft will be too heavy. The adage "the only time you have too much fuel is when you are on fire" does not apply in mountain flying; you can also have too much fuel for safe arrivals and departures. Always manually check fuel quantity during preflight, as you need to know precisely how much fuel you have, and plan your reserves carefully.

Several airplane parts suppliers sell hollow glass fuel sticks you can calibrate to your airplane, or you can make your own fuel stick. Cut a dowel or stick to a length twice as long as the depth of the tank so if it is accidentally dropped it will not be as likely to fall into the tank. Drive a nail into the bottom of the stick so the head is flush with the stick. That will allow you retrieve it with a magnet, since wooden sticks can float and lodge against the upper surface of the tank, often far from the filler port. Empty the tanks of usable fuel, park the airplane on a level surface, and ensure the nose strut is properly inflated; then mark the stick as you fill the tank incrementally.

Planning for adequate reserves will vary with the conditions and your personal limits. Reserves should be at least that required by Federal Aviation

Regulations (FARs), and usually more. Mountain weather can change rapidly, and you may have to divert around weather or make an unplanned stop, which could require extra time to descend and climb out again.

Terry (2000) stated, "Never use your reserve fuel for anything less than emergencies or unexpected, important events. Do not use reserve fuel for unplanned, unnecessary actions, possibly putting you and your passengers 'up a creek' for no good reason. Reserve fuel is for emergencies only—it is a good rule."

R.K.'s
Rule

Carry enough fuel to make a complete round trip plus 50%, or plan a fuel stop. The 30-minute rule is for flat land!

Skunberg (2018) said he finds a lot of fuel caps near the fuel pit and has had to loan gas caps to many pilots because they leave them off after fueling, probably because they were distracted. Airflow over the wing could create a suction and draw fuel out of an open tank during flight, so always double-check caps after refueling. This can happen with a bad gasket, even with the cap properly tightened. Skunberg also thinks pilots should pay more attention to fuel caps and adapters because they can corrode or dry out, allowing water to get into the fuel tank. He has seen engine failures resulting from bad fuel cap gaskets and suggests putting light fuel-compatible grease on the gasket as a preventive measure. Also, according to Skunberg, more than one-half (½) teaspoon of water in a fuel sample should be investigated.

Engine and Propeller

Whether you own or rent the airplane you intend to use, become familiar with the powerplant and its systems. Have a mechanic conduct a thorough inspection of your engine and repair any problems before you fly into remote areas. Once you are away from maintenance facilities, you could be stranded by something as simple as a broken hose or wire, so inspect the engine as thoroughly as possible before each flight. Check for anything loose or missing, such as hoses, wires, or clamps, even if you don't know what they are. Listen closely to the feel and sound of the engine, and be suspicious of vibrations or noises, or anything that does not seem right, and have a mechanic inspect it. Engine speed should be low enough that the airplane does not move when power is set to idle. Skunberg recommends 600–700 RPM for small aircraft engines. Verify that the tachometer is accurate and the gauge reaches redline at maximum power.

Inspect the engine baffling for cracks to ensure there is a tight seal against the cowling. Loose seals can change the airflow around the engine and cause it to run hot. Inspect the cowling, tighten any loose screws, and have cracks repaired. Have a mechanic determine the source of oil leaks or streaks on the engine and firewall and make necessary repairs. Keep your engine clean so you can see new oil or fuel leaks, and ensure the oil dipstick and fuel cap are tight. Skunberg has lost track of the number of times he has had to wash down an airplane engine because a pilot left the dipstick out after checking the oil or left the oil cap completely off.

Skunberg also advocates for frequent oil changes, at least every 30–33 hours, or 3 changes every 100 hours. He does not think pilots fly as much as they used to. Lengthening the calendar time between oil changes can be harmful, so it is best to do frequent oil changes, since engines are expensive and oil is cheap insurance for engine health. He says, "keep your airplane's belly clean. How can you see a fresh leak with a dirty belly?"

Skunberg recommends checking firewall **fuel strainers** for drips and leaks before you go into a remote mountain area, and he notes, "Some pilots don't like to check their strainers because they might tend to leak. It's better to know strainers are working properly before you head for the hills and then have a problem." Also, some aftermarket strainers have odd-size O-rings, so pilots should keep spares for themselves and their mechanics.

Inspect the engine intake and exhaust hoses for leaks and check that clamps are tight and hoses are seated properly. Check your ignition harness wires for wear and make sure spark plug and magneto connections are tight. Have frayed or damaged connections repaired. Skunberg has seen a lot of bad magnetos over the years and states:

> I recommend two tests. Do the first somewhere under 1000 RPM, and momentarily turn the key to the off position to see if the engine stops. You don't need to let it quit completely; you are just checking for a hot mag. With a hot mag the engine won't quit. The second test is to see whether the switch itself has integrity. With the engine off, put the key in the different mag positions and wiggle and pull gently on it. If the key comes out of the ignition, the switch should be replaced because the key can be removed with a mag in the on position. (Skunberg, 2018)

Engine cowl flaps should work smoothly without binding, and hinges and rods should be tight. Air filters and intakes should be clean and unobstructed. Have your mechanic check the throttle, mixture, propeller, and carburetor heat controls for smooth operation and lubricate them to prevent sticking or binding. Inspect the cabin heater and have leaks repaired so carbon monoxide does not escape into the aircraft cabin. Skunberg also advocates using a reliable carbon monoxide detector in the cockpit.

The propeller should be inspected before every flight, and blade nicks, cuts, or gouges must be properly dressed. Propeller seals should be checked for leaks and the hub inspected on constant-speed propellers. Make sure the propeller spinner is secure and the propeller is operating properly.

Skunberg believes newer cylinders and replacements are better than they were years ago. He encourages the use of engine monitors to keep track of engine health, and recommends that pilots write down accurate descriptions of the symptoms to help mechanics troubleshoot engine problems. Skunberg suggested the following:

One good engine check pilots can do occasionally, after warm-up, is to do about 1700 RPM, pull the prop and leave it to make sure the RPM drops at least 200. If it doesn't, it means mis-rigging or a crack in the transfer collar. This checks the integrity from the governor through to the prop.

However, it is not necessary to deep cycle props repeatedly during the run-up. I've seen that procedure sling oil on to the face of the prop. (Skunberg, 2018)

Skunberg also thinks cylinder thermal shocking is not as common as it used to be, and he does not see nearly as many cracked cylinders from shock-cooling as he has in the past. He said, "I think a good general rule during descent is to keep bringing the manifold pressure back about an inch for every 1,000 feet of altitude, which would be 2 inches—one for the lower altitude and one for the power reduction."

Check with the engine manufacturer regarding your particular engine; some have a high rate of crankshaft failure and others exhibit chronic engine case cracks. An awareness of weaknesses of your particular engine is an important part of your preflight planning. Be sure to regularly check **airworthiness directives** (ADs) and **service bulletins** that affect your aircraft.

Landing Gear, Wheels, and Brakes

Any unimproved airstrip can be rough, with dirt, holes, rocks, gravel, sand, turf, and ditches. Before operating off pavement, have a mechanic thoroughly check the landing gear, wheels, brakes, and tires, and make necessary repairs. Inspect each of them often, especially after landing at a rough airstrip. Skunberg says good landing gear is critical, and he advocates running larger than standard tires and flex brake lines for optimum performance and safety (Figure 1-3).

Figure 1-3. (A) A Cessna 182 with oversize Airglas nose strut, 800 nosewheel, and 850 main tires. **(B)** A King Katmai conversion with 850 nosewheel and oversize mains. **(C)** A Cessna 185 has low-pressure, high-volume Alaskan Bushwheel tundra tires. *(Photos by Amy Hoover)*

Oversize tires are a compromise, so you must weigh the advantages and disadvantages relative to the mission you wish to accomplish with larger-than-normal or low-pressure tires. **Tundra tires**, such as the Alaskan Bushwheel (manufactured by Airframes Alaska), Alaska Tundra Tires (formerly Gar-aero), and Goodyear brands are popular high-volume, low-pressure tires used on many bush planes. Low-pressure tundra tires can roll over rough ground, rocks, and holes and act as shock absorbers to minimize potential damage to the landing gear and propeller, which gives them an advantage during an emergency, off-field landing. Big tires and extended gear also increase the angle of attack of the wing for tailwheel airplanes sitting on the ground, which can improve takeoff and landing performance. Tundra tires can dampen pilot-induced rudder oscillations and make conventional gear handling easier. Glacier pilot Paul Claus opined that larger tires are one of the best modifications you can make to the airplane for mountain and bush flying because they can actually prevent incidents and accidents (Claus, 2018).

A disadvantage of tundra tires is poorer braking action due to the larger mass and diameter of the tire. Some early design low-pressure tires had high friction coefficients on pavement and would cause the tire to "grab," but newer tires are much improved. Grooved tires are better than smooth tires on slick surfaces such as wet grass or mud. Smooth tundra tires have extremely poor braking action on slippery surfaces and can also reduce controllability in crosswinds. Oversize tires may also require installation of larger rims and heavier-duty brakes, which increases purchase and operation costs. You can expect lower cruise speeds (by 5–10 knots) and excessive wear from landing on pavement. Tundra tires also have the potential to give pilots a false sense of invulnerability. They are not a substitute for skis, although it is possible to land in light powder. However, due to their greater mass, they can dig into crusted snow and cause the airplane to flip upside down. See the Reader Resources page at www.asa2fly.com/reader/mountain for a comprehensive review of the various tires, including cost and maintenance considerations.

For tricycle-gear aircraft, make sure oleo struts are properly charged and inflated. Repair any leaking seals and cracked or loose scissors links or hinge joints, and ensure the nosewheel tire is properly inflated. Inspect and repair loose or sagging tail springs. Inspect tail stingers and cable attach points, and keep your tail wheel greased and free of dirt and debris to minimize the chance of it locking up or malfunctioning. If the tail wheel has any shimmy or is loose, it needs to be inspected and repaired by a mechanic.

Most retractable-gear aircraft have relatively more fragile landing gear and smaller wheels and tires than fixed-gear airplanes. Have the gear thoroughly inspected and serviced before operating from dirt or unimproved airstrips. Carefully consider the surface conditions of an airstrip before choosing to operate retractable-gear airplanes, and accept that there are additional hazards and a greater opportunity for damage. Sources of information include internet sites, blogs, airplane type clubs, and airport descriptions. One of the best methods is to ask local pilots for information about the surface conditions of a particular airstrip.

Wheel fairings (or pants) can collect grass and dirt and break apart on rough strips, potentially jamming or obstructing the wheels and brakes. Remove them prior to operating off pavement. Without fairings, you will be able to better see and inspect the wheels for cracks and be able to inspect tires for wear and damage. Worn, cracked, scuffed, or bald tires should be replaced immediately. It is a good idea to look at all wheels, brakes, and tires each time you land at a backcountry strip.

Amy's Axiom

Protect your gear; take your pants off!

Before you go, check your brake lines, bushings, flex hoses and connections for cracking or leaking, and repair broken or worn components. Check the brake master cylinder for fluid level and leaks. Hydraulic fluid expands with temperature, and in some older master cylinders, topping them off can cause the brakes to lock up as the day warms up. Ensure that the parking brake is fully disengaged when in the off position. Inspect brake linings (pads) and rotor discs carefully before every flight because dust and dirt can accumulate quickly. Skunberg sees a lot of airplanes with worn brake pads, so ensure they are within legal limits for your airplane.

Worn or dragging brakes can cause longer takeoff rolls, loss of brake effectiveness, or loss of directional control, which could be extremely hazardous on a short or narrow airstrip. Skunberg suggests rolling the airplane during preflight, which allows you to look and listen for dragging brakes and see flat spots or weather checking on the tires. Do not fly with damaged brakes or tires.

Exterior and Interior

Prior to venturing into remote areas, thoroughly inspect the airplane's exterior, paying particular attention to the underside of the fuselage, wing, and tail surfaces. Inspect the skin, rivets, screws, hinges, control surfaces, and moving parts for damage. Make a "damage map" of the airplane, including photos, to record where all the little dings and nicks are, so you will be able to notice new damage.

Flap tracks, hinges, and rollers should not have excessive play or show cracks; repair damaged flap tracks before flying. Check control surfaces for proper movement and ensure there is no sticking or binding. Elevator, rudder, and aileron push rods and hinges should work smoothly, and regularly lubricate hinges and rod ends with an approved lubricant (one that will not collect dirt and grime).

Skunberg notes insects seem to plug pitot tubes more than fuel vents. He says he has unplugged hundreds of pitot tubes, which have to be disassembled to be properly repaired. He has seen problems with the flip-type pitot covers and recommends using a standard pitot cover with streamer attached.

Aircraft anti-collision lights should be clean and operational. Also, make sure the aircraft's **emergency locator transmitter (ELT)** is working properly. Chapter 9 presents types of **personal locator beacons (PLBs)** and other emergency devices you may want to have on board.

The airplane interior should be kept clean and neat so you can see damaged or missing items. Seats should move freely and adjust properly without binding on seat rails, and seat stops should be locked in place. Check seat belts and harnesses for wear and ensure that the attach points are secure and that buckles latch smoothly and lock properly.

The cargo area should be clear of debris; use a cargo net or other means of tying down and securing the aircraft load. Inspect the attach points for proper operation and repair frayed or broken lines, ropes, webbing, or nets.

Windscreen

The windscreen should be clean and free of scratches and crazing. Cracks should be repaired immediately. Polish a crazed windshield as best you can or replace it, since you could be blinded during early morning or late evening flights into low-angle sun. That could be deadly in a canyon.

Clean the windscreen when you do your post-flight inspection so you can see and attend to any new scratches or problems. A clean windscreen will repel dew and moisture better. Rub up and down, not horizontally or in circles. Wiping side to side can polarize the Plexiglas, and you may not be able to see when flying toward the sun. Rubbing in circles will cause "spider webs" that are hard to see through.

The invention of microfiber greatly influenced the ability to clean a wet windscreen. For heavy morning dew, you may need several microfiber cloths to wipe off all the moisture. Any fabric other than an absorbent microfiber will disperse the dew into tiny droplets that cling to the windscreen, which can blind you on takeoff and departure, especially looking toward low-angle sun. Do not wipe the windscreen if you cannot remove all of the water; instead allow the propeller wash to blow it off during the taxi and takeoff roll.

Skunberg discourages the use of windshield covers unless they are just used overnight for frost prevention when there is no wind. He has seen many ruined windshields caused by wind pushing and trapping dust particles between the cover and the windshield, which is effectively like taking sandpaper to the windscreen surface (Figure 1-4).

Figure 1-4. Backcountry airstrips can be dusty, which can damage windscreens. *(Photo by Fred Williams)*

Sun visors should be large enough to block out low-angle sun, and you might consider investing in movable visors like the ones manufactured by Rosen or Vantage Plane Plastics. Portable visors that adhere directly to the windscreen with suction cups or static charge can be repositioned as necessary.

Tool Kit

Carry some tools so you can make minor repairs to your airplane. U.S. regulations allow aircraft owners to do preventative maintenance and make certain repairs, including fabric repair, small simple repairs to fairings, cover plates, cowlings, safety belts, certain hose connections, and more (14 CFR Part 43, Appendix A). Skunberg suggests a tool kit that you can make yourself (Figure 1-5), or you can purchase one of the commercially available kits from an aircraft supplier.

Lenny's List—Tools for the Back-Country Airplane

- ☐ Gorilla Tape or high-quality duct tape
- ☐ For tubeless tires, a repair kit with hand pump and tire gauge
- ☐ For tubed tires, a can of Fix-a-Flat or similar product
- ☐ Safety wire
- ☐ A 4-in-1, 6" screwdriver or a magnetic screwdriver with multi-bits
- ☐ A short handled crescent wrench
- ☐ Pliers or diagonal cutters
- ☐ A small kit of common nuts, bolts, and screws
- ☐ A spare fuel quick-drain
- ☐ Jumper cables or a new-style battery power supply such as the Lightning Power Pack.
- ☐ A spare spark plug and socket wrench
- ☐ Red chalk—this is to mark exhaust manifolds if the engine is misfiring. Warming the engine will cause the red chalk to burn off, showing which cylinder is bad
- ☐ Vise grips
- ☐ Cable ties
- ☐ A small double-end wrench (spanner) for common-size nuts and bolts in your airplane (e.g. 5/8, 7/16, 1/2 inch)

Figure 1-5. Some suggestions for a tool kit from Lenny Skunberg, of Lenny's Airmotive.

Amy's Ignominious Interruption
By Amy Hoover

Years ago, a group of us went airplane camping in the Frank Church Wilderness of Central Idaho. I was flying my 1955 Cessna 180 that was always hangared. After spending the night, we decided to head to a nearby airstrip in the next canyon over to have breakfast at a backcountry lodge. During my preflight, some other pilots who were camped nearby came over to chat, and we talked about various things including weather, the day's plans, and our airplanes. Then I loaded my passenger, a friend's 13-year-old grandson, for the short flight. After run-up and pre-takeoff items, I took off on the long airstrip without issue. As discussed in Chapter 6, I had identified an abort point that was well down the airstrip and used an eyes-outside, correct pitch attitude takeoff, allowing the plane to lift off when it accelerated to flying speed. After liftoff, as the plane climbed out I heard a "whack-whack-whack" sound and, suspecting the culprit, looked at my airspeed indicator.

Zero.

Then I looked out at the red "remove before flight" hangtag on the pitot tube that was making all the noise. Fortunately, it was

Preflight and Post-Flight Inspections

A thorough preflight inspection is a must, and Skunberg also advocates that a thorough post-flight inspection be conducted after every flight. Skunberg says, "An important part of the preflight, after you have completed your close-up inspection, is to stand away from the airplane 20 or 30 feet and walk around the airplane looking at it from different angles. The first thing you may see is a tow-bar attached" (Skunberg, 2018). Skunberg says he has done probably $50,000 worth of repairs on a single airplane due to tow bar damage, including propellers, cowlings, and gear doors. He told of one incident in which three pilots were flying together, all doing the preflight, then took off with the tow bar still attached. Another pilot got distracted by a cell phone call and left the tow bar on.

Skunberg cited distractions as one of the biggest dangers to proper preflight inspections. The most prevalent, according to him, are pilots interrupting their preflight inspection to answer their cell phones. He advocates pilots turn off their phones to avoid being distracted while doing such important tasks. Skunberg said, "Answering or looking at the phone breaks the safety link, which continues down the dangerous chain of events."

severe clear, and I knew how to fly the airplane by the way it looked, felt, and sounded, so I had no problem returning for a landing to remove the pitot cover. We took off again with no issues, and I deserved the ribbing I got at breakfast from all the other pilots who had witnessed my blunder.

We camped another night and the next morning readied to return to town. As I was preflighting my airplane, I felt a tap on my shoulder and turned around. My friend's grandson had removed the pitot cover and now was handing it to me to stow in the cockpit.

The lesson learned that day is how easy it is to get distracted and miss checklist items. After I was interrupted, I should have started the walk-around inspection over again from the beginning, rather than continuing from where I thought I had left off. Additionally, I did not normally use the pitot cover in the hangar, which made it especially important to follow the preflight inspection checklist since it was not part of my normal habit to remove it during the walk-around.

After every flight, do a complete inspection of the airplane. That is the best time to clean off the bugs and dirt from leading edges and the aircraft belly. While cleaning, you will be able to note any new damage, missing screws, leaks, or other problems and attend to them immediately, rather than find them on your next preflight.

Skunberg noted the numerous times he has seen pilots leave the master switch on after a flight, and the battery freezes in cold temperatures after it runs down, causing "one heck of a mess with acid everywhere." An easy way to avoid that is to leave the anti-collision light on as a visible warning. As Skunberg pointed out, "In the backcountry, a dead battery means a hand-prop or a jump start, and that can be difficult with the 24-volt systems," which means you could be stuck in the middle of nowhere (Skunberg, 2018).

Finally, Skunberg recommended that pilots should make a checklist to supplement the manufacturer's checklist. The list should include all the extra items for backcountry flying and will help organize the pre- and post-flight inspections.

Was it the Preflight?

By R.K. Williams

I was a low time tailwheel pilot flying an old stock Super Cub. It was a club airplane and therefore did not need 100-hour inspections, only annuals. It was flown by nine different pilots, and although kept in a hangar, it was a poorly lit, dirt floor arrangement. I was also a low time backcountry pilot, but on this day, I was out practicing at a couple of airstrips along the Selway River in Idaho.

On climb-out from one of these strips, the right rudder suddenly became completely limp and useless. Not a good thing! I pondered the situation as I headed back towards home base. It is hard to move around and look at things inside a Super Cub cockpit, but I could squint down onto the dark floorboards and see the cable that links the primary rear rudder to the front lying useless on the floor. By hanging my right arm straight down, I could easily put my hand on the right rear rudder pedal and operate it, which meant I had to hold the stick with my left hand instead of the normal right-hand position. This also meant I didn't have my left hand available for the throttle, again the normal position.

There was no one to talk to at the quiet little Unicom home base airport, but fortunately there was very little wind blowing. I would have to land on pavement, power off, with my left hand on the stick and my right hand on the rudder. Did I mention I was a low time pilot? This situation definitely had my attention. I planned a stall landing to be as slow as possible and figured that in a bad bounce, I could quickly trade hands back to normal, forget right rudder, and go around. Not pretty, probably, but maybe okay if I didn't ram the throttle and cause a lot of torque and P-factor requiring a lot of right rudder that I didn't have.

I practiced flying this way for a few minutes and set up as stable an approach as I could, power off. I remembered reading something about flight control issues being one of the most critical in emergency flight situations. That didn't make me feel any better. It was an odd feeling, maintaining directional control with one foot and one hand.

Well, as they say, a good approach has a good possibility of leading to at least a decent landing. And that's what I got. It was actually surprisingly easy to taxi in that configuration!

We advocate post-flight inspections as well as post-flight briefings. This situation definitely called for both! The inspection quickly revealed that the weld at the tab connecting the cable to the rudder pedal had failed and that it had been cracked at the weld for some time.

My next task, although I wouldn't have called it that at the time, was to post-flight brief—to ponder what had happened, how it had happened, and how I could have prevented it. It had never been my habit to inspect rudder cable connections inside the cockpit, although one of the beauties of the Cub is that so much is exposed and easy to inspect. I had conducted my preflight in poor light without a flashlight (probably because I didn't have one). A more thorough preflight, in good light, *might* have shown the problem. I'll never really know, but this was an unforgettable lesson. This was an older airplane, flown by several pilots, with minimal maintenance and professional oversight. I also had the responsibility to notify all the other pilots, kind of like a mini **service bulletin**, so they could be aware and learn from my experience.

Accident Scenario

On March 26, 1991, a Cessna 337 Skymaster collided with terrain after takeoff. The NTSB cited an inadequate preflight and failure to remove the control lock as the cause of the accident (Figure 1-6).

National Transportation Safety Board
Aviation Accident Final Report

Location:	BOISE, ID	**Accident Number:**	SEA91FA071
Date & Time:	03/26/1991, 0748 MST	**Registration:**	N2107X
Aircraft:	CESSNA 337	**Aircraft Damage:**	Destroyed
Defining Event:		**Injuries:**	1 Fatal
Flight Conducted Under:	Part 91: General Aviation - Positioning		

Analysis

THE PILOT OF THE CESSNA 337 FAILED TO REMOVE THE AIRCRAFT'S CONTROL LOCKS. THE AIRCRAFT CRASHED ONTO THE AIRPORT RAMP AREA AFTER TAKING OFF, CLIMBING STEEPLY, AND ROLLING PARTIALLY INVERTED BEFORE IMPACTING NOSE LOW AND LEFT WING DOWN, IN AN APPROXIMATE 95 DEGREE BANK.

Probable Cause and Findings

The National Transportation Safety Board determines the probable cause(s) of this accident to be: THE PILOT'S FAILURE TO REMOVE THE AIRCRAFT CONTROL LOCKS PRIOR TO ATTEMPTING FLIGHT. FACTORS INCLUDE AN INADEQUATE PREFLIGHT.

Findings

Occurrence #1: LOSS OF CONTROL - IN FLIGHT
Phase of Operation: TAKEOFF

Findings
1. (C) REMOVAL OF CONTROL/GUST LOCK(S) - NOT PERFORMED - PILOT IN COMMAND
2. (F) PREFLIGHT PLANNING/PREPARATION - INADEQUATE - PILOT IN COMMAND

Occurrence #2: IN FLIGHT COLLISION WITH TERRAIN/WATER
Phase of Operation: DESCENT - UNCONTROLLED

Figure 1-6. NTSB accident final report stating the probable cause of the Cessna 337 accident on March 26, 1991.

The following narrative was provided via email by Michael Stockhill, who was the NTSB investigator for the accident:

Due to fog in Spokane, the freight pilot arrived in Boise the night before the accident and got lodging, expecting to complete his last leg home when the fog lifted. As originally equipped, like many Cessnas, the airplane had a control column gust lock with a metal flag that blocked either switches or power levers. In this instance, another party had replaced the factory control lock with a bolt to go through the control column, with a piece of rope with a piece of dowel similar to a broom stick attached. My recollection is that the rope was a foot or two long and the dowel was eight or ten inches long. It appeared customary to insert the bolt and then wrap the rope (about the diameter of clothes line) around the throttles, leaving the dowel to dangle.

With either the control lock or the bolt in place, the airplane's elevator was secured with its trailing edge up. It appeared that the pilot took off without removing the improvised control lock. As the airplane accelerated, it pitched nose up with the ensuing loss of control and impact. There was some evidence that the pilot attempted to remove the control lock, but it was not conclusive. I also suspected that the early morning glare in the cockpit was not helpful to the pilot observing the rope or dowel of the gust lock.

Pre-takeoff checklists generally specify checking controls for freedom of motion, of course. But it is also worth noting that the factory control lock would have limited the likelihood of even starting the engines before it was removed. Too often in aviation, it is not the big things, but the little things that lead to accidents. (Stockhill, 2018)

Review Questions and Exercises

Answers to review questions are provided in Appendix B.

Circle the correct answer:

1. Total flight time is a good indicator of your ability to fly mountainous terrain. (**True** / **False**)

2. Sailplane (glider) experience can be helpful in flying around the mountains. (**True** / **False**)

3. Airspeed has no correlation to turn radius. (**True** / **False**)

4. Practice maneuvers at only one weight and CG location. (**True** / **False**)

5. It is a good idea to leave the beacon switch on all the time, whether the master switch is on or not. (**True** / **False**)

6. Use flaps during flight at slow airspeeds to increase the limit load factor of the wing. (**True** / **False**)

7. The airplane will be (**more** / **less**) stable at a forward CG, the maneuvering speed will be (**higher** / **lower**), and the stall speed will be (**lower** / **higher**).

8. The airplane will be (**less** / **more**) maneuverable when loaded to a rear CG and the stall speed will be (**lower** / **higher**), allowing for (**slower** / **faster**) approach speeds.

Short answer:

9. What are some important aircraft preflight items you should conduct before venturing into the mountains and canyons?

10. Describe your personal level of pilot skill and experience and explain what you would do to prepare for flying in the mountains, canyons, and backcountry. Your answer should include (but not be limited to) the following:

   · What flight maneuvers and situations would you practice, and why?
   · What gross weight and CG loading position will you use?
   · What limitations would you impose as to where and when you would fly?
   · What type of aircraft would you choose to operate in the mountains, and why?
   · Will you have an experienced pilot or instructor accompany you? Why or why not?

Flight lesson:

Determine what exercises you will practice for mountain, canyon, and backcountry flight, and at what gross weight and center of gravity. Based on your current experience level, indicate whether you will take a mountain flying instructor with you, the current weather conditions, and what aircraft you will be using. Ideally, do this on a relatively cool and calm day. Take note of the various power settings needed for the different exercises.

Consider performing the following maneuvers:

   · Dutch roll coordination exercise
   · Flight at constant altitude with airspeed and configuration changes, in straight flight and in turns
   · Climbing and descending turns
   · Climbs, descents, and turns at V_A, V_{FE}, V_{LE}, and V_{CANYON}
   · Short-field and soft-field approaches and landings
   · Maximum performance takeoffs
   · Power off emergency glides to spot landings

Post-flight critique:

Use the FAA practical test and airman certification standards, private or commercial, as a basis for evaluation.

- How was your general aircraft control, including altitude and airspeed control?
- Did you maintain situational awareness as well as see and avoid other aircraft in the practice area?
- Did you practice stall/spin awareness throughout the maneuvers?
- What was your general comfort level?
- Does your performance warrant more sessions?

2

MOUNTAIN

and

CANYON

METEOROLOGY

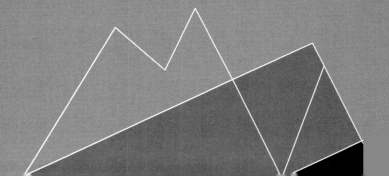

> *The storm starts, when the drops start dropping. When the drops stop dropping then the storm starts stopping.* 〝〞
>
> **Dr. Seuss**[1]

What is weather? What should pilots consider when planning flights into remote and mountainous areas? How does weather vary from region to region and from season to season? Does canyon weather differ from that over the top of mountains? How do sun and wind affect local flying conditions? What kinds of clouds should pilots expect to see, and how are clouds used to interpret weather? Those questions and more should be an integral part of your preflight planning before venturing into remote mountains and canyons. In addition to large-scale weather, smaller-scale weather phenomena are created by solar heating, wind, and pressure changes. You can use knowledge of both large- and small-scale weather patterns to enhance flight planning, avoid weather hazards, improve aircraft performance, and make critical decisions to mitigate risk and operate safely and efficiently.

The discussion of weather presented here assumes the reader has a working knowledge of weather theory at least comparable to that required to obtain a private pilot license, including study of frontal systems, precipitation, clouds, fog, mountain waves, microbursts, thunderstorms, wind shear, and other weather encountered in mountains and canyons. There are a multitude of resources on aviation-related weather theory and processes. The Federal Aviation Administration **Advisory Circular** (AC) 00-6, *Aviation Weather*, is free and available online (Federal Aviation Administration [FAA], 2016b). A good hard copy book is *Aviation Weather*, by Lester (2013), and an excellent online resource is Rod Machado's Understanding Weather—Interactive eLearning Course (Machado, 2017).

Flying in adverse weather remains a major cause of both fatal and non-fatal **general aviation (GA)** accidents (Knecht & Lenz, 2010; Price & Groff, 2013). Price and Groff (2013) cited studies showing that unfavorable winds, updrafts, and downdrafts were most associated with nonfatal GA accidents, while visibility-related weather conditions such as fog, rain, snow, or low ceilings increased the risk of fatal accidents. Defining "weather-related" as "fog, rain, snow or low ceilings," they found "the fatality rate for weather-related GA accidents is approximately three times higher than that for all GA accidents, and fatality rates for weather-related GA accidents have been consistently high over the years, ranging between 58% and 72%" (Price & Groff, 2013).

Mountain and canyon flight in adverse weather can amplify the already high risk, as there may be unique meteorological phenomena not encountered elsewhere. Anderson (2003) gives an overview of mountain weather patterns, which includes examples from the U.S. Rocky Mountains, and Potts (1993) provides excellent descriptions of weather phenomena at different times of year and during "transition periods" between seasons. This chapter explores several mountain and canyon weather phenomena, including situations unique to areas

---

[1] Dr. Seuss (1979). *Oh Say Can You Say?* New York, Random House Publishing.

with deep canyons. It also presents tips on how to avoid weather-related risks and maximize aircraft performance, primarily during warmer months. Chapter 7 includes information on winter weather and cold weather operations.

Preflight Weather Knowledge

Before any flight, you should obtain all available information about the weather, as dictated by 14 CFR §91.103. There are many sources of weather information, including phone weather briefings from an **Automated Flight Service Station (AFSS)** or through one of several online resources discussed in the next section. You will want to identify position and movement of major fronts, precipitation, convective activity, winds aloft forecasts, and adverse weather reports and forecasts. However, mountain weather can change rapidly, and forecasts may not be valid for more than a few hours. Major weather concerns during summer are morning fog in valleys and canyons, turbulence, wind shear, mountain waves, and afternoon or evening thunderstorms. Rain and snowstorms can form quickly in spring, fall, and winter, and daylight can be short-lived or nonexistent, depending on latitude. Wind and weather can be unpredictable and may vary greatly between locations only a few miles apart.

Online Weather Resources and Apps

You can obtain FAA weather briefings, including forecasts and **Notices to Airmen (NOTAMs)**, on the phone or from www.1800wxbrief.com in the United States. Another useful weather site is the **National Oceanic and Atmospheric Administration (NOAA)** Aviation Weather Center site at www.aviationweather.gov. A more complete list of websites and online pilot weather resources is available on the Reader Resources page at www.asa2fly.com/reader/mountain.

There are many weather and flight planning mobile apps. Two of the most popular are **ForeFlight** and **Garmin Pilot**. Both are subscription services that include weather information and also provide VFR and IFR charts, flight planning tools, live in-flight weather, and more. **AeroWeather** is an app that shows weather reports and forecasts with updates every hour, as well as live radar and links to airport information and webcams.

Doppler weather radar can predict and track weather systems, but it may provide limited coverage over remote mountain and canyon areas. It can provide information about the upper atmosphere, but Doppler radar signals may be blocked by terrain in much of the lower atmosphere over mountains and canyons. Doppler radar sites are widely spaced in the mountain west and Alaska (Vivion, 2018), and low-level precipitation or weather may be invisible due to terrain interference.

Pilot Reports and Webcams

Make a **pilot report (PIREP)** with FSS, whenever possible. However, you may not be able to do so due to terrain interference. Make reports over the common traffic frequency in remote areas (usually Multicom on 122.9 in the United States) and listen for other pilots making weather reports. Ask their position and inquire about fog, smoke, surface wind conditions, and convective activity unique to that area. It is important to accurately report weather at your location. This "backcountry telegraph" is often the best source of up-to-date weather information.

Some mountainous areas have live webcams and remote weather reporting stations. Webcams can prove invaluable. However, backcountry webcams usually rely on solar power to uplink to satellites and can have downtime, so refresh your browser or web viewer and check the date and time stamp to ensure you have the current image.

In-Flight Weather Information

As described by Vivion (2018), accessing good weather data in flight can be difficult. The **Automatic Dependent Surveillance–Broadcast (ADS-B)** system (see Chapter 3) may provide weather information over flatland areas, but it has limited coverage over mountainous and canyon terrain. **XM Satellite Weather** is a satellite-based system that provides most of the weather information necessary to make good weather decisions in remote areas. It requires a subscription and a device to display the data. You may also be able to use a satellite phone to obtain weather information when out of cell service or Wi-Fi range. However, the availability of up-to-date weather information is invaluable. One of the key features of a satellite-based system, even in flat country, is that you can receive weather data to help with your decision-making before takeoff, rather than having to get airborne before acquiring weather data via radio or the ADS-B system (Vivion, 2018).

Global Circulation and Pressure Patterns

General mid-latitude (30–60 degrees) circulation in the northern hemisphere is from the southwest to northeast. Southern hemisphere circulation is from the southeast to northwest. Summer brings southwesterly and westerly flow aloft to the Canadian and U.S. Cascade Mountains and the Sierra Nevada. Mountain waves are not uncommon to the east of the ranges up to flight level altitudes. Westerly winds exceeding 50 knots are not uncommon in the Colorado Rocky Mountains. Since the ranges are mostly perpendicular to prevailing winds, extreme turbulence can occur, and mountain waves can exist hundreds of miles "downstream" (east) of the mountains (Anderson, 2003). Generally, high-pressure systems bring good visibility and stable air, and low-pressure systems bring unstable air, turbulence, and possibly precipitation. During fall, winter, and spring, winds and circulation patterns are less predictable. Study the large-scale weather patterns and climate for any mountainous area in which you plan to operate, and gain as much knowledge as you can from persons familiar with the area before flying there.

When I was flying sailplanes in the Sun Valley, Idaho, area years ago, we would always watch for eagles that nested near the ridge where we usually dropped from the tow plane. The eagles were the best indication of the strongest—although sometimes narrow—thermals. One unforgettable time, I saw one of the eagles watching me as I climbed in a strong thermal. He decided I had chosen a better one than he had (only by dumb luck) and came over to join me. We soared together for several minutes, with the eagle making his turns inside my glider's turns. I could clearly see him watching me and maneuvering his winglets for fine bank control.

Raptors, however, are not always so accommodating. Consider our friend Michael Stockhill's experience: "I found myself on a head-on collision course with an eagle in my single-seat glider. He decided I was a threat at the moment I spotted him. He extended his legs and talons, ready to attack, for a moment, and then retracted his landing gear again. He was ready to tear off my face." (Stockhill, 2018)

Mountain Winds

Mountain and canyon winds create shear, lift, sink, and turbulence, and it is prudent to maintain a constant awareness of wind direction and strength. The flow of wind over terrain is similar to water flow in a shallow, fast-moving stream. It may help to study a whitewater river and try to visualize how wind, which is also a fluid, might flow around and over terrain. Visualize this while flying and also when studying an aeronautical chart before your flight. Winds aloft forecasts will give you an idea of where you might expect to encounter various wind phenomena. Try to determine from the terrain or the chart locations where wind might accelerate or decelerate as it blows through mountain passes or canyons. Envision where it could create updrafts and downdrafts over hills, mountains, ridges, and other obstacles. Imagine how winds might mix and create turbulence at the confluence of canyons or divert into a valley before being forced over a mountain or ridge. Several of these effects are covered later in this chapter, and the end-of-chapter exercises will give the opportunity to apply them to preflight planning.

Look at trees, smoke, and mountain lakes to ascertain local wind direction and speed. Cloud shadows give an indication of the prevailing wind at the level of the cloud layer. Observing birds can give you an indication of the effects of wind, as large birds may use thermals or ridges to catch updrafts. Always be alert, because wind speed and direction can be inconsistent and change rapidly, even from one ridge or canyon to the next.

In general, wind velocity increases as wind blows across a mountain or ridge (Figure 2-1). This will produce updrafts on the upwind side and downdrafts on the downwind, or lee side, sometimes without much turbulence.

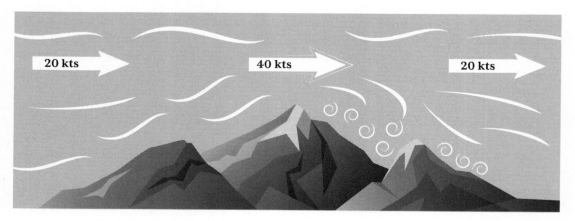

Figure 2-1. Wind velocity increases as it blows over a mountain range. Due to the restriction of air as it is forced over the obstruction, velocity will increase, similar to what happens when air flows over a cambered airfoil. *(Courtesy of Civil Aviation Authority of New Zealand, 2012.)*

R.K.'s Rule

The wind doesn't blow, it sucks!

Use extreme caution crossing ridges, and always do so at a 45-degree angle so you can turn away should you encounter downdrafts. Narrow mountain passes may increase wind velocity, even with only light to moderate prevailing winds.

Knowing the winds on the ground is critical when operating from mountain and canyon airstrips. During summer, many mountain airstrips, especially those in canyons, are unsafe to fly into or out of by late morning because of wind. Landing with a headwind at a one-way strip means you would be departing with a tailwind (see Chapters 5 and 6). In high winds, consider returning to land later after the wind has calmed down, or plan to stay at a one-way strip until it decreases.

Mountain Waves

Given relatively stable air and winds aloft of more than 25 knots perpendicular to a mountain range—such as the Rocky Mountains, European or New Zealand Alps, U.S. and Canadian Cascades, the Alaska Range, or the Sierra Nevada—a mountain wave effect may result. Conditions can be fairly calm on the windward side of the mountains but turbulent on the leeward side with rotors and downdrafts. Mountain waves may extend many miles downwind of the mountain range, and wavelengths can vary, but they generally are about eight to ten miles (FAA, 2016b),

Figure 2-2. Photo of a cap cloud taken from the upwind side of Mt. Adams in the Washington Cascades. Cap clouds are formed when moist air is forced upward and is cooled to its condensation point. As the moist air is compressed on the downwind side, the cloud evaporates, making the cloud seem to hover above the mountain. The lenticular shape is caused by winds aloft blowing over the mountain. *(Photo by Amy Hoover)*

and the shorter the wavelength, the greater the amplitude of the wave. For more information regarding mountain wave formation, see Lester (2013) or FAA (2016b).

Use extreme caution if you suspect mountain wave activity. Forecast high-velocity winds aloft, **cirrus clouds**, and **lenticular clouds** all indicate increased wind speed over the mountains.

Cap clouds, **rotor clouds**, and **standing lenticular clouds** may form over mountaintops or in a mountain wave if there is enough moisture. Those clouds warn of high winds and turbulence. Figure 2-2 shows a cap cloud taken from the upwind side of a mountain.

Avoid flying too close to a ridge or mountain on the downwind side, as you could encounter extreme turbulence and downdrafts that exceed the climb capability of your aircraft. Do not attempt to out-climb a downdraft. Winds aloft as little as 25 knots can create downdrafts of more than 2,000 feet per minute (fpm) when blowing over even small ridges or mountains (Lester, 2013). Most GA airplanes will not be able to climb at a rate that exceeds the downward air, especially at high altitudes over mountainous terrain. Pitching for V_Y (**best rate of climb**) is not recommended, as it will slow the airplane down and increase the amount of time spent in the downdraft. The best course of action is to immediately turn away from the source of the descending air (e.g., ridge, mountain, obstruction) and fly out of the downdraft toward lower terrain, if possible. Use normal cruise speed in smooth air. Fly at **maneuvering speed** (V_A) in turbulence to avoid exceeding the wing's limit load factor. Always approach a ridge or mountain at an angle and do so with sufficient altitude to clear the terrain should you encounter downdrafts.

Amy's
Axiom

Do not try to out-climb a downdraft! Turn and fly away, to live again another day.

Cloud Types and Weather Systems

For classification purposes, clouds are divided into four families: high, middle, low, and those with extensive vertical development (FAA, 2016b). Additionally, clouds are given a prefix or suffix describing other characteristics. For example, a **stratus cloud** is layered. A **nimbostratus cloud** is also a layered cloud, often widespread, that produces precipitation. Familiarizing yourself with the various types of clouds and their relationship to global weather patterns, as well as the significance of certain cloud types, will help you anticipate adverse weather conditions.

Thunderstorms are particularly hazardous because of the effects of high winds, turbulence, and precipitation as storms move over ridges and through canyons. Associated cloud formations include **cumulonimbus** and **mammatus** clouds, and you should never fly in or near them. These clouds can develop rapidly—much faster than a jet can climb at altitude. **Microbursts** can also be associated with convective activity and thunderstorms, regardless of whether moisture or precipitation is present. **Virga** is precipitation that evaporates before it reaches the ground and is common during summer months in dry areas, such as the mountainous western United States. Exercise caution around clouds that produce virga because there could be severe turbulence and downdrafts—or even microbursts—underneath them. Also note that forest fires can create their own weather systems, including convective activity and thunderstorm formation.

Some of the most dangerous mountain and canyon flying conditions are widespread areas of low clouds and steady precipitation, such as occur in a stable air mass. Visibility is usually poor and can change rapidly from **visual meteorological conditions (VMC)** to **instrument meteorological conditions (IMC)**, both spatially and temporally. Marginal weather in canyons, such as rain or snowstorms and low clouds with restricted visibility, is dangerous. It is possible to suddenly encounter a "whiteout" condition and lose sight of all visual reference to terrain. Flying in these conditions is not advocated; it is best to wait until the weather improves.

Figure 2-3. Widespread cloud cover at ridge-top level obscures the terrain below. Deep canyons and mountain ridges cannot be seen through the overcast layer. *(Photos by Amy Hoover)*

Fog

In mountainous terrain, the temperature often drops below the dew point overnight, and if there is moisture, usually from the previous night's thunderstorms, fog will form in the valleys and canyons. You might take off from a valley and cross a ridge to find a large area of fog blanketing the next canyon or a wide area of terrain (Figure 2-3). Fog can form very quickly, especially close to the time of sunrise, so it is good to have an alternate airport that is clear within range.

Is it safe to fly over the top of a broken or overcast layer in the mountains? The answer depends on many variables and will change from one day or flight to another. For example, you might depart from an airport that is VMC and know your destination airport is also VMC as reported by **ASOS/AWOS**, live webcam, or another reliable source. Then ask yourself several questions. What is the risk of flying over mountainous terrain blanketed by clouds, since you will not be able to see the ground to navigate or to make a landing in an emergency? Is the weather system stable or unstable? Are conditions likely to improve or to deteriorate? Cold, stable weather, such as during fall or winter, can cause the cloud layer to remain in place most of the day. Winter temperatures close to the ground may be colder than those aloft, creating a temperature inversion. This stable air condition resists vertical motion and widespread areas of freezing fog can last days or even weeks.

In summer months, solar heating may cause fog and low clouds to break up and rise out of the canyons and off ridge tops, with good visibility underneath. You will then have to make a decision whether to fly in a canyon under the cloud layer or go over the top. Either choice may present hazards. You might have adequate clearance under the clouds, but not be able to climb up and out

Figure 2-4. The overcast cloud layer is below ridge-top levels. You might descend through a "hole" into the canyon below. However, if you fly under a cloud layer in a canyon, you might not be able to climb back out again. *(Photo by Amy Hoover)*

of the canyon through a broken or overcast layer. Your choice may be based on familiarity with the terrain and your own personal minimums, as discussed in Chapter 9. Generally, if you are not confident you will be able to climb out of a canyon or do not know the twists and turns of the terrain, do not attempt to fly up or down a canyon under a cloud layer that is at or below ridgetop level (Figure 2-4).

Another hazardous situation, as described by the Civil Aviation Authority of New Zealand (CAA, 2012), is high-level clouds lacking a defined base lowering to blend with lower-level scattered clouds. The CAA notes "this can sometimes be difficult to detect and may trap the unwary... Do not be suckered into flying between ill-defined cloud layers."

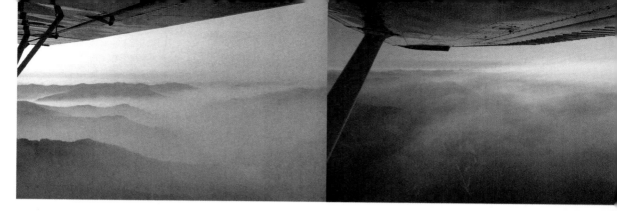

Figure 2-5. Smoke from forest fires settled into the canyons during stable air conditions. Note the terrain at the bottom of the canyon is visible in the foreground. However, once in the canyon, it may not be possible to see terrain ahead of the aircraft. *(Photos by Amy Hoover)*

Haze and Smoke

In smoke and haze, even though weather may be reported as visual meteorological conditions (VMC), it may not actually be possible to navigate by outside visual reference. Vivion coined the term **"Pretend VFR"** (PVFR) and defined it as:

> A situation where the meteorological conditions meet the definition of "basic VFR," but conditions are such that there are too few visual references within the range of the prevailing visibility to keep the airplane upright by reference to a visual horizon, and to safely navigate... PVFR prevails when one is in VFR weather conditions but can't see anything except the weather. (Vivion, 2008)

Based on the concept of PVFR, you might deem it safe to operate in widespread haze or smoke with 3 to 5 miles visibility over flat terrain without obstacles, where you can fly close enough to the ground to see the terrain, but what about in a canyon? Figure 2-5 shows an area of widespread smoke that has settled into canyons that are 4,000 to 5,000 feet deep. Although flying and navigating via visual cues above the ridge tops may be possible, forward visibility after descending into the smoke might not be enough to allow you to see the canyon walls and to maneuver without impacting terrain.

Small-Scale Local Weather Phenomena

An important component of mountain and canyon flight is identifying where to find lift and using it to improve climb performance and terrain clearance. Mountain pilots typically expect wind to flow down into a canyon and then up the other side, creating an updraft on the downwind side of the canyon. However, that is not always true since actual lift is the result of the interaction between orographic lift (created by wind and mountains) and solar lift, or heat. Additionally, the updraft side may change from one side of a canyon to the other as the canyon twists and turns and different sides face the sun or wind. This concept is explored in the following sections on orographic and thermal effects adapted from "Canyon Weather Part 1: Effects of Wind and Sun" (Hoover, 2001a).

Solar Lift

Every process of weather is related to uneven heating of the earth's surface. As morning sun strikes east-facing slopes, they heat up more quickly than the surrounding terrain, causing the warmed air to rise as thermal (**anabatic**) lift. This early morning lift may not last more than an hour or two. Thermal lift in the northern hemisphere is found on south and west facing slopes for most of the day, and in the southern hemisphere on north and west facing slopes as the day progresses. Thermal lift can be quite significant during summer, and mountain pilots seek it out. Rising air must be replaced by downward moving air at a different location, so where there are thermals, there will also be downdrafts. With practice, you can learn to anticipate the location of each, use the thermals to your advantage, and stay out of the downdrafts. There may be no lift in winter as there is not enough heat from the sun to cause a temperature differential.

Amy's Axiom

What goes up must come down. Be alert for downdrafts near thermals.

Anabatic lift typically extends approximately 100 to 300 feet from the slope (Conway, 1969). On steep slopes or canyon walls, it can be as close as 50 to 100 feet from the face of the ridge, or directly above the ridgeline, depending on the degree of slope. That means you need to be close to mountain faces or canyon walls to take advantage of thermal lift. Bare rocks and slopes will heat up faster and generate more lift than areas that are heavily forested, so look for the "brighter" slopes. Expect to find a lift differential between areas in sun and shadow, and possible

---

[2] Curtiss, Glenn H. and Post, Augustus (1912). *The Curtiss Aviation Book.* New York, Fredrick A. Stokes Company

turbulence at the boundary between those areas (Figure 2-6). There may even be enough difference between bare slopes and forested areas to create turbulence at the boundary between them due to wind shear produced by differential lift.

Figure 2-6. Rocky canyon walls are exposed to morning sunlight. Expect thermal lift on the "bright" sides and either no lift or negative lift (sink) on the shadowed side. Vertical wind shear could be present at the boundary between the light and dark areas. *(Photo by Amy Hoover)*

Orographic Lift

Orographic lift is mechanical lift created by wind flowing over terrain. As air flows over mountains, it rises and cools. Moist air can form clouds (such as the cap cloud shown in Figure 2-2), orographic precipitation, or upslope fog. Heavy, cool air is heated and dries out as it descends down a mountain slope or canyon, which can cause local winds, such as the Santa Ana winds of Southern California, the Mistral winds downwind of the French Alps, or Chinook winds east of the North American Rocky Mountains.

In Western North America, prevailing winds are generally from the west and southwest. Thus, you usually find upslope winds on west-facing slopes and downslope winds on east-facing slopes. This is especially true with well-defined, major north–south mountain ranges oriented perpendicular to the prevailing westerly winds, such as the Canadian and U.S. Cascades, the Sierra Nevada, or the Rocky Mountains. Using thermal lift from terrain to gain altitude is called "contouring" and entails repeated trips along the ridge or mountain face to gain altitude. When circling back toward the lift, always make turns away from the ridge to avoid being blown into the terrain.

In areas where more randomly oriented mountains and canyons prevail, determining local wind directions and locations of orographic lift is not straightforward. For example, the mountains of Central Idaho and Western Montana are formed by a large mass of randomly oriented ridges cut by deep, sinuous rivers. Prevailing wind flow over those areas is more like waves crashing over a jumble of rocks, creating local winds on a smaller scale that produce patterns of random, unpredictable areas of lift and sink, and ridge-top winds are often hard to predict and vary widely with respect to speed and direction.

Combination of Orographic and Solar Lift

Summer sun shines for the longest amount of time on southwest and west facing slopes in the northern hemisphere, and prevailing wind is usually out of the southwest or west. Thus, orographic and **thermal lift** can combine and greatly augment the lifting force. But what if the wind is blowing from a different direction and thermal and orographic lift work against one another? Thermal lift will create updrafts on a sun-facing slope, but if that slope is on the lee side of a ridge or canyon, orographic effects produce downdrafts. The updrafts meet the downdrafts and create turbulence (Figure 2-7).

Turbulence can reach deeper into the canyon as wind velocity increases and become severe to extreme. In very deep, rocky canyons exposed to the sun over a long time, thermal lift may cause updrafts powerful enough to create a "cushion" of air in the canyon bottoms that deflects orographic downdrafts. Turbulence may occur at any level and depends on the relative strength of the opposing thermal and orographic effects. Such turbulence is often greatest at ridge-top level (Figure 2-7B). At lower levels, solar lift on the upwind side may be stronger than orographic lift on the downwind side, depending on temperature and geographic location, thus making it better to fly on the upwind, or "wrong" side of the canyon. After departing from

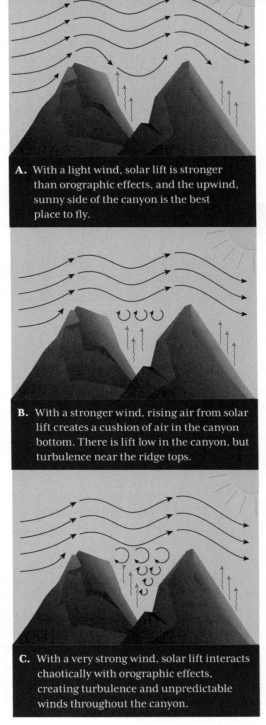

A. With a light wind, solar lift is stronger than orographic effects, and the upwind, sunny side of the canyon is the best place to fly.

B. With a stronger wind, rising air from solar lift creates a cushion of air in the canyon bottom. There is lift low in the canyon, but turbulence near the ridge tops.

C. With a very strong wind, solar lift interacts chaotically with orographic effects, creating turbulence and unpredictable winds throughout the canyon.

Figure 2-7. Effects of orographic and solar lift (Hoover, 2001a). *(Courtesy Pilot Getaways Magazine)*

an airstrip in the bottom of such a canyon, you could encounter updrafts during initial climb that change to turbulence and downdrafts as you gain altitude.

Very strong winds create turbulence and wind shear at all levels in a canyon. Predicting which of these phenomena will occur is difficult, so it is best to stay out of canyons during strong winds (Figure 2-8). Local pilots can be a great resource since they may know where and when to expect turbulence and lift. It could be safe to fly with winds of 15–20 knots in one area but not another. A good practice is to consult with local pilots before attempting to mix mountains, canyons, and wind.

Figure 2-8. (A and B) Airstrip located in the bottom of a deep river canyon with forested north-facing slopes to the left and "brighter" south-facing slopes to the right will have differential lift. Expect wind shear at the boundary between the two slopes, which can be exacerbated by downdrafts over the cooler river water. This airstrip also has a drop off of approximately 100 feet to the river on the approach end. *(Photos by Amy Hoover)*

(C) This airplane ran into a ditch and flipped after a late afternoon landing attempt with wind shear and gusts, causing the pilot to overshoot the approach and land long on the 1,500-foot runway. *(Photo courtesy Mike Chapman, Flying Brokers)*

I had the opportunity of a lifetime to bring my Super Cub up to Anchorage, Alaska, while stationed at Elmendorf Air Force Base. One day I'd be flying the F-22 in a large training exercise over the Alaska range, and the next day I would hop in the Super Cub to catch fish on one of the countless rivers and lakes. My background in mountain and canyon flying skills applied across both aircraft. However, in the F-22 I had the power to get out of situations that could prove disastrous in a small airplane. There was a day where the mission had eight F-22s training in the Stony MOA west of Anchorage. At the end of the mission, four of us had some remaining fuel prior to Bingo and took the opportunity to refresh our low-altitude skills. We had a standard training route that we called "Star Wars canyon" and would fly either a north-to-south flow or vice versa. The weather initially was great, but as we progressed in a trail formation down the canyon, it changed quickly. An overcast layer was descending and began occluding our follow-on route. The decision was easy—light the afterburners, go straight up to 25,000 feet, and take it home for the day. During the time down low, it was easy to see the changing signs of the weather moving in: dust blowing down the canyons, clouds rolling over the tops of the peaks from multiple sides, and increased turbulence. Making a quick decision to climb was important, and we had the excess power and options to take it to the max.

A couple months later—this time in the Super Cub—I was returning from a caribou hunt in north Alaska. I was approaching the Alaska range just southwest of Denali, having passed Galena two hours prior, and bucking a 20-knot headwind. As I got closer to the mountains, I saw some of the same warning signs across the range that I had seen in the F-22. Dust and haze were blowing out of every canyon exit, reducing visibility and increasing

Reverse-Direction Winds

Anderson (2003) described the occurrence of "**reverse-direction**" **winds** in the Colorado Rocky Mountains and cited studies showing surface winds (extending up to as high as 1,000 feet above ground level) that blow opposite the prevailing wind direction over a mountain pass and against the normal pressure gradient. Similar winds can occur on a much smaller scale in deep canyons (Figure 2-9). With moderate winds, updrafts occur on the downwind side of the canyon. However, as wind velocity increases, a reverse "scooping" effect is sometimes observed, and downdrafts are encountered on the downwind side of a canyon, with updrafts on the upwind side. Remain vigilant and be ready to alter course immediately if you encounter downdrafts. Lift is where you find it, and not always where you expect it to be.

the turbulence and wind—a clear sign of major downdrafts. This time I didn't have the afterburners to carry me up and over in a matter of seconds. The route through the mountain passes was the best for contingency plans and efficiency, but that was quickly showing signs of not being an option for the day. I briefed my passenger and began a climb while offsetting to the most "updraft" part of the canyon entrance I could find. With 3,500 feet now below me, I tried rounding the first corner and, sure enough, the performance decreased. At full power there was no climb, and then I hit the downdrafts. Having prepared my out-maneuver with this expectation, I quickly dropped the nose and dove out towards my safe zone. Once several miles away from the mountains, I began to assess my options. I could return to Galena and refuel to try again later in the day, land on a gravel bar and camp for the night, or climb up and assess the VFR capability and conditions. Since I had long-range fuel tanks, I decided to try the on-top option. I was balancing risks, but in the end it was the best way across the range while the weather was still holding up. Fighting a 30-knot headwind with a crawling 50-mph ground speed all the way home was much better than forcing a potentially disastrous situation through a mountain-canyon pass in poor conditions.

Reading weather takes many forms, including wind over lakes and rivers, blowing trees, dust devils, virga, blowing dust, the direction of cloud movement, types of clouds, thermals, likely updraft/downdraft areas, cold or warm front indications, the smell of the air or humidity level, pressure changes seen on the altimeter, and the feel of the air as you fly through it. Interpreting all of the environmental conditions that you are flying in will allow you to make proactive rather than reactive decisions.

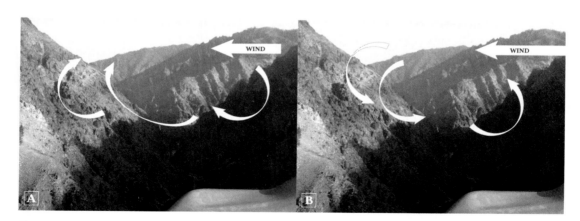

Figure 2-9. Reverse-direction flow can occur as wind velocity increases. **(A)** Updrafts will be on the downwind side of the canyon and downdrafts on the upwind side in moderate wind. **(B)** As wind increases, downdrafts occur on the downwind side of the canyon, which is the sunlit side in this example and opposite to what you might expect. *(Photos by Amy Hoover)*

One calm morning, I flew into Stehekin airstrip in the Washington Cascades. The airstrip lies at the bottom of a deep canyon between glacially formed Lake Chelan to the southeast and high mountain peaks to the northwest. Diurnal winds are common, and the deep glacial lake canyon is more than 30 miles long, so winds can be significant. Generally, the diurnal winds start around mid-morning during spring and summer months, blowing up the lake to the northeast and toward the mountains.

After I made a landing to the NW and took off to the SE, over the lake, I returned and landed to the SE. The lake showed no indication of wind, the trees were not moving, and the windsock was still. After landing, I turned around, verified the sock was still dead, and took off to the NW toward the mountains. After the airplane lifted off the ground and into ground effect, I felt a significant gust of tailwind; the sock shot straight out, the trees waved, and I felt "the bottom drop out" as the tailwind hit the wing of my Cessna 180. Since I was past my pre-determined abort point

(see discussion of takeoff abort planning in chapter 6), I immediately pushed the nose over to gain airspeed and clear the trees at the

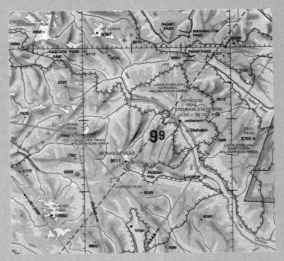

Aeronautical chart of Stehekin State airport. High terrain to the west and northwest cause diurnal winds to form, which are accelerated down the narrow glacial lake to create a venturi effect and increase wind velocities. Diurnal winds can pick up suddenly in the mornings.

Diurnal Effects

Phenomena that occur daily, known as diurnal, are caused by uneven heating of the earth's surface throughout the day and by uneven cooling at night. Factors such as varying slope, color, latitude, and elevation contribute to uneven surface heating. **Diurnal winds** are observed on a large scale near major mountain ranges and also occur in canyons. Many canyons are hundreds of miles long, and the river elevation between their upper and lower ends may differ by thousands of feet. Daily cyclic changes through these deep, long canyons are the result of the interplay between heat from the sun, rising and falling air, and the shape and elevation of the terrain. Diurnal changes are greatest in summer when the sun is higher in the sky and the days are longest. As described by the FAA (2016b) and shown in Figure 2-10, a valley breeze is a wind that ascends a mountain valley during the day because the air above the mountain slope heats up faster than the

end of the airstrip. The wind intensified as I continued to climb up the canyon, so rather than attempting to turn around at low altitude, I headed for the canyon wall directly in front of me, since I could visualize the wind hitting the rocks and being forced upward. I flew over to the side of the canyon at an angle and caught an updraft of more than 1,500 fpm that lifted me like an elevator. The diurnal wind started almost instantaneously, and had I remained over the middle of the canyon I might still be there trying to climb out!

Stehekin airstrip: **(A)** photo looking southeast toward the lake and **(B)** northwest toward the Cascade mountain range. After takeoff to the northwest, a tailwind will cause updrafts on the rocky slopes.

cooler valley air, becomes less dense, and rises, causing wind to flow from the valley up the mountain slope. A mountain breeze refers to the downslope winds that occur at night when the sloping terrain cools the air faster and it becomes denser, thus flowing downslope to replace the warmer air above the valley.

The valley/mountain breeze phenomenon is magnified as wind blows through a canyon. As the morning sun strikes canyon walls, air from the lower part of the canyon heats up. Rather than rising directly upward, the air follows the canyon upstream toward higher terrain (valley breeze). Thus, winds normally blow up-canyon (or upstream) beginning midmorning. These winds can become quite strong by mid-afternoon. Air cools more quickly in the evening at the upper (higher altitude) end of a canyon, becomes dense, and sinks downstream. Thus, canyon winds (mountain breeze) normally flow down-canyon (downstream) during evening and nighttime hours.

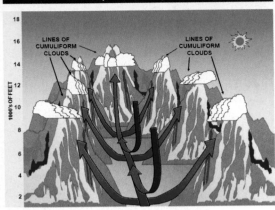 

Figure 2-10. Valley and mountain breezes: (**A**) During the daytime, wind blows up the mountain slope and the resultant cooled air sinks over the valley, creating a circulation. Clouds and precipitation may develop over mountain slopes. (**B**) At night, the surface wind blows down the mountain slope and warmer air rises over the valley, reversing the direction of circulation. *(From FAA, 2016b, figures 9.8 and 9.10)*

This cycle of winds blowing upstream in the mornings and downstream in the evenings is a dynamic process that repeats daily, but there can be many exceptions locally due to the shape of the canyon itself, as well as the influence from winds entering the canyon from tributary canyons. Several of those effects are described next, as adapted from "Canyon Weather Part 2: Convergence, Turbulence, Venturis, and More" (Hoover, 2001b).

Convergence Effects

A unique wind phenomenon that occurs where canyons join is called a **convergence effect**. Canyons may converge at various angles and directions. Diurnal winds can be stronger and develop early in the day through large canyons, but they may develop later or not at all in smaller tributary canyons. This means the wind might be blowing upstream through a major river drainage but downstream in one of the side canyons that feed into the main canyon. Expect turbulence at the confluence, and the turbulence could be severe depending on the relative strength of the opposing winds. Because of converging rivers or streams, canyons are typically wider at confluences, and sandbars or benches tend to form there. Thus, airstrips are often located near river confluences (Figure 2-11). Study the aeronautical chart ahead of time and pay special attention to areas where canyons converge so you can anticipate flying conditions. At airstrips near confluences, be alert for varying winds, wind shear, and turbulence.

Many canyon airstrips have more than one windsock, and it is not unusual for them to point in different directions. Variable wind can be due to microbursts, a thermal over the runway, or convergence.

Figure 2-11. The confluence of two river canyons. Late morning and afternoon winds often blow upstream in the main canyon (in the canyon from top left toward right in the photo) and may blow downstream in the side canyon (from bottom left toward the confluence in the photo), and they can cause turbulence at the juncture. Note two airstrips located near the confluence, one on the side canyon in the lower left in the photo, and the other on the main river in the right side of the photo. There is often turbulence with unpredictable winds. *(Photo by Amy Hoover)*

When it comes to wind shear and microbursts, often what comes to mind is the tragedy at Dallas–Fort Worth with a Delta L-1011 on August 2, 1985. The Delta Air Lines Flight 191 flew through a microburst on approach to land and crashed a mile short of the runway, killing 137 people. It is easy to think a smaller aircraft might be able to avoid a catastrophe like that. In fact, a Learjet had just completed a successful approach ahead of that airliner, and its success was later attributed to its size and power. Even though that particular wind shear was thunderstorm related, I experienced almost uncontrollable mountain wind shear in Idaho in a Learjet 45 many years later.

We were operating at an airport I was very familiar with and from which I had flown sailplanes years earlier. I also knew that the control tower was under public pressure to conduct landings on runway 31 and takeoffs on 13 whenever possible for noise abatement. On our approach, we noted strong, gusty winds out of the southwest (coming across and down a ridge to the west adjacent to the runway) with a forest fire and thunderstorm in the vicinity to the north. The tower was advertising landings on 31, with a quartering tailwind, and the entire area was clearly unstable.

We started experiencing some strong turbulence as we entered the canyon south of the airport, and I suggested to my co-captain, and flying pilot, that we request a landing on 13 to avoid the tailwind component and facilitate an easier go-around if necessary. He agreed and

Unconnected Drainages

Atmospheric pressure patterns and local winds can vary considerably from one location to another only a short distance away. Pressure usually equalizes between two canyons in the same drainage system and altimeter settings are similar. However, if you fly from one canyon across a ridge or divide into a canyon in a different drainage system, there may be a pressure differential between the two canyons. Expect wind and turbulence at the divide between the two drainage systems; this pressure difference may cause your altimeter to be off by several hundred feet.

Other pilots may have originated their flights from an area of different pressure, so be aware they may be reporting altitudes with a different altimeter setting from yours. Set your altimeter to the field elevation each time you land and verify altimeter settings with other pilots in flight. Remember: flying from high to low pressure, or hot to cold, your altimeter will indicate higher than your true altitude, so "look out below."

the tower complied. As we entered downwind, it was obvious the flying pilot had his hands full just flying the airplane. At about 1,500 feet, as we turned base, he called for full flaps, and just about then it really broke loose as we entered the shear. I had just moved the flap handle to full, but instantly put it back to 20 degrees. The pilot initiated the go-around from that point and we got to hear every bad aural warning the aircraft had to offer:

"Wind shear, wind shear!"

"Pull up, Pull up!"

Then the stick shaker and the warning, "Stall! Stall!"

"Sink rate! Sink rate!" "Don't sink! Don't sink!"

We attended simulator training every six months and routinely went through the Dallas reenactment. This was worse, but at least we were up on the correct procedures, and the pilot flew them perfectly. The airplane pulled through and eventually initiated a climb and recovery, but it was an experience neither of us will soon forget. We were fortunate to initiate recovery at that altitude, with 7,000 pounds of thrust. I would not have wanted to be there in a less powerful airplane.

Ten minutes later, we made a successful approach on 31, still uncomfortable but safe. Wind shear is not something to mess with in any airplane, and it generally changes in ten to fifteen minutes or less.

Venturi Effects

The **venturi effect** is an increase in wind speed through a constriction or bottleneck, such as a mountain pass or narrow canyon. A wide valley or intermountain basin that narrows to form the entrance to a canyon will accelerate the wind, causing a pressure decrease and horizontal and/or vertical wind shear. An extreme example of this is the Columbia River Gorge where it cuts through the Cascade Mountains between Oregon and Washington (Figure 2-12).

In winter, the semi-desert terrain east of the Cascade Mountains has a higher pressure than the maritime areas west of the mountains, and winds blow from east to west. The dry and more barren terrain east of the mountains heats up more quickly during summer, resulting in an opposite pressure differential. Summer winds blow from west to east as the relatively denser air west of the range rushes to replace the rising air in the east. The Columbia Gorge is the "windsurfing capital of the world" for this reason.

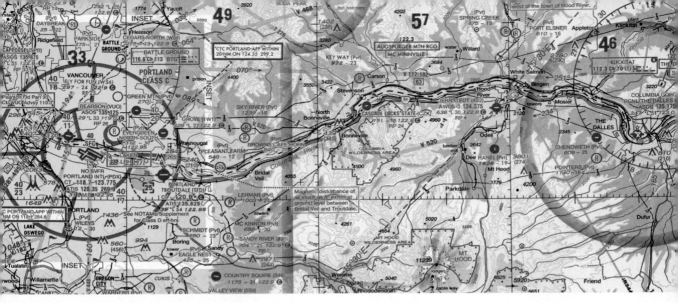

Figure 2-12. The Columbia River Gorge in the Cascade Mountains creates a venturi. Several airports in and near the Gorge experience high winds year-round, although the prevailing wind direction changes from summer to winter.

At the west end of the Gorge, the narrower terrain opens out into a wide valley, and the wind diverges and flows outward away from the constricted area, causing vertical and horizontal wind shear. An example of this is at the east end of the Columbia River Gorge (Figure 2-12). In winter, Troutdale airport (KTTD), which is located at the mouth of the Gorge, can have strong east winds while airports only a few miles to the north or south will have calm or only slight winds.

There can be turbulence and wind shear during approach and departure to an airport located at the mouth of a canyon, regardless of wind direction. Study the charts ahead of time and identify terrain constrictions to anticipate a venturi effect. Also, anticipate a venturi in a narrow canyon that makes a sharp bend, causing the wind to change direction rapidly. The "formula" for a venturi is the presence of relatively high terrain relief and an abrupt narrowing of a valley or canyon that constricts the flow of wind.

Venturi effects can cause significant threats. Wind shear and downdrafts are often insidious; however, there may not be much associated turbulence. This can be particularly hazardous after departure from an airstrip in a canyon that narrows beyond the end of the strip (Figure 2-13). After takeoff, you could encounter horizontal or vertical wind shear, or both. Downdrafts may not dissipate and can extend through trees all the way to ground level. Even if a downdraft decreases close to the ground, the airplane still has downward momentum and can impact terrain.

Figure 2-13. The airplane is taking off from a one-way airstrip in a canyon that narrows downstream of the strip, creating a venturi effect. When departing toward the venturi, you may encounter wind shear and downdrafts and not be able to climb out, even though departing toward lower terrain. *(Photo by Amy Hoover)*

Turbulence

This chapter has described many situations and locations where you might find turbulence in mountains and canyons (Figure 2-14).

Turbulence is Found:
· On the lee side of mountain ridges
· Near abrupt changes from sunlit to shaded, or wooded to bare, terrain
· Above ridges separating canyons that are not connected
· In canyons when winds aloft exceed 15–25 knots
· In canyons where orographic and thermal effects are in opposition
· In areas of convergence (at the confluence of two drainages)
· In areas where a valley narrows to a canyon or canyon opens into a valley
· In canyons that narrow abruptly or have a radical change in direction

Figure 2-14. Some of the more common areas where turbulence can be encountered while flying in mountain and canyon terrain.

Turbulence can make a flight uncomfortable and potentially damage your aircraft or cause dangerous wind shear (Table 2-1). Light turbulence can cause enough of an airspeed fluctuation to stall a GA airplane at slow speeds, such as during approach and departure. Moderate turbulence can create significant wind shear, and vertical gusts could easily exceed the climb capability of your aircraft. Therefore, be vigilant for phenomena such as convergence and venturi effects and learn to anticipate areas of turbulence.

Table 2-1. Effect of wind gusts on an aircraft's airspeed and G-load. Extreme caution is advised for flights in mountain and canyon terrain with any reported turbulence, as even light to moderate turbulence could prove hazardous. *(Derived from FAA [2016c].)*

	Light	Moderate	Severe	Extreme
Derived gust (fpm)	300–1,199	1,200–2,099	2,100–2,999	>3,000
Airspeed fluctuation (kts)	5–14.9	15–24.9	>25	NA
G-load (g)	0.2–0.49	0.5–0.99	1.0–1.99	>2.0

Amy's
Axiom

Lift is where you find it; stay clear of downdrafts, always be wary of turbulence, and if the winds aloft over the mountains and canyons exceed 25 knots, consider not flying.

Although there are some general rules pertaining to wind, lift, and turbulence, conditions in mountainous and canyon areas can be unpredictable. Often, lift is simply where you find it; actively seek out updrafts and always be wary of ridges and areas that can produce downdrafts. Have a plan to escape toward lower terrain at all times. Reassess your flight plan if the winds aloft are strong; you may need to change your route of flight, departure time, or decision whether to go or not.

Knowledge of these phenomena can help make your mountain and canyon flight safe and enjoyable. A good rule is shown in Amy's Axiom at left.

Accident Scenario

On March 3, 2013, at 1320 MST, the pilot of a Mooney M20E lost control while flying in a turbulent mountain-wave environment shortly after takeoff from Angel Fire Airport (KAXX) in New Mexico. The NTSB listed the pilot's overconfidence in his ability to safely pilot the airplane in gusting wind conditions and his lack of experience operating in mountainous areas as contributing factors to the accident. All four people on board were fatally injured (NTSB, 2014).

Figure 2-15 shows the VFR sectional chart of Angel Fire Airport, which is located in a narrow, deep valley surrounded by high terrain. High mountains to the west and northwest are as much as 5,000 feet higher within 10 miles of the airport, and the narrow valley is perpendicular to the prevailing winds.

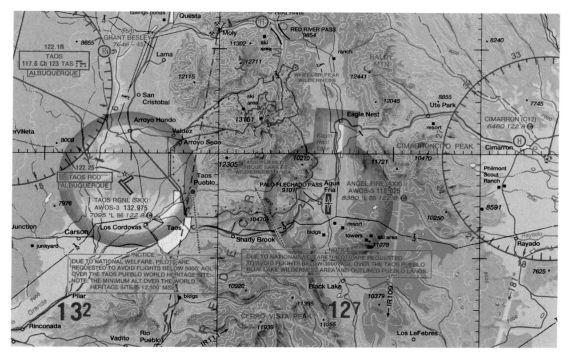

Figure 2-15. Sectional chart for Angel Fire Airport, New Mexico (KAXX). The narrow canyon is deep and perpendicular to the wind, setting up a situation that will form a venturi, wind shear, and high winds.

The Accident report states:

> Winds as high as 55 knots could occasionally reach the surface. Satellite imagery between 1300 and 1400 MST recorded a large amount of standing lenticular cloud near all of the mountainous terrain around the accident site. These clouds indicated the presence of a mountain wave environment. At 0322 and 1134, the National Weather Service issued wind advisories for the accident area that warned of a west of southwest wind between 25 and 35 miles per hour (mph) with gusts to 50 mph. (NTSB, 2014)

The NTSB conducted a weather research and forecasting model, which showed the area to be in a turbulent mountain wave environment at the time of the accident, with low-level wind shear, updrafts and downdrafts, downslope winds, and an environment conducive to rotor formation. Additionally, satellite imagery taken at the time of the accident showed a large amount of standing lenticular clouds near all of the mountainous terrain around the accident site. The *Airport/Facility Directory* (now referred to as the **Chart Supplement U.S.**) current on the date of the accident noted strong gusty winds are possible and high density altitudes probable for KAXX airport. The NTSB analysis stated:

Before takeoff, strong, gusting wind from the west was present, so a fixed-base operator (FBO) employee asked the pilot about his intent to fly. He stated that the pilot seemed "confident" about his ability to fly the airplane and that he was not concerned about the wind. As the airplane departed, the reported wind was 33 knots gusting to 47 knots. The FBO employee stated that he saw the airplane "crab" into the wind about 40 degrees right of the runway's heading. The airplane rose and fell repeatedly as its wings rocked. When the airplane was between 75 and 150 feet above the ground, the left wing dropped, and the airplane then rolled left, descended inverted, and impacted terrain in a nose-down attitude. A post impact examination of the airframe and engine revealed no evidence of mechanical malfunctions or failures that would have precluded normal operation. (NTSB, 2014)

Based on findings from interviews with the deceased pilot's relatives and employees at the fixed-base operator (FBO), the pilot stated he was not concerned about high winds, although KAXX was the highest-elevation airport from which he had operated, and he had no prior experience there. There is no record of the pilot receiving an FAA weather briefing, and it is unknown what other weather information he might have received prior to the flight.

This accident was avoidable had the pilot heeded the warnings given him by printed material such as the *Airport/Facility Directory* and the **FAA Aeronautical Information Manual** on safety in mountain flight, among the many other resources. Additionally, he did not utilize advice given by local personnel familiar with the area who questioned his intention to depart into the known adverse conditions, and he reportedly told a relative that flying in wind did not bother him (NTSB, 2014). Even without the windy conditions of the accident day, an informed study of the aeronautical chart would reveal the conditions ideal for mountain wave formation and possible venturi effects.

Review Questions and Exercises

Answers to review questions are provided in Appendix B.

Circle the correct answer:

1. Microbursts can be associated with convective activity and thunderstorms, regardless of whether moisture or precipitation are present. (**True** / **False**)

2. Wind velocity decreases as wind crosses a ridge, providing a cushion of upward-moving air on the downwind side of a mountain or ridge. (**True** / **False**)

3. Wind blowing up or down a canyon that opens out into a wide valley will typically flow outward away from the constricted area, causing horizontal and vertical wind shear. **(True / False)**

4. If you encounter downdrafts when approaching a ridge, you should pitch for best rate of climb speed (V_Y) to ensure clearing the ridge with adequate altitude. **(True / False)**

5. A valley breeze blows **(upslope / downslope)** and occurs during **(morning / evening)** in mountainous areas and canyons.

6. A mountain breeze blows **(upslope / downslope)** and occurs during **(morning / evening)** in mountainous areas and canyons.

7. While on approach to an airstrip, you can expect **(updrafts / downdrafts)** over darker or shaded terrain and **(updrafts / downdrafts)** over lighter or sunlit terrain.

For questions 8–11, you can reference any aeronautical chart that shows mountainous or canyon terrain.

8. Find a location where you would expect to encounter venturi effects, and describe the following:
   - What combination of wind and terrain features will cause a venturi at that location?
   - What conditions might you anticipate while operating around this area?
   - What precautions should you take to avoid an adverse flight situation due to the venturi?

9. Identify an area where you might encounter a mountain lee wave, and describe the following:
   - What kinds of clouds might you see form in the wave system?
   - Where would you expect to encounter downdrafts and turbulence?
   - What precautions would you take to avoid an adverse flight situation in that area?

10. Identify an area where you would expect to encounter diurnal winds, and use that specific location to describe the mechanism that creates diurnal winds in mountainous areas.

11. Find and describe a location where you would expect to obtain orographic lift, and describe how you would use that orographic lift to your advantage when flying in the area.

3

——

FLIGHT PLANNING

and

NAVIGATION

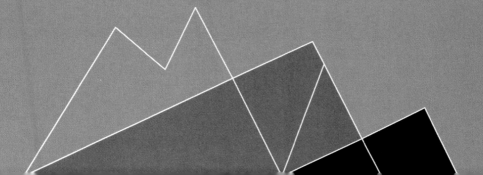

Depending on the time of year, pilots flying in mountains and canyons will be planning for a variety of terrain conditions and flight parameters, including the possibility of high density altitudes and severe thunderstorms during spring and summer, rain and snow storms in fall and winter, and strong winds at various times of year. For any cross-country or local flight, much of the success of an enjoyable and safe adventure starts with thorough and thoughtful preflight planning. Once you venture into a remote mountain or canyon area, you could be operating far from improved airports and maintenance or repair facilities and with large distances between fuel stops. For trips into the wilderness or backcountry to camp, hike, fish, hunt, or participate in other recreational activities lasting several days or more, you may not be able to obtain current weather information before a return flight.

The planning stage begins with preparation of your aircraft, your skills, your attitude, your experience, and your personal goals and limitations, as outlined in Chapters 1 and 9. Once you have determined that both you and your airplane are capable with respect to performance and limitations, you will need to carefully consider the weather and environment (see Chapter 2). Next, it is time to plan your flight.

VFR Charts

VFR **Sectional Aeronautical Charts** are published at a scale of 1:500,000 and are excellent for distinguishing terrain and other geographical features. Electronic sectional charts displayed on a tablet can be zoomed or expanded as needed in the cockpit. For more detail, refer to topographic maps for a particular area or use an application such as Google Earth™. Study chart terrain features carefully so you have an idea of the overall geography of the area, not just along your planned route. Building a good mental picture enhances **situational awareness**, which helps you to avoid becoming lost and to stay oriented to the general direction of lower terrain and more populated areas.

In remote backcountry areas, where there are no roads, cities, towns, or human habitation, it can be easy to get lost. Note the position of prominent landmarks on the aeronautical chart so you can positively identify features from the air. The appearance of landmarks will change with the seasons as vegetation, snow pack, and water levels change. Also, terrain features look different under

---

[1] Kern, Tony (1998). *Flight Discipline*. New York, McGraw Hill.

various lighting and weather conditions as well as from various angles and different altitudes.

Learn common flight routes for a particular area. Commercial operators, local flight schools, and pilots familiar with the area are good resources; ask about their knowledge of safety practices and hazards associated with various routes. Indeed, "the local mountain operators would rather spend 15 minutes giving you a briefing on their area of expertise than 15 hours rescuing you." (Civil Aviation Authority of New Zealand, 2012). Charts such as the **Canada VFR Navigation Chart** plot recommended routes for flight in mountainous terrain (Figure 3-1).

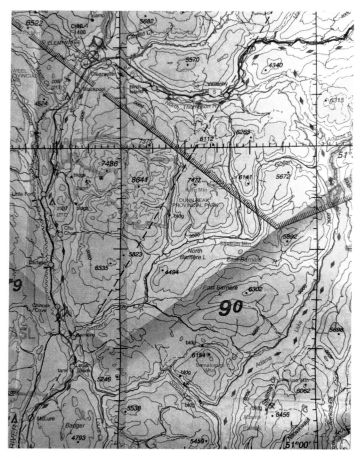

Figure 3-1. Canada VFR Navigation Chart showing the recommended route through mountainous terrain, indicated by the line of blue diamond symbols. These are usually located in wider valleys, with lower terrain, and over more populated areas.

[2] Gann, Ernest (1961). *Fate is The Hunter: A Pilot's Memoir.* New York, Simon and Schuster.

Westward Wanderings

By Amy Hoover

In the early 1990s, I was instructing at the FAA Mountain Flying clinic based in Challis, Idaho (KLLJ, see figure at right). The Challis Airport lies to the east of the Frank Church Wilderness, where most of the flights were conducted for the clinic. Early one morning, I set out with a student in his Cessna 182 to conduct training in the Middle Fork Salmon River Canyon, which entailed crossing over the high ridge to the west of Challis and following a river canyon westward toward our destination.

The pilot was sharing the flight with his brother, also a pilot, who was in the back seat for the first leg of the day. This was in the days before GPS. Some pilots used LORAN, but the coverage was sparse, so setting a compass course and using pilotage was the primary means of navigation.

We departed around 6:30 a.m. on a beautiful June day, and the sun had already been shining on the east-facing slopes, providing some thermal lift. I decided to help the pilot

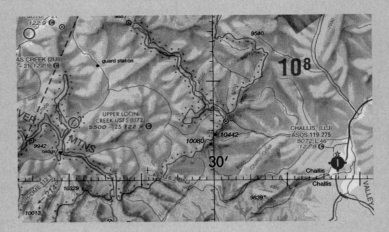

VFR sectional chart of Challis, Idaho (KLLJ). After departure from Challis toward the west, you must climb over the high ridge to enter the backcountry area in the Frank Church Wilderness. Thermal lift can be helpful in the mornings, but with winds aloft out of the west or southwest, as is common in summer months, you will encounter downdrafts when approaching the ridge from the east and should gain sufficient altitude before attempting to cross.

learn about where to find and use that lift to gain altitude (as described in Chapter 2) in preparation for crossing the ridge at the lowest pass. We headed toward the sunlit slopes and circled around a few times, contouring the terrain to gain altitude. Once we were high enough to clear the terrain, the pilot set the course and leveled off. As we continued, the dialogue went like this:

Detailed study of an area's geography is helpful. In addition to VFR charts, most areas have topographic maps available to the public. The U.S. Geological Survey and Natural Resources Canada both produce maps at scales varying from 1:250,000 to 1:50,000 that are available in hard copy or electronic format. Check similar sources for flights in other areas of the world. Your goal is to become

Me: "So, we are headed into the Middle Fork, right?"

Pilot: "Yep!"

Me: "What direction is that from here?"

Pilot: "West!"

Me: "Beautiful day. What is that?" (*pointing out the front of the airplane*)

Pilot: "The sun?"

Me: "Yep! What time is it?"

Pilot: "I have 6:45."

A few moments pass.

Me: "So, we want to fly west to the Middle Fork, right?"

Pilot: "Yep!"

Me: "What is that?" (*again, pointing at the sun*)

Pilot: "The sun!"

Me: "Yep! I also show about 6:45 a.m. for the time."

I look over my shoulder at the brother in the back seat, who is almost in tears trying to keep from laughing out loud...a few more moments pass.

Me: "So...everything looks OK? We are on course?"

Pilot: "Well, we should be...."

Me: "So, what is that?" (*pointing dead ahead at the sun*)

Pilot: "Man, that's the sun. Why do you keep asking me that?"

By now the brother cannot help himself and is howling with laughter. I figure it is time to help the pilot before he suffers too much sibling ribbing.

Me: "OK, so we want to go west. Check your DG."

Pilot: "Wow, is that right? Yep. It checks with the compass. We're flying east. How did that happen?"

Me: "We did a lot of maneuvering over those hills to get lift and it is easy to get turned around when you are contouring the terrain like that. It's a good lesson to make sure to double-check your position, your heading, and match the landmarks with the chart."

Pilot: "I guess. Wow! I won't do that again! And shut up back there, Mr. Smarty Pants (*to the brother*) 'cause you're next!"

The lesson that day is a common one; it is easy to become disoriented and lose **situational awareness** during low-level maneuvers. The pilot was over an unfamiliar area doing something he had not done before: flying close to the terrain to contour it and use lift to gain altitude, which entailed several turns and circles. Although he was taking all the correct precautions not to fly into a blind canyon and to always have room to turn back, upon reaching altitude he simply continued flying toward the same direction he was headed without checking his instruments, or even making the mental connection that he wanted to go west, and the sun rises in the east!

familiar enough with an area that you can visualize the general orientation of mountain ranges, valleys, canyons, and drainage patterns, which will greatly enhance situational awareness and decrease your overall workload.

Basic Navigation

Since you will be conducting flights under **visual flight rules (VFR)**, your primary means of navigation should be **pilotage**, which is navigating by reference to visual landmarks and checkpoints. Pilotage should be backed up by **dead reckoning** (calculating time, airspeed, distance, and direction), satellite navigation, such as **Global Positioning System (GPS)**, or other radio navigation aids whenever possible. Although you will probably not follow a straight-line route, it is a good idea to know the direction of flight so if you are blown off course by wind or lose the GPS signal, you will know what compass heading to fly. Limitations of GPS for mountain and canyon operations are discussed later in this chapter.

Know your position at all times. Although pilotage should be the primary means of navigation, GPS is useful to track your flight progress by verifying your position, confirming the distance from navigational aids and airports, and updating your time en route and fuel burn. Many ground-based navigation aids, such as **VOR** or **NDB**, have limited range in mountainous areas and may not be reliable at the altitudes used for **VFR** flight. Refer to an **IFR chart** to determine the **minimum en route altitude (MEA)** for VOR airways that will guarantee reliable signal coverage. The MEA is often above the service ceiling of light GA aircraft over high or remote terrain, and the signals cannot be used.

Navigation Software and Apps

Navigation Apps such as **ForeFlight Mobile**, **Garmin Pilot**, and the free App **FltPlan Go** have revolutionized flight planning and in-flight navigation (Figure 3-2).

These apps include moving map displays that mimic much more expensive panel units and can greatly enhance situational awareness. Pilots can file and amend flight plans and get visual displays of real-time weather, special use airspace, **Temporary Flight Restrictions (TFRs)**, and more. Some even include **synthetic vision** and **electronic flight instrument system (EFIS)** displays. However, in confined areas such as canyons or over remote terrain, these apps should be considered useful aids to navigation but not be used as the primary means of maintaining situational awareness. It is extremely easy to become complacent when relying on such technology to the extent that pilots are distracted from using pilotage as the primary navigation method.

Flying in canyons entails a constant heads-up and eyes-out-of-the-cockpit level of attention (see Chapter 4), especially when maneuvering at low levels during initial climb out or descending into a confined area for landing. Overreliance on a tablet or other devices, or even glancing down at the wrong time, can be a deadly distraction. Unfamiliar backcountry or remote areas are not the places to start using apps. As described later in this chapter, GPS satellite signals may not always be reliable in deep canyons, so your primary reference should always be pilotage; you need to be proficient at visual identification of landmarks and terrain features.

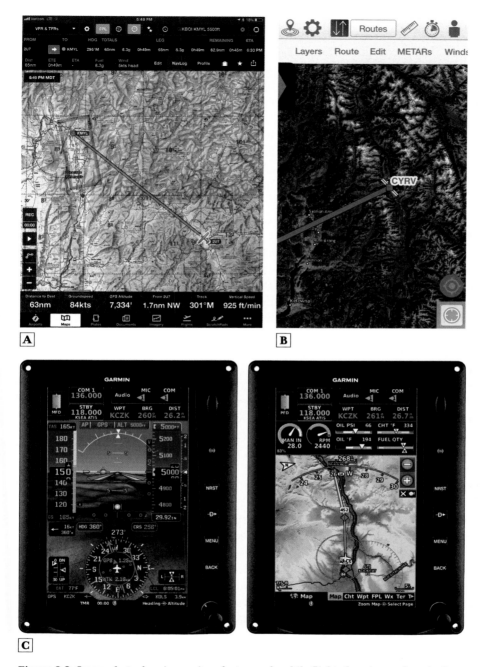

Figure 3-2. Screenshots showing various features of mobile flight planning and navigation apps. (**A**) A terrain feature moving map display from the ForeFlight app. *(Photo Courtesy Katie Dorris)* (**B**) FltPlan Go, a free app that includes flight planning and weather. *(Photo by Amy Hoover)* (**C**) Garmin's portable unit synthetic vision view with overlay of HSI and flight instruments similar to in-panel Garmin units. *(Photo by Garmin)*

Route Selection

The best route in mountain and canyon terrain may not be a straight line. Wind, weather, lighting conditions, and aircraft performance will influence route selection. Consider your familiarity with the area, availability of fuel and other services, emergency and forced landing options, communication, and aids to navigation when selecting your route.

In general, it is best to fly major river drainages, canyons, passes, or highways and to stay near populated areas when possible. A basic understanding of airflow over terrain can help you select a route that minimizes flight in turbulence and downdrafts and maximizes flight in smoother air and updrafts (see Chapter 2). Wind, weather, and turbulence are dynamic processes that are not always predictable, and you must constantly assess their influence on your flight path.

It is always a good idea to plan at least one alternative route in case your first choice is not feasible, so you have more than one option. For example, if you plan to follow a river canyon to your destination but conditions are not ideal, have a plan to climb, cross into a different canyon, and follow a different route. Fuel planning should consider the possibility you may not be able to fly your first choice.

Even with more than one type of navigation aid such as GPS at your disposal, it is still a good idea to practice pilotage and dead reckoning. One example is the concept of **offset navigation**. In an unfamiliar area, you might have trouble identifying your target visually, so navigate to a nearby prominent linear feature such as a river, mountain ridge, or road a few miles off the left or right of your destination, and then turn and follow it. If you try to fly directly to your destination and cannot identify it, you may not know which way to turn and search.

Time of Day and Sun Angle

Early morning, late afternoon, or evening sun at low angles can cause shadows that hide features and make it difficult to see the valley sides, canyon wall, or a lower ridge in the foreground. You may need to adjust your flight path in order to see the terrain. A deceptive phenomenon occurs during early morning or evening: you may be in daylight at altitude, but the sun has not yet risen, or has already set, in the canyon. This is especially dangerous when descending into a canyon after sunset, as you may suddenly find yourself flying VFR at night in a canyon. That is an extremely hazardous situation over uninhabited terrain with no sources of light. The immediate response should be to climb back to altitude where you have daylight and navigate toward a populated area where you can make a landing at a lighted runway.

Climbing toward a ridge when facing directly into the sun makes it almost impossible to judge the height of terrain and whether you will clear it. You may not be able to see at all. One technique heading toward low-angle sun is to "zig-zag" by changing your heading 30 degrees or so every minute or less, depending on how confined an area you are in. Low sun angles also present problems while maneuvering in a canyon for landing or after departing an airstrip located at the bottom of a canyon. Assessing the effects of low-angle sun on your approaches and departures is addressed further in Chapters 5 and 6.

Terrain, Wind, and Weather

You should not attempt to fly in an area where most of the terrain is close to or higher than the service ceiling of your aircraft. Aircraft performance is based on **density altitude (DA)** and not indicated or true altitude (see discussion in Chapter 8), so you must consider the temperature when estimating whether you will be able to clear terrain. It may be possible to fly a route during the cooler temperatures of fall or spring, while that same route becomes hazardous in hot summer conditions due to the higher DA.

Plan a route that uses the terrain to your advantage as well as minimizes hazards. During flight planning, how will you know where to look for lift and how to avoid downdrafts and turbulence? Some of that comes with practice, but a good way to visualize it is to compare the prevailing winds aloft to water as it flows up, over, and down ridges and canyons. Look for lift on the upwind side of mountain ranges, on the sunny side of mountains and canyons, and other places described in Chapter 2. Expect turbulence and be wary of abrupt changes in wind speed and direction, especially around mountain passes.

If you have a major mountain range to cross, have more than one plan in case you have to turn back due to high winds or turbulence through a mountain pass or over a ridge. Also learn to identify features on a smaller scale so you can anticipate possible wind patterns in canyons.

Canyons are useful because they provide identifiable routes and can be used to execute cruise climbs and cruise descents into and out of airstrips located next to rivers. However, following a canyon to navigate requires you to positively identify the correct drainage and make sure you are following it in the right direction. It is easy to fly up the wrong canyon at low altitude, especially in a complex system of tributaries branching off a main canyon (Figure 3-3). Plan ahead so you know the orientation of the canyon you want to follow. For example, if you want to fly downstream toward the east to follow a canyon but are instead heading upstream to the north, you are in the wrong canyon. Circle and climb to a higher altitude until you are out of the canyon and can re-orient yourself.

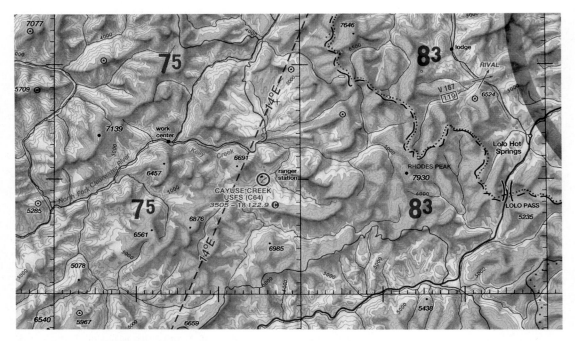

Figure 3-3. VFR sectional chart of an area with canyons that are oriented in many different directions. Pilots need to positively identify the correct drainage, especially when using canyons to climb and descend. For example, after takeoff from Cayuse Creek airstrip, it would be easy to turn up the wrong canyon and enter a dead-end that rises faster than the airplane's climb capabilities.

Study the chart and identify whether you want to be flying upstream or downstream, and then verify the direction during flight. It may be harder to determine the direction of flow for large rivers with shallow gradients, but they are usually in wider valleys with more room to maneuver. In narrow canyons with steep rivers, look for the whitewater; it is always downstream of rocks and obstacles, which will point you toward downhill. A good practice is to avoid going uphill or upstream in canyons formed by small, narrow streams. Such drainages can rise steeply, and you might encounter a dead-end or box canyon and not be able to reverse course. See Chapter 4 for a discussion of canyon flying, canyon turns, and emergency turns.

Mountain and canyon terrain can look very different during various seasons, such as when covered in snow or when parched and dry from drought. Additionally, landmarks look different when viewed from different altitudes or directions. A good way to familiarize yourself with a new area is to initially fly at a higher altitude. Once you are comfortable just above the ridge tops, fly at lower levels and note the different landmarks at lower altitude. This will help with navigation during climb into and out of airstrips situated at the bottom of canyons

Figure 3-4. An overcast layer can obscure terrain and make it difficult to positively identify the correct drainage. *(Photo by Amy Hoover)*

or when there is an overcast layer. An overcast can obscure landmarks and make navigation difficult. It can be very easy to turn up the wrong valley or canyon when flying under an overcast (Figure 3-4).

As described in Chapter 2, flying with low ceilings in a canyon may not be practical or safe, and you might not be able to recognize landmarks when there is a ceiling that obscures ridge tops. Avoid the temptation to venture into a canyon under a low ceiling unless you are positive there is a way out.

Fuel and Services

Your aircraft's range and the distance between airports with fuel and services will be a major planning factor. You want to have enough fuel to provide a margin of safety in case of weather delays or diversions, but excess fuel adds weight, which can compromise performance and safety at high DA. Careful fuel planning is essential and may change over the same route on different days, seasons, or conditions. During hot weather, it may be better to make flights with shorter legs and more fuel stops to reduce the weight and still have sufficient fuel and reserves for safe operations. For example, instead of topping off long range tanks to fly seven hours nonstop, it might be more prudent to leave with a partial fuel load and plan a fuel stop halfway through. Alternatively, if there are long distances between available fuel, it might be best to carry a full load of fuel in the event of weather or unexpected headwinds.

Plan for possible weather delays should the conditions change, especially for overnight stays at a backcountry destination. Additionally, if it takes more than one trip to haul your gear into an airstrip, make sure you have enough fuel for multiple trips, or refuel. Fuel planning is not necessarily more complicated in remote areas, but you certainly want to pay attention and monitor your fuel closely at all times. Fuel gauges may not always be accurate, and fuel flow monitors are only as good as the data entered by the pilot; use caution with unfamiliar airplanes. It is better to land at an airstrip and check your fuel than to exhaust your supply in the air. The section on dispatching and flight following introduces technology you can use to send information and update your status with someone who is following your flight progress.

Accuracy means something to me. It's vital to my sense of values. I've learned not to trust people who are inaccurate. Every aviator knows that if mechanics are inaccurate, aircraft crash. If pilots are inaccurate, they get lost—sometimes killed. In my profession life itself depends on accuracy. 99

Charles A. Lindbergh [3]

Global Positioning System (GPS) Navigation

Satellite-based navigation is accurate and reliable, and it can significantly reduce pilot workload. A well-designed GPS receiver is capable of accuracies of 3 meters or better horizontally and 5 meters or better vertically 95% of the time. Although GPS has become the primary form of navigation around the world, it does have disadvantages. There can be errors associated with satellite position and signal failures, and sometimes in deep canyons there may not be enough satellite signals "visible" to the receiver, giving an erroneous position. Do not rely solely on GPS

---

[3] Lindbergh, Charles A. (1953). *The Spirit of St. Louis*. New York, Charles Scribner's Sons.

or any other form of navigation; rather, use a combination of pilotage, dead reckoning, and GPS to constantly update your position. The biggest drawback to satellite-based navigation is noted by Williams (2018): "GPS deserves every bit of praise it receives, but…its dark side is that it can tempt pilots into complacency and a potentially dangerous loss of situational awareness." Each form of navigation has its strengths and weaknesses (Figure 3-5).

	Assets	Liabilities
Pilotage	· Simple, relatively easy · Doesn't require any equipment in the aircraft or on the ground · Excellent for maintaining situational awareness when done properly	· Relies upon good visibility and readily identifiable landmarks · May require a more circuitous routing
Dead Reckoning	· Easy to execute · Doesn't depend on ground stations or satellites · Allows for direct routing · Not necessarily contingent on good visibility	· Requires more detailed planning than pilotage · Requires instruments like magnetic compass and preferably a directional gyro · Vulnerable to changing conditions like wind and aircraft performance when used in isolation
VOR	· Reliable · Provides clear position information · Precise · Relatively easy to use · No requirement for visual reference	· Requires nav radios and antennas · Limited range and reception · Dependent on ground station · Can't fly "direct" · Fewer VORs than there once were
ADF	· Reliable · Simple · Easy to use · No visual reference required	· NDBs are fast disappearing from the NAS · Not as precise as VOR/GPS · Vulnerable to distortion around water · Positional information dependent on proximity to the NDB · Limited range
GPS	· Accurate · Reliable · Excellent position information · No visual reference required · "Direct to" anywhere · No range limitations	· Weak GPS signal can be jammed · "Direct to" can limit situational awareness · Complexity and variety of avionics requires more familiarity with the specific unit · Requires recurring database updates

Figure 3-5. Assets and liabilities of each form of navigation, from Williams (2018). Pilotage is the best form of primary navigation for mountain and canyon flying, backed up by GPS to maintain SA.

Carol Jarvis, one of my early mentors, told me I would not really know the Idaho backcountry until I had flown it in all seasons. The different coloring of the hills and mountains, not to mention approaching areas from different altitudes and directions, would completely change the look of things. And boy, was he right! Over the years since then, I have also learned that currency in an area is just as important. It is one thing to fly an area on a very regular basis, and a completely different situation to go back to an area you have not flown for several years or have only flown sporadically over the years. Age and experience do not always make you a sage old master; they can also make you an un-current oldster who has forgotten the land you once knew so well.

I was doing a reconnaissance flight for a friend a few years ago, trying to locate some old historic trails in a mountainous area with several similar-sized creek drainages. As we wound around several different creeks at fairly low altitude, I realized that I didn't know what drainage I was in, even though years before I had been intimately familiar with the country.

We were not in any danger, as the airplane could easily climb out or turn around, so I began playing with my GPS and using the zoom feature to help get oriented. Almost immediately, even flying at canyon speed in a slow airplane, I realized it was dangerous and distracting to play with the unit while flying at a few hundred feet in a twisting canyon. Rather than climb—my other good option—I continued downstream until joining with another creek and eventually recognizing familiar terrain. It was a little embarrassing to get turned around on a beautiful VFR day in country I used to know. And the GPS was not much help.

Now imagine if the weather is marginal VFR, and you are flying with a heavy load in a faster airplane—not doing a recon, but just trying to get from A to B. If you cross a flat summit area where there are several creek

Pilots have gotten themselves into trouble by misidentifying a primitive airstrip and attempting to land at the wrong place, resulting in an accident, a confrontation with an angry private landowner, or an unsuitable takeoff situation. GPS should mostly eliminate that problem, but as just discussed, it should be used as a backup rather than a sole means of navigation in mountainous terrain, particularly in deep and sinuous canyons. Generally, equipment errors should not affect VFR flight unless you are relying on the GPS to navigate in marginal weather, unfamiliar territory, or both. Always check your signal accuracy and use pilotage to verify your position.

Potential problems with direct-line GPS routes are obstacles (high peaks) and exposure to high winds, downdrafts, turbulence, and other micro weather patterns around mountain and canyon topography (see Chapter 2). Pilots ignorant of those phenomena, as well as of search and rescue limitations and communication issues, can unknowingly put themselves and their passengers at

drainage headwaters, a turn of just a few degrees might put you in a drainage other than the one you intended. With marginal ceilings, this can be very easy to do, and the GPS often is no help because you are too busy flying the airplane. This has not only happened to me; it has happened to virtually every professional mountain pilot I know. At this point, it is essential that you continue downstream, and the worst scenario could be ending up down in a bowl with weather preventing you from going anywhere. I have been in this situation, too. If you are fortunate, the squalls will be moving fairly quickly, and circling safely over a tree to stay oriented (another Carol Jarvis lesson) might be your best option for several minutes (five minutes will seem like an eternity). This is a survival technique, however, and not someplace you want to be. If you end up in this situation, it means you made some errors, and the only other option is to enter the clouds and fly in IMC. Even if you and your airplane are capable, which is not likely in mountainous terrain with icing, you would be taking a big risk using this option. Knowing several friends who met their demise that way (both inadvertently and intentionally entering clouds), I always declined transitioning from VFR to IFR.

The lessons I learned:

- GPS is a secondary tool for mountain navigation. It is nice to have, but you should be able to do without it.
- Currency trumps experience. Older pilots will have to relearn things they once knew.
- Know and practice the basics of pilotage in the mountains and canyons. Going downstream might be one of the most important things to know, or be very sure of yourself when heading upstream.

Anyone and almost everyone becomes at least "a little turned around" at times.

risk by trying to fly a GPS direct route. As demonstrated by the accident scenario at the end of this chapter, pilots have flown into blind canyons from which they did not return or could not out climb. Fatal crashes have occurred because pilots were following the GPS without positively identifying the correct canyon or river drainage they wanted to follow. You may be able to use map displays on the airplane GPS, or apps such as ForeFlight, to plan your route using several shorter segments, rather than a straight line, to avoid some of those issues.

If using a map display, it is a good idea to study the charts ahead of time and be familiar with the route and airstrip of intended landing. Use pilotage to orient yourself, and if in doubt, climb until you can get a better view. A valuable use of GPS is to obtain accurate ground speeds and winds aloft estimates. Significant changes in ground speed could signify a change in winds aloft and associated weather patterns. Knowing the winds aloft can help you to better determine possible areas of turbulence and where you can look for updrafts and avoid downdrafts.

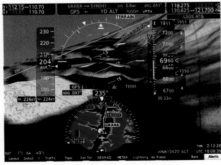

Figure 3-6. (A) Terrain view on moving map. *(Photo by Amy Hoover)* **(B)** Synthetic vision display of terrain on Primary Flight Display. *(Photo courtesy Garmin)*

The terrain feature is another useful display. Used properly, it can reduce the risk of **controlled flight into terrain (CFIT)**. Color-coded terrain warnings on moving maps and synthetic vision displays are common even on some portable GPS units (Figure 3-6), and most have audible warnings as well.

Although terrain displays can help avoid CFIT, do not rely on them for primary navigation. GPS units are a useful and valuable tool, but your primary navigation in mountains and canyons should always be pilotage.

Automatic Dependent Surveillance Radar—Broadcast

Automatic Dependent Surveillance–Broadcast (ADS-B) is a system in which properly equipped aircraft broadcast their identification, position, altitude, and velocity to other aircraft and to **air traffic control (ATC)**. Broadcasting this information is called **ADS-B Out**, and receiving it is known as **ADS-B In**. The **Traffic Information Services–Broadcast (TIS–B)** feature provides traffic information to aircraft using Automatic Dependent Surveillance–Broadcast (ADS-B) Out and In. ADS-B technology will eventually replace radar as the primary surveillance method for ATC monitoring and separation of aircraft worldwide (ICAO, 2014).

The system requires the aircraft to be equipped with a **WAAS**-enabled GPS and some kind of ADS-B data link, such as a **Mode S transponder-based 1090 extended squitter (ES)** or a **universal access transceiver (UAT)**. The aircraft position, as determined by the GPS, broadcasts identity, altitude, and velocity information at rapid intervals (approximately every 0.5 seconds) over discrete frequencies. Dedicated ADS-B **ground-based transmitters (GBTs)** receive the broadcasts and relay the information to ATC and to other aircraft in the area that are equipped for ADS-B In. ADS-B equipped aircraft may be able to "see" other equipped aircraft even when not in range of a GBT. ADS-B In equipped aircraft may also receive weather data over the link.

After 2020 in the United States, Mexico and Europe, all aircraft must be equipped with ADS-B Out to operate in certain controlled airspace. Other countries have similar mandates, so check before flying in a particular area. For example, at the time of this writing, the Airservices Australia mandate is only for IFR aircraft, and Canada has not yet mandated it.

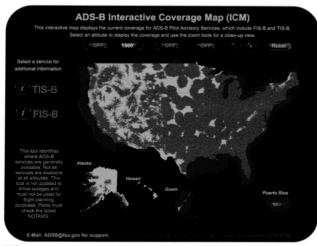

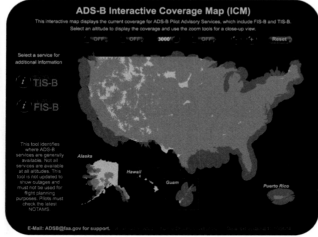

Figure 3-7. ADS-B coverage (**A**) at 1,500 feet AGL and (**B**) at 3,000 feet AGL (FAA, 2017). Note that much of the mountainous areas in the western continental United States and most of Alaska do not have coverage below those altitudes. When flying in canyons, below ridge-top level, it is unlikely you will have ADS-B coverage.

ADS-B has many potential benefits, including collision avoidance, ATC surveillance in a non-radar environment, and enhancing pilot situational awareness. However, for operations in remote mountain and canyon areas, you will need to understand the limitations of ADS-B. Since it is a line-of-sight signal, mountainous areas—and canyons in particular—may not have coverage below 1,500 feet or even 3,000 feet above the highest terrain (Figure 3-7).

Although you may be flying an aircraft equipped with ADS-B Out or ADS-B In, data will not always be available in mountainous terrain, so plan accordingly. You will still need to rely on visual scanning, position reporting over the radio, and maintaining situational awareness to safely avoid other aircraft as well as tracking your flight progress.

Dispatching and Flight Following

If you are flying high enough, you may be able to obtain VFR flight following from an ATC facility. However, radar services and flight following are not possible over many remote areas. Radar coverage may be limited due to terrain interference, and as described in the previous section, ADS-B may not be available below 3,000 feet AGL. Also, it may

One late November, three hunters departed Fairbanks, Alaska, in a Cessna 185 en route to the Upper Nowitna River area, approximately 200 miles west of Fairbanks, to hunt moose. The hunters intended to access the general hunting area, scout for moose from the airplane, and then choose an area to land and camp. Because no specific destination or route of flight was planned, filing a flight plan with FSS would have been impractical. The pilot of the airplane informed his wife of the hunter's plans. He told her they would return in a few days and explained the destination as the Nowitna River, which is a long river. When the hunters did not return that Sunday, the wife of the pilot was not sure what to do. Eventually, she called the Alaska State Troopers, who initiated an air search. The size of the search area was huge, covering thousands of square miles of territory. Short winter days limited the search time. Eventually, the wreckage was found seven miles south of Fairbanks. There were no survivors.

The message here is to not only leave a plan with someone but to be as specific as possible about your intended route of flight and time of arrival.

not be possible to contact a Flight Service Station to file an FAA flight plan or to close it when you land at an airstrip deep in a canyon. Cellular coverage is sporadic over mountainous areas and is non-existent below certain altitudes. However, you may be able to get a signal some of the time. Apps such as **ForeFlight** rely on Wi-Fi or cellular coverage for filing, opening, and closing flight plans, so you may not be able to use those functions. Although you might not be able to contact ATC directly, you should know the ATC frequencies for the area. During an emergency or if you need assistance, you may be able to contact other aircraft at higher altitudes, such as those on IFR flight plans, who are communicating with ATC.

Often an FAA or other official flight plan may not be possible or practical, so dispatch your flight and "file" a flight plan with someone on the ground. Leave your planned route of flight, estimated flight times, destination, and time of return with someone you trust who will begin a search if you do not report back as scheduled. For longer trips, you may want to give a "window" of dates you are expected back. However, the more accurate you are, the better equipped your contact will be to help if you go missing.

In an unfamiliar area, check in with a local FBO or flight school or club, as most will be happy to take your information and track your flight. Once you have done that, fly the planned itinerary as closely as possible, since that is the route your contact will assume for initiating a search. You can also email or text your itinerary and make updates en route at high enough altitudes to receive a cellular signal or through use of a GPS tracker or texting device, as described next.

Satellite Locators and GPS Trackers

GPS based flight trackers, such as the **Garmin InReach**, **Spidertracks**, and **SPOT**, use satellites for real-time tracking and allow you to send and receive text messages and trigger an SOS for emergency help. These relatively inexpensive devices have revolutionized the way flights are followed and greatly increased safety as well as peace of mind for those checking your flight progress. Choose a device that has satellite system coverage in your area. Many backcountry charter services now use GPS-based tracking for their dispatching and flight following. Ensure that the person who is following your track understands how the system operates and its limitations.

Consider getting a satellite phone for emergency use in remote areas. Chapter 9 expands on emergency and survival equipment, and a GPS tracker and/or satellite phone is an excellent addition to your kit.

Position Reporting

Even with ADS-B In coverage, a satellite tracking device, and dispatching, make periodic position reports "in the blind" on the appropriate radio frequency for the area. This will alert other aircraft as to your position. Use landmarks that are on the chart and easily identifiable, such as airports, mountain peaks, fire lookouts, or marked bodies of water. Radio calls should be concise and contain sufficient information for other pilots to understand where you are and where you are going; the calls should include your position, altitude, and direction of flight or destination. It may help to use a position and a GPS mileage; for example, "Piper 12345 is over Moose Peak, 10 miles west of Bull Elk Airport, at 9,500 feet, headed north."

Listen for other pilot's position reports and determine their relative location. You can coordinate with the other pilot, and either of you can modify your route or altitude to enhance separation. Also, check your altimeter setting against that of the other pilot to make sure you are using the same setting, since it could be incorrect if you departed from different locations.

In summary, dispatching your flight, filing some kind of plan, and reporting your position are critical elements when flying in rugged, remote mountain and canyon terrain. If you are delayed or have to make a precautionary landing or a diversion, GPS trackers and satellite phones are invaluable tools. Satellite phones are also an ideal option for emergency communications.

Accident Scenario

Late one September morning in 2003, two airplanes departed from Indian Creek airstrip (S81) in the Idaho backcountry en route to Upper Loon airport (U72) (Figure 3-8).

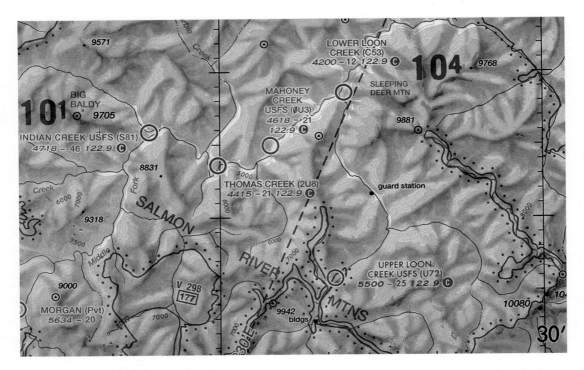

Figure 3-8. VFR sectional chart of a portion of the Idaho backcountry. The accident airplane took off with another airplane as a flight of two from Indian Creek USFS airport (S81) en route to Upper Loon airport (U72). According to the eyewitness statement from the pilot of the other airplane, the plan was to fly downstream on the Middle Fork Salmon River to Lower Loon airport (C53) and fly upstream on Loon Creek to U72 (NTSB, 2004).

The eyewitness statement from the second airplane described what happened while the pilot of the lead airplane followed his GPS and turned up the wrong drainage, descended toward rising terrain, and fatally crashed trying to turn around in a tight box canyon (Figure 3-9).

Figure 3-10 shows the location of the accident site. The NTSB final report stated: "The narrow valley is bordered by steep rising terrain. Post-accident inspection and teardown of the airplane's engine revealed no evidence of a pre-impact mechanical malfunction or failure."

According to the NTSB eyewitness report, Ray Arnold of Arnold Aviation descended into the canyon to investigate the crash site. Arnold stated that even several hundred feet above the altitude of the accident airplane, he would not have been able to make a tight enough turn to reverse course in the narrow canyon (Arnold, 2018). This is a clear case of a pilot failing to use pilotage and instead relying on the GPS for direct-to navigation, resulting in flight into a box canyon with no way out. Tragically, the pilot of the other aircraft alerted him to the hazard, but reliance on the GPS overruled the warning.

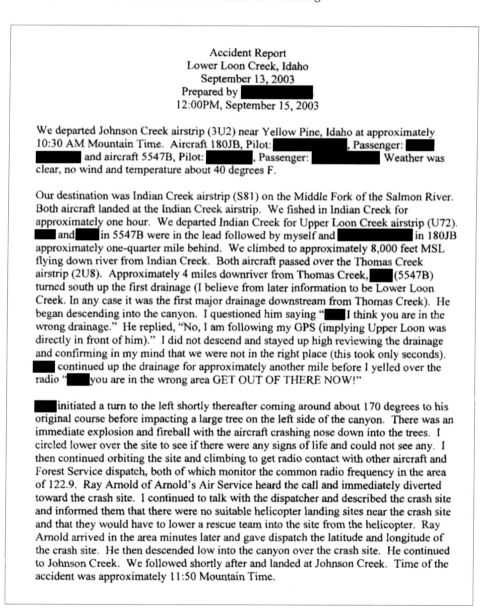

Accident Report
Lower Loon Creek, Idaho
September 13, 2003
Prepared by ███████
12:00PM, September 15, 2003

We departed Johnson Creek airstrip (3U2) near Yellow Pine, Idaho at approximately 10:30 AM Mountain Time. Aircraft 180JB, Pilot: ███████, Passenger: ███ ███████ and aircraft 5547B, Pilot: ███████, Passenger: ███████ Weather was clear, no wind and temperature about 40 degrees F.

Our destination was Indian Creek airstrip (S81) on the Middle Fork of the Salmon River. Both aircraft landed at the Indian Creek airstrip. We fished in Indian Creek for approximately one hour. We departed Indian Creek for Upper Loon Creek airstrip (U72). ███ and ███ in 5547B were in the lead followed by myself and ███████ in 180JB approximately one-quarter mile behind. We climbed to approximately 8,000 feet MSL flying down river from Indian Creek. Both aircraft passed over the Thomas Creek airstrip (2U8). Approximately 4 miles downriver from Thomas Creek, ███ (5547B) turned south up the first drainage (I believe from later information to be Lower Loon Creek. In any case it was the first major drainage downstream from Thomas Creek). He began descending into the canyon. I questioned him saying "███ I think you are in the wrong drainage." He replied, "No, I am following my GPS (implying Upper Loon was directly in front of him)." I did not descend and stayed up high reviewing the drainage and confirming in my mind that we were not in the right place (this took only seconds). ███ continued up the drainage for approximately another mile before I yelled over the radio "███ you are in the wrong area GET OUT OF THERE NOW!"

███ initiated a turn to the left shortly thereafter coming around about 170 degrees to his original course before impacting a large tree on the left side of the canyon. There was an immediate explosion and fireball with the aircraft crashing nose down into the trees. I circled lower over the site to see if there were any signs of life and could not see any. I then continued orbiting the site and climbing to get radio contact with other aircraft and Forest Service dispatch, both of which monitor the common radio frequency in the area of 122.9. Ray Arnold of Arnold's Air Service heard the call and immediately diverted toward the crash site. I continued to talk with the dispatcher and described the crash site and informed them that there were no suitable helicopter landing sites near the crash site and that they would have to lower a rescue team into the site from the helicopter. Ray Arnold arrived in the area minutes later and gave dispatch the latitude and longitude of the crash site. He then descended low into the canyon over the crash site. He continued to Johnson Creek. We followed shortly after and landed at Johnson Creek. Time of the accident was approximately 11:50 Mountain Time.

Figure 3-9. Eyewitness statement from the NTSB Public docket file (NTSB, 2004).

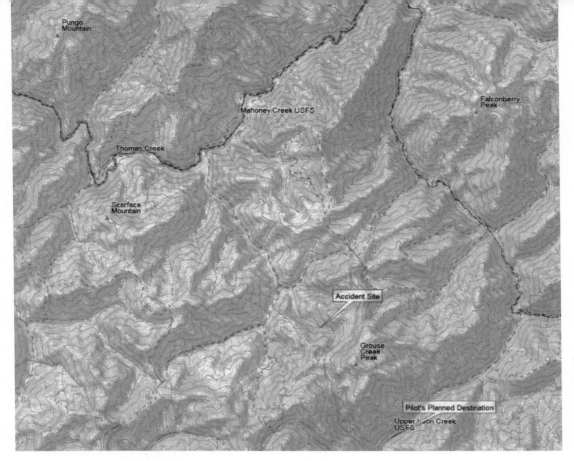

Figure 3-10. Location of the accident site, from NTSB (2004). The pilot stated he was following his GPS and descended toward rising terrain, and he impacted terrain and trees in an attempt to turn and exit the steep, narrow drainage. The red boundary line on the map shows the route the pilots intended to take down the Middle Fork of the Salmon River to Loon Creek, and up Loon Creek to Upper Loon airstrip.

Review Questions and Exercises

Answers to review questions are provided in Appendix B.

Circle the correct answer:

1. Following river drainages is preferable to flying in a straight line over mountainous terrain. (**True** / **False**)

2. If you become disoriented, you should descend to a lower altitude to better identify terrain features. (**True** / **False**)

3. Filing an FAA flight plan may not be possible in remote areas. (**True** / **False**)

Figure 4-1. Position of the actual horizon and the perceived horizon. In level flight, a typical response is to climb, which can cause a dangerous loss of airspeed. *(Photo by Amy Hoover)*

Baldwin captured the essence of the dangers to pilots who fail to recognize this visual illusion:

> We are born into a level world. We crawl on level floors, sit at level tables, play sports on level playing fields and otherwise spend our lives leveling cabinets, refrigerators, and picture frames. When we start out in our flying career we learn to level off, level our wings and go straight and level. We are so level oriented that we psychologically crave level even in our uneven world. It is so pervasive that we will assign level to something even if it isn't and fail to acknowledge the obvious signs that scream out the contrary. (Baldwin, 2010)

The obvious signs are an increase in pitch attitude and decreasing airspeed. This is a good reason to cross-reference your airspeed indicator and use all your senses to help understand the situation. For example, your engine sound will change in a climb. Continuously having to advance the throttle to "stay level" is a warning that you are either in a downdraft or are climbing due to a visual illusion. Regardless of which it is, the response should be the same. Look straight ahead and envision level, cross-reference your airplane instruments, and do not climb. Visual reference to upsloping terrain perceived as level will cause you to ascend and your airplane might not be able to out-climb the gradient.

Another factor that contributes to spatial disorientation is uneven terrain. Using the slope of the mountainside or canyon wall as a visual horizon, especially during turns, can cause you to lose sense of the actual horizon, especially with no sky visible. For example, in the traffic pattern at a canyon airstrip, terrain can block all reference to the actual horizon, and you may not be able to see anything but sheer rock and canyon walls everywhere you look. Developing a visual sense for this type of maneuvering takes practice, and novices can quickly become disoriented. Some methods to overcome visual illusions while turning are discussed later in this chapter.

Before flying in mountain and canyon terrain, there are ways you can develop depth perception. For example, glider pilots develop depth perception to accurately estimate altitude above the ground in case they need to make an off-field landing during cross-country flights. That training transfers well to mountain and canyon flight. Practice by covering your altimeter (first ensuring it is correct), estimating your height above the ground over a known elevation, and then checking it with the altimeter until you can be accurate within 200 feet or less.

Crossing Ridges

The safest way to cross ridges is to have plenty of altitude. Most mountain flying recommendations suggest a clearance of at least 1,000–2,000 feet of altitude above ridge level, depending on the conditions (Imeson, 2005; Anderson, 2003; Levi & O'Meara, 1992). Try to cross at the lowest point or through a mountain pass or saddle. Choose a location that is more like a knife-edge rather than a broad, flat plateau that takes more time to cross.

Performance limitations may require you to fly at lower altitudes, so you need to know how to cross ridges at or near ridge-top level. Ensure you have adequate terrain clearance before attempting to cross. If more terrain becomes visible beyond the ridge as you approach, then you should clear the ridge (unless there is a downdraft). If the ground beyond the ridge disappears as you approach, you will not clear it, so turn away and gain more altitude before attempting to cross. An overlying cloud base may restrict your altitude, so make sure the mountain tops are not obscured by clouds or you could enter the cloud before clearing the ridge. Use caution in this situation, as it is easy to head down the wrong canyon under low ceilings (Figure 4-2). Avoid cutting through a ravine or drainage when ridge tops are obscured, as there may not be room to turn around to the other side.

Constantly monitor the conditions behind you if the weather is deteriorating and ensure you will always be able to continue ahead or turn back. It may help to periodically make a 360-degree turn to assess the weather behind and to the sides of your flight path.

Expect downdrafts on the downwind (or leeward) side of a ridge. Allow sufficient altitude to provide a wide margin of safety when crossing. On the windward side, updrafts might help you gain altitude to clear the ridge, but do not

Figure 4-2. Low clouds and ceilings obscure mountain and ridge tops, making it hard to distinguish canyons. A low ceiling may obscure the ridge tops and you might not be able to clear the terrain before entering the cloud. *(Photo by Amy Hoover)*

count on that. However, be aware that severe updrafts could carry you upward into an overlying cloud layer. Try to determine the wind direction at all times and seek out lift and updrafts to help remain at safe altitudes.

Regardless of which side you approach a ridge, saddle, or pass, always cross at an angle that allows a turn back or escape toward lower terrain, preferably a 45-degree angle or less. Avoid entering directly into small cul-de-sacs where it is not possible to turn around. Continuously update your mental "picture" of how you will turn back, and update your escape plan often.

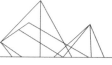

Amy's Axiom

As you cross a ridge, have a back door and keep your hand on the doorknob.

A smaller approach angle can give you a better view of terrain on the other side of the ridge and requires a shallower bank if you need to turn away from the ridge. Your planned escape route must be downhill or downstream and free of obstacles. Once you have cleared the ridge or pass, fly away from it at a 90-degree angle, if terrain permits. That will get you out of turbulence and downdrafts as quickly as possible. As stated by the Civil Aviation Authority of New Zealand:

It was a late November day, windy, low, and squally, and I was trying to get a Cessna 185 ski plane to Cold Meadows airstrip in the Idaho wilderness for a hunter pickup. I was westbound to the area, and strong headwinds slowed my progress. I remember being glad I had put on some extra fuel. There was a high ridge perpendicular to the wind on the direct route, and I foolishly attempted that route trying to save time—a decision that turned out to do the opposite, as it usually does. Even though I was not heavily loaded, the skis added significant drag, and I hit a strong downdraft as I approached the ridge. I turned away, climbed as much as the low ceiling would allow, and tried it again. The same thing occurred. I might admit to foolishly even trying it a third time, aware of the risks and compensating for them, but to no avail. After wasting time, money, and fuel, I spent a mere five minutes going a longer but lower way around.

Unfortunately, this was not my first experience with similar conditions trying to go direct under adverse conditions. A few years earlier, I had scared myself quite badly trying to cross the Wyoming Tetons in a Super Cub in high winds. Sometimes it makes one wonder how many lessons it may take to make one learn!

Remember Murphy's Law of mountain flying: when you need to turn back, it will be through sink, turbulence and a tailwind—so make sure you have the space and height available to do it safely. Don't rely on aircraft performance to get you out of trouble—good anticipation and good decisions are required. (CAA of New Zealand, 2012)

Slow to **maneuvering speed** (V_A) or below in wind, and anticipate wind shear as you cross a ridge, especially those that separate drainage divides (see Chapter 2 for a description of unconnected drainages and turbulence). It is not a good idea to approach a ridge from below in a climb attitude, since you will be at a slower speed and have less margin above the stall should you encounter wind shear or downdrafts. Also, it will be more difficult to judge whether or not you have enough altitude to cross the ridge.

Terrain Flying

Mountain and canyon regions are characterized by irregular topography. Ridges may be broad and flat or sharp and narrow. Rock outcroppings called mesas and buttes can stand high above the surrounding terrain. Valleys formed by glaciers are usually broad with wide, gentle turns. Canyons in younger mountains, or those formed by rapid geological uplift, are characterized by rivers with steep gradients, which form canyons that can change direction or end abruptly. Depending on the type of rock formations, canyons walls vary from gentle slopes to vertical cliffs. Vertical relief—the distance from the highest ridge to the bottom of a canyon or valley—can vary from only a few hundred feet to more than 10,000 feet. In deep canyons, relief occurs over a very short distance.

Although the term "terrain flying" may bring to mind the military term "Nap of the earth (NOE)" flying, it is not the context for this discussion. During NOE flight, military aircraft operate in, rather than over, valleys and folds in the topography to avoid enemy detection and fire. For the purpose of this discussion, terrain flying means using knowledge of the topography to plan your route, climbs, descents, and airport operations to take full advantage of terrain features. For example, knowledge of locations where updrafts and downdrafts usually occur enables you to use thermal or orographic lift and remain clear of turbulence and downdrafts (see Chapter 2).

Fly at an altitude high enough to clear terrain. Always be able to reverse course or turn toward lower areas. During cruise flight over mountainous areas, holding a constant altitude is not as important as maintaining safe terrain clearance and an altitude that provides for emergency options at your current position. VFR cruising altitudes in the United States are for flights more than 3,000 feet AGL. Below 3,000 feet over the mountains, consider using updrafts for "free" altitude, as you might encounter a downdraft later. Do not try to outclimb a downdraft (see Chapter 2). Maintain cruise speed (or V_A in turbulent air) and fly through the downward-moving air as quickly as possible.

Baldwin introduced the term **situational altitude**, which he described as "the altitude above the ground level (AGL) that permits maneuvering to a suitable landing site in the event of complete power loss. It is unique to the place and conditions you are in and continually changes as you move in space" (Baldwin, 2010). The concept of situational altitude entails constantly updating your situational awareness with respect to terrain clearance, obstacles, wind, and your airplane's turn and glide performance. Even along the same route, a different day with different wind, weather, and DA conditions will necessitate a different altitude be flown for safe operations.

Amy's Axiom

When flying close to terrain, the cardinal rule is: Don't hit anything!

When flying toward rising terrain, it is important to be able to reverse course toward lower elevations. Imeson (2005) defined two important positions, the turn-around point and the point of no return, described below.

Turn-Around Point

According to Imeson (2005), "The turn-around point is determined as the position where, if the throttle is reduced to idle, the aircraft can be turned around during a glide without impacting the terrain." Since the position is determined with throttle at idle, the airplane should be able to reverse course safely unless there are downdrafts. The challenge will be to establish where that point is. Flights toward rising terrain, toward a more confined area, or in a narrow valley or canyon require constant scrutiny of your position and altitude to ensure you do not continue past the turn-around point. Imeson stated that the point is "a gauge to judge and establish the point over the ground where an escape turn must be made. For most light aircraft this will be approximately 500-feet AGL" (Imeson, 2005).

Point of No Return

As defined by Imeson (2005), "The point of no return is defined as the point on the ground of rising terrain where the terrain out climbs the aircraft." Regardless of whether this occurs due to lack of situational awareness or poor decision making, it is an emergency situation. Your only option may be a controlled emergency landing straight ahead or within a few degrees of your course, or an emergency turn, as described in the next section. However, both of those options are fraught with hazards, and your best option is to identify the turn-around point and execute a normal turn before it becomes an emergency.

Flying in Canyons

Follow drainages that have large rivers or streams flowing down them. Large canyons will be wider and have shallower gradients, and the terrain will be less likely to rise more steeply than the climb performance of your aircraft. Avoid the middle of a canyon; the middle is where you will encounter the most turbulence and wind shear (see Chapter 2). Flight in the middle of a narrow canyon may not allow enough room to reverse course (Figure 4-3).

Do not fly up a blind canyon. Without positively identifying a drainage or knowing how quickly the terrain rises, you could get boxed in and not be able to turn around. If you are unsure of the outcome, do not attempt it. Take the time to turn around and gain more altitude before flying up a canyon.

You will be flying closer to terrain than you may be accustomed to, especially during approaches and departures (Figure 4-4). The best route for descending or climbing will often follow valleys and canyons. Stay close to one side of a canyon, wind and weather permitting, to allow room to turn around, while constantly assessing your planned "escape route" should you encounter adverse weather or other hazards. Use the right side in no-wind conditions to allow traffic to flow safely and pass in relatively narrow canyons. That is based on right-of-way rules for passing and overtaking aircraft as defined by the FAA. Check the right-of-way rules for other parts of the world, as they may be different. Use strobes, position lights, and landing lights to increase your chances of being seen by other pilots.

Amy's
Axiom

If the rocks and trees are your enemies, keep them close!

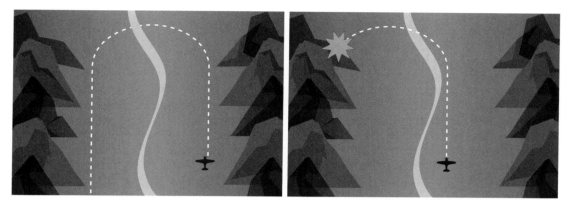

Figure 4-3. Fly along one side of a canyon to allow room to turn. Positioning to the side leaves maximum room to turn in case a 180-degree reversal is required. Flying in the middle means a steeper turn is necessary and there may be insufficient room to reverse course. *(Courtesy of the Civil Aviation Authority of New Zealand)*

Figure 4-4. When flying along the side of a canyon, you will be close to terrain, particularly during approach and departure, and you must learn to accurately judge distance and your airplane's position. *(Photo by Amy Hoover)*

Winds and Turbulence

Fly in smooth air. Winds in mountainous terrain and canyons are unpredictable, and high winds or turbulence can be hazardous (Chapter 2). Fly on the "updraft" side of the canyon in wind or turbulence, but be wary, as oncoming aircraft may be on the same side. The updraft may change sides as the canyon changes direction, and wind and turbulence patterns are unpredictable. Your best option with strong winds may be to climb out of the canyon or land at an airstrip to wait out the weather.

Turning Safely

In canyons, it is important to understand the relationships between your aircraft's speed, rate and radius of turn, wing load factor, and stall speed. You can directly control some of those variables to maximize your margin of safety, especially during critical phases of flight, such as arrival and departure from airstrips in mountain and canyon terrain. For normal operations, consider the following basic concepts adapted from "Canyon turns: between a rock and a hard place" (Hoover, 2001) to help maximize performance, minimize risk, and keep your passengers happy.

Medium-Bank Turns

At constant airspeed, steeper bank angles produce a smaller turn radius and a faster turn rate. At a constant bank angle, slower airspeed produces a tighter turn radius and faster turn rate (Figure 4-5). Since tighter turns are needed in confined areas, you will have to either steepen the bank or slow down, or do both.

As shown in Figures 4-6 and 4-7, increasing the bank angle beyond 30 degrees rapidly increases the load factor required for a level turn. Stall speed, and the corresponding risk of stalling, increase as well. For example, the load factor in a level turn at 30-degree bank is only 1.15 G with a corresponding 7.5% increase in stall speed. However, a level turn at 60-degree bank requires a 2G load factor with a corresponding 41% increase in stall speed.

In addition to increasing load factor and stall speed, steep-bank turns in mountain and canyon terrain can cause visual disorientation. As discussed in the previous section, it may be difficult to visually reference the airplane's attitude, and you can quickly lose reference to the horizon. Excess G-forces imposed by steep turns can alter your perception of which direction is down and exacerbate the sense of disorientation. The best way to avoid becoming disoriented and overbanking is to limit bank angles to 30 degrees or less for normal maneuvering in a confined area, such as a narrow canyon. Many pilots are intimidated when turning close to terrain because the view out the front is nothing but rock wall. You can help overcome this by visually "leading" the turn and looking ahead of the airplane's flight path in the direction of the turn.

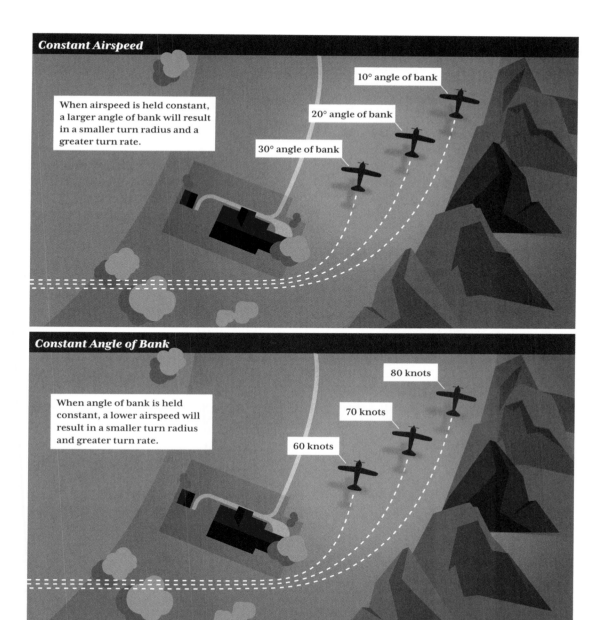

Figure 4-5. Relationship between airspeed, bank angle, and turn radius.

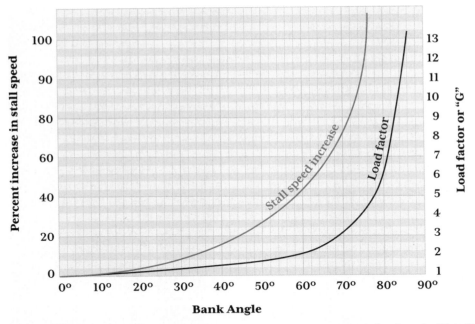

Figure 4-6. Increase in stall speed and wing load factor with increase in bank angle (FAA, 2016d). Stall speed increases significantly past 30 degrees of bank, and load factor goes up dramatically past a 60-degree bank angle.

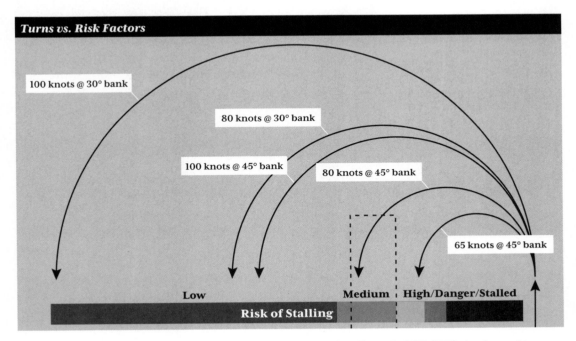

Figure 4-7. Turns versus risk factors for various bank angles and stall speeds (TSB, 2011). As airspeed is reduced and bank angle simultaneously increased, the risk of stalling increases.

Slow Down

If you limit the angle of bank to 30 degrees or less, that means you will need to fly at a slower airspeed to accomplish a tighter turn. By slowing down, you can maneuver or reverse course in a relatively narrow space. Flying slowly also gives you more time to react and decreases the aircraft turn radius while maneuvering in confined areas. Slow at least to **maneuvering speed (V_A)** or maximum **flap extended speed (V_{FE})**, or you may want to use **canyon speed (V_{CANYON})**, as introduced in Chapter 1, to slow down and configure your airplane for maneuvering.

Determine ahead of time the correct target power settings and airspeeds to use at various weight and **center of gravity (CG)** positions so you are not distracted while turning in a narrow canyon. Determining target power settings in advance will enable you to slow down smoothly and with confidence while maintaining situational awareness (See Chapter 1 for expanded procedures).

For operations in canyons more than about 3/4-mile wide, V_A is a good target airspeed for most **general aviation (GA)** aircraft. In narrower canyons, with no turbulence, you could slow to V_{FE} and extend flaps to stabilize the airplane. This can also be a good time to use your predetermined V_{CANYON} speed. Use appropriate speeds, power settings, and configurations.

Use of Flaps

Lowering partial flaps decreases the stall speed of the wing and can stabilize the airplane at slower speeds. However, lowering flaps may drastically decrease the limit load factor of the wing (Chapter 1). Familiarize yourself with the effects of flap extension on limit load factor prior to operating in various configurations.

Airspeed and Turn Radius

You can determine your turn radius at various airspeeds in a given bank angle. This can be calculated using the formula:

$$R = \frac{V^2}{11.26 \times \text{tangent of bank angle}}$$

Where:
R = radius in feet
V = velocity in knots true airspeed (TAS)

You can also use Table 4-1, which shows the approximate turn radius in feet for a given TAS and angle of bank. For example, an airplane in a 30-degree bank flying at a TAS of 80 knots will have an approximate turn radius of 985 feet. The airplane will require twice that distance, or approximately 1,970 feet, to reverse course 180 degrees. G-load is a function of bank angle and is independent of airspeed.

Table 4-1. Turn radius in feet for various bank angles and airspeeds. *G-load factor is shown in parentheses.*

True Airspeed	Bank Angle in Degrees (G-load factor)				
	20° (1.1)	30° (1.2)	45° (1.4)	60° (2.0)	70° (2.9)
50 kts	611	385	222	128	81
60 kts	880	554	320	185	116
70 kts	1198	754	435	251	158
80 kts	1565	985	568	328	206
90 kts	1980	1246	719	415	261
100 kts	2445	1538	888	513	323
110 kts	2958	1862	1075	621	390
120 kts	3521	2215	1279	738	465
130 kts	4132	2600	1501	867	545
140 kts	4792	3015	1741	1005	632
150 kts	5501	3462	1998	1154	726

Let's look at another example: What airspeed will allow you to turn around in a canyon one-half nautical mile (3,000 feet) wide to circle over an airstrip or to turn away from weather (Figure 4-8)?

Figure 4-8. The airplane is flying in a canyon that is approximately one-half nautical mile wide. The pilot must determine how much to slow down to ensure a turn can be made without impacting terrain. *(Photo by Amy Hoover)*

For an airplane with a cruise speed of 120 knots TAS in a 30-degree bank, turn radius will be:

$$R = \frac{V^2}{11.26 \times \tan \text{bank angle}} = \frac{120^2}{11.26 \times 0.578} = 2,215 \text{ ft}$$

It would require twice that distance (4,430 feet) to execute a 180-degree turn and reverse course at a cruise speed of 120 knots in a 30-degree bank. You would have to make a steeper bank turn to avoid impacting terrain, and risk other hazards of steep banks just discussed.

However, at a reduced speed of 80 knots TAS, the new turn radius would be:

$$R = \frac{V^2}{11.26 \times \tan \text{bank angle}} = \frac{80^2}{11.26 \times 0.578} = 985 \text{ ft}$$

Now the 180-degree turn can be executed comfortably and safely in 1,970 feet, much less than the 1/2 NM wide canyon, while still maintaining terrain clearance (Figure 4-9).

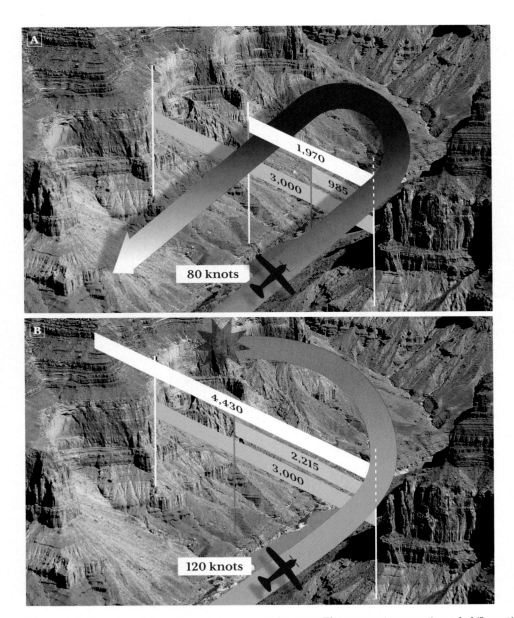

Figure 4-9. Two aircraft have flown into a canyon by error. The canyon is approximately 1/2 nautical mile (3,000 feet) across with sheer cliffs on both sides. **(A)** This pilot is flying at 80 knots. After realizing the error, the pilot uses a 30-degree medium bank angle to reverse course. This aircraft requires about 1,970 feet to turn 180° and makes it out of the canyon safely. **(B)** This pilot is flying at 120 knots and also uses a 30-degree angle of bank in an attempt to reverse course. The aircraft requires 4,430 feet to reverse course to safety. Unfortunately, the canyon is only 3,000 feet across, so the aircraft will hit the canyon wall. Airspeed is the most influential factor in determining how much distance is required to turn. Many pilots have made the error of increasing the steepness of their bank angle when a simple reduction of speed would have been more effective.

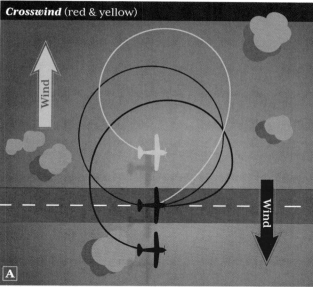

Crosswind (red & yellow)

Wind

Wind

A

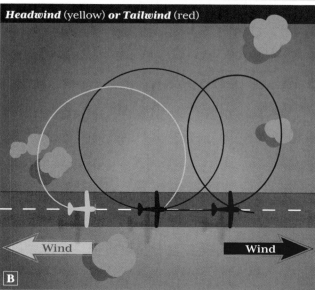

Headwind (yellow) **or Tailwind** (red)

Wind

Wind

B

Figure 4-10. Effects of wind on ground track of an airplane at a constant TAS with constant turn radius. In no wind, the ground track will mimic the actual turn radius (shown by the blue airplane). (**A**) shows the effects of a crosswind on the ground track (shown by the yellow and red airplanes). (**B**) shows the ground track resulting from a headwind or tailwind.

Turn radius may vary depending on pilot technique (i.e., maintaining a constant airspeed and bank angle). At a specific bank angle and airspeed, you will always have the same rate and radius of turn regardless of weight, CG location, or type of airplane. However, a heavier airplane, or one loaded to a forward CG, will require more power to sustain altitude in a turn. At high **density altitude (DA)**, power may be limited, so you will need to lower the nose and sacrifice altitude to maintain airspeed and avoid stalling the airplane. As Parfit (1977) wrote about veteran Idaho backcountry pilot Carol Jarvis, "His turns at this [slower] speed were between 20 and 35 degrees banks and were usually accompanied by a distinct lowering of the nose. Backpressure in a turn, he said, can be fatal."

The important factor with respect to not impacting terrain is ground speed, which is a function of **true airspeed (TAS)** and wind. Since TAS increases at a rate of 2% per thousand feet increase in DA, a given bank angle will result in a higher turn radius than at sea level at the same **indicated airspeed (IAS)**.

Wind will affect the airplane's ground track and alter the flight path, which could cause the aircraft to impact terrain in a narrow canyon (Figure 4-10). When turning in a confined area, if you are uncertain how much bank to use, it is best to start with a steeper bank and gradually decrease the bank angle through the turn as necessary. If you start with a bank that is too shallow and increase it through the turn, there is a chance you could exceed the wing's load factor or become disoriented.

Overbanking Tendency

Due to design properties such as wing dihedral or keel effect, most GA aircraft tend to be laterally stable in a shallow turn (tend to roll out of bank), neutrally stable in a medium-banked turn (stay in the selected bank attitude), and laterally unstable in a steep turn (tend to increase bank). For that reason, medium-bank turns are the most stable, least distracting, and require the least amount of pilot input, since the tendency to overbank is not as great. It is important to note that climbing turns have a greater tendency to overbank than descending turns, and you may need to vary control inputs accordingly. You may need to hold opposite aileron in a climbing turn to avoid overbanking. In contrast, during a descending turn, you may need to hold aileron into the turn to maintain a constant angle of bank. Always keep the aircraft coordinated and maintain situational awareness throughout the maneuver.

Emergency Turn

The emergency turn, also known as blind canyon escape or box canyon turn, is a potentially life-saving maneuver if a 180-degree course reversal is the only way out. However, in this case it means you already flew past the turn-around point, as discussed earlier in this chapter, and are now in a critical emergency. As emphasized by Imeson (2005), "The box canyon turn is an emergency procedure. The best advice is to avoid a situation that might require a box canyon turn course reversal." The Transportation Safety Board of Canada noted:

> There is no single, universally accepted canyon turn procedure, and there is no preferred method of determining the ideal canyon turn procedure for a specific aircraft type. However, it is widely accepted that planning is a critical aspect of the canyon turn procedure. While canyon turn procedures may share a number of similarities, one generic procedure will not work for every aircraft type. It is important that an appropriate canyon turn procedure be customized for each aircraft type, to ensure proper aircraft configuration. If an aircraft is improperly configured, performance will be degraded, and safety margins will be reduced. (TSB, 2011)

It is possible to turn most GA airplanes around in a distance as small as 4–5 wingspans (See Table 4-1). As previously discussed, medium-bank turns are best, but if you find yourself needing to steepen the bank, keep in mind that at a 60-degree bank, the airplane requires a sustained 2G load by the pilot to remain in level flight. The required G-load increases exponentially past 60 degrees (Figure 4-6). Thus, at steeper bank angles you will need to pitch down (lose altitude) to unload the wing and avoid a stall. Do not attempt to make a steep-banked emergency turn unless you have researched the best bank angle and airspeed to use and have practiced it ahead of time with your airplane loaded the way you are going to fly it and at a DA similar to where you will be operating. Also, 14 CFR §91.307 dictates that you must wear a parachute if you execute any intentional maneuver that exceeds 60 degrees of bank or a nose-up or nose-down attitude of more than 30 degrees.

If you decide to practice emergency, steep-banked turns, take an experienced instructor with you. Climb to the DA for which you want to practice the maneuver, preferably over flat land. You can simulate an emergency by slowing to V_A, V_{FE}, or V_Y, as appropriate for the situation you wish to simulate. When below V_{FE} (in no turbulence), apply maximum lift flaps for your airplane before initiating the turn. Pitch down as you enter the turn and transition to a descent to unload the forces on the wing while applying power as needed.

Progressively increase the bank angle as you practice tighter and tighter turns. You may need to pitch down even more as bank increases to reduce the G-load and to prevent a stall, which means you will have to sacrifice altitude during the maneuver. There could be a large altitude loss to start with, especially in a heavy airplane at high DA, until you get the feel of the airplane.

The goal is to practice your chosen technique until you can perform the smallest-radius turn safely with an acceptable altitude loss. Once you determine how tightly you can turn and how much altitude is lost, you will be better prepared to make a choice whether to turn or land straight ahead if ever faced with a box canyon scenario. Remember that TAS, and thus ground speed, increases as altitude increases, so turns at higher DA will take more room. Most importantly, plan ahead so you will not need to actually use the maneuver.

Both Imeson (2005) and Geeting & Woerner (1988) recommend only partial flaps in an emergency canyon turn, and Anderson makes a strong case for not using full flaps:

> **The 40° flap turn.** The only reason I discuss this very frequently recommended method of canyon turns is to tell you emphatically *not* to do it…. The idea is that dumping in 40° of flaps throws on the brakes, balloons you up with extra lift, greatly reducing the turn radius because you are going so much more slowly…. At high altitudes, it is easy to get a small, low-powered aircraft behind the power curve with full flaps. In this mode, you are going so slowly at such a high angle of attack that lifting the nose does not result in a climb. In fact, full power is required to just hold altitude. Lifting the nose actually *increases* your sink rate, so now you are going down with full power almost stalled. The only way to recover from this situation is to lower the nose. (Anderson, 2003)

The Transportation Safety Board of Canada determined the use of full flaps to be a contributing factor in the fatal crash of an airplane whose pilots attempted a canyon turn during a mountain training flight in a narrow canyon. The report stated, "The application of full flaps produces high drag, and therefore lowers the performance of the aircraft during a turn where maximum performance may be necessary" (TSB, 2011). Use of full flaps at high angles of bank can also exceed the limit load factor, as discussed in the previous section. However, according to Vivion (2018), some airplanes, such as the Aviat Husky, do well with full flaps in steep turns.

In summary, executing an emergency turn requires practice. Do not attempt it in a real emergency situation unless you have mastered the technique. The safest course of action is to avoid such a situation altogether through careful planning and maintaining situational awareness.

Low-Level Maneuvering

Low-level maneuvering can set pilots up for visual illusions and distractions that lead to stall/spin scenarios from which recovery is not possible. Wind worsens the situation, since drift can cause distinct visual illusions. The end result is often an uncoordinated turn that results in a low-level, cross-controlled stall/spin accident. A classic scenario is the "moose stall." The term is commonly used to describe a crash that occurred when the pilot was circling at very low level over an animal or object, such as a moose, as depicted by Baldwin:

> A strange thing happens when you are turning very steeply over a moose. First, the inside wing of your Cub starts getting in your line of view. A simple solution is to roll toward the outside of the turn and step on a little bottom rudder. That "solution" raises the wing so you can see and also keeps the turn tighter than normal—to stay close over the animal. The final nail in your coffin is the "safe" feeling you get from the skid you have created, because you feel you are being pushed up and away from the center of the turn. Suddenly, the low wing stalls and drops out rolling you from 60 to 70 degrees of bank angle to an immediate upside down attitude. Now, even if you can break the stall, you have too little altitude to roll upright and pull out of the dive. (Baldwin, 2010)

The amount of cross control required to produce such a stall/spin varies with the airplane. However, the fact that loss of control in flight remains the number one cause of fatal accidents in the United States (FAA, 2018) means pilots either may not be able to recognize an aerodynamic stall or spin and execute immediate corrective action, or they may not be at a high enough altitude to recover before impacting terrain.

The primary illusion during turns at low altitude occurs when the airplane is below its pivotal altitude. At any given ground speed, the projection of a visual reference line (such as the airplane's lateral axis) will pivot around a point on the ground that appears stationary from the pilot's perspective (Figure 4-11). Pivotal altitude is calculated based on the airplane's ground speed, and bank angle does not affect pivotal altitude unless it is steep enough to affect ground speed (FAA, 2016a). However, distance from the object on the ground affects bank angle. The closer the object, the greater the necessary bank angle (Figure 4-12).

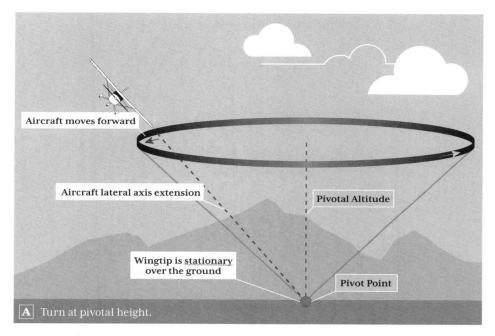

Figure 4-11 (above and next page). Pivotal altitude during a turn. **(A)** At the pivotal altitude, the point appears stationary from the pilot's perspective and the airplane pivots around it. In any turn **(B)** above pivotal altitude or **(C)** below pivotal altitude, the point will move in the pilot's vision.

Figure 4-11 continued...

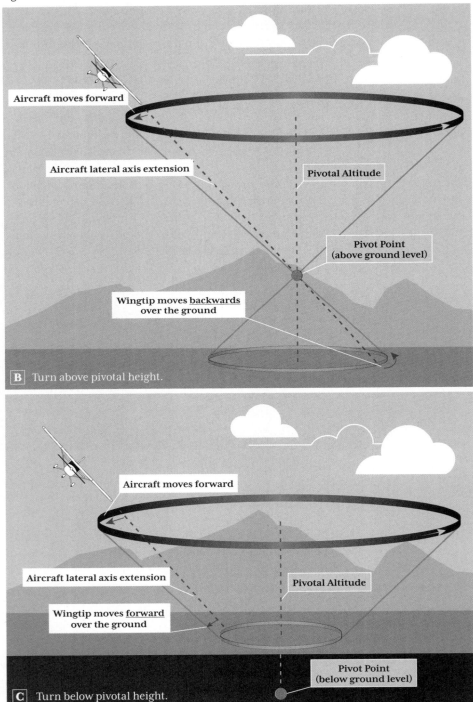

B Turn above pivotal height.

C Turn below pivotal height.

Labels in panel B:
- Aircraft moves forward
- Aircraft lateral axis extension
- Pivotal Altitude
- Pivot Point (above ground level)
- Wingtip moves <u>backwards</u> over the ground

Labels in panel C:
- Aircraft moves forward
- Aircraft lateral axis extension
- Pivotal Altitude
- Wingtip moves <u>forward</u> over the ground
- Pivot Point (below ground level)

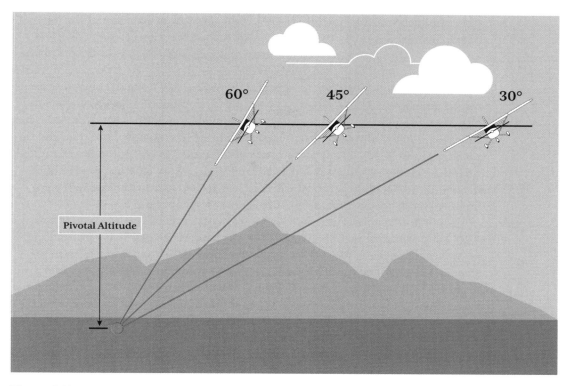

Figure 4-12. Various bank angles at the pivotal altitude. The angle of bank does not affect the pivotal altitude. However, the closer the airplane is to the object on the ground, the steeper the bank angle at pivotal altitude.

During the maneuver eights-on-pylons, pilots practice varying the pivotal altitude by climbing or descending as ground speed changes throughout the turn from upwind to downwind. Stowell described it this way:

> I recommend sighting down the wing to the ground reference (GR). Note the position of the GR relative to something on the wing or wingtip, e.g., along a line of rivets, or a series of rib stiches. While flying a coordinated turn, keep the GR in the same place relative to your wing/wingtip references throughout the maneuver. If the GR moves ahead of the references on your wing/wingtip, push forward and catch up to the GR (descend down to pivotal altitude). If the GR moves aft of the references on your wing/wingtip, pull back to the GR (climb up to pivotal altitude). (Stowell, 2018)

The danger occurs when the airplane is flown at an altitude below the pivotal altitude and the pilot's attention is focused on a point or object, such as an animal or structure, near the center of the turn. There is a natural tendency to try to fix the movement of the GR by applying rudder toward the inside of the turn (rather than pulling back), thus inducing a skid. If the airplane is slow enough, or the bank angle steep enough, the skid could cause the lower wing to stall and lead to an incipient spin. If the airplane is already critically slow, pulling back may not be a good idea either.

For a very slow airplane, the height above ground (AGL) of the pivotal altitude can be quite low. The FAA states: "a good rule of thumb for estimating the pivotal altitude is to square the ground speed, then divide by 15 (if the ground speed is in miles per hour) or divide by 11.3 (if the ground speed is in knots), and then add the mean sea level (MSL) altitude of the ground reference" (FAA, 2016a). For example, a STOL airplane traveling at 50 mph ground speed would have a pivotal altitude of $50^2 \div 15 = 167$ feet AGL. The typical scenario occurs at low altitudes and steep angles of bank, from which a stall/spin is not recoverable and usually fatal.

Another illusion occurs when turns are made in wind. As shown in Figure 4-10, wind affects the ground track of the airplane. When practicing ground reference maneuvers, such as S-turns and rectangular patterns, pilots learn to steepen the bank angle and increase backpressure to maintain altitude when ground speed is fastest. This happens most often during the turn from downwind to base in the traffic pattern. The problem is that at low altitude, or close to terrain such as in a canyon, the visual sense of drift may cause pilots to overbank or to incorrectly perceive the drift as a skid and use improper rudder inputs. The turn from upwind or crosswind to downwind can also be deceiving. The pilot may confuse the increased ground speed with an acceleration in airspeed and pull back on the yoke or stick and increase the bank angle, resulting in a stall and/or spin. The illusions are best avoided by always remaining coordinated and limiting bank angles. According to Potts:

> Tight downwind turns in strong winds should be avoided whenever possible. If necessary, they should be performed without ground reference. Here you are making your turn in a rapidly moving body of air, and the turn has to relate to the air mass, not some spot on the ground. During the turn, sideways drift will be quite pronounced, and trying to remain over a landmark—say a trophy moose or bear—will just lead you into tightening the turn until you stall and go spinning in. (Potts, 1993)

Baldwin advocates "Our solution to minimize risk is virtually never circle in high winds. We fly away downwind then make a low altitude, wings level upwind pass to get our [photo] shot" (Baldwin, 2010).

In the following story, Michael Vivion provides an insightful and chilling description of a different scenario that might lead to a loss of control.

do this flight, *don't* go below 100 knots. If it dips to 90 temporarily in a gust or something, OK; but if it is more than a few seconds, lower the nose and get more speed immediately."

Years ago, a pilot flew across a pass in a Cessna 180, stalled, and fell probably 500 feet upside down, killing all four people on board. I guessed the wind at the pass was 25–30 knots, and on the downwind side it probably made 50–60 knots straight down. We get no second chance in this scenario!

Use cruise climbs, or better yet, cross passes at cruise speed with plenty of altitude and a flat attitude or nose down. My very worst experience in a pass was one time when I was going up at 2,000 feet per minute, and suddenly it shifted to a huge downdraft. To compensate with a fully loaded de Havilland Beaver, I had to point the nose down about 40 degrees to keep enough speed to fly out of the downdraft. The end of the canyon had a particular S-turn to it, and all the wind that day was compounded by the terrain. Fortunately, I was still at my usual 500 feet above the ground. I have not flown through that pass since then unless I am much higher!

Using Terrain

Determine the location of updrafts, downdrafts, turbulence, wind shear, and other weather that could affect your flight (see Chapter 2). Use the terrain by climbing in orographic or thermal lift. You may want to stay out of updrafts during descents as they can hinder your ability to lose altitude. Maintain visual reference to terrain to ensure situational awareness while climbing or descending and plan ahead so you arrive at the appropriate altitude to enter the airport traffic area at your destination.

Accident Scenario

Mountain pilot and author Sparky Imeson wrote about and gave educational presentations describing an accident he was involved in on June 3, 2007. His reflections and insights are presented at www.mountainflying.com/pages/crash/crash1.html and discussed here as they are an invaluable contribution to the subject.

Imeson was giving mountain flight instruction to the owner of an Aviat Husky A1-B, J.C. Kantorowicz, when the airplane impacted terrain in a canyon near Winston, Montana. Both he and the pilot were injured, and the airplane was consumed by a post-crash fire. The National Transportation Safety Board determined the probable cause(s) of this accident to be: "The pilot's failure to maintain an adequate airspeed while maneuvering at low altitude in a canyon that led to a stall. The pilot's decision to fly along the canyon wall at a low altitude and low energy state was a factor" (National Transportation Safety Board [NTSB], 2007).

As described in the NTSB report:

> The airplane stalled and impacted terrain during flight in a canyon at low altitude and a slow airspeed. The pilot was participating in a mountain flying seminar and was flying with a CFI. The purpose of the flight was instructional in nature intending to practice short canyon turns. They flew the first canyon at 300 feet AGL, 70 mph, 20 degrees of flaps, along the south side of the canyon, and rode a few thermals. Identifying areas where thermal lift could be found was part of the instructional flight. He then crossed into another canyon that was full of burned out terrain and dead fall trees. This canyon he flew at 300 to 350 feet AGL, 60 to 65 mph, and full flaps. The pilot angled his plane towards a rock cliff expecting to pick up thermal lift from the warm rocks. He flew with the wing tip about 10 feet from the cliff. The climb stopped, the airspeed fell off, and the wing stalled. He turned left, applied full throttle, and lowered the nose of the airplane. The descent was rapid as he tried to direct the airplane between deadfall trees into a drainage gully. The airplane's descent continued and he tried to land the airplane as gently as he could. After the collision with the sloped terrain, both pilots egressed the airplane just before it was engulfed in flames. The pilot stated that the airplane and engine had no mechanical failures or malfunctions during the flight. (NTSB, 2007)

The crash and subsequent search and rescue was widely publicized, including news interviews as well as narratives from both Imeson and the other pilot that circulated on social media sites, chat rooms, and published in aviation newsletters. From those, some interesting stories resulted. Not only did both pilots initially recount memories of the event that were very different from one another, but some of those accounts changed over time (Lincoln, 2007a, 2007b; Imeson, 2007). For example, Imeson initially reported they encountered a downdraft with wind shear that sheared to a tailwind, and that the pilot caused the airplane to stall by turning the wrong direction and attempting to climb, which caused the airplane to stall (Lincoln, 2007a). In a rebuttal to that article, the pilot stated that he added power, lowered the nose, and initiated a turn toward lower terrain in an attempt to avoid stalling and hitting trees (Kantorowicz, 2007). As a result, the original article was updated; the initial quotes from the instructor were removed, and the probability that the airplane might have been hit by two downdrafts in succession was posited (Lincoln, 2007b). These changes are mentioned not to specify whether either account is right or wrong, but to demonstrate that people's perceptions of an event, particularly in a high-stress environment, can be highly varied and will change once new input is received, such as occurred after the rebuttal to the initial report. In fact, Imeson later posted the original article along with Kantorowicz's rebuttal on his website (see previous link).

Ultimately, the NTSB determined the accident was caused by failure to maintain an adequate airspeed while maneuvering at low altitude in a canyon that led to a stall. Additionally, the decision to fly along the canyon wall at a low altitude and low energy state was a factor (NTSB, 2007).

There were some notable outcomes as described by both pilots. The downdrafts were described as "very strong" and "a surprise" (Lincoln, 2007a, 2007b). Imeson told a reporter that downdrafts are a normal cycle of the air; however, so far that day they had only encountered updrafts, and "the one spot where we needed one (a downdraft) not to be there, there was one" (Lincoln, 2007b). Conway (1969) pointed out that where there are updrafts, there will always be downdrafts, and both pilots admitted afterward they had not exercised good judgment in entering a narrow canyon at low altitude, where a downdraft would be hazardous (Imeson, 2007; Kantorowicz, 2007).

Valuable lessons learned and articulated by both pilots included information about poor decision-making as well as post-crash survival equipment and procedures. For example, Imeson did not bring his survival vest on the flight. Kantorowicz was not wearing his, and instead placed it behind the seat. When they had to jump out of a burning airplane, neither had any survival gear or emergency signaling devices with them. They also deviated from their flight plan, so no one from the mountain flying seminar in which they were participating knew where to look for the crash. Imeson, who was injured, left the scene of the crash and was not found by search and rescue personnel until almost a day after they found the pilot (Kantorowicz, 2007; Imeson, 2007). Additional points include the following:

- "It was stupid to modify my personal safety standards. I have developed them after years and years of flying. Had we been at my comfort level of 500 feet AGL, this would not have happened...after flying for more than 40 minutes and evaluating the aircraft performance I revised my comfort level to about 300 feet AGL." (Imeson, 2007)

- "I had felt entirely comfortable in the first green canyon. I was uneasy in the second canyon. I should have listened to [another instructor's] little voice in my head saying 'Do we really need to be in here?'" (Kantorowicz, 2007)

- "If I had stayed at 70 mph and 20 degrees flaps perhaps I would have noticed the loss of lift a little earlier." (Kantorowicz, 2007)

- "If I had used [another instructor's] short turn around learned the day previous, I probably would not have stalled and the turnaround would have been successful." (Kantorowicz, 2007)

Although the crash and subsequent survival and rescue efforts could have ended in tragedy, Kantorowicz did several things that facilitated their success and survival. After encountering the downdraft, he lowered the nose, kept flying speed, turned toward lower terrain, and flew the airplane all the way to the ground (Imeson, 2007; Kantorowicz, 2007). He also maintained a positive mental attitude after the crash, lighted a fire, and signaled a rescue helicopter with a piece of broken glass (Lincoln, 2007b; Kantorowicz, 2007). Probably most important, both pilots honestly evaluated their actions, reactions, and lessons learned to make decisions about their future attitudes toward safety and flight operations (Imeson, 2007; Kantorowicz, 2007).

Review Questions and Exercises

Answers to review questions are provided in Appendix B.

Circle the correct answer:

1. It is best to fly down the middle of a canyon to give yourself more maneuvering room. (**True** / **False**)

2. Cross ridges at a 45-degree angle so you can turn toward lower terrain if you encounter a downdraft. (**True** / **False**)

3. Overbanking tendency is greatest in a descending turn because the outside wing is traveling faster. (**True** / **False**)

4. An emergency turn at a high angle of bank should always be used to turn around in a canyon. (**True** / **False**)

5. When determining what power settings to use while maneuvering and turning in a canyon, power required to maintain a given airspeed in level flight depends on aircraft weight and position of the (**center of gravity** / **center of lift**).

6. During maneuvers, more power is required for an airplane that is (**heavier** / **lighter**) and with a center of gravity that is more (**forward** / **rearward**).

7. The (**turn-around point** / **point of no return**) is determined as the position where, if the throttle is reduced to idle, the aircraft can be turned around during a glide without impacting the terrain.

Short answer:

8. It is best to slow down and use medium-bank turns in canyons.
    - Why do you want to slow the airplane down?
    - What are three reasons why you should not exceed a medium-bank turn?

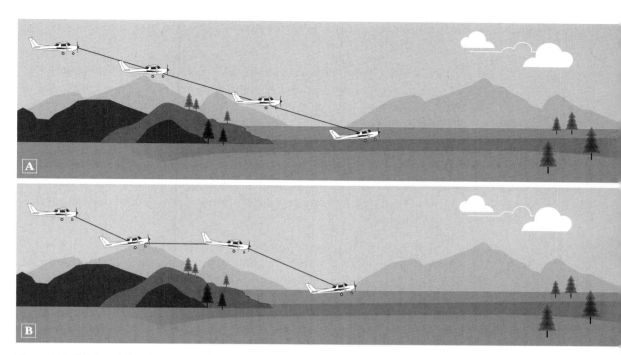

Figure 5-2. (A) A stabilized, power-on approach to landing: The airplane has locked onto a constant airspeed and power setting, and the pilot can adjust pitch and power for wind shear or turbulence to remain on glide path to the landing point. **(B)** An unstabilized approach: The airplane shows a path with constantly changing airspeed and power settings, and it is never stabilized. When the airplane arrives at the landing zone, it will be either too fast or too slow, thus causing it to overshoot the landing spot or land short or hard.

The basic principles referred to by Hoover are those necessary to fly a power-on stabilized approach to a precise aim spot. Flying this type of approach requires you to use visual references to accurately judge your position and glide path and to precisely maintain the proper airspeed. The descent angle and approach path you choose will be based on obstacle clearance and may vary from a standard 3-degree approach to as much as 5 degrees (steep approach) for maximum obstacle clearance and visibility. As emphasized by Potts:

> Control of airspeed is arguably the single most important factor involved in an approach. A couple of knots too fast or too slow at the threshold will guarantee a less than satisfactory landing. Make a point of being precise in this area. (Potts, 1993)

To set up for a stabilized approach, you must first determine the correct airspeed and power setting for the weight and CG you are going to use and the descent angle you want to fly. Lean the mixture for the DA at your landing destination. Assuming no wind shear, you will then be able to descend directly toward an aim point at the appropriate airspeed and trimmed for "hands off" flight. According to the FAA:

> A fundamental key to flying a stabilized approach is the inter-relationship of pitch and power. At any targeted airspeed in any configuration, adding more power will make the glide path shallower; reducing power will make it steeper. Experienced pilots know the power settings and airspeeds for different landing weights, drag configurations and rates-of-descent for their airplanes. (FAA, 2008a)

A key component to perfecting your ability to fly a stabilized approach is to practice, and then practice some more. Highly experienced mountain and glacier pilot Paul Claus noted:

> We all start to learn by the numbers, and instrument flying is a good example of everyone doing things pretty much the same way. Although using numbers is a good base, [this type of flying] goes beyond to the technique of "feeling" the airplane. It is very difficult to teach, and is a long, hard process to learn. (Claus, 2018)

Claus sometimes requires pilots to fly for three years with his operation before allowing them to fly passengers. He stresses the importance of practice and logging at least 2,000 short takeoffs and landings before advancing to his type of work. Claus says his best pilot flies every single day, and that—combined with good skills and natural ability to start with—puts him at an almost unreachable level of skill in the one airplane he flies. Claus also notes that some of the best respected pilots are ones who did not learn particularly quickly, but attained their skills through steady, tedious repetition. Although years ago, primary teaching involved a seat-of-the-pants feel, it really isn't done anymore (Claus, 2018).

The next section describes techniques you can use to determine appropriate airspeed, power setting, and configuration to use for a stabilized approach.

Airspeed and Power

Williams (1986) contended that backcountry approaches should always be flown with power on to allow for gusts, lift and sink, and turbulence, such as that encountered when landing over rivers, ledges, ridges, and trees. Approaches made without power require pitch changes or slips to control both airspeed and descent angle, and those are not conducive to precision (Terry, 2000). For example, when you are too high on a power-off approach and the nose is lowered, your airspeed will increase, which could cause an overshoot or long landing. Conversely, if you get too low on a power-off approach, you may not have enough power to climb and might not make it to the runway. Power-off approaches can be hazardous and are not recommended for normal operations.

Power-on approaches allow for better aircraft control and mitigate the risk of the airplane getting "behind the power curve," a situation that develops when drag exceeds power required and the airplane begins to "mush" and sink; the slower you fly, the more power you will need to maintain altitude. When flying a power-on approach, "If you are fast and low, a pitch correction can get you back on the glideslope at good airspeed; conversely, if you are high and slow, you can pitch down some for airspeed and pull power and flaps to get lower" (Williams, 1986). Ultimately, you want to learn how to set your airplane up for a stabilized approach so that required changes to pitch and power are minimal; then you can anticipate where you might encounter downdrafts or wind shear on the approach and make smooth and prompt adjustments to pitch and power as needed. Terry (2000) stated, "If the air is rough, you'll still be prompt but you won't be so smooth due to the size of upsetting gusts or shears and the required size of your corrections."

The first step toward perfecting your backcountry power-on approach is to determine an appropriate airspeed. Most pilot's operating handbooks (POH) for GA aircraft recommend approach speeds only at gross weight, although some may list speeds at different weight and CG positions. For normal approaches, if no speed is listed, the FAA recommends using 1.3 V_{S0}, where V_{S0} is the **calibrated power-off stall speed** of the airplane in the landing configuration and usually with a forward **center of gravity (CG)**. For sufficiently long runways, a normal approach speed at 1.3 V_{S0} is a good place to start. However, for constricted approaches into short, rough airstrips, it is common to use 1.2 V_{S0}.

If your POH does not list speeds at different weights, you can estimate them using the following rule of thumb from the FAA (2008b):

FAA Rule of Thumb:
To estimate approach speed as a function of reduced weight: reduce the calibrated *approach airspeed for the maximum weight of your aircraft by **one-half of the percentage of the weight decrease**.*

Example: Your airplane has an approach speed of 70 knots calibrated airspeed (CAS) at full gross weight (GW).

> Subtract 20% weight (e.g., airplane now at 80% GW)
> New approach speed = 70 knots − 7 knots (10% of 70 knots)
>   = 63 knots CAS

When determining what speed to use based on V_{S0}, make sure you know what the **calibrated airspeed (CAS)** for V_{S0} is, since it could vary significantly from **indicated airspeed (IAS)** on the instrument itself. Most POHs give values for converting IAS to CAS in various configurations (Figure 5-3) and you can interpolate the values.

FLAPS UP													
KIAS	50	60	70	80	90	100	110	120	130	140	150	160	- - -
KCAS	57	64	72	80	90	99	109	118	128	138	147	157	- - -

FLAPS 20°													
KIAS	40	50	60	70	80	90	95	- - -	- - -	- - -	- - -	- - -	- - -
KCAS	51	57	64	72	80	90	95	- - -	- - -	- - -	- - -	- - -	- - -

FLAPS 40°													
KIAS	40	50	60	70	80	90	95	- - -	- - -	- - -	- - -	- - -	- - -
KCAS	50	56	64	72	81	90	95	- - -	- - -	- - -	- - -	- - -	- - -

Figure 5-3. Airspeed calibrations at different flap settings for a Cessna 182P at gross weight. Note that at slow speeds, such as approaching the stall, IAS can be highly inaccurate.

If there is wind or turbulence, you will need to fly at a faster approach speed. The general recommendation is to add one-half the gust factor to the approach speed. Effects of wind on your landing approach are discussed later in this chapter. For highly technical approaches to very short fields, usually by pilots flying STOL aircraft, an approach speed of 1.1 V_{S0} might be used.

Airspeeds listed in the POH will not be accurate for airplanes that have been altered with STOL components, engine and/or propeller upgrades, or other modifications. Also, for some airplanes, the POH does not list speeds for various loading configurations. An exercise you can do is load your airplane at different weight and CG locations, then perform some stalls at different power, flap, and gear (if applicable) settings. Record the IAS stall speed for the different weights and configurations (Table 5-1) and notice how the flight controls feel and respond.

Table 5-1. Power-off stall speeds recorded at different flap settings and weights for a Cessna 182P and Piper PA-18 Super Cub.* *All speeds were recorded with CG at mid-range.*

Example only—not intended for actual use.

Cessna 182P (IAS)				Piper PA-18 (IAS)			
Flap Setting	Gross Weight (lbs)			Flap Setting	Gross Weight (lbs)		
	2,950	2,500	2,000		1,750	1,525	1,350
0° Flap	57 kts	54 kts	52 kts	0° Flap	45 mph	43 mph	36 mph
20° Flap	53 kts	53 kts	50 kts	10° Flap	43 mph	40 mph	35 mph
40° Flap	51 kts	49 kts	48 kts	25° Flap	41 mph	37 mph	33 mph
				50° Flap	39 mph	35 mph	31 mph

* These are empirical numbers for specific airplanes and are not to be considered generally representative.

After determining the stall speed at different weight and CG locations, you can find the target approach speed for calm wind by determining V_{S0} for each weight and multiplying by the desired factor (for example 1.2 V_{S0}). Remember to convert IAS to CAS before calculating the correct speed, and then you will need to convert back to IAS.

Example: To determine the correct IAS to use for an approach speed of 1.2 V_{S0} for the Cessna 182P at 2,950 pounds GW, use the recorded numbers from the flight tests (Table 5-1) and convert to CAS using the chart from the POH (Figure 5-3):

$$
\begin{aligned}
\text{IAS for } V_{S0} \text{ at 40 degrees flaps} &= 51 \text{ knots (Table 5-1)} \\
&= 57 \text{ knots CAS (Figure 5-3).} \\
1.2 \times 57 \text{ knots CAS} &= 68 \text{ knots CAS} \\
\text{Then, convert back to IAS} &= 65 \text{ knots IAS (Figure 5-3)}
\end{aligned}
$$

Before you get too bogged down with numbers, realize a primary reason to do this exercise is to "play" with your airplane. The more you learn how it feels, sounds, and behaves at **minimum controllable airspeed (MCA)** and during incipient and full stalls, the better equipped you will be to recognize and avoid hazardous situations that could lead to stalls and spins when maneuvering and flying approaches to short backcountry airstrips. Some airplanes exhibit markedly different approach to stall and stall recovery characteristics at a full-forward or full-aft CG, so make sure to practice over the entire range of possible CG positions. This exercise will also provide you with speeds to determine the V_{S0} for the different loads and configurations.

Once you have established your target airspeed for calm wind conditions, you can adjust it accordingly for gusting conditions or wind shear. However, as discussed later in this chapter, if there is a lot of wind, consider not landing until conditions improve. The next step is to choose a descent angle, or approach path, you want to use for the conditions and the airstrip, as described next.

Descent Angle

Terry (2000) suggested pilots might choose an approach angle as low as 1.5 degrees for bush flying operations, while Imeson (2005) advocated for an approach angle of 4.5 degrees. A normal 3-degree approach path should work unless there are large trees, terrain, or other obstructions, and it is familiar to pilots since most airport visual approach indicators are set to 3 degrees. However, the majority of approaches to backcountry airstrips entail maneuvering around and over terrain, trees, and other obstructions in the approach path. For that reason, a steeper-angle approach is usually best since it allows for better visibility and obstacle clearance (Figure 5-4). Steeper approach path angles also make it easier to detect a change in your projected touchdown point. The following section describes the aim point technique.

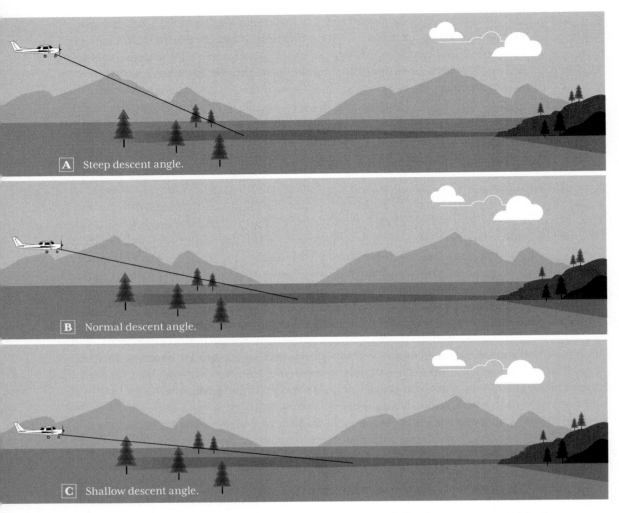

Figure 5-4. A comparison of various descent angles for an approach (angles are exaggerated for the purpose of illustration). Note the steeper descent profile (**A**) provides better visibility and clearance over obstacles.

A steeper approach requires less power than a shallow one when flown at the same airspeed, since the forward component of aircraft weight acts in the direction of thrust and opposes drag; this is a distinct advantage at high DA when there is less power available (Figure 5-5). The more excess power you have available, the better equipped you will be to compensate for downdrafts or wind shear on the approach. Generally, you will use a normal to steep approach, but there will be exceptions based on surrounding terrain, sun angle, or other unique characteristics of a particular airstrip. With experience, you can learn to judge those factors and choose the best approach angle for the given conditions; by using the aim spot technique discussed later in this chapter, you will ensure a landing on the correct spot regardless of your approach angle.

The opposite of a steep approach is a flat approach at minimum airspeed and high angle of attack, which may require maximum power just to sustain level flight (Figure 5-6). The airplane is then flying in the "region of reversed command," also known as the back side of the power curve, as described by Figure 5-5.

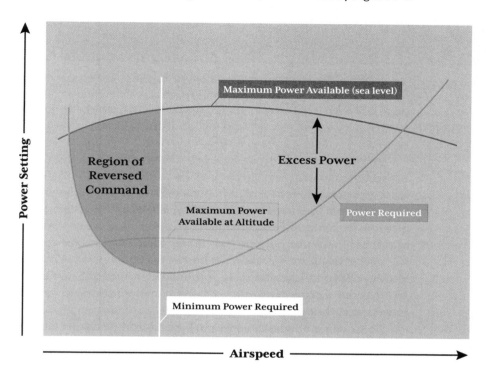

Figure 5-5. Power versus speed relationship for an airplane. The power curve is directly related to drag: parasite drag increases as a function of speed, and induced drag is inversely proportional to speed. When an airplane is flown at speeds lower than the minimum drag speed, large amounts of power are required to fly slower because the wing is at a high angle of attack. That is known as the region of reversed command or flying "behind the power curve." It takes more power to fly slower at constant altitude, and at high DA the maximum available power may be less than the power required to sustain minimum controllable airspeed in level flight.

Figure 5-6. The "drag-and-drop" approach is not advocated for normal mountain and canyon operations, as it reduces forward visibility and places the airplane in the region of reverse command. If there is insufficient power to compensate for wind shear or downdrafts, this could result in collision with obstacles or landing short of the airstrip.

The flat "drag-and-drop" approach is not recommended at high DA for backcountry approaches. This type of approach makes visibility over obstacles difficult and requires a lot of power due to the high amount of induced drag. There may not be enough power available at high DA to sustain flight at minimum airspeeds, and the aircraft also may not have any reserve power to compensate for wind shear or downdrafts during the approach. The airplane could drop below the level of terrain or trees and not be able to climb back up. With the flat drag-and-drop approach, power must be immediately reduced after clearing obstacles, which could require a large pitch change to maintain airspeed and can result in a hard landing or bounce.

Paul Claus is an Alaskan operator who has competed and won the Valdez Alaska short field takeoff and landing competition several times. During an interview, he noted that although an extremely short landing can be accomplished with the flat, slow airspeed, high angle of attack approach, he does not consider the **short takeoff and landing (STOL)** competitions to be real bush flying (Claus, 2018). Claus prefers what he calls a "flight path" approach (at an angle) since it affords good visibility and is safer in turbulence with a better go-around option. He has seen short takeoff and landing (STOL) competitions won using the flat approach, yet he has won many himself using his "flight path" approach. Claus stated at the STOL competitions it ultimately comes down to personal preference. Terry (2000) also pointed out, "Drag-and-drop is used in spot landing contests, and such contests do have merit. However, not too many of those contests are held in gusty crosswinds...with only the wild, hungry carnivores watching with interest."

Descent Rate

The **descent rate** needed for any given approach angle is based on the **ground speed (GS)**. Instrument pilots are familiar with the practice of setting pitch and power to achieve a desired descent rate and maintain a fixed vertical path over the ground, such as a glide slope. Once you have decided what airspeed you want to use (for example, 1.2 V_{S0} at your weight), simply note your ground speed and set the power for the appropriate descent rate at the desired angle of descent (Table 5-2).

Table 5-2. Rate of descent in feet per minute (fpm) for specific descent angles at different ground speeds. (*Adapted from FAA, 2008a*)

Angle of descent (degrees)	Ground Speed (knots)			
	45	60	75	90
2.5	200	265	330	395
3.0	239	318	398	478
3.5	271	370	465	555
4.0	315	425	530	635
4.5	355	475	595	715
5.0	395	530	660	795

This is where a GPS is useful, since you can read ground speed directly from the instrument. Without a GPS, you will need to estimate ground speed based on **true airspeed (TAS)** and wind. You should always fly the same IAS for your weight and CG configuration, regardless of the DA. However, TAS increases 2% per 1,000-foot increase in DA. Therefore, ground speed increases by the same amount, which will increase the descent rate needed for a given approach angle. This is demonstrated using the Cessna 182P from the previous example and extrapolating the values from Table 5-2 as shown below:

Amy's
Axiom

Always fly your approach at the same IAS for a given weight, regardless of DA.

Approach at sea level with no wind		Approach at 7,000 ft DA with no wind	
CAS = 1.2 V_{S0}	= 64 knots	CAS = 1.2 V_{S0}	= 64 knots
TAS	= 64 knots	TAS = 64 knots × 1.14	= 73 knots
Ground speed	= 64 knots	Ground speed	= 73 knots
Approach angle	= 4°	Approach angle	= 4°
Rate of descent	≈ 450 fpm	Rate of descent	≈ 520 fpm

In most light airplanes, every one-inch reduction of manifold pressure (MP) increases the rate of descent at a constant airspeed by approximately 100 fpm. For example, in a descent at 90 knots and 300 fpm, simply reduce the MP by 2 inches to descend at 500 fpm while maintaining airspeed. For airplanes with fixed-pitch propellers, a reduction of 100 RPM on the tachometer increases the rate of descent at a constant airspeed by approximately 100 fpm.

You can also use the following rules of thumb to quickly estimate your desired power setting to fly at a specific descent angle.

> To maintain a **3-degree approach angle**, *multiply ground speed in knots by 5 to find the required descent rate in fpm:* **GS (kts) × 5 = descent rate (fpm)**
>
> To maintain a **4.5-degree approach angle**, *multiply ground speed in knots by 8 to find the required descent rate in fpm:* **GS (kts) × 8 = descent rate (fpm)**

For example, at a ground speed of 70 knots, a 3-degree approach angle requires 70 × 5 = 350 fpm descent rate, and a 4.5-degree approach angle requires 70 × 8 = 560 fpm descent rate.

The reason to do these exercises before heading into the mountains is to determine airspeeds, power settings, descent angles, and descent rates and help you become intimately familiar with your airplane's performance. At first when practicing, you will need to reference the power instruments, airspeed indicator, and vertical speed indicator to fine-tune your approach and give you visual and kinesthetic references for your target speeds and power settings. Once you know those targets, you will practice until they become automatic and are part of your muscle memory and visual perspective. By knowing how the airplane should look, sound, and feel before you venture into a canyon to land at a backcountry airstrip, you will be able to quickly set up the desired pitch and power without having to fumble with the controls or focus too much attention on the instruments. That in turn will increase your ability to assess other inputs and maintain a higher level of situational awareness when flying approaches to land at backcountry airstrips.

Aim Point Technique

The final step to mastering the stabilized approach is perfecting the aim point technique. The aim point is the spot on the ground toward which you will descend at a constant angle for landing; it is the point where your visual approach path intersects the ground. As the FAA recommends, "Select an appropriate touchdown point on the runway surface and adjust the glide path so that the true aiming point and the desired touchdown point basically coincide" (FAA, 2008a). Where you place the aim point (discussed later in this chapter) depends on factors such as the airstrip length, shape, and slope; obstacles; and your approach path. For the purpose of practicing, you should be able to fly a stabilized approach and land on your pre-selected spot every time.

landing surface. Compare what you see with the information you gathered during your preflight planning. Use the same pre-landing checklists and procedures to which you are accustomed. Also, consider using a simple memory aid to help recall items so you can focus on looking outside the airplane. The pre-landing checklist GUMPS is effective:

Gas—select proper tank, fuel selector and/or pump set
Undercarriage—down and locked, or check condition visually for fixed gear
Mixture—leaned for DA*
Propeller—set and **P**assengers briefed
Seatbelts—secured and **S**witches set

* For a normally aspirated engine, the mixture will not be set at full rich at higher DA. Set the mixture for the appropriate DA to achieve maximum power for changes during the approach or during an abort or go-around.

Some additional things you want to consider include:

· Terrain and obstacles
· Approach path and touchdown point
· Takeoff and departure path
· Escape routes
· Wind
· Surface condition
· Animal or human activity
· Slope
· Length, width, and shape of airstrip
· Temperature, DA, and performance
· Abort plan and alternate landing spots
· Go-around options and hazards

It may seem intimidating at first to attempt to assess all these features, but with time and practice you will gain the ability to observe and judge what to expect. Flying with someone familiar with the airstrip can be invaluable to help with your observation and planning.

Terrain and Obstacles

You will most likely be flying much closer to rocks, trees, and canyon walls than you are accustomed. When landing at airstrips in canyons, the shape of the surrounding terrain may dictate how you fly the approach. Determine at what point you will begin your descent and whether you will have to fly over the top of a ridge or rock outcropping or maneuver around it. A logical traffic pattern often contours the terrain and may not be a standard rectangular shape.

Bare rocks that have been heated by the sun are sites of potential updrafts, and downdrafts or sinking air could be in areas of shadow (Chapter 2). The line between sun and shadow can be an area of potential wind shear, so look for where you can anticipate updrafts or downdrafts when crossing shadow lines on the approach (Figure 5-10).

Figure 5-10. Looking down an airstrip toward the approach end. A left-hand turn downwind to land toward the photographer will be in shadow from the canyon wall. On the turn to base, the airplane will cross the shadow line into sunlit, bare terrain and the pilot should anticipate wind shear at the shadow line and updrafts over the bare terrain. *(Photo by Amy Hoover)*

Observe where your traffic pattern and approach might encounter orographic updrafts, downdrafts, or wind shear and plan accordingly. You may want to modify the landing pattern to stay out of downdrafts and areas of potential wind shear. Expect downdrafts and sinking air over rivers or lakes, and even with light wind expect updrafts or downdrafts over abrupt ledges at confluences.

Look for obstacles in the approach and landing path, such as trees and brush. Bushes and brush can grow rapidly and block the approach path, so check out an airstrip again if you have not been there for a while. Dead trees and burned snags are a particular hazard because they are hard to see, especially when looking toward the sun.

Carefully observe the position of sun and shade in a canyon, especially when the sun is at a low angle during early morning or late evening. At those times, rock walls will cast a shadow across a canyon, making it easier to see obstacles and terrain features. However, when flying out of the shadow or turning into the sun, you can be blinded (Figure 5-11).

Figure 5-11. Since the airstrip is in the bottom of a canyon, the airstrip is in shadow, but the pilot could be blinded when turning into the sun. Avoid that risk by circling and assessing the shadow line before making your approach. *(Photo by Amy Hoover)*

In a narrow canyon, the shadow line can move rapidly. You might be in shadow with good visibility when you circle to assess the airstrip, but you could be in sunlight during the approach. Although it sounds mundane, flying toward the sun when close to terrain is hazardous, as you might not be able to see obstacles and terrain. One technique you can practice is circling while looking down or to the side to avoid looking directly into the sun. When doing that, you will need to maintain sufficient clearance from the canyon walls, and you should not attempt it unless you have surveyed the terrain from above or know the area well. Another option might be to wait, or leave the area, and return when the sun is at a higher angle. A difference of only five to ten minutes can be significant in steep-walled canyons. This is also a time when it is critical to ensure your windscreen is not crazed to avoid being completely blinded, and a time when windshield visors are valuable. It is also a good reason to wear a hat or cap with a bill to shade your eyes.

Approach Path and Touchdown Point

While maneuvering for landing, keep the airport within sight and within gliding distance, if possible. You may be able to fly a normal traffic pattern, but non-standard approaches are common and often consist of a 180-degree turn to final from downwind. You could lose sight of the strip momentarily until you are on final, so you want to identify landmarks to help you maintain situational awareness. Plan for a final of at least 1/2 mile and you will probably have time to stabilize the approach. Sometimes you will fly a different approach into the same airstrip depending on the time of day, sun angle, and wind. Fly with someone who has local knowledge of the airstrip and who can familiarize you with the best patterns to use at each location. Long, straight-in approaches are not recommended because it is easy to get too low or become disoriented if flying down in a canyon. Additionally, you may not be able to see the runway or hear other traffic until the last minute, which could cause a collision hazard with departing aircraft.

After determining the location where you want to start your descent, simply set the airplane up as you practiced, and you will be able to easily and quickly stabilize the approach. Your selected aim point will not necessarily be at the approach end of the airstrip. It may be farther down the strip to clear obstacles or avoid landing on soft or rough ground. It should be at the approach end for very short airstrips, and for extremely steep ones it might be farther along the strip, as discussed later in this chapter. Look for tire tracks in the dirt or grass that indicate where other airplanes have been touching down, which could be the best indication for where to place your aim point.

On a curved airstrip or one with a dogleg, either land short and slow down as much as possible before the dogleg, or if the airstrip is long enough, land past it. Landing in a turn is an advanced maneuver that should not be attempted without practice. In his book *Guide to Bush Flying*, F.E. Potts (1993) provides a detailed description of preferred techniques to use when landing in turns.

Each airstrip is unique, and your aim point can change from one approach to the next, depending on the conditions. Regardless, you should choose an aim point that ensures you have enough distance to land and stop; otherwise, do not land.

In very narrow canyons with lots of turns, you may have to fly a "blind approach" to an airstrip. Overfly the entire area to ensure you know where the airstrip is and which way the canyon turns, as well as to carefully select a position from which you can safety abort the approach.

Alternate Landing Spots

Identify potential emergency landing sites around the entire area before you begin your approach, and also plan your departure route. Once you land, you may not be able to see the departure path from the ground, especially if it entails flying around a corner or up or down a canyon. Therefore, before you land, it is prudent to determine your takeoff path and any alternate landing spots should you encounter downdrafts, turbulence, or have an engine failure after takeoff.

as necessary, and climb back to altitude safety (Figure 5-12). Once you fly past that point, you are committed to land.

Positively identify the point in your mind, visualize it, and state its location verbally when flying the approach. A good practice is to mentally note, or say out loud, something like "no go-around from here" or "I am committed to land." Doing that will help you avoid indecision and the risk of acting too late.

You also need to identify what your flight path would be after aborting an approach, as it may follow a canyon or necessitate maneuvering around terrain or obstacles, and you need to know which way to turn. The best way to accomplish that is to overfly the area at a higher altitude and identify the main route as well as side canyons so you do not turn the wrong way into a blind or box canyon that your airplane cannot out climb.

According to Hoover:

> In a go-around you are not just starting a climb, you are transitioning from a descent, or a bounce, to a climb, which could take a considerable amount of time and distance. A heavily loaded airplane has a lot of inertia, and an attempted go-around in the landing configuration could take an amazingly long time to achieve a positive rate of climb. It would be better to ground loop, run off the end of the airstrip, or run into obstacles on the ground than to attempt a go-around too late and hit obstacles, trees, or terrain while airborne, or to enter a departure stall, both of which can be deadly. Many fatal stall-spin accidents occurred when pilots tried to clear obstacles in an ill-attempted go-around. (Hoover, 2000)

Go-arounds from a botched landing pose additional problems. A typical bounce results from excessive airspeed, which usually results from a fast approach. If you are too fast on final approach, ask yourself, "Would I take off in the landing configuration from mid-field?" because that is what you will be attempting to do during a go-around from a float or bounce.

There have been many fatal accidents in remote mountain and canyon areas because pilots attempted go-arounds from a bounce or bad landing. For some airplanes set to the landing configuration, with full flaps and trim, application of power causes an enormous nose-up pitching moment, which the trim setting exacerbates. The pilot may have to push forward hard on the yoke or stick to avoid a stall. In a heavily loaded airplane with an aft CG, the force may be too great for a pilot to overcome. At lower altitudes the engine will be producing maximum power, which can make it even harder. Additionally, an immediate and strong application of right rudder might be necessary to avoid loss of directional control due to asymmetrical thrust (P-factor) at a high angle of attack.

An example is an accident that occurred with a Cessna 185 at a private airstrip at sea level near the Oregon Coast; the airplane crashed during an attempted go-around and the pilot was killed in a post-crash fire (NTSB, 1999). The NTSB noted the flaps were found fully extended. The report states:

According to witnesses, the pilot appeared to be high and fast on his approach to the airstrip. One witness said the pilot 'S'-turned and side-slipped on final approach. The airplane touched down from 1/2 to 3/4 of the way down the 1,950-foot grass runway, shortly after which power was applied (with what was described as the sound of full power) and the airplane climbed out at a steep angle. When the airplane was near the end of the runway, at an altitude that witnesses estimated as from 30 to 75 feet above ground level, with full flaps extended, the right wing dropped and the airplane descended at a steep angle into a ravine at the end of the runway, about 100 feet below the runway elevation. (NTSB, 1999)

The key to a successful go-around is to decide early, make a positive decision, and implement it without hesitation before a critical situation develops. Plan ahead and practice the actual sequence of the maneuver. For example, a typical scenario would be to simultaneously add power, right rudder, and push forward on the yoke or stick; retract flaps incrementally to takeoff setting after the descent is arrested; trim to relieve control pressures; and then retract landing gear after a positive rate of climb is achieved.

It is essential to practice the go-around transition sequence at different weights and CG positions so you will know what to expect. Take the airplane to a safe altitude that is close enough to the airport elevation you will be using so that you will have similar power and P-factor effects (FAA regulations specify 1,500 feet AGL for recovery from maneuvers). Set the plane up for a normal approach descent with gear and flaps down and trimmed for landing. Ensure the mixture is leaned properly for the DA (see Chapter 8 for more on this technique). Then, add full takeoff power and note several items, including: (1) how much forward force you must apply to the yoke or stick to avoid a departure stall; (2) altitude loss from the time of power application until you arrest the descent and initiate a climb; and (3) the time and distance required to transition from the descent to level flight, and then a climb. Do the transition to best rate and best angle of climb speeds and note the pitch attitude and the different control pressures required. Then do some transitions "hands off" and let the plane enter a departure stall on its own, which may surprise you. You may want to take a capable instructor with you to practice the maneuver.

All too often, a go-around is executed as a "knee-jerk reaction" maneuver, which can have disastrous results. By planning ahead, you can add go-around safety to your flying mindset. Consider any go-around to be an emergency procedure; plan for it, practice it, and use it wisely. Many backcountry airstrips are one-way, and go-arounds are not an option. In those cases, you must take the idea of going around out of your thought process and out of your vocabulary. Think instead about how you will plan the approach and at what point (location and altitude) you will firmly state that you are committed to the landing with *no option to go-around.*

The Airstrip

In addition to evaluating the surrounding environment while circling, determine as much as you can about the airstrip before landing. As described by Potts (1993), "Sometimes the job will require a pilot to land in fairly unsavory areas, where the strip is a mélange of hard gravel, gullies, rocks, and sand pits." Although not all remote airstrips are as unsavory as Potts describes, surface hazards are a primary concern. Resources discussed earlier can be useful as can information from other pilots who have recently visited the airstrip.

Landing Surface

Use tracks made by other airplanes since they probably indicate the best surface. On dirt or gravel airstrips, look for areas that have a different color or texture, as they could indicate moisture under the surface, ditches, or sandy or rocky areas. Sloped airstrips may have rubber water diverters to direct runoff and prevent erosion. While they may look intimidating from the air, the diverters are made from rubber skirting and do not damage airplane tires (Figure 5-13).

Figure 5-13. A dirt/gravel airstrip equipped with water diversion strips made from rubber skirting. The airplane will roll over the flexible diverters during landing or takeoff. *(Photo by Amy Hoover)*

Early one June morning I was giving flight instruction to a pilot in his Cessna Turbo 206. We flew into an approximately 1,700-foot-long private airstrip in the Salmon River canyon where he had just bought a cabin. The airstrip was partially shaded, and we did several take-offs and landings until he felt comfortable with the approaches and departures though the narrow canyon. After our last takeoff, I suggested we visit a 1,500-foot-long, public-use airstrip a little more than a mile upstream. Although he did not plan to use that airstrip regularly, we agreed it was a good idea for him to fly the approach and departure should he ever want to land there during an emergency. It is a one-way airstrip with a blind approach that requires maneuvering in the canyon on short final and immediately after departure. We looked the airstrip over and noted it was still in shade, which was good with respect to the sun angle for departure. Since we had just landed at the nearby private airstrip, we knew the temperature and DA would be the same.

The pilot asked if I would do the first landing while he watched, so I took the controls and made the approach. I touched down on the main wheels at the appropriate spot and added brakes to slow down. Instead, we sped up! We

Try to determine how tall the grass is. Airstrips in wilderness areas are not maintained. Grass can grow tall in spring and early summer and will create drag for both landing and takeoff. You might be able to land successfully but not have enough airstrip to depart again. Rodent holes, rocks, or other hazards are hard to see under the grass. Some strips that are maintained may have sprinklers—either above-ground pipes or underground "pop-up" sprinklers. Locate their position so you can avoid them.

Most unimproved backcountry airstrips have uneven surfaces, and water will collect in low spots. It is difficult to tell water depth in pools or ditches when viewed from the air, so try to avoid standing water or water running across an airstrip. It is also hard to tell how wet the grass is, but when the strip is in shade, especially in the morning, there is a good possibility it will be wet. Although you might be able to land and get stopped, consider how wet grass might affect your takeoff and departure.

The ground can remain wet long after snow has melted, depending on how soft the ground is and how much sun the airstrip gets. Some strips in narrow canyons get only a few hours of sun during the day. Airplanes have become stuck in spring mud and left for days or even weeks at mountain strips until the conditions dried out. Sand can absorb a lot of moisture, although it may not look wet, and it can be soft. One reason to avoid landing on wet airstrips is to minimize damage to the surface (Figure 5-14). Do not land if you are unsure of the conditions.

immediately realized the wheels were hydroplaning on the wet grass, which had been in the shade all morning with temperatures a few degrees above freezing. Later inspection revealed the grass was about two inches long, with lots of clover and a consistency much like lettuce that has been left in the refrigerator about a week too long. When the plane started sliding, I kept the weight on the main wheels and worked the brakes, alternating left and right much like a car's anti-lock brake system so that they would not lock up. Thanks to the approximately 3% slope for the last 300 feet of airstrip, we were able to come to a stop with room to turn around in the narrow space at the end. Stupidly, I gave the controls to the pilot and said "OK, now it is your turn," and we took off and made another landing, with him at the controls. He conducted the landing pretty much the same way, and we slid up the hill at the end and turned around in the same place.

The lesson learned that day was although the surface conditions were fine at the first airstrip, only a mile away, it did not guarantee the same conditions at the second airstrip. The grass was longer, wetter, and a different consistency.

Figure 5-14. Ruts formed by four-wheel recreational vehicles that operated on the strip when it was wet in the spring. Any use, including airplane operations, can cause such damage. *(Photos by Amy Hoover)*

Animal and Human Activity

There could be wild game, birds, domestic stock animals, or people on the airstrip. Survey the area around the strip for evidence of animal activity. Deer, elk, moose, sheep, caribou, antelope, and other herd animals often leave easily discernable game trails in the forest, sagebrush, or tundra. Bears, wolves, coyotes, and other animals also use the same trails. A trail that crosses the airstrip is a signal that animals could be nearby. They can be obscured by brush or trees and when spooked might run onto the strip. Horses, mules, and cattle might also use the airstrip to graze. Because many mountain and canyon airstrips are one-way, with no go-around option, animals can be a particular hazard just before or during touchdown. Therefore, accept that it is better to hit an animal rather than attempt a go-around from low altitude or after landing.

Birds of prey are common around areas where they might be hunting for rodents or small animals, and waterfowl are found near lakes and rivers. While maneuvering to check out the airstrip, be wary of large flocks of birds on the water, as they could take off en masse. A bird strike can be a serious hazard, and you might consider returning later when the birds have moved on.

Many backcountry airstrips have camping either adjacent to or on the airstrip itself (camping under the wing) and there could be pedestrians. Airstrips near ranches, towns, or recreational areas could have motorized vehicles such as four-wheelers or tractors. People on motor vehicles may not be able to hear an airplane over the noise of their vehicle. Do not assume that they will see or hear you if you make an approach or that they will move out of the way of a landing aircraft. Do not land until you have ensured the area is clear of all human activity.

Shape and Width

Sometimes airstrips are not straight. Obstacles, terrain, or other factors determine their shape. When checking out a curved strip, consider where to touch down and how to fly the approach. Once on the ground there may be no line of sight between the ends of the strip due to the curvature (Figure 5-15). You can place your aim point and land at a position that will minimize side loads on the airplane landing gear. The slower the airplane is moving while turning, the less stress will be imposed on the gear.

Many rough fields are narrow; some consist only of two ruts the width of a typical light airplane's landing gear. A narrow airstrip can appear to be longer than it is; carefully consider visual cues surrounding the field as well as your selection for the landing aim point. Also, determine how much room there is to the trees, brush, rocks and other obstacles off to the sides of a narrow airstrip.

Airstrips that are wide compared to their length present the opposite illusion; they appear to be shorter than they are (Figure 5-16)

Figure 5-15. A curved airstrip in the mountains. The two ends are misaligned by approximately 30 degrees (Runways 14 and 35), so there is no line of sight between the ends. *(Photo Courtesy Galen L. Hanselman, QEI Publishing)*

Figure 5-16. A wide airstrip surrounded by tall trees. The airstrip is 2,640 feet long and 100 feet wide. Wide airstrips may look shorter than they actually are. *(Photo by Amy Hoover)*

Figure 5-17. The airplane is on short final to an airstrip that is a relatively wide landing zone between tall trees. However, the right side is extremely rough and not suitable for landing. The center is rough, but usable, and the best place to land is where the tracks from other airplanes are seen slightly to the left of center. *(Photo by Amy Hoover)*

Wide airstrips sometimes have markers delineating the landing zone or indicating which side to use. Observe where other airplanes have been taking off and landing and follow suit (Figure 5-17).

Because each airstrip and its surroundings are unique, the best insurance for a safe approach and landing is not to rush. Circle the airstrip as many times as needed, and ensure you observe as many of the criteria discussed here as possible. Then, have a plan for the approach and landing before committing. Even when landing at an airstrip you have been to many times before, it is not advised to land without first checking it out, since every time will be different; animals, surface conditions, wind, and other factors constantly change.

The effects of wind and gradient on approaches and landings is discussed in the next sections.

Landing with Wind

An important aspect of your pre-landing assessment is to evaluate the wind at the airstrip as well as the surrounding area. More than one windsock positioned at various locations along or around an airstrip indicates the wind can be irregular. For example, if one end of the airstrip is near a terrain feature such as the convergence of two drainages, wind direction and speed could be very different only a few hundred feet away or at the other end of the airstrip. Trees surrounding an airstrip may block the wind at the surface and the windsock(s). Look for other wind indicators, such as nearby bodies of water (large rivers or lakes) or movement in the treetops to alert you of wind direction and intensity. Trees swaying near the airstrip with no wind indication on the sock means you could encounter wind shear during the approach.

Expect turbulence or rotors at treetop level when landing, regardless of the direction from which the wind is blowing. Trees can block surface wind and the shear could destabilize your approach. As you descend below the level of trees, a headwind could shear to zero wind. When that happens, your indicated airspeed will decrease by an amount equivalent to the wind shear, lift will be lost, and the airplane can pitch down or descend rapidly. The opposite will occur for tailwind landings made over trees: the shear will cause the airspeed and pitch attitude to increase, which could result in a long landing. To compensate, anticipate wind shear when descending below the level of trees and add power to keep the airspeed from degrading too fast. Even without trees and obstacles, wind can become more turbulent and shear closer to the ground due to friction of the earth's surface (Lester, 2013).

In addition to assessing how the wind will influence your approach and landing, you need to determine how it might affect your takeoff and departure (see Chapter 6). Study the surrounding terrain and visualize where you might expect updrafts, downdrafts, venturi effects, or convergence effects under various wind conditions. Wind changes constantly, so it is important to visualize its effects for various wind directions, including your future takeoff. You may decide not to land, even with a favorable wind as it could prohibit your ability to take off and depart safely.

Headwinds

Landing with a headwind is good because it allows the airplane to touch down at a slower ground speed, which reduces the landing ground roll. Most airplane POHs give the amount of reduced ground roll with a headwind as a percentage of the total. You can use the following rule of thumb (Porter, 1986) to estimate the effect of a headwind on landing distance, all other variables being equal (slope, surface conditions, DA, pilot technique).

> **Porter's Rule of Thumb:**
> *A headwind equaling 1% of the landing airspeed will cause about a 2% decrease in landing distance.*

For example, given:
Landing airspeed = 70 knots
Headwind = 7 knots
Landing distance = 7 ÷ 70 = 10%
10% × 2 = 20% decrease in landing distance

Such rules of thumb can be used to estimate effects of wind up to a point, but as wind speed increases, the relationships become more complicated. Other variables such as wind shear, updrafts, downdrafts, and turbulence can destabilize your approach and counteract the positive contribution of a strong headwind. Careful study of the windsocks, surrounding trees, and other wind indicators will help you make the right decision when checking out the airstrip. However, the wind can change from the time you make your assessment until you are on final approach, so constantly check it during the approach.

Figure 5-18. (A) The airstrip atop a mesa has a drop off into the canyon below at both ends. *(Photo courtesy of Galen Hanselman, QEI Publishing.)* **(B)** Landing into a wind, expect downdrafts off the approach end of the airstrip. *(Photo by Amy Hoover)*

Anticipate downdrafts on final approach into a headwind when landing over a drop-off, such as atop a mesa (Figure 5-18).

When landing over water, such as a lake or river, there may be an area of sink caused by the cooler water (Figure 5-19).

Figure 5-19. A one-way airstrip in a mountain area. The elevation is 5,646 feet MSL and the strip is 2,870 feet × 50 feet. Go-arounds are not possible on final approach due to rising terrain at high altitudes, and the approach must be made over the lake. While planning the approach and landing, it is necessary to determine whether you will be able to take off and depart over the lake, as terrain rises past the end of the lake after departure. *(Photo by Amy Hoover)*

Lakes or rivers can exacerbate the downdraft caused by a headwind blowing over a drop-off and create sink (Figure 5-20). There might not be enough power to compensate for the downdraft and the airplane could land short. Full power might be required, resulting in an overshoot, as happened to the pilot in Figure 2-8C (see Chapter 2).

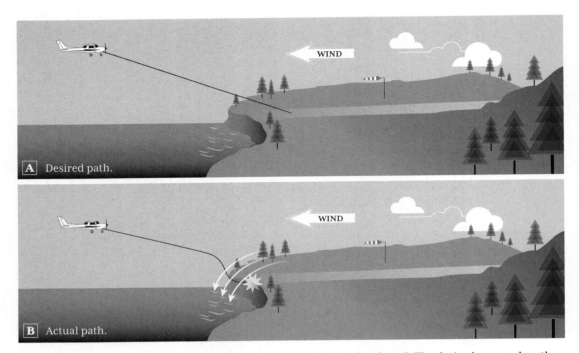

Figure 5-20. Effects of wind on the landing approach made into a headwind. The desired approach path (**A**) will be modified by downdrafts over a bench, ledge, or edge of a mesa, which can be magnified by a river or lake off the end of the airstrip. As the airplane flies an approach into the wind, it can encounter sinking air over the river and a downdraft over the drop-off. The downdrafts can cause the airplane to land short (**B**).

An approach flown into the wind at the same rate of descent as in calm wind will be at a steeper angle due to the lower ground speed, as demonstrated by Table 5-2. Conversely, if you want to fly at the same angle as a no-wind approach, you will need to carry more power to fly at a lower descent rate.

Tailwinds

It is best not to land with a tailwind. Most GA airplane landing performance charts indicate an increase of around 10% for each 2 knots tailwind (up to 10 knots). Thus, it takes only a slight tailwind to greatly increase the landing distance. The fact that most airplane manufacturers do not list effects of tailwinds above 10 knots should be an indication not to attempt a tailwind landing in strong winds.

However, many airstrips in backcountry mountain and canyon terrain are "one way" for landing, with no go-around. You will have to decide whether to land with a tailwind or not land at all. At airstrips above a bench or drop off, you can expect an updraft over the edge, which could cause the airplane to float down the strip and land long (Figure 5-21).

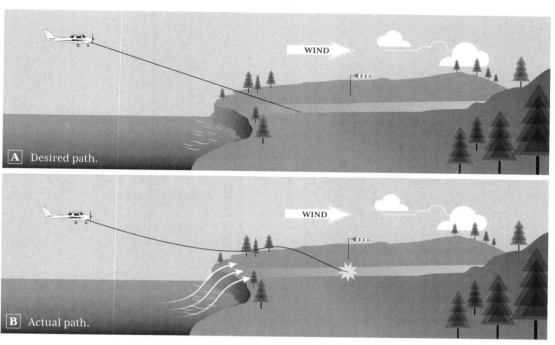

Figure 5-21. Effects of a tailwind on the landing approach. The desired approach path (**A**) will be affected by updrafts over a bench, ledge, or edge of a mesa, which can cause the airplane to "balloon" and land long (**B**).

Landing with tailwinds should not be attempted unless you have experience doing so and are familiar with the hazards associated with them. To practice tailwind landings, find an experienced instructor and start out with only very light winds to observe the significant effect on your landing distance and approach path. Approaches flown at a normal descent rate will be shallower due to the higher ground speed. A specific approach angle will require a higher descent rate (and less power) at the faster ground speed (see Table 5-2).

As previously noted, approaches should always be flown at the same IAS for the aircraft's weight and wind conditions regardless of DA. Since TAS increases 2% per 1,000-foot increase in DA, ground speed increases by the same amount. For pilots unaccustomed to that increase, adding a tailwind to the already higher ground speed can be visually disorienting; the pilot will think they are flying too fast and may erroneously reduce their airspeed, which could result in a stall on short final.

Figure 5-22. A backcountry airstrip with a 6.35% gradient (as measured by Hanselman, 2015). The gradient may not be obvious from the air due to the surrounding terrain or the angle at which the strip is viewed. This is a one-way airstrip with no go-around. The elevation varies between 4,205 feet and 4,313 feet, and it is 1,700 feet long. *(Photo by Amy Hoover)*

Crosswinds

Mountain and canyon winds can be highly unpredictable. Gusting crosswinds at an airstrip that also has obstacles, turbulence, downdrafts, or wind shear, and no go-around option, can destabilize the approach to the extent that the best option is not to land unless it is an emergency.

Sloped Airstrips

This section is adapted from *Uphill, downhill; airstrips with a gradient* (Hoover, 2002).

Airstrips located atop mesas, in hill country, in canyons, or along rivers may have a gradient varying from small to significant. It may not be possible to accurately judge gradient when checking out an airstrip from the air, and for some airstrips it can be visually deceiving (Figure 5-22).

Gather as much information as you can from airport directories and other publications and apps, or ask local pilots familiar with the airstrip to determine the gradient before you attempt to land and depart. Hanselman (2015) conducted ground surveys of several hundred runways around the western United States and produced a runway elevation profile (REP) for each one (Figure 5-23), which can be helpful when planning your approach and landing into a backcountry airstrip with a gradient.

Atlanta
Runway Elevation Profile (REP)

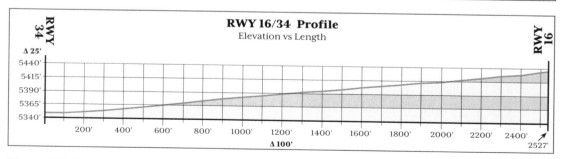

| ARP: **55H** | RWY 16 Elev: **5438'** | Length: **2527'** | Elevation Gain: **90'** | Survey Date: **06/30/10** |
| ARP Elev: **5438'** | RWY 34 Elev: **5348'** | Width: **60'** | RWY 34 Uphill: **3.56%** | Surveyors: **glh, sjh** |

Figure 5-23. (A) A runway with a 3.56% gradient and **(B)** the surveyed runway elevation profile (REP). The gradient in percent is the difference in the elevation between ends divided by the total length. This is a one-way airstrip with no go-around due to the high elevation and rising terrain beyond the airstrip. *(Photo and figure courtesy of Galen Hanselman, QEI Publishing)*

Gradient is usually indicated in percent slope, which is the difference in elevation between the ends divided by the total length of the runway. Surveyors call it the "rise over the run," which is simply the vertical elevation change compared to the horizontal distance.

Gradient in percent slope should not be confused with slope angle in degrees. Slope angle is the amount of deviation from horizontal expressed in degrees. Percent slope is the tangent of the angle; thus a 45-degree angle equals a 100 percent slope (Figure 5-24).

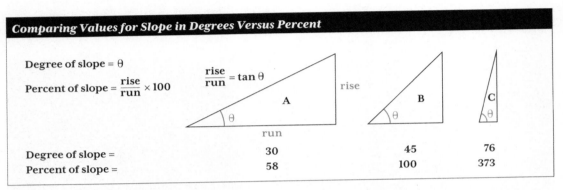

Comparing Values for Slope in Degrees Versus Percent

Degree of slope = θ

Percent of slope = $\dfrac{\text{rise}}{\text{run}} \times 100$

$\dfrac{\text{rise}}{\text{run}} = \tan \theta$

	A	B	C
Degree of slope =	30	45	76
Percent of slope =	58	100	373

Figure 5-24 The relationship of slope in percent gradient compared to degree angle of slope. To convert percent slope to degrees, use the tangent to the angle, and vice versa.

On the ground, you can determine the gradient by finding the altitude at each end of the airstrip and dividing it by the total length. For an irregular slope, you will only be able to determine the average gradient. The easiest way to determine altitude is with a GPS device or an altitude app on your smartphone that uses GPS to calculate position (including altitude). Since the apps use GPS, and not Wi-Fi or cellular service, they should work anywhere satellites are visible to the device. Another method is to use the airplane's altimeter; taxi to one end of the airstrip and record the altitude, and then taxi to the other end to obtain the altitude there and divide the elevation change by the total length. However, if you landed halfway up a very steep airstrip and needed full power to get to the top end, it might not be wise to taxi downhill for this exercise, as you might not have enough power available to make it back up the hill. You can pace off the airstrip to obtain a fairly accurate measurement of its length.

Some POHs include factors for gradient in their performance charts, but some do not. Various rules of thumb are cited in the literature regarding how gradient affects landing (and takeoff) performance, but the relationships are complex and, for more than a slight gradient, are not linear. As with all rules of thumb, the relationships are meant to help pilots estimate the effect of different variables and should be used with caution. Porter (1986) presented the following rule of thumb:

> **Rule of Thumb:**
> *Each 1% of runway slope will cause about a 3% change in landing distance.*

Rather than relate the slope to landing distance for the airplane, a different rule of thumb can be used to estimate effective (or theoretical) runway length (Hoover, 2002).

> **Rule of Thumb:**
> *When computing runway gradient, every 1% grade is about equal to a 10% change in effective runway length.*

Using the rule of thumb, you would add 10% to the theoretical length for every 1 percent upslope. For example, a landing on a 2,000-foot-long runway with a 3% uphill gradient would be similar to landing on a flat runway with length 2,000 + (2,000 × 0.3) = 2,600 feet. If the gradient were downhill, it would be roughly similar to landing on a 2,000 − 600 = 1,400-foot-long runway. However, other factors, such as the runway surface and braking action, will also influence stopping distance. Additionally, for an uphill landing, a component of weight acts rearward as drag; however, in a downhill landing a component of weight acts forward as thrust.

Because there are so many uncontrolled variables that influence the outcome, rules of thumb represent estimates only and are meant to alert pilots to possible hazards. Backcountry airstrips rarely have a consistent slope and their surfaces can be irregular, which compound the issues with respect to gradient and stopping distance. An airstrip might have a hump in the middle (Figure 5-25B), so landing will be uphill for the first part and downhill after the hump, and the strip may appear to be shorter than it actually is because one end is not visible from the other. Some airstrips are U-shaped in profile view, with a dip in the middle (Figure 5-25A), so landing is downhill initially and then transitions to uphill. Landing on the downhill portion will cause the plane to float; then power will have to be added to taxi uphill to the end. Finally, some airstrips are irregular with some sections steeper than others (Figure 5-25C).

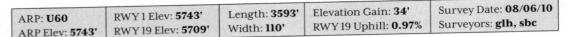

A

Big Creek
Runway Elevation Profile (REP)

ARP: **U60**	RWY 1 Elev: **5743'**	Length: **3593'**	Elevation Gain: **34'**	Survey Date: **08/06/10**
ARP Elev: **5743'**	RWY 19 Elev: **5709'**	Width: **110'**	RWY 19 Uphill: **0.97%**	Surveyors: **glh, sbc**

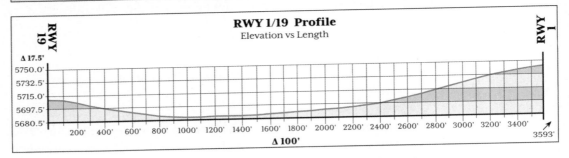

B

Reed Ranch
Runway Elevation Profile (REP)

ARP: **I92**	RWY 16 Elev: **4143'**	Length: **2185'**	Elevation Gain: **2'**	Survey Date: **08/05/10**
ARP Elev: **4157'**	RWY 34 Elev: **4145'**	Width: **100'**	RWY 16 Uphill: **0.09%**	Surveyors: **glh, sbc**

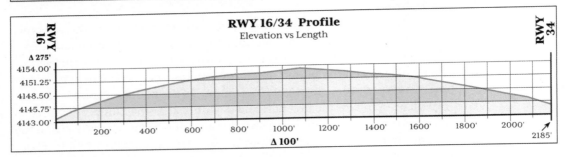

Figure 5-25 (above and right). Runway elevation profiles (REP) for three different runways. Profiles may show **(A)** a dip in the middle, **(B)** a hump, or **(C)** be irregular along their length. *(Courtesy Galen Hanselman, QEI Publishing)*

Grand Gulch Mine
Runway Elevation Profile (REP)

ARP: **667** ARP Elev: **4527'**	RWY 2 Elev: **4510'** RWY 20 Elev: **4527'**	T Length: **2146'** U Length: **same**	T Gain: **+17' -0' = +17'** U Gain: **same**	T Avg Slope: **0.79%** U Avg Slope: **same**

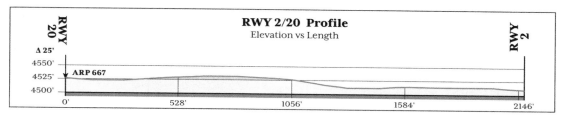

ARP: **667** ARP Elev: **4527'**	RWY 16 Elev: **4515'** RWY 34 Elev: **4537'**	T Length: **3157'** U Length: **same**	T Gain: **+39' -17' = +22'** U Gain: **same**	T Avg Slope: **0.70%** U Avg Slope: **same**

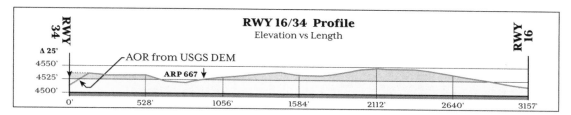

Landing Uphill

Wind permitting, it is generally best to land uphill and take off downhill. With practice, approach and landing to uphill airports can be accomplished safely, and most pilots find the ground roll delightfully short. However, as strips get steeper, shorter, and higher, planning for approach, landing, takeoff, and departure becomes more critical. Specific techniques for taking off on sloped strips are discussed in Chapter 6. However, you want to consider the effects of gradient on both landing and takeoff performance during your preflight planning and when circling to check out the airstrip for approach and landing. You will need to decide whether a takeoff would be prudent with a given aircraft weight, wind, and density altitude before landing.

Unless the airstrip is extremely steep (see R.K.'s recipe for success above), it is generally best to fly a normal approach and use the aim spot technique described earlier to avoid being fooled by visual illusions. Landing on an upsloping airstrip can create the illusion that the aircraft is higher than it actually is, causing the pilot to fly an approach that is too low and creating a danger of landing short or colliding with trees on the approach path (Figure 5-26).

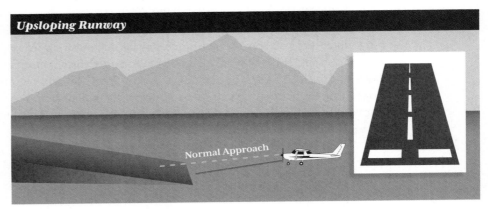

Figure 5-26. An approach to an upsloping airstrip. The visual illusion can cause pilots to fly too low of an approach to an uphill airstrip.

to amend your power and approach speed. As you develop a feel for your aircraft while you practice this, you will find some approximate numbers to guide you.

Generally, these airstrips are short, and I recommend full flaps. I also recommend that your aim point be about one-third of the way up the airstrip and that you consider approaching at a flatter angle than normal, perhaps as low as 1.5 degrees (this will help decrease the necessary angle difference). Give yourself enough room and the previously determined airspeed and power to fly *up* the slope rather than *at* the slope (which would require an exaggerated flare) and use your peripheral vision to match the aircraft pitch to the slope of the hill. This technique tends to minimize the hazard of a hard landing into the hill, and looking out the side to match the airplane to the slope will aid in a proper flare. If you see yourself approaching too flat, increase the pitch, and power as required to slow the rate of descent in the flare.

If you are landing too fast or over flare, you might bounce. A bad bounce might require some power to recover, but since you are landing on a steep slope you can stop in a very short distance compared to when landing on a level, short airstrip.

Landing uphill on a gradient of more than 10% requires special techniques and practice. Get training from an experienced instructor before attempting this.

One method you can try is to set your airplane up at a safe altitude, preferably the same DA of the airstrip where you intend to land, at normal approach speed and configuration. Then, pitch up to approximately the angle that matches the slope of the airstrip on which you intend to land and observe how quickly the airplane slows and at what airspeed it stabilizes (See R.K.'s recipe for successful steep-sloped landings above).

Landing gear configuration will influence the actual pitch-up angle when using the techniques described by R.K.'s recipe. For example, when landing on a strip with a 15% slope (8.5-degree angle) in a nose wheel airplane, you can pitch up to approximately 8.5 degrees, which would simulate a touchdown on all three wheels. A slightly larger pitch up (maybe 10 degrees) would provide for a slight flare. However, the pitch up will need to be greater in a tailwheel airplane. For example, an airplane that sits on the ground in a 3-point attitude at 10 degrees would require a pitch up to 18.5 degrees for a full stall landing. You might not be able to pitch up enough before the airplane stalls, which should be a warning it will not work: the pitch up might cause an abrupt stall, or the plane can sink into the hillside. In fact, after practicing this technique several times, you will get a feel for the way your airplane is going to react and may be convinced it is smoother and more accurate to fly the airplane up the slope rather than abruptly pitch up to match the incline.

Figure 5-27. The airstrip slope was estimated at approximately 22%, which equals an angle of about 11 degrees. On level ground, the airplane sits at approximately 12 degrees, so it would need to pitch up to about 23 degrees to match the slope on landing. *(Photos by Amy Hoover)*

At high DA, it could take almost all available power to fly up the slope at the high angle, which takes practice and a keen eye. The visual illusion that you are too high will be much more pronounced when approaching steeper slopes, so it is particularly important to use the aim spot technique at the approach angle you

choose and use peripheral vision as you transition into the landing and match the airplane's angle to the slope. Figure 5-27 shows a tailwheel airplane landing at an airstrip in a canyon that has an estimated 22% slope. The strip is approximately 700 feet long.

Landing Downhill

Landing downhill is not a common practice on more than a very slight gradient. You may choose to land down a slight incline to compensate for wind or sun angle. If that is also the takeoff direction, there is usually a possibility for a go-around. The airplane may float for a long distance when landing downhill, and it may be hard to touch down as the ground continually drops away from the airplane. Once on the ground, you must count on brakes to stop, which could be a problem on wet or slick surfaces. Heavier airplanes have more inertia and will be harder to stop. Turbulence and wind shear could make landing downhill extremely risky in high winds.

Approaches made to a down-sloping runway will cause the opposite visual illusions to landing uphill: the pilot will perceive the airplane to be too low and will fly a high approach (Figure 5-28). Davisson posited:

> The problems are further complicated if the runway's end is sloping either up or down to the threshold. If it's sloping down so that you're, in effect, flying down the face of a hill, then you'll probably feel that you're low. If it slopes up to the threshold, you'll feel high. Thus, if you're flying down a hill to a down sloping runway, you'll need to fight the illusions and land it short. Truth is, the illusions are a problem only if you're one of those pilots who aims at the runway rather than at a distinct spot on the runway. If you pick a spot—whether it's the numbers, a clump of grass or the threshold—and ignore the runway itself, then none of these illusions will be an issue. (Davisson, 2010)

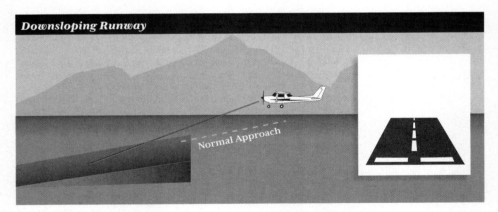
Downsloping Runway

Normal Approach

Figure 5-28. An approach to a down-sloping runway. The visual illusion can cause pilots to fly too high an approach to a downhill runway.

Wind versus Slope

Ideally, pilots would always be able to land uphill and take off downhill. But what about the times when gradient and wind are in opposition? Is it better to land uphill with a tailwind, or downhill with a headwind? Or should you even land at all? As described by Davisson (2010): "trying to understand the energy trade-offs involved in an uphill/downhill landing versus an into/out of the wind landing is critical—and frustratingly complex." For long, paved runways with shallow gradients and the option to go around, the decision of which way to land with wind versus slope may be relatively straightforward. However, as gradients become steeper, typically more than 5%, and winds are more than 8–10 knots, a whole new set of problems will arise.

Landing Uphill with a Tailwind

This should be done with caution. A tailwind that blows over an airstrip ending in a drop-off (Figure 5-21) can cause the airplane to balloon or float. For an airstrip with a slope larger than a few degrees, the updraft could push the airplane into the hill prematurely. You will need to compensate for increased ground speed in a tailwind landing by either shallowing the approach angle or increasing the rate of descent (Table 5-2), which can exacerbate visual illusions. On a one-way airstrip, such as in a canyon or on a hillside with rising terrain beyond the departure end, an attempted go-around could be fatal; even if the airplane is able to fly up the slope initially, the climb profile will be flatter due to the higher ground speed from the tailwind, and the airplane would likely impact terrain or obstacles beyond the end of the airstrip.

Landing Downhill with a Headwind

Compare performance charts from a typical GA airplane's POH, or the rules of thumb with respect to wind and gradient. It takes a strong headwind to overcome the increased landing roll that a downhill landing creates. Wind strong enough to cancel the effects of a large downhill slope will probably create turbulence on the approach, particularly around obstacles or trees. Flying the approach at a faster airspeed to compensate for gusts and turbulence will also increase the landing distance. The only advantage to trying this situation would be a landing in the same direction as the takeoff direction on the particular airstrip, which more than likely means you would have a go-around option until late in the approach.

Use caution when mixing wind and slope. Airstrips with gradients often have surrounding obstacles and terrain that can exacerbate the effects of downdrafts, wind shear, and turbulence on approach. Ultimately, for more than a slight gradient or wind, the best option is probably to wait until the wind dies before attempting a landing, particularly if you have not yet mastered landing on sloped runways without wind.

Touchdown and Rollout

Flying a stabilized approach at the proper pitch attitude and airspeed should minimize the need to make large changes to pitch and power during the final flare and touchdown. For tricycle-gear airplanes, the wheels should touch down at the one-G stalling speed at your landing weight; however, the actual touchdown speed will probably be slightly above the stall.

Pilots of tailwheel aircraft should be proficient in at least the maneuvers required by 14 CFR §61.31, which include (1) normal and crosswind takeoffs and landings; (2) wheel landings (unless the manufacturer has recommended against such landings); and (3) go-around procedures. You might vary the landing technique (three-point or main wheel landing) depending on the conditions, such as wind, slope, surface conditions, or other factors. Regardless of the type of landing you choose, you must have practiced before attempting to use it on a short, unimproved backcountry airstrip. Ultimately it will come down to personal preference. However, it is best to land on very steep inclines or truly soft fields in the three-point attitude with power on and be prepared to add more power immediately.

Forward thrust should be at a minimum for the shortest landing roll, unless you are landing uphill and need power to keep the airplane moving (see R.K.'s recipe for successful steep-sloped landing). On level surfaces when conditions permit, reduce power to idle at the moment of touchdown. A windmilling propeller with the engine at idle power gives a large negative thrust value during the first part of the landing (before approximately 25% reduction in airspeed) and aerodynamic braking is greatest, after which it becomes negligible (Porter, 1986). As the airplane slows, wheel braking becomes the dominant decelerating force during the last part of the landing roll. Thus, the heaviest braking should be immediately after touchdown, and braking force should be reduced as the ground speed decreases. Brakes should be applied smoothly and evenly to avoid locking them up. Heavy braking at slow speeds has been known to cause tailwheel aircraft to nose over.

Large flaps, like on Cessnas, can help slow the airplane during initial roll out. Alternatively, raising the flaps soon after touching down places the weight on the wheels, and increases braking effectiveness. However, doing so during the landing roll on short, narrow strips can be distracting as you reach for the flap handle or switch, and you could run off the side of the airstrip. So, practice this technique ahead of time or consider waiting until you have slowed or stopped to adjust flaps.

A go-around from a bounce or long landing may not be possible, and you may have to commit to running off the side or end of an airstrip. If the airplane is still in the air, a last-ditch maneuver is to raise the flaps to dump the lift and get on the ground, then apply brakes as soon as the wheels touch down. An intentional ground loop may be a better option than running over a cliff or into the river off the end of the airstrip.

Taxi and Ground Operations

Unimproved airstrips can have uneven slopes and hidden surface hazards such as holes, rocks, wet or marshy areas, or other obstacles (Figure 5-29).

Figure 5-29. Rocks and ruts on the surface of a backcountry airstrip. Taxi slowly over rough areas to avoid damage to landing gear, propeller, and tail surfaces. *(Photo by Amy Hoover)*

Rodents and other small animals may dig large holes that are not visible from the air (Figure 5-30). Once you have landed, slow the airplane to taxi speed to avoid obstacles and holes. Taxi fast enough to keep the airplane moving over soft or wet ground, but slow enough that you can see and avoid surface hazards. You may need to add a significant amount of power when taxiing up a slope, and it could be hard to see rocks and other hazards over the nose of the airplane. Keep the plane moving until you reach the top of the hill.

Figure 5-30. A large hole made by ground rodents in the middle of a narrow runway. The hole is deep enough to break a nose wheel or tail wheel, or cause a propeller strike, if taxied over. *(Photo by Amy Hoover)*

Most POHs recommend taxiing with the elevator control in the full aft position for tricycle-gear airplanes to keep weight off the nose wheel and maximize propeller ground clearance. Full aft stick in conventional-gear airplanes will keep the weight on the tail wheel to enhance tail wheel steering; however, a small or fragile tail wheel can be damaged, and you may want to keep it light when rolling over rough or uneven surfaces. When turning toward downhill on a slope or turning away from a tailwind, you will need to vary the pressure on the tail wheel as you make the turn, particularly at a more forward CG.

If either the nose wheel or tail wheel bounce, you will not have steering capability any time the wheel loses contact with the ground, which is a primary reason to taxi slowly over rough surfaces. You may need to hold the elevator in the neutral position on some airplanes to avoid damaging elevator counterweights. Unless you have checked out the surface to the sides of the airstrip, stay on the strip during taxi as the surface to the sides could be even rougher and more hazardous.

When parking, the prudent procedure is to shut down, get out, walk around, and look for hazards before taxiing into a tie down or parking area if there is any question about the condition of the surface. Park on a level, dry surface if possible and tie your airplane down. Tie down areas may be rutted deep enough to cause a prop strike, so beware. Oversize tires can help eliminate this risk (see Chapter 1). Use wheel chocks, especially on a sloped surface, and do not rely on the parking brake to hold the airplane. You can use rocks to chock the wheels, but make sure to remove them from the parking area before you depart so they do not present a surface hazard to other airplanes.

Airplanes parked on a hill should face up or down the slope, rather than sideways, to avoid fuel draining onto the ground or into the downhill tank in airplanes with fuel cross-feed. Fuel that runs out of the tank may not be noticeable if it drains onto sand, gravel, or grass. Always visually check the fuel quantity after you have left your airplane unattended. Some airplanes retain enough fuel in the lines to run for several minutes before the fuel is exhausted. Selecting the off position, or single tank on a cross-feed system while parked, requires an extra pre-flight check to ensure the fuel selector is repositioned correctly.

Do a walk-around inspection of the airplane after every shut-down since landing gear, control surfaces, propellers, tires, brakes, and other components can sustain damage at any time. Planes left unattended, even for a short time, attract insects, birds, rodents, or other animals that perch or nest in the engine compartment or climb up the tailwheel spring or stinger, so do a thorough preflight check before departing.

Many backcountry mountain and canyon airstrips have parking tie-down areas adjacent to campgrounds, cabins, barns, corrals, or other structures. Always taxi cautiously around congested areas and be alert for human and animal activity. Persons and animals not familiar may be unaware of the hazards associated with moving aircraft. Be cognizant of where the tail of your airplane is pointed at all times and turn so your propeller blast is directed away from other airplanes, camping areas, people, animals, and structures. These practices are not only courteous flying, they are vital to maintain safe operations at all times.

Accident Scenario

The saying "hindsight is 20/20" is the reason to analyze accidents and incidents to help pilots understand a set of circumstances and hopefully avoid duplicating them. Analysis of an accident in the Oregon Coast range exhibits how several concepts discussed in this chapter not only caused but could have prevented the accident (Figure 5-31).

National Transportation Safety Board
Aviation Accident Final Report

Location:	FLYING M RANCH, OR	**Accident Number:**	SEA98LA184
Date & Time:	09/20/1998, 1350 PDT	**Registration:**	N95318
Aircraft:	Taylorcraft BC12-D	**Aircraft Damage:**	Substantial
Defining Event:		**Injuries:**	2 Minor
Flight Conducted Under:	Part 91: General Aviation - Personal		

Analysis

While landing with a tailwind at the 2,125 foot grass airstrip, the aircraft was hit by a wind gust that pushed it toward the side of the runway. The pilot, who had landed to the west, decided to execute a go-around. While attempting the go-around toward rising terrain and tall trees, the pilot allowed the airspeed to fall below stalling speed (Vs), and the aircraft stall/mushed into the terrain. A note in the Airport/Facility Directory stated, 'Land to West, takeoff to East.'

Probable Cause and Findings

The National Transportation Safety Board determines the probable cause(s) of this accident to be: The pilot's failure to maintain an airspeed above stalling speed (Vs), and the resultant stall/mush of the aircraft into the terrain. Factors include the pilot's improper decision to attempt a go-around into rising terrain, landing with a tailwind, and trees and rising terrain off the end of the runway.

A

Figure 5-31. (A) The NTSB accident analysis and **(B)** the VFR sectional chart of the accident location. The Flying M Ranch is relatively low elevation but is surrounded by higher terrain that rises rapidly to the west toward the Oregon Coast Range mountains.

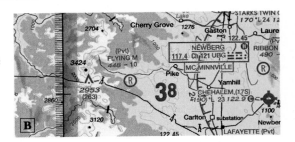

Next, add several items to the checklist specific to each airstrip. Have some operating parameters established for the following:

- Density altitude
- Wind (direction, intensity, gusts)
- Mixture set for best power (lean the mixture for taxi to avoid fouling spark plugs)
- Shape and gradient
- Takeoff abort point
- Departure abort plan and emergency plan

Find a relatively smooth spot with no gravel and debris to do a run-up, and make sure you are not "blasting" other airplanes, people, structures, or campground areas. You may not be able to do a static run-up without damaging the propeller or airplane on gravel, sand, or dirt strips. Engine and control checks can be done during the taxi, but only if safe to do so without hitting obstacles or running off the sides of the airstrip. It is usually best to keep the airplane moving slowly throughout the taxi and turn for takeoff to line up and continue into the takeoff roll. Do not attempt these techniques for the first time on a narrow airstrip unless you have practiced them on smooth, wide surfaces.

Keep the airplane moving from taxi to takeoff roll over soft or rough surfaces and avoid large bursts of power. Power changes should always be made smoothly and precisely. On unimproved airstrips at high DA, the best technique

is a combination short–soft field takeoff. Holding brakes while applying maximum power is not recommended. The propeller wash can blow rocks and debris into the propeller, fuselage, and tail surfaces (Figure 6-1).

Figure 6-1. This damage to the top of the horizontal stabilizer was caused by a rock that was picked up by a 26-inch Goodyear tire and thrown onto the top of the tail surface by the propeller wash when full power had to be applied to move the airplane out of a gravel tie-down area. *(Photo by Amy Hoover)*

You can lean the mixture for the DA before takeoff and do a quick check during the takeoff roll to ensure you are producing appropriate RPM and manifold pressure. If not, abort the takeoff.

Refer to the pilot's operating handbook (POH) for specific short- and soft-field takeoff instructions, as various make and model of aircraft have slightly different characteristics. For a general technique in tricycle-gear aircraft, use enough back pressure at the start of the takeoff roll to lighten the nose wheel as soon as possible. When the airplane is ready to lift off, it will do so if properly trimmed. You should not need to make large pitch changes.

In most taildraggers, let the tail wheel come up and take off tail low; however, the technique may vary with aircraft type and position of the load. Techniques will also vary for airplanes modified with STOL features; for some STOL aircraft the wing may fly before there is enough airflow over the tail surfaces to render them effective. In that case, you will need to raise the tail to lower the wing's angle of attack momentarily until the elevator and rudder become effective.

The key is to find and hold the correct **pitch attitude** that provides maximum acceleration (generally slightly nose high, with the nose wheel or tail wheel barely off the ground). The best way to maintain the proper pitch is to use a visual sight picture. Trim the airplane for takeoff speed at the weight and CG, maintain the visual sight picture, and the airplane will accelerate and fly into ground effect. Precision is critical for the airplane to lift off at the earliest possible position and get the wheels off the ground as soon as possible on rough or soft surfaces. Potts noted that "During the takeoff run, aircraft attitude must be maintained within two degrees of optimum no matter how rough the airstrip" (Potts, 1993).

Regardless of landing gear configuration, at high DA the airplane will need to accelerate to climb speed in ground effect. After the main wheels break ground, decrease the pitch attitude to stay in ground effect and hold it there. The airplane will climb once it accelerates to the correct airspeed, with only minimal control inputs; you should not have to pull or push much on the yoke or stick. The sight picture for correct pitch attitude at high DA will be much flatter (lower angle) than what you are used to at lower DA, which can make obstacles seem more intimidating; a quick check of your airspeed indicator will verify you have the proper pitch attitude for the airspeed you choose. This technique minimizes takeoff roll and maximizes safety by allowing the airplane to fly itself off without the pilot forcing it to rotate before climb speed is obtained.

Pilots who have no experience with high-altitude takeoffs are usually amazed at how long an airplane takes to accelerate. However, at high DA, ground speed will be higher than IAS, giving a false sense of acceleration. A common and dangerous mistake is to over-rotate in an attempt to force the airplane off the airstrip. Over-rotating can result in a climb out of ground effect and a stall, with the airplane dropping back onto the ground. That can greatly increase the takeoff roll. Patience is the primary skill needed to perform a high DA takeoff, especially from a soft or rough field.

Use the flap setting recommended by your airplane's manufacturer for maximum performance takeoffs. For airplanes with POHs that do not list takeoff flap settings, you can experiment to attain the optimum balance between additional lift and drag caused by various flap extensions. The technique is described by Imeson:

> Match the flap deflection to the aileron deflection. This provides the maximum amount of lift versus drag for the airfoil considering the effect of drag. Maximum aileron deflection is a compromise providing the greatest performance for the particular airfoil section. (Imeson, 2005)

Extending flaps after starting the takeoff roll can help unstick the airplane from snow or soft ground by suddenly increasing lift. However, do not attempt it on a narrow or short airstrip without practicing the technique first, since reaching for a manual flap handle or to activate an electric or hydraulic flap switch can be distracting and cause loss of directional control. The abrupt configuration change requires a concurrent change in pitch attitude and a subtle feel for how the lift/drag is affected as configuration and speed change. Unless you are proficient at the technique, it is best to set takeoff flaps prior to the start of the takeoff roll to avoid the distraction. Potts advocated the technique eloquently:

> To put it briefly, the airplane is lifted into ground effect with flaps; then, while still in ground effect, it is allowed to accelerate to its best angle of climb speed, whereupon climb-out is initiated. The trade-off here is decreased ground run for increased pilot skill, and, needless to say, this is a pro's technique that has the potential to get the amateur who does not understand how it works into trouble. (Potts, 1993)

Takeoff Abort Planning

A takeoff abort plan is critical, particularly on unimproved backcountry strips. Refer to the POH to estimate the distance required for takeoff over an obstacle and add a percentage for safety. Determine ahead of time the point by which you need to be airborne and what climb performance you will need to clear obstacles and terrain off the departure end of the airstrip given the wind conditions at time of departure (see the following section for more about the effects of wind). Consider reducing aircraft weight or waiting for cooler temperatures (see Chapter 8) before attempting a takeoff with questionable performance. According to Imeson (2005), for airstrips without much gradient, a general aviation airplane must attain 71% of its liftoff speed halfway down the strip for a successful takeoff. Imeson did not specify whether that rule of thumb included takeoffs requiring obstacle clearance but recommended aborting the takeoff if the airplane does not attain that speed prior to the halfway point. Stopping may not be possible on slippery surfaces, on very short strips, or when taking off downhill with a steep gradient (see next section). In such cases, make a mental note that an abort is not possible and be prepared for emergency options, especially with regard to emergency landing spots along the departure path.

The best way to select a takeoff abort point is to walk the airstrip. Look at the surface and note obstacles, holes, ditches, soft spots, and places to avoid during the takeoff roll. Pace off the airstrip to gauge the midpoint or establish how much distance is needed to stop safely and choose an easily identifiable visual abort point. Make the decision to abort if the airplane is not accelerating in ground effect, with engine instruments indicating full power, by a certain prominent rock, stump, tree, bend in the strip, windsock, etc., that you chose while walking the strip. For most pilots, there is a great temptation to continue the takeoff for just a little longer after they pass the abort point. Since you chose the abort point on the ground, through thoughtful consideration while not under pressure, you need to trust your choice and *use* it. You may find it helpful to verbally call out the abort point as it approaches to make a definitive decision.

For takeoffs on curved airstrips or those with a "dog-leg" or bend, carefully select your abort point. The primary concern is how much speed you will be able to carry around the bend without drifting or skipping sideways. The best technique, provided the airstrip is long enough, is to smoothly apply power so you accelerate to the precise speed and can turn without drifting at the dogleg or curve. Then, once around the curve, continue to apply full power. Start with full aileron deflection toward the turn, similar to a crosswind takeoff (e.g., yoke or stick to the right in a right turn, and vice versa). As airspeed increases, your ailerons will become more effective and provide an aerodynamic assist to the turn. The amount of aileron deflection will need to change as speed increases. Feel for a balance between sideways drift and excessive side loads on the landing gear when determining at what speed you will make the turn. Left turns may be easier, since the airplane at high power is already producing left-turning tendencies (torque and P-factor), but be careful, especially in tailwheel airplanes, not to over-control or allow the airplane to be pulled sideways and off the airstrip.

Surface Conditions

Sand, long grass, and wet or uneven surfaces all lengthen the takeoff roll unpredictably. For example, Imeson (2005) recommended adding anywhere from 20–30% to your estimated takeoff distance for long grass (4 inches or more), 45% for sand, and anywhere from 20–75% for mud or a soft surface. This means you should be extremely conservative taking off from unimproved surfaces and learn to develop what Potts (1993) called a "sixth sense" regarding your airplane's performance and the shifting conditions of the airstrip. He recommended pilots should estimate where they "feel" the airplane will lift off before every takeoff, after considering all factors such as wind direction and speed, slope, condition of the airstrip, DA, condition of the airplane, engine and propeller, obstructions, psychological pressures and fatigue, and flying ability at that precise point in time. Potts wrote:

During each takeoff, carefully monitor the feel of the airplane (seat of the pants; shifting control pressures), and pay close attention to where and how these sensations relate spatially to your estimate of the liftoff point. This is very important, for these shifting relationships are not only the key to precisely determine takeoff requirements under varying conditions, but will also allow you to pinpoint possible problems or miscalculations prior to reaching the point of no return [the abort point]. (Potts, 1993)

According to Potts, you can expect erratic progress at first, but with experience you should be able to develop an accurate sense of where to expect your airplane to lift off under various conditions within 50–75 feet; that kind of precision will take a lot of formal practice.

Departure

Use recommended power, propeller, and flap settings during initial climb. There can be areas of lift, sink, turbulence, or wind shear in canyons or over irregular topography, even without wind (Chapter 2). The ground typically drops away from the airstrip after a takeoff downhill or downstream in a canyon or river valley. When clear of obstacles, it is always better to have extra airspeed to provide a safety margin for unexpected wind shear or downdrafts rather than to climb at a high angle and slower speed to gain additional height above the ground.

To clear obstacles, maintain **best angle of climb (V_X)**, and then accelerate to **best rate of climb (V_Y)** or **cruise climb** as soon as possible. Cruise climb is recommended, as it provides better forward visibility and allows for increased engine cooling. Refer to techniques described in Chapter 2 to use orographic and thermal lift to

Amy's
Axiom

Faster and lower beats higher and slower.

help with climb after takeoff, which typically means you will move either right or left of the centerline to take advantage of lift or avoid downdrafts coming off canyon walls. You can turn away at an angle from the airstrip's centerline if there is space to provide more turning room back to the landing area after an engine failure (at a high enough altitude). However, do not attempt to return to an airstrip for landing unless you know precisely how much altitude your airplane will take to make such a turn, which can only be established with practice. For more information and resources about how to plan for and execute this "impossible turn," visit www.asa2fly.com/reader/mountain.

Pilots unaccustomed to flight at high DA may be alarmed at the enormous reduction in climb rate and make the mistake of pitching the nose up too much, especially just as the airplane leaves ground effect. A nose high attitude is dangerous at high DA. It can abruptly lower the airspeed, increase drag, and cause a departure stall. For a given IAS, pitch attitude decreases with altitude, and the angle for both V_X and V_Y are much lower (flatter) at high DA than at sea level. For example, you might use a 7–8 degree nose-up attitude to maintain your chosen IAS for climb at sea level, but use only 3–4 degrees to hold the same IAS at a higher DA. It is imperative to learn the correct pitch attitude and sight picture for the aircraft's climb speeds at higher DA and vigilantly reference the airspeed indicator. Also, the IAS for V_X increases with altitude, and the IAS for V_Y decreases with altitude, until they converge at the absolute ceiling for the airplane; it cannot fly higher than that altitude (Figure 6-2). For takeoff and climb at DA near the airplane's service ceiling, the pitch attitude will be almost the same for V_X and V_Y. A good general rule of thumb at high DA is that if you can't see the ground over the nose of the airplane, the angle is too high.

Changing aircraft configuration while climbing at low altitude over obstacles can be distracting and potentially dangerous. Concentrate on climbing and maneuvering before decreasing power or retracting flaps, particularly in canyons or confined areas. Know the amount of drag reduction and the retraction time for landing gear for complex airplanes. It may be best not to change propeller, gear, or flap settings until clear of obstacles and established in a positive climb unless making changes results in significant drag reduction. Retracting the gear in some aircraft, such as an older Cessna 210, creates significant drag, which could cause the aircraft to go from a climb to a descent and settle back to the ground or into an obstacle.

A normal traffic pattern departure may not be possible at backcountry and canyon airstrips. Terrain, wind, sun angle, turbulence, and locations of lift or sink may dictate the desired departure path. Plan your takeoff and departure while studying the terrain before landing (see Chapter 5). Planning should include identification of emergency landing spots along the departure route. Your departure route often will follow a river, valley, or canyon during climb-out. Always assess the route in advance and know whether you will be able to make the required climb gradient. Keep in mind that as you climb, your airplane's performance will decrease with altitude, and you might not be able to outclimb steeply rising terrain. Slow to maneuvering speed in turbulence, wind shear, or unstable air (refer to Chapter 4 for enroute climbs). If conditions worsen as you climb out of a canyon, consider returning to land and waiting until conditions improve.

Absolute and Service Ceiling

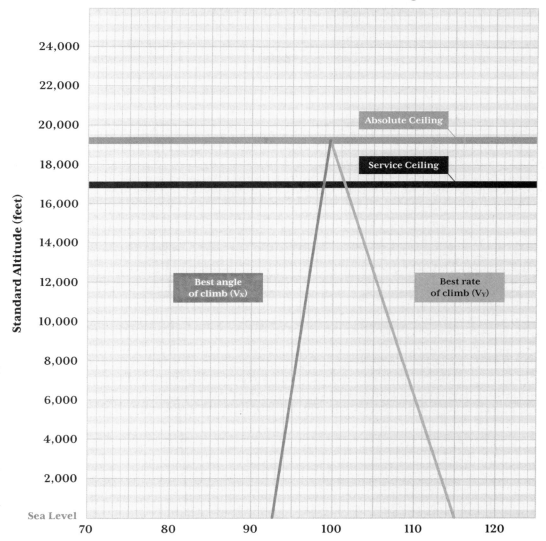

Figure 6-2. Variation in V_X and V_Y with altitude for an airplane. The IAS for the two speeds converge at the absolute ceiling and the airplane will no longer be able to climb. The service ceiling is the altitude at which the airplane can sustain no more than a 100 feet per minute rate of climb. *(From FAA, 2016)*

Dick's Derelict Dixie Departure

By R.K. Williams

View of Dixie Town airstrip looking north toward higher terrain. Departures to the south can follow the creek downstream toward lower terrain but require maneuvering immediately after takeoff. Departures to the north toward rising terrain may be hazardous, especially into the wind, since downdrafts and turbulence can be expected. *(Photo courtesy Galen Hanselman, QEI Publishing)*

I began flying into the Dixie Town airstrip in Central Idaho during the mid-seventies in a stock PA-18 Super Cub. I was told it was a two-way airstrip, depending on the wind. Since I came and went from the northwest, it made sense to land to the south and take off to the north, wind permitting. I never had any issues doing that, and I did not fly there in wind. The airstrip, which is 2,865 feet long, is at an elevation of 5,600 MSL and is situated in a valley surrounded by higher terrain (see photo above).

I never really evaluated the terrain from the air, as discussed in this chapter, and I had not been taught to do so. However, materials available today make it clear this unique airstrip is lower in the middle than on either end; the higher end is toward the south, and the terrain rises dangerously in a bowl to the north of the airstrip, as shown in the runway elevation profile at right (Hanselman, 2015). Even though the airstrip is higher at the departure end, the preferred takeoff direction is to the south because the terrain drops more than 3,500 feet elevation down the creek to its confluence with the Salmon River.

Years later, on a charter flight in a Cessna 206 with three large passengers, I was still ignorant. The locals (non-pilots) recommended I take off to the south, even with that steep uphill slope at the end. There was no wind, and

Dixie Town
Runway Elevation Profile (REP)

| ARP: **none** | RWY 17 Elev: **5608'** | Length: **2865'** | Elevation Gain: **10'** | Survey Date: **08/13/10** |
| ARP Elev: **5600'** | RWY 35 Elev: **5618'** | Width: **80'** | RWY 17 Uphill: **0.35%*** | Surveyors: **glh, bpc** |

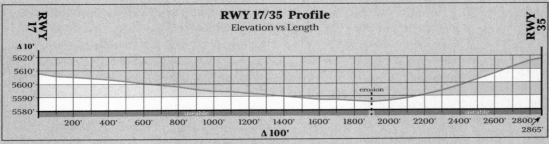

RWY 17

RWY 17/35 Profile
Elevation vs Length

RWY 35

Δ 10'
5620'
5610'
5600'
5590'
5580'

200' 400' 600' 800' 1000' 1200' 1400' 1600' 1800' 2000' 2200' 2400' 2600' 2800'
2865'

erosion

useable   useable

Δ 100'

*Gradient of RWY 17 past 1900' exceeds 5% uphill

I just couldn't make myself do it. Consequently, I took a heavy non-turbo-charged Cessna 206 into a very bad place to the north. With 20 degrees flaps and full power, I massaged the airplane through a shallow left turn against the terrain with the stall horn blaring—a very scary lesson learned the hard way. Just because you might get away with something in a STOL aircraft, don't blindly think that it is the proper way to do it!

Trying to evaluate this airstrip while on the ground was nearly impossible for me, and the only accurate appraisal would have been to take a good hard look from the air before landing.

Runway elevation profile and view to the north of Dixie Town airstrip. The initial takeoff is downhill in both directions for the first part, then changes to an uphill slope, with the south end being much steeper, exceeding 5%. *(Figure and photo courtesy Galen Hanselman, QEI Publishing)*

Taking Off with Wind

By visualizing where you might expect updrafts, downdrafts, venturis, or convergence effects (Chapter 2), you will be able to make a better decision about how much wind is acceptable and from what direction you can safely take off and depart the airstrip. It is usually best to take off with a headwind, but at one-way airstrips you could have a tailwind for takeoff (especially if you just landed with a headwind). You will have to weigh many factors to decide whether a takeoff is safe or not, including the wind and terrain beyond the airstrip, not just at the surface. As described in the following sections, you might have to decide how much wind is acceptable, balance that against the gradient and terrain in the departure path, and then make a decision whether to take off under the existing conditions. Observe the wind for 5–10 minutes to discern whether it is changing direction or intensity. Observe whether there is a pattern or if the gusts and variations are random. To make things more complicated, none of the variables are straightforward, and even the POH or commonly cited "rules of thumb" become imprecise as wind strength and slope increase.

Headwinds

Evaluate the potential effect of obstacles, such as trees in the departure path. Trees surrounding an airstrip can block the wind, so expect rotors below treetop level and wind shear over the trees. Also, trees can block the windsock so that wind above the airstrip might be significantly stronger and from a different direction than on the ground. Visualize how the wind will be blowing around bends in canyons or drop-offs from benches or mesas and where you can expect to encounter downdrafts, turbulence, and wind shear during your departure.

A common—and deadly—mistake made by pilots new to high-DA, confined-area takeoffs is to depart into the wind toward rising terrain; although the airplane may become airborne, orographic downdrafts beyond the departure end of the airstrip can drastically reduce the climb or force the airplane down before there is enough altitude to maneuver (Figure 6-3).

Even without ridges or hills in the immediate departure path, climbing toward rising terrain can be hazardous, especially at high DA. Learn to identify potential orographic downdrafts while studying the chart during your preflight as well as while maneuvering for landing. For example, Figure 6-4 shows an airstrip surrounded by higher terrain on three sides; an airplane departing into the wind toward terrain could encounter downdrafts before having enough altitude to reverse course or maneuver.

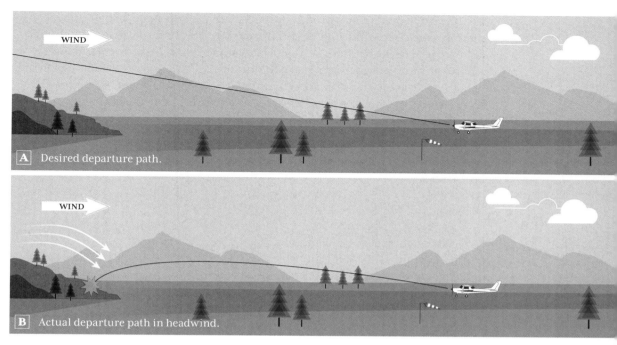

Figure 6-3. (**A**) The desired departure path and (**B**) the actual path resulting from the airplane being forced down by orographic downdrafts off the departure end of the runway.

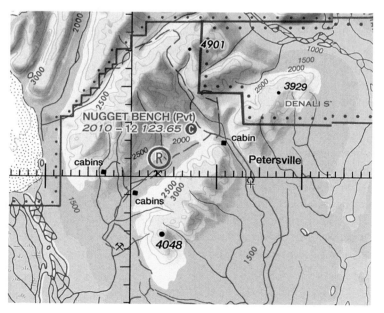

Figure 6-4. The Nugget Bench airstrip is surrounded by higher ridges, except to the southwest down the canyon. Although the airstrip is at a low altitude, an airplane taking off toward the northeast into a headwind would encounter orographic downdrafts and wind shear, and the airplane might not be able to outclimb the ridge or turn before impacting terrain.

Consult your POH or aircraft owner's manual to estimate takeoff performance into wind, and especially consider the effects of surface conditions, as discussed in the previous section. For example, most Cessna performance charts recommend decreasing takeoff distance by 10% for every 9 knots headwind, all other variables (slope, surface conditions, DA, pilot technique) being equal. Porter (1986) presented a general rule of thumb to estimate the effect of a headwind on takeoff performance:

> **Porter's Rule of Thumb:**
> *A headwind equaling 1% of the takeoff airspeed will decrease the takeoff distance about 2%.*

For example, given:
Takeoff airspeed = 60 knots
Headwind   = 12 knots
Takeoff distance = 12 ÷ 60 = 20%
20% × 2   = 40% decrease in takeoff distance

Rules of thumb are to help you think critically while planning and are not meant to substitute for the information in the POH or aircraft owner's manual.

Tailwinds

On a one-way airstrip, you may have to consider whether or not to take off with a tailwind. In general, tailwind takeoffs are not recommended with more than a very light wind, as they greatly increase the takeoff roll. For example, most Cessna POHs recommend adding 10% to the takeoff roll for every 2 knots tailwind (up to 10 knots). That means after landing with a 10-knot headwind, an immediate departure in the same wind would be increased by at least 50%. Most airplane POHs do not list tailwinds more than about 10 knots, which should serve as a warning that it is considered a dangerous maneuver.

In addition to drastically increasing the takeoff distance, tailwind takeoffs also increase the risk of loss of directional control, as gusts and shifting wind can lift the airplane's tail prematurely and even cause it to nose forward and strike the ground with the propeller. If a pilot plans to operate frequently from a one-way airstrip and tailwinds are expected on departure, it is a good idea to practice under known conditions on a longer runway to become familiar with the aircraft's performance. For tailwheel airplanes, keep the tail on the ground through the takeoff until the mains fly off first to avoid a pitch-over caused by the tailwind and to maintain adequate ground control until flying.

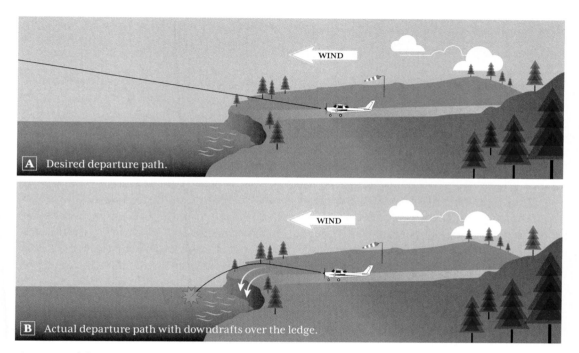

Figure 6-5. (A) The desired departure path and **(B)** the departure through downdrafts created by a tailwind blowing over a bluff or drop-off. Downdrafts can force the airplane into the terrain.

The hazards continue past the takeoff itself, since a tailwind will produce a shallow climb gradient that could force the airplane into terrain or obstacles unexpectedly. Downdrafts caused by a tailwind blowing over a ledge, ridge, or drop-off can force the airplane into the ground, as shown in Figure 6-5. If you do encounter downdrafts after departure, lower the nose and fly out of it as soon as possible. Always maintain airspeed in a downdraft and do not try to outclimb it. A departure will often require following a canyon or valley, and the tailwind may persist during the climb.

Crosswinds

Mountain and canyon winds can be highly unpredictable. Taking off with a crosswind at an airstrip that also has obstacles in the departure path, turbulence, downdrafts, or wind shear might not be a prudent option. Best to wait until the wind quits. Remember, takeoffs are optional, and it may be worth it to wait rather than to depart into a marginal situation, risking your welfare as well as that of your passengers to the whims of shifting winds.

When you fly sophisticated aircraft such as the de Havilland Twin Otter, you might think the books will tell you everything, but they do not. The certification standards do require advanced performance charts, including accelerate-stop distances, engine-out performance, and wind component factors.

The company I worked for really wanted to get in-depth performance data at the airstrip they used for their lodge support, Thomas Creek in the Idaho wilderness. However, we found that sometimes even the best data did not give us what we really wanted.

Thomas Creek is at the bottom of a deep canyon, at 4,400 feet elevation and 2,100 feet long, with a dogleg (see Figures 6-8 and 6-9 later in this chapter). The normal departure is made downstream to the northeast. We experimented with upstream takeoffs to the southwest, but they were limited due to a ridge that produced downdrafts, a sharp turn in the canyon, and a tributary entering the main canyon that often causes mixed air currents. The wind usually blows downriver at the airstrip, which normally dictates a tailwind takeoff.

We wanted to know something that couldn't be gleaned from the performance charts: How much weight could we take off with, with how much tailwind, and at what temperature and then lose one engine and still climb out safely? After departing downstream in the canyon, we had to first make a right turn and then a left turn, making a turn into the dead engine inevitable, and downdrafts were predictable behind the ridges during those turns. For twin-engine operations, turns made toward the inoperable (dead) engine increase drag, increase minimum control airspeed, cause an over-

Sloped Airstrips

See Chapter 5 for a description of how gradients are measured and specifics of sloping and oddly shaped airstrips. For example, backcountry strips might be sloped up or down toward a dip or hump, or even irregular along their length, so the takeoff might change from uphill to downhill, or vice versa, midway through the takeoff roll (Figure 6-6).

For takeoffs on airstrips that are low in the middle (Figure 6-6A) the airplane may become airborne and be able to fly in ground effect. However, at high DA the airplane might not have the climb performance to clear the uphill gradient toward the departure end and could end up landing again. Aborting such a takeoff is easy, since the plane will decelerate more rapidly going uphill. Study the terrain past the departure end, as discussed earlier, to determine if the airplane will have sufficient climb performance once departed the airstrip.

banking tendency, and result in a performance loss as much as 80% in some light twins.

There was nothing to do except some trials. We started at light weights with light winds and gradually worked our way up. We eventually found that our company limits would be a gross weight of 10,500 pounds (certified gross weight was 12,500 pounds), at 70°F with a 5-knot tailwind. Experimenting with zero thrust from either engine, we found that we could make both turns downriver with acceptable performance.

We did exactly what we are advocating in this chapter on performance. Know your airplane and glean everything you can from your airplane charts. However, to really fine-tune your planning, make your own performance tables. A few years after this exercise, our training facility was able to upgrade their simulator to the degree that we could plug in most of these variables, and we were pleased to see we had duplicated the performance very closely!

A quick word on multi-engine operations in mountainous terrain: Remember that loss of one engine will mean an 80% loss of total performance, and turns in canyons will reduce that performance even more. It is also important to know and remember the single-engine service ceiling on your twin-engine aircraft and understand that the service ceiling is a DA. On a warm day in the canyons, many light twins are operating at a DA higher than their single-engine service ceiling, which means you are in effect flying a single-engine airplane that may not be able to hold altitude above the height of surrounding terrain. This is critical in your takeoff planning.

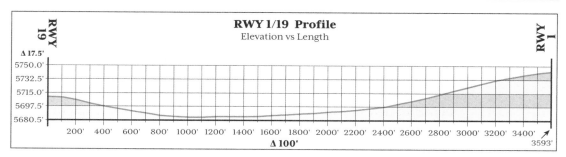

A

Big Creek
Runway Elevation Profile (REP)

| ARP: **U60** | RWY 1 Elev: **5743'** | Length: **3593'** | Elevation Gain: **34'** | Survey Date: **08/06/10** |
| ARP Elev: **5743'** | RWY 19 Elev: **5709'** | Width: **110'** | RWY 19 Uphill: **0.97%** | Surveyors: **glh, sbc** |

Figure 6-6 (above and next page). Elevation profiles for runways with (**A**) a dip in the middle, (**B**) a hump near the midway point, and (**C**) an irregular profile. Taking off from such runways will alter the takeoff roll and the abort plan since the pilot may be unable to see one end of the runway from the other and will need to decide whether the airplane can be stopped on a downhill slope. *(Figures courtesy Galen Hanselman, QEI Publishing)*

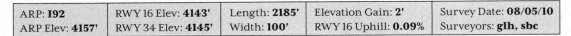

B

Reed Ranch
Runway Elevation Profile (REP)

ARP: **I92**	RWY 16 Elev: **4143'**	Length: **2185'**	Elevation Gain: **2'**	Survey Date: **08/05/10**
ARP Elev: **4157'**	RWY 34 Elev: **4145'**	Width: **100'**	RWY 16 Uphill: **0.09%**	Surveyors: **glh, sbc**

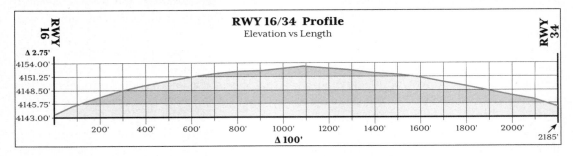

C

Rogersburg, WA
Runway Elevation Profile (REP)

ARP: **D69**	RWY 9 Elev: **872'**	Length: **1473'**	Elevation Gain: **3'**	Survey Date: **09/23/10**
ARP Elev: **869'**	RWY 27 Elev: **869'**	Width: **35'**	RWY 27 Uphill: **0.20%**	Surveyors: **glh**

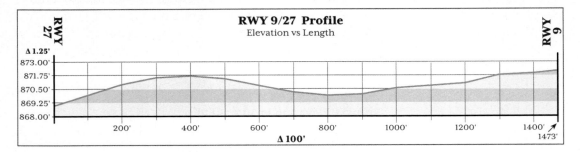

For airstrips with a high point in the middle (Figure 6-6B), the airplane will need to accelerate uphill, and you must choose an abort point that gives sufficient room to stop going downhill. A disadvantage to a humped airstrip is the inability to see from one end to the other, which makes it seem shorter than it is. Choosing a physical abort point is critical for takeoff planning when you cannot see the entire strip. On very steep slopes, it may not be possible to stop.

Departing downhill from airstrips with more than approximately 5–6% gradient can be visually intimidating, particularly in tailwheel airplanes, since you may not be able to see the ground over the nose of the airplane as it drops away from view. On steep gradients of 10% or more, you will probably see nothing but sky ahead of the airplane. When taking off downhill on steep strips, keep the airplane straight. As it accelerates and the ground drops away, pitch down and follow the slope until you gain enough airspeed to fly. The airplane will probably bounce over rough surfaces; keep it straight and hold the pitch attitude until it accelerates to climb speed. Once sufficient speed is attained, you may not need to climb steeply since the terrain will drop away from the airplane (Figure 6-7).

Figure 6-7 (above and next page). A tailwheel airplane departing from a backcountry airstrip with an approximately 22% gradient. The pilot will not be able to see the ground at the start of the takeoff roll and should keep the airplane tracking straight with rudder. As the airplane accelerates, the pilot will need to pitch down to maintain airspeed as the ground falls away down the slope. Once climb speed is attained, the airplane can be trimmed for a climb. *(Photos by Amy Hoover)*

C Fly down the slope to gain airspeed.

D Once sufficient airspeed is attained, pitch for climb.

E Terrain typically drops away from the airplane in a downhill takeoff.

Wind versus Slope

Similar to mixing wind and slope for landings (Chapter 5), the combination presents hazards for takeoff operations. Variables including surface, engine performance, aircraft weight, and the relative effects of wind and gradient are difficult to quantify. This section is adapted from *Uphill, downhill; airstrips with a gradient* (Hoover, 2002).

Use caution when mixing wind and gradient. Airstrips with gradients often have surrounding obstacles and terrain that can amplify downdrafts, wind shear, and turbulence on both the approach and departure. Taking off with more than a light wind may not be a good idea, especially on short strips with obstacles in the departure path.

Taking off Downhill with a Tailwind

The balance between a shortened downhill ground roll and increased takeoff distance from a tailwind is not straightforward for more than a few percent slope or a light wind. For example, using the Cessna POH from the previous section, a 10-knot tailwind may increase the ground roll by 50%. Any advantage from a downhill takeoff must account for the surface, irregular slope, and pilot technique, which make generalizations and estimates difficult. Each airstrip must be evaluated for its unique characteristics, including the surrounding terrain, obstacles, and the need for maneuvering after departure. The airplane may become airborne or fly in ground effect on a downhill airstrip, but if it ends at a river or edge of a mesa (similar to Figure 6-5), expect a downdraft over the drop-off. A river or lake can amplify the downdraft; the only option is to lower the nose and maintain airspeed.

Taking off Uphill with a Headwind

An airplane will generally require a significant headwind to counteract more than a slight uphill slope, since it will not only need to accelerate to flying speed but be able to climb at a higher gradient than the slope of the terrain. At high DA, the airplane might not be able to do that, so choose an abort point just as you would on a level strip. The advantage to attempted uphill takeoffs is they are easier to abort; stopping takes less distance than with no slope. Similar to the situation shown in Figure 6-3, you can anticipate wind shear and turbulence over trees or obstacles after departure.

Terrain beyond the departure end of an uphill airstrip usually rises and may exceed the climb capability of the aircraft, so you must carefully study the departure path ahead of time. Even if the airplane becomes airborne, it could impact terrain during climb out.

Dial a Flight Instructor

By Amy Hoover

One afternoon many years ago, I got a phone call from (the late) John Kounis, editor of *Pilot Getaways Magazine*. After exchanging pleasantries, John asked me what I thought about taking off on a runway with about a 3–4% downhill gradient and an approximately 8–10 knot tailwind versus taking off uphill with the same amount of headwind. Since I had just sent John an article for publication entitled "Uphill, downhill; airstrips with a gradient," I figured he had called to chat about it. So, I asked him what the theoretical runway looked like: How long was it? What kind of surface? Was it in a canyon, or was there a drop-off to a river or from the edge of a mesa at the downhill end? What did the terrain look like past the uphill departure end? Were there trees or obstacles? Was the wind steady or gusting? When John

started giving me some very specific answers, and I noticed the wind noise in the background, I became suspicious. "Where are you?" I asked. He confessed he was standing by his Cessna 185 at a grass strip somewhere in Oklahoma having just finished lunch at a BBQ joint, and he was trying to decide which way to take off on the sloped airstrip with wind blowing.

Uh-oh.

I was *not* going to tell him which way to take off because I was not there, but I started asking more questions to help him with some critical thinking about the situation. As he continued to describe the area, I got a visual picture of a sloped runway that ended at a bluff approximately 200 feet down to a river bed, which ran perpendicular to the runway. The river draw was about 500 feet wide with a

Accident Scenario

The purpose of reviewing and analyzing aviation accidents is to learn from them. Pilots who have first-hand knowledge of an accident, or the area where it occurred, usually remember it and the lessons learned. Here is one scenario that emphasizes the need to plan ahead for the takeoff and departure, including assessment of surrounding terrain, wind, DA, and procedures, and following recommendations and advice of people who have local knowledge.

The following scenario is shared by author R.K. Williams based on his own experience.

It was the spring of 1979 and I had flown into Thomas Creek airstrip deep in the canyon on the Middle Fork of the Salmon River in Idaho (Figure 6-8) to pick up some guests at the Middle Fork Lodge.

As I waited for my passengers, I chatted with the lodge manager, and we began talking airplanes. I expressed a desire to get my hands on one of the new Cessna T206s that had come out in 1977. They had 310 horsepower with a big, three-bladed, square-tipped propeller, and their performance was already legendary. Bud, the manager, said they were only as good as the way they were flown. I asked what he meant, and he told me about this accident that occurred the previous summer.

cliff about the same height on the other side. We discussed how there would be a downdraft off the end of the airstrip that could push his airplane down, and he would need to make a turn either right or left in order to avoid the bluff on the other side of the river. If the tailwind was gusting, it could shear and affect his airspeed, and he would also be making a turn with a tailwind, which would increase the turn radius and possibly carry him across to the other side at low level. The picture looking uphill included a fence and terrain that rose at approximately the same gradient as the strip itself, so we discussed that he would have to be able to take off and continue a climb at that angle just to stay in ground effect and might not be able to make any turns.

We spent the better part of half an hour with me asking lots of questions and John really paying attention to the airstrip, wind, surrounding terrain, and the whole environment to answer them. Then, I wished him luck with his decision, and we hung up.

About a week later, John sent me an email thanking me for the "dial an instructor" session and said after we assessed the situation, he decided to go back to the grill house. He had a wonderful afternoon sipping sweet tea at the restaurant until the wind subsided, after which he had an uneventful takeoff and departure.

Speaking with John that day reminded me it is often knowing what questions to ask that keeps us on our toes and out of trouble.

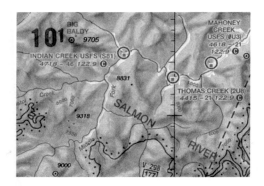

Figure 6-8. VFR sectional chart of Thomas Creek Airport in Central Idaho. The airport is situated deep in the canyon and surrounded by high terrain. The Idaho airport directory recommends landing Runway 21 (upstream on the river) and departing Runway 03 (downstream).

On August 10, 1978, a Cessna T206 departed the Thomas Creek airstrip. The private pilot had three passengers on board and was planning a return flight over the mountains to Boise, Idaho. Conditions were poor. The time was 5:45 p.m. and the temperature at that hottest part of the day was 90°F. The corresponding DA on the ground would have been approximately 7,300 feet.

The pilot and his three passengers had stopped to see the lodge and were preparing to leave in the late afternoon, against Bud's advice. Bud asked him about his airplane, the new model, and the pilot bragged about its tremendous power and capability. He said he would take off upstream into the slight headwind and climb straight out and up and over the west fork of Thomas Creek, above the lodge, instead of turning and climbing up the main river toward Indian Creek (Figure 6-8).

Figure 6-9. Thomas Creek airstrip looking upstream toward the south. A takeoff into the wind in this direction will be towards rapidly rising terrain and downdrafts. *(Photos by Amy Hoover)*

The Idaho airport directory recommends taking off downstream. Upstream takeoffs are never a good idea, especially in a loaded airplane, even with a downstream wind. In this case, the reason is that the ridge to the south (upstream) of the airport creates a strong downdraft off the departure end of the airstrip, and any takeoff will be into that downdraft. Also, the airplane would have to make a hard-right turn of more than 150 degrees to fly behind the ridge and up the main canyon or try to climb straight ahead into rapidly rising terrain and more downdrafts (Figure 6-9). Bud advised the pilot against taking off upstream, telling him no one did that. Although the lodge employees did not see the accident happen, they saw the smoke up the creek soon afterward and notified authorities. The pilot was killed, but somehow the passengers survived.

The NTSB report (Figure 6-10) stated:

- PIC failed to follow approved procedures, directives, etc.
- PIC—improper in-flight decisions or planning.
- Fire after impact.
- PIC didn't follow published departure from canyon strip. Unable to outclimb terrain.

NTSB Identification: SEA78FA054

14 CFR Part 91 General Aviation
Aircraft: CESSNA T206, registration: N756LV

```
------------------------------------------------------------------------------------
 FILE    DATE        LOCATION        AIRCRAFT DATA     INJURIES    FLIGHT                    PILOT DATA
                                                       F  S M/N    PURPOSE
------------------------------------------------------------------------------------
3-2836  78/8/10  NR.CHALLIS,ID      CESSNA T206      CR-  1 0  0   NONCOMMERCIAL           PRIVATE, AGE 50, UNK/NR
        TIME - 1745                 N756LV           PX-  0 1  2   PLEASURE/PERSONAL TRANSP  TOTAL HOURS, UNK/NR IN
                                    DAMAGE-DESTROYED  OT-  0 0  0                            TYPE, NOT INSTRUMENT
                                                                                            RATED.
        NAME OF AIRPORT - THOMAS CREEK
        DEPARTURE POINT           INTENDED DESTINATION        LAST ENROUTE STOP
          BOISE,ID                   RETURN                     CHALLIS,ID
        TYPE OF ACCIDENT                                 PHASE OF OPERATION
           COLLISION WITH GROUND/WATER: CONTROLLED          IN FLIGHT: CLIMB TO CRUISE
        PROBABLE CAUSE(S)
           PILOT IN COMMAND - FAILED TO FOLLOW APPROVED PROCEDURES,DIRECTIVES,ETC.
           PILOT IN COMMAND - IMPROPER IN-FLIGHT DECISIONS OR PLANNING
        FACTOR(S)
           AIRPORTS/AIRWAYS/FACILITIES - AIRPORT FACILITIES: OTHER
           TERRAIN - HIGH OBSTRUCTIONS
           WEATHER - HIGH DENSITY ALTITUDE
        WEATHER BRIEFING - NO RECORD OF BRIEFING RECEIVED
        WEATHER FORECAST - UNKNOWN/NOT REPORTED
        SKY CONDITION                              CEILING AT ACCIDENT SITE
           UNKNOWN/NOT REPORTED                       UNKNOWN/NOT REPORTED
        VISIBILITY AT ACCIDENT SITE                PRECIPITATION AT ACCIDENT SITE
           5 OR OVER(UNLIMITED)                       NONE
        OBSTRUCTIONS TO VISION AT ACCIDENT SITE    TEMPERATURE-F
           NONE                                       90
        TYPE OF WEATHER CONDITIONS                 TYPE OF FLIGHT PLAN
           VFR                                        NONE
         FIRE AFTER IMPACT
        REMARKS- DIDNT FOLLOW PUBLISHED DEPARTURE FROM CANYON STRIP.UN OUTCLIMB RISING TERRAIN.DENSITY ALT 9900FT.

                                Full narrative is not available
```

Figure 6-10. NTSB accident report showing the elevation, temperature, and time of day of the accident. The DA at the crash site, up the Thomas Creek drainage to the south of the airstrip, was 9,900 feet.

It is unknown whether the pilot had an abort plan for the takeoff, but his disregard for recommended procedures and advice from the ranch manager cost him his life.

Review Questions and Exercises

Answers to review questions are provided in Appendix B.

Circle the correct answer:

1. On a gravel airstrip, you should hold the brakes and apply maximum power for takeoff. (**True** / **False**)

2. A takeoff abort point should be chosen for every airstrip and should consider wind, slope, length, and obstacles. (**True** / **False**)

3. During initial climb, use normal power, propeller, and flap settings recommended for the aircraft. (**True** / **False**)

4. The best takeoff technique at high DA is to accelerate the airplane with all three wheels on the ground until you reach flying speed, then abruptly pitch up to a high angle for maximum climb. (**True** / **False**)

5. Only a slight headwind will counteract the effects of taking off uphill. (**True** / **False**)

6. You should immediately apply full power when taking off on an airstrip with a curve or dogleg so the airplane reaches maximum speed around the curve. (**True** / **False**)

7. Normal traffic pattern departure may not be possible at airstrips in mountain and canyon environments. (**True** / **False**)

8. Best angle of climb speed (V_X) is the IAS that gives a climb to altitude over the (**shortest horizontal distance** / **shortest amount of time**) and (**decreases** / **increases**) as altitude increases

9. Best rate of climb speed (V_Y) is the IAS that gives a climb to altitude over the (**shortest horizontal distance** / **shortest amount of time**) and (**decreases** / **increases**) as altitude increases.

10. For a given IAS, pitch attitude (**increases** / **decreases**) with altitude, and pitch attitude for both V_X and V_Y is much (**higher** / **lower**) at high DA than at sea level.

7

—

COLD WEATHER

and

SKI FLYING

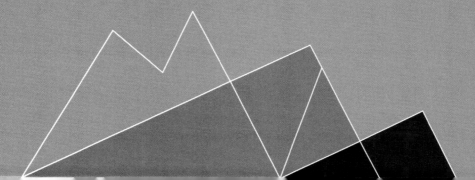

Although the long cold nights and short days of winter may seem like a time to leave your airplane snug in a nice warm hangar, flying during the colder months can be fun and safe. However, winter in remote and mountain environments presents unique situations and hazards not encountered elsewhere. Whether you plan to operate from paved (and plowed or maintained) airports or decide to venture into the world of ski flying, thorough planning and preparation is essential.

This chapter, which is divided into three sections, presents technical information on equipment, weather, and other concepts and operational considerations for winter and ski flying. The first section is written by guest author Michael Vivion and gives valuable insight into winter weather, ski equipment, and ski operations. Vivion has extensive experience flying skis in the Alaskan bush, which is characterized by unique weather and snow conditions and a wide variety of landing areas.

The second section includes insight from an interview with Paul Claus, whose expertise as an Alaskan glacier pilot and operator gives a glimpse into that highly specialized type of flying. Finally, long-time Idaho backcountry pilot Mike Dorris shares his experience in the Rocky Mountain west, where short, steep runways create a particular set of challenges and hazards for ski-equipped airplanes.

Guest Author Michael Vivion

Mike Vivion is retired from a 34-year career with the U.S. Fish and Wildlife Service (FWS), nearly 30 years of which were as a wildlife biologist/airplane pilot in Alaska. For 20 of those years, his assigned area of operation was the Upper Yukon Valley north of Fairbanks. Vivion has extensive experience on all types of skis and a variety of aircraft in the interior of Alaska. In December 2005, he retired from FWS and accepted a faculty position at the University of Minnesota, teaching and advising in the Aviation program. After seven years, he re-retired and now resides in Bozeman, Montana, with his wife Gina and Wiley the Brittany. Vivion currently flies a Piper PA-11 Cub Special.

In the following sections, Vivion shares his expertise on weather, equipment, operations, and other important considerations for ski flying.

Why Ski Flying?

As the leaves fall and winter arrives, pilots are faced with many challenges: the need to preheat the aircraft's engine; fitting engine and wing covers if the airplane will spend nights outdoors; assembling an eclectic collection of not-very-stylish clothing; the development of a proclivity toward hot beverages; and more.

While some aviators may let a little thing like winter restrict their flying adventures, the dyed-in-the-wool aviation junkie will just shift gears. Landing gear, that is—from wheels to skis. For those who have not experienced ski flying, you don't know what you're missing. Many of those scenic destinations you couldn't quite find time to visit last summer are even more spectacular under a blanket of snow. Many resorts and communities promote year-round tourism, and attractions of all sorts are available to the traveler willing to brave the cold. Ice fishing is a great way to extend the season, and competition for good "holes" is almost nonexistent with an airplane on skis. Finally, the challenges and splendors of winter camping in wilderness scenery are unmatched in any other season. The air in winter is often smooth as glass and crowds are generally easier to avoid than during the summer. Most aviators are somewhat restricted to runways of some sort during the summer months, but ski landing gear offers a whole new range of possible "airports," in locations like Alaska and Montana, with literally thousands of level landing sites within reach. These landing sites are often lakes and rivers, but with sufficient snow cover, ski-equipped aircraft can land virtually anywhere, from frozen lakes to farm fields to remote glaciers.

A set of skis on your airplane may open a lot of doors to winter adventure that you never dreamed of. Once your airplane is equipped with skis, you need to consider essential winter flying equipment, ski operations and general winter operations, as described in this section. Ski flying really isn't too difficult, but the environment is very different from what most pilots are used to, and there are some traps the novice ski pilot can slide into. Most are easy enough to avoid with just a bit of experience, training, and thoughtful preparation. Ski flying in Alaska and many other parts of the world is an off-airport operation, so dual instruction is strongly advised. Following are steps and considerations to prepare for your ski flying adventure.

Weather

Winter weather can be more difficult to predict than weather in other seasons. Part of the problem is the relative speed with which storm systems develop and move during winter, as well as the difficulty of predicting the rate of movement. While weather can be harsh and change fairly rapidly, the pilot will benefit from some winter phenomena. Because of limited solar radiation, there is little convective activity and afternoon turbulence from rising air is minimal. Thunderstorms are rare. Cold air can reduce the negative effects of **density altitude (DA)** on aircraft performance, although it can still be a factor during winter in the mountains. Winter is also usually free from obscurations to visibility due to smoke and from airspace restrictions associated with forest fires. Winter weather can provide some of the clearest blue skies of any season.

Current weather information and forecasts are even more important in winter than in summer, both during planning for a flight and during the flight itself. The weather sources listed in Chapter 2 provide weather data for decision-making prior to launch. Accessing good weather data once the pilot is in flight is more difficult. The ADS-B system may provide weather information in many locales in the flat lands but has very limited coverage in mountainous terrain. **XM Satellite Weather** is an excellent option that allows the pilot to obtain weather data before takeoff as well as when airborne. Additionally, **Doppler radar** should be used with caution in the mountains, as outlined in Chapter 2.

Airframe icing can be a significant threat during winter. Most ski-equipped airplanes are not equipped for flight in known icing conditions, and in winter almost any precipitation can cause airframe icing. Enter an area of precipitation only after considering your escape options should you encounter airframe icing. Very cold temperatures suggest that atmospheric moisture is likely to be frozen, but atmospheric water in liquid form can exist to temperatures well below zero in rare instances. Airframe icing and mountainous terrain are a very bad combination.

Flatland pilots accustomed to flying in restricted visibility may find that flying in mountainous terrain presents an additional dimension—or rather, lack of dimension—to visibility. Generally, in restricted visibility or lower ceilings, a cautious pilot will keep his or her head on a swivel, always evaluating any possible "escape route" in case the weather worsens. Mountainous terrain severely restricts the options available and limits the available escape routes.

One of the problems forecasting weather in the mountains is that the mountains themselves modify the weather. A system approaching a mountain range may contain high moisture content, but the first few ranks of mountains can strip much of that moisture out of the system as it passes, leaving little precipitation on the lee side of the mountains. But a stronger system may power over the mountains in its path and continue to deposit large quantities of precipitation as it continues on the leeward side of the range. The barometric pressure of the low-pressure center associated with a front can offer clues to the relative strength of the system, as can winds aloft. However, the somewhat subtle differences between a storm that pushes over a mountain range and one that dissipates as it passes the mountains can make forecasting difficult.

Just as in summer, strong winds at the height of the peaks can create severe turbulence, rotors, and other phenomena that are best avoided in light aircraft. Cautions recommended in Chapter 2 regarding winds should be applied by the mountain pilot year-round.

Fog and other **obscurations to visibility** can be common in winter, particularly in air temperatures which are above freezing during the day and drop below freezing at night, saturating the atmosphere near the surface. While fog often dissipates fairly quickly in summer due to solar effects, it may hang on much longer in winter due to low sun angles and short daylight periodicity. Fog generally occurs in the bottom of the valleys and canyons—precisely where the ski plane pilot is likely to land and stay overnight.

While true at any time of year, pilots flying in winter should always look at weather from both a strategic and tactical perspective. A careful examination of the weather patterns for the intended area of flight should be started well in advance of the flight. As the day of the flight approaches, the pilot should study the forecasts including the existence and movement of frontal systems. Then, follow up by checking to see how accurate that forecast was. This strategic view will offer some insight to at least what the weather systems have been doing in the area of interest—how fast they have been moving, their direction of movement, and the resulting weather. This can help the pilot better understand how the weather patterns have been behaving. Checking the veracity of the forecasts can offer clues as to the predictability of a particular system.

Once the day of the flight arrives, the pilot needs to view the weather in a more tactical manner, but knowing the characteristics of recent weather patterns in the area can help to evaluate forecasts and make better weather-related decisions. Weather cameras may be available in some areas and offer important clues to weather in the area you're interested in. The state of Alaska has developed a system of aviation weather cameras at avcams.faa.gov. There are also numerous cameras in passes and at airstrips in the Continental United States and possibly elsewhere. See www.asa2fly.com/reader/mountain for a non-exhaustive list. The ability to visualize weather through a pass or at an airport is a useful tool to improve decision-making.

After departure, continue to evaluate the weather en route and at your destination, either via radio or XM Satellite Weather. Remember to check the date and time on images or data you receive; you don't want to make critical assumptions based on outdated observations.

If you watch the weather carefully and decide to abort the flight, continue to check the actual weather for the intended route over the period of time the flight would have taken. This will help to affirm your decision, or perhaps it will turn out that the weather would have been flyable along the route. Either way, you will learn to better understand weather systems in the area. This process will improve your weather predicting skills, and prudence is always the best option.

The Ski-Equipped Airplane

Traditionally, most ski-equipped aircraft have been tailwheel types, but this is not an absolute requirement. Some high-wing, tricycle-gear models, such as Cessna singles, can and do make capable and versatile ski aircraft (Figure 7-1). Also, de Havilland Twin Otters and Lockheed Hercules C-130s are successfully used at both the North and South Polar regions and other areas throughout the world.

Figure 7-1. A ski-equipped Cessna Turbo 206. *(Photo by Michael Vivion)*

The aspiring ski pilot is advised to research whether ski approvals exist for their aircraft. Field approvals for ski installations used to be common, but currently installations must be approved either on the aircraft **type certificate** or with a **supplemental type certificate (STC)**. Nonetheless, a number of ski approvals are available for many aircraft. While there are few current ski manufacturers and not a lot of recent ski approvals, new ski models are on the horizon and manufacturers are looking to expand their market by working on new STCs.

What other characteristics should you look for in a candidate ski aircraft? Besides the obvious requirements for good heat and defrost capability, lots of power and a propeller optimized for takeoff and climb are essential ingredients for a good ski plane. While ski conditions can occasionally make a pilot wish for a little more braking action, more often the issue is whether you have enough thrust to overcome the drag caused by the snow.

A high-wing design is more flexible than a low-wing for ski operations, but there are successful low-wing ski planes. Tasks like draining the wing sumps can be somewhat more "interesting" on a low-wing airplane in snow, and the low-wing design can be a liability in deep snow due to snow berms and other obstacles. Deep powder snow can turn that low wing into a submarine.

Sufficient cabin space to carry all the necessary winter gear is important in cold weather flying, whether on skis or wheels. Wing and engine covers, a snow shovel, snowshoes, and survival gear, including sleeping bags, all add up to a lot of bulk but not necessarily a lot of weight. The ski pilot often runs out of room in the airplane well before reaching maximum gross weight in winter. A large aft compartment where light gear can be stowed helps, particularly in smaller, two-seat aircraft. Extended baggage compartment modifications provide more storage area. Cargo pods have become available for many aircraft in recent years and offer additional space for stowage. In very deep powder snow, however, pods can add considerable drag in a situation where that is the last thing you need.

Favorites of the ski flying world are most of the fixed-gear, single-engine Cessnas, Champion/Bellanca/American Champion models, several de Havilland models, Aviat Husky, Maules, most high-wing Pipers, and most Taylorcraft models. This list is certainly not exhaustive, but the point is that a number of airplane choices are available for the ski flying enthusiast. Finally, the list of very capable experimental homebuilt designs is increasing rapidly, and many of these aircraft would make excellent ski planes as well. The beauty of the experimental aircraft in this regard is that certification of skis is not a requirement, so the aircraft owner has the option of choosing virtually any ski model or design and adapting the skis to the aircraft.

The Skis

Many different ski models have been built over the years for use on a wide variety of aircraft. Most of these skis are no longer in production and would be difficult to install legally today since their original applications were limited, and they were often installed via field approvals. Nonetheless, many of the aircraft mentioned above have ski approvals noted in their type certificate data. As an example, the type certificate for the Cessna 170B lists several approved models of straight and retractable skis. Find a set of the appropriate model skis, get a mechanic to install them per the type certificate and good operating practices, and you will be ready for some ski flying adventures. Finding a set of Wesco straight skis might be a bit difficult, but there are still lots of AWB 2500 retractable wheel skis around. Ski manufacturers have also developed numerous after-market STCs that provide a basis for installation on various aircraft models.

The ski types in common use today are straight skis, wheel penetration skis, semi-retractable skis, and fully retractable wheel skis. There is also considerable variety in the material from which skis are made, including metal, fiberglass, high-tech carbon fiber composites, and the original composite material—wood. Let's discuss the pros and cons of the various ski types.

Straight Skis

Straight skis, also known as **wheel replacement skis**, are purely ski landing gear—no wheels, no actuator mechanisms, and no brakes—just basic skis (Figure 7-2).

Figure 7-2. Piper PA-18s on straight skis. The skis attach directly to the airplane's landing gear. *(Photos Courtesy Paul Claus)*

For performance in deep snow or challenging conditions, nothing can beat a good straight ski. They are lighter than any other ski type, and they generally have more bottom surface area as well, affording maximum "float," which is desirable in deep or difficult snow conditions. Straight skis are also the simplest ones to rig, and they require almost no recurring maintenance.

Straight skis are installed by removing the wheel and brake assemblies (in some installations the brake calipers are left in place, but safety-wired and non-functional) and mounting the skis on the same axles, using the same attachment hardware as the wheel assemblies. The typical straight ski rigging consists of a rear, or aft, limit cable fastened between the rear of the ski and a point on the fuselage aft of the main gear attach point (the rear float fittings, if installed, are often used). The aft limit cable prevents the front, or toe, of the ski from rising too high in flight, and the length of this cable determines the angle of incidence of the ski in flight.

A forward limit cable, which is generally attached between the toe of the ski and a point near the firewall of the airplane or the forward landing gear attach point, prevents the toe of the ski from going down in flight, which would be a very bad thing. The forward limit cable is rigged with a significant amount of slack to permit the skis to conform to the surface as the airplane slides on the snow. A bungee or spring attached between the front of the ski and the same (or separate) fuselage attach point as the forward limit cable takes up slack in the forward limit cable (Figure 7-3).

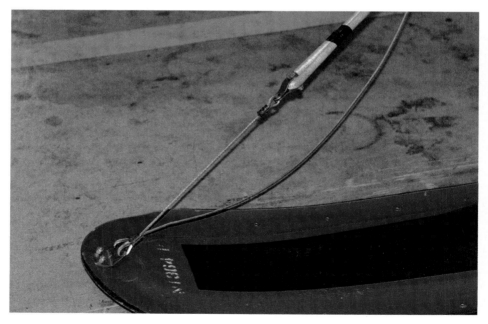

Figure 7-3. The forward limit cable is connected with slack and a leading length of "crust cutter" cable to protect the bungee from crusty snow. *(Photo by Michael Vivion)*

The bungee or spring keeps the toe of the ski at the proper landing attitude by keeping tension on the aft limit cable in flight. Skis are typically rigged just slightly nose up with reference to the wing's angle of incidence (generally from one to six degrees nose up, with reference to the bottom of the wing).

Although straight skis have many advantages, they also have disadvantages. The straight-ski airplane becomes an almost exclusively off-airport machine—your only option is to taxi, take off, and land on snow or ice. Straight skis may not be the best choice for pilots who operate from airports that do not offer a snow-covered surface that remains usable for a substantial part of the season. However, if you operate from an airstrip that can be groomed, straight skis may be best. Handling wheels are available on the market or made from scratch and are available for nearly any ski arrangement. Hangaring a plane equipped with straight skis can be problematic. Fuel availability may also be an issue, though some marinas still offer auto fuel in winter months. Otherwise, you may have to devise a fueling strategy—cans, a small tank in the back of a pickup, etc. You will also need to develop a technique for propping the skis up off the snow when parked outside to prevent them from freezing to the surface.

Wheel Penetration Skis

Wheel penetration skis offer a bit more flexibility than straight skis by providing the ability to operate on either runways or snow-covered surfaces. Penetration skis use the standard landing gear, complete with wheels and brakes, but install a ski with a cutout or opening for the landing gear tire to protrude from (Figure 7-4).

The skis themselves attach to the landing gear axles via axle extensions, or stub axles. They are rigged in similar fashion to straight skis, and the ski height is set so that on pavement or gravel surfaces only the main tire, which protrudes below the ski bottom by an inch or so, is in contact with the surface. Generally, a small "tail wheel" is attached to the rear of the ski to prevent it from dragging on hard surfaces.

Figure 7-4. A Cessna 185 with Airglas wheel penetration skis. *(Photo courtesy Paul Claus)*

The biggest advantages of penetration skis include their lower price compared to retractable skis. They also offer the ability to use either snow-covered or bare surfaces—a major advantage over straight skis. Unfortunately, penetration skis are still a compromise. The primary disadvantages are that they are heavy and do not perform as well as straight skis, particularly in deep snow. Penetration skis are heavy because they include two complete sets of landing gear: the skis and the wheels.

The opening in the ski through which the wheel runs, the protruding tire itself, and that tiny tail wheel (or tail wheels) create a lot of drag in deep snow, so takeoff performance suffers significantly compared to straight skis. Nonetheless, many pilots opt for these skis because they are simple, cost-effective, and require minimal effort to install and remove. If most of what you do with a ski plane is fly to lakes with a foot or so of loose snow or generally operate on well-packed snow, these skis should be fine. The industry is coming out with new penetration skis, and the designs are improving, so performance may also improve.

Retractable Wheel Skis

The "ultimate" ski setup for many pilots is the **retractable wheel ski**. These skis are "ultimate" in many ways, not the least of which are cost, weight, and complexity. Retractable wheel skis offer the best of both worlds (Figure 7-5).

Figure 7-5. A Cessna 185 with the Fluidyne Fli-Lite 4000 hydraulic wheel skis. *(Photo by Amy Hoover)*

Retractable wheel skis install either on a separate stub axle or on an extension to the existing landing gear axle. The skis have a cutout through which the wheel protrudes during wheel operations. Prior to landing in snow, the ski is extended downward, thus "retracting" the wheels (though the wheels themselves never actually move). There are as many types of operating mechanisms for retractable wheel skis as there are models. Some use purely hydraulic retraction systems, some use electro-hydraulic retraction systems, and at least one uses purely mechanical, spring-actuated gear, which is capable only of extension but not retraction. For a more detailed description of the different types and manufacturers of retractable wheel skis, visit www.asa2fly.com/reader/mountain.

A modification of the retractable wheel ski is manufactured by Aero Ski of Brooten, Minnesota. These semi-retractable (for want of a better description) wheel skis look similar to wheel penetration skis, except they can be repositioned. For runways, the skis are in the "up" or wheels position, with the wheel protruding from an opening in the ski. Snow landings are made with the wheels protruding, similar to a penetration ski. Once on the surface, the skis have to be manually extended one at a time using a pry-bar lever. After a snow takeoff, the skis can then be retracted by pulling a handle inside the cockpit, which releases a catch on the skis, allowing spring pressure to raise the skis and permitting the wheels to once again protrude through the openings in the skis for a runway landing. The advantages of these skis are their simplicity and relatively inexpensive cost compared to fully retractable skis. The primary disadvantage is they can't be lowered to the ski position in flight. Some snow landings must be done with the wheels extended, then the pilot must get out of the airplane to move the skis to the down position. As described later in this chapter, skis with wheels protruding make site evaluation by dragging the skis difficult if not impossible.

Another current production, fully retractable ski is the Rösti-Fernandez 8001 retractable wheel ski, manufactured by Solo Aviation in Germany (Figure 7-6).

These skis utilize an electro-hydraulic actuation mechanism, so retraction and extension are accomplished with a gear lever similar to the one in most retractable gear aircraft. The skis are supported by a carbon fiber arm that attaches to the axle. With skis extended, the tire rests on top of the ski, supporting the weight of the airplane on the main gear axles. They are approved in Europe on several aircraft types, but in the United States they are approved only on the Aviat Husky and the Piper Super Cub. They are in use by many aircraft in Europe, where approvals have been available for longer than in the United States. Landings as high as 14,000 feet MSL have been performed on these skis...followed by takeoffs, of course. These skis are by far the lightest retractable skis on the market at about 76 pounds total weight for the installation, and they are lighter than some straight skis. They perform as well or better than any straight skis.

Figure 7-6. Rösti-Fernandez 8001 retractable wheel skis. *(Photo courtesy Michael Vivion)*

Materials

A variety of materials are now available for the manufacture of aircraft parts, and this is becoming true for skis as well. Originally, most skis were made of wood. F. Atlee Dodge Aircraft Services in Anchorage, Alaska, manufactured a very nice set of wood straight skis until a few years ago, and some are still in service in Alaska. More recently, this company is manufacturing a similar ski with carbon fiber bottoms instead of wood.

Historically, many manufacturers transitioned from wood to metal skis, as produced by the two big ski manufacturers, Federal and Fluidyne, both of which built straight skis and hydraulic retractable wheel skis. The Fluidyne type certificates are now owned by Wipaire, Inc., which has restarted production of some of the retractable Fluidyne skis.

Landes Airglas began manufacturing aircraft skis in the 1950s, when Wes Landes used his boat building skills to manufacture aircraft skis from fiberglass. An extensive line of fiberglass skis followed, including thousands of sets of skis and tundra pads for helicopters. Many military heavy-lift helicopters operating today utilize Airglas "tundra pads." Airglas, Inc., has manufactured a line of straight and wheel penetration skis for years. More recently, the company was sold, and the current management has continued the tradition of producing a quality line of skis and ski designs. Their new skis are made from lightweight carbon fiber.

Virtually all ski bottoms today are covered with a plastic material such as **ultra-high molecular weight (UHMW) plastic** to reduce friction and help prevent the skis from sticking down after being parked. UHMW is commonly used in the food preparation industry because it provides a very slick surface and is non-porous, and thus it is easy to clean. UHMW is available in various thicknesses, but 1/4 inch or 3/16 inch are the most commonly used for ski bottoms. The material is cut to fit the outline of the ski bottom and then riveted or bolted to the ski. Some users extend the UHMW bottom an inch or so beyond the edge of the ski bottom itself to provide more bottom area. Most skis are equipped with a metal **skeg** or **wear strip** to prevent the ski from sliding sideways in snow and to prevent damage to the ski bottoms from movement on hard surfaces. It is beneficial to replace those wear strips with a similar-dimension strip made from UHMW. The steel strips that most skis come equipped with will freeze down with the skis at rest on snow, and that frost layer is incredibly tenacious. Once the steel strips have frosted, full power will not move most ski planes. At that point, the pilot must dig out under the skis and clean that frost off. By comparison, skis that have had the steel strips replaced with UHMW of similar dimension provide good directional control and are much less prone to freeze down.

Tail and Nose Skis

The tail wheel on an airplane can serve as a very effective anchor in certain snow conditions. This occasionally can be beneficial, but it is more often a hindrance. If your ski plane is equipped with a tail wheel, consider adding a penetration tail ski (Figure 7-7). The heavier the airplane's tail is, the more beneficial a tail ski will be.

Figure 7-7. Penetration tailwheel skis. *(Left photo by Amy Hoover; right photo courtesy Paul Claus)*

Burl Rogers in Anchorage, Alaska, manufactures a great-performing and durable tailwheel penetration ski called the "Magnum 1 Tailski," which comes in sizes for use on a number of different aircraft models. Another benefit of a tail ski is that it will significantly reduce wear and tear on your tail surfaces and tail wheel, particularly in crusty snow conditions. For tricycle-gear aircraft, Airglas produces a nose ski that will fit most tricycle-gear ski planes.

Other Equipment

Once your aircraft is outfitted with skis and your mechanic has rigged them properly and completed the appropriate paperwork, you are ready for some winter flying fun. Well...almost. Before you tackle the great outdoors in that newly ski-equipped airplane, understand that a ski pilot must always be prepared to spend the night wherever the airplane lands. Getting stuck is always a possibility, and winter weather can change rapidly, so you want to be well prepared; you'll need to equip your aircraft and yourself with some basic equipment in addition to the skis.

One of the first pieces of required equipment is a good set of snowshoes. In deep snow, they can be worth their weight in gold. You can use them to stamp out a snow runway, which will permit your ski plane to depart in much less distance than it might in untracked snow, or even use it to get unstuck. If you do get stuck, snowshoes are useful to make camp, gather firewood, and move around more easily. Bigger snowshoes are better; choose ones at least 3 feet long and very wide. The small snowshoes in vogue these days may be fine on packed trails, but they would be useless in deep, unconsolidated snow.

The ski airplane also needs a comprehensive survival kit customized for winter. Shelter-making equipment, sleeping bags, fire-making supplies, etc., are necessary tools of this trade. Even more important, the pilot needs the basic skills to deploy this equipment and set up a good camp almost anywhere. One of the most important of those skills is the ability to start a good, warming fire in a matter of minutes under virtually all conditions.

There are many books and articles available to help you put together a good winter survival kit, and the best place to test both your survival kit and your winter survival skills is right in your back yard. If the exercise does not work out, go inside where it's warm, and rethink your gear and/or skills.

The late Ray Tremblay was a trapper, game warden, and pilot in Alaska for decades. Ray told me that survival gear is the stuff that's in your pockets when you go out the door of the airplane. That bag in the back of the airplane is camping gear, *not* survival gear. It's important to understand this philosophy and adapt to the possibility that the airplane and its contents may not be available to you after an incident. Suppose you land on a remote lake, and you are unfortunate enough to discover thin ice. The airplane sinks to the wings in icy cold water, and you get out and pull yourself up onto the ice, but you're not going to dive down and try to retrieve that gear bag in the baggage compartment. Another scenario might involve fire. These kinds of incidents are extremely rare, but it would only take one to ruin your day. Tremblay's answer was to wear a fisherman-type vest and fill the pockets with essential survival equipment. When I flew for a natural resource agency, our policy was that everyone aboard the airplane was required to wear such a survival vest. Survival vests and their contents are discussed in more depth in Chapter 9. Finally, comfortable winter clothing is essential for ski flying. Layering is important since periods of activity will alternate with periods of sitting in the airplane. Always fly a ski plane dressed to survive in the country over which you are flying.

In addition to the challenge of keeping your body temperature warm, your aircraft's engine also needs to retain heat, and if you are parked for long, you will need some means to preheat the engine. Engine preheating can be simple if you have electricity. Tanis and Reiff both offer excellent certificated electric engine heat systems for most aircraft engines. Other more basic engine heaters are also available. In a pinch, small electric automotive interior heaters can warm an aircraft engine well enough to safely start in cold temperatures.

If there is no electricity, a combustion heater is required. One such device is the Northern Companion heater. This is a small, lightweight, tubular device designed to work with a backpacking camp stove that has a separate fuel tank. The burner goes inside the metal tube, and a piece of scat hose fits over the upper end of the tube and is routed into the lower cowl of the engine compartment. With a good insulated engine cover, you will be ready to fly in a couple hours, even at very cold temperatures. You might also make your own device, keeping in mind that combustion heat safety is essential; any type of heater needs to be continuously monitored during the preheat process.

During preheat, you need to get the crankshaft and its associated bearings and the oil in the sump to reasonably warm temperatures. A short burst of heat, even very intense heat, will warm the outside of the engine, but it takes more time for that heat to penetrate to the core of your engine. Take your time during preheat.

What conditions require engine preheat? Opinions vary on this topic. Lycoming recommends engine preheat any time the temperatures are at or below 10°F, but it is best to err on the safe side and preheat any time the engine is below freezing. Although getting heat to the engine is essential, retaining heat is just as important. The best way to do so is with a fitted, insulated engine cover (Figure 7-8).

When flying in the winter, with or without skis, the first thing you should do after engine shut down is cover the engine and cowling to retain the engine's heat. With a well-insulated engine cover applied, most engines can stay warm enough to start nicely after three or four hours at temperatures close to 0°F.

Figure 7-8. An insulated engine cover, which is essential to keep the engine warm after shutting down in cold temperatures. *(Photo by Michael Vivion)*

Wing covers should be used for overnight or longer stays to prevent the wings from becoming frost-covered. Trying to remove frost from an airplane without a warm hangar or de-icing fluid is difficult. Wing covers are easy to apply, and they also serve secondary duty as potential shelter-building materials in the event of an emergency. There are a few varieties of wing covers, but they all do basically the same task. A number of companies produce good-quality, fitted engine and wing covers for many aircraft models. If you can't find fitted covers for your airplane, you can order custom covers for your specific aircraft model. Covers take up considerable space in a light aircraft's baggage area, but the utility is well worth the space.

A good shovel is an essential piece of equipment that should be aboard any ski plane. Small aluminum shovels are best and are available in mountaineering outlets. These shovels come in handy in routine operations and are essential equipment if you get stuck.

Factors Affecting Ski Flying

Novice ski pilots are strongly encouraged to find an instructor with ski flying experience, preferably one who is also experienced in the aircraft type. Do some training on skis before venturing out on your own. In Switzerland, a pilot is required to complete a glacier flying course and a series of instructional flights including 200 ski landings in different seasons prior to being licensed to fly onto the glaciers solo. While U.S. pilots are not required to complete any training or obtain a rating to fly skis, it's wise to remember that a few hours of instruction from an expert is the cheapest insurance policy you'll ever buy. However, it can be difficult to find such an instructor, particularly if you live in a part of the country where ski flying is uncommon. Internet forums offer the ability to network with pilots who operate similar aircraft, and you may find a qualified instructor via one of those. Visit www.asa2fly.com/reader/mountain for links to several forums to help you get started.

It is important to consider some of the unique challenges presented by the frozen winter environment. Snow is the main character in ski flying and should be studied well before departing. Following are some things to consider.

Snow Quality

Snow varies greatly in both texture and character. The ski pilot must learn to read snow conditions from the air prior to landing and understand their effects on the aircraft's performance. Perhaps nowhere in the world of flying does the term "site evaluation" have more meaning and importance than in ski flying. Many people think of snow as being soft and smooth, but the truth can be far different.

Wind moves snow into drifts, and once snow "sets up," it can become incredibly solid. At flying speed, even crossing a snowmobile track that has set up can damage a ski plane. There is an old saying that there are dozens of words that describe snow in the Inuit languages of northern native cultures. People who ski recreationally have a number of different names for snow, as well: "powder snow," "corn snow," etc. These are descriptors for differing snow composition and texture that also affect the performance of your ski plane.

Visibility and Light Quality

Visibility is an important issue to the ski pilot, and not just the effects of precipitation on visibility. Winter sun angles are low in the north, and this, coupled with overcast weather and a white environment, can create a condition commonly referred to as "flat light" (Figure 7-9). It can be nearly impossible for even the most experienced ski pilot to determine height above the surface in flat light. This is different from "whiteout" conditions, which generally involve significant obscuration to visibility as well as flat light.

Flat light can occur with no obscuration to visibility, just an overcast and low sun angle, and can be dangerous. If flat light is combined with an overcast and an all-white environment, it may be unsafe to fly by use of visual references, let alone land on the snow. The European glacier pilots understand the dangers of flat light, and glacier flying operators in the Alps have a policy that no glacier flying is permitted on any day with continuous cloud cover, even with a high ceiling.

Figure 7-9. An airplane landing on an alpine glacier, illustrating the difficulty of seeing the surface in flat light conditions. *(Mikadun/Shutterstock.com)*

Figure 7-10. Flat light is such a risk that obstacles around airports, like this snow berm, are often spray-painted with day-glow paint to prevent taxiing aircraft from colliding with the snow. *(Photo by Michael Vivion)*

Humans rely heavily on depth perception, which depends on fairly subtle cues. Shading and shadows are both high on the list of cues that we constantly rely on without conscious thought. Enter into a world with no shadows, no color for contrast, and little shading, and it can be difficult or impossible to see obstacles that are partially masked by a blanket of snow (Figure 7-10).

One year during a recurrent semi-annual checkride, I was flying a Cessna 185 on retractable skis near Fairbanks, Alaska. The weather was barely VFR with a solid overcast and 3 to 5 miles visibility. The check airman pointed out a small lake and told me to land there. I started the process of site evaluation. After a few passes, I landed, and slid to the opposite end of the lake. We turned around and took off in the same tracks. The check airman instructed me to land there again, turn around, taxi back, and take off in the same direction I had landed—an exercise in turning, which can be difficult at times. So, we landed, turned around, and taxied back to the touchdown point. As I was turning around into the tracks where we'd been touching down, I saw a very large beaver house right beside where we'd been landing. This house was perhaps 7 feet tall, and neither of us had seen it during several passes. It was, of course, covered with snow and nearly invisible. That was the end of the checkride and a valuable lesson learned.

Temperature

Temperature affects our function, the performance of the airplane, and the performance of the skis in the snow. There are some fascinating physics involved in ski flying, and it is important to understand at least some basics. On a snow surface, the pressure between the ski bottom and the snow causes some physical changes at the near-molecular level within the snow. This creates a very thin layer of water at the ski bottom/snow interface, even in fairly cold temperatures. This is one reason skis slide well. In temperatures colder than about -20°F to -30°F, the snow eventually becomes too cold for this to occur, which degrades ski performance. It is important to understand that a spot where you operated yesterday may demand significantly different performance from your airplane to manage today, and much of this relates to temperature.

On the other hand, reciprocating engines produce more horsepower in cold temperatures due to the density of the induction air. If you are operating at -20°F, you don't necessarily need to use all the power the engine is capable of generating at those temperatures, so keep the throttle back a bit to save wear and tear on the engine, unless you really need maximum power. Some aircraft have available "cold weather kits," the most essential component of which is a plate that restricts induction air. This prevents the engine from being damaged by limiting available horsepower to maximum rated power. In addition, some sort of cover for the engine oil cooler should be considered for operation in cold weather.

Above all, ski flying should be fun. I generally cut off my personal flying at a minimum of -10°F, but at work -40°F was our cutoff. Remember that at these very cold temperatures, the atmosphere is generally very stable. Cold sinks can form in lakes and other low areas, creating pockets of very cold air with temperatures much lower than surrounding areas. Most pilots will likely limit their ski flying to temperatures around 0°F or warmer. Just remember, though, that very warm snow can severely degrade aircraft performance. The longest I've ever been stuck on skis was due to cool temperatures that warmed to +40°F during the day, while we were in deep spring snow. The airplane would not climb up out of this "corn snow." It simply flowed out, around, and over the skis. We shut down and waited until very early the next morning, when freezing temperatures caused the snow to consolidate again, and facilitated our escape.

Snow and Ice Stability

Overflow is unfrozen liquid water lying on top of ice, which can exist as free water under a crust, or turn the snow nearest the ice into thick, icy slush. It is common in areas where large amounts of snow have fallen on relatively thin lake ice, pushing the ice down and cracking it, thereby permitting water to flow out over the top of the ice. It can also occur where water levels have continued to drop after freeze-up, allowing water from a stream to flow out on top of the ice and settle in the low spot in the center of the waterbody. Geeting & Woerner noted:

Remember, overflow always drains to the lowest point on any type of surface. Normally the center of a lake will have the worst overflow. Inlets and outlets of lakes should also be avoided. And if small amounts of fog are present on the lake, a pilot can expect overflow in that area of the lake. Overflow can be detected by its greenish color. If overflow is a problem, take off or land close to shore, keeping in mind, of course, that if you are too close to shore you may encounter mechanical turbulence. (Geeting & Woerner, 1988)

I have found overflow in areas subjected to -50°F and colder temperatures. Deep snow that lies on top of the water can provide enough insulation to prevent this water from freezing. If you land your ski plane in this stuff, you may be in for some real winter "fun." If the skis break through the top layer of snow and settle into the water, they will immediately start to freeze in cold temperatures. As you step out of the plane, soaking wet boots and feet may be another consequence. There you are, with a stuck airplane, which is starting to become an integral part of the lake you landed on, and you have wet feet. And, it is really cold.

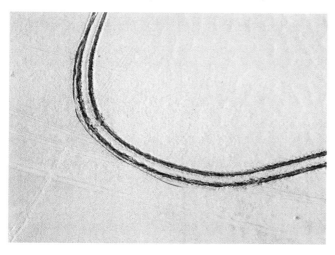

Figure 7-11. Overflow in ski tracks. The pilot made a pass with the skis on a frozen lake, and several minutes later water soaked into the tracks from the lake below. *(Photo courtesy Brad Thornberg)*

Here is a typical scenario involving overflow. The pilot puts down tracks on a lake surface and does not observe any dark areas in his tracks, where the skis broke through a crust into water. Sometimes it takes quite some time for overflow to show itself in tracks (Figure 7-11). Had the pilot waited another ten minutes or so, he may have noted that the airplane's tracks gradually darkened as the free water soaked through the tracks to the surface. The lake is of insufficient length to land, stop, and take off straight ahead, so a turnaround will be required. On landing, everything seems fine, until the pilot starts to turn, at which point the outboard ski (the one on the outside of the turn) breaks through the crust, which had just barely prevented the airplane from breaking through earlier. This swings the airplane around, so that it is now pointing at the shoreline, and one gear leg is deep in slush.

Now the pilot has a job on his hands, because the longer he waits, the more "stuck" the airplane will become. But, if you find yourself in this situation, there are several things you can do to mitigate the danger. First, always carry several extra-large plastic trash bags in the plane for just this eventuality. Slide the trash bags over the skis, and you will minimize the freezing of the skis to the lake. Cutting a long pole to lever each ski up out of the free water, and then sliding spruce boughs, branches or anything else you can find under the skis, one at a time, will lift the skis above the water level, and once the water freezes, you may be able to escape with minimal effort. You might also carry a long (100 foot) section of aircraft cable, a few ice screws (used in ice climbing and available at mountaineering outlets), and a small rope come-along (manual winch). With these devices, you can carefully turn an airplane that is pointed in the wrong direction or pull a stuck airplane out of a tight spot. Sometimes.

As you turn the airplane, be very careful not to damage the landing gear. The skis can apply significant torque to the ski axles, which are easily damaged with twisting loads. Above all, do not risk your health to try to extricate the airplane. Remember the camping gear in the back of the plane. Don't get yourself so "sweated up" struggling with a stuck plane that you risk hypothermia. If it looks like a really big job, get the trash bags on the skis, do the preliminaries, and then set up camp, get a fire going to dry yourself out, and tackle the problem a step at a time, with the camp and fire to back you up. Survival is your first priority.

Overflow can be relatively common some winters and virtually non-existent in others. In interior Alaska, overflow has frozen up by March, so it tends to be seasonal. I carefully look for it prior to any ski landing. Any hint of grey or black showing up in the ski tracks will mean going somewhere else to look for a landing site.

Ski Operations

Once you have an understanding of the kinds of hazards to expect in the ski flying environment, it is time to discuss actual operation of the ski plane and how it can differ from operating on wheels.

Taxiing

Your first exposure to ski flying will be taxiing. Taxiing on straight skis may be some of the tenser moments of a flying career. There are no brakes, so pay attention and give yourself lots of room to maneuver and stop. You may still have some braking action with wheel skis except on glare ice. Takeoff from a packed ski strip is pretty straightforward, and most tailwheel aircraft are more forgiving on skis than on wheels.

Just like landing and taking off, taxiing on skis is dependent on the depth and consistency of the snow. The key is to do whatever is necessary to get the main skis in a pitch attitude that is just slightly nose up, and the tail wheel sort of "floating" behind the airplane. That is not easy to do without using big blasts of throttle, and in fact, that is one of the best ways to turn around: sudden, full applications of all controls.

While taxiing on a really slick surface, a short loop of rope tossed over the nose of a ski can help to turn around in some situations by providing a little differential friction. If you really get jammed up and can't turn around in the space available, tie a long piece of rope to your tail wheel and have someone pull sideways on the line as you power around to the desired heading. If you are by yourself, you can use a come-along and long piece of light cable. Attach the cable to an ice screw (available from the ice climbing counter at your local outdoors store) that you have screwed into the ice surface. Use the come-along to winch the tail around.

I have done all of these at one time or another. Be aware, however, that turning a ski plane around in snow exerts a *huge* amount of torque to your axles, and it is quite possible to break an axle turning a ski plane around manually while exerting an external force like pushing or pulling on the airframe. All things in moderation: turn it *slowly*, and a little bit at a time. When using a come-along, I winch just a bit, stop and walk to the toe of the ski, give it a gentle kick sideways to release pressure on it, and then winch some more. And finally, sometimes you just get properly stuck, which leads us into the next topic.

Site Evaluation and Landing

Skis behave pretty much like tires in flight, although they create more drag. As you approach your intended destination and prepare to land, your first priority will be to find what appears to be a usable landing zone nearby. While that sounds intuitive, there are times that conditions dictate a landing site farther from your actual destination than you'd like. Rough snow may preclude landing on the south side of a lake, but landing on the northeast side of the lake and then taxiing to the south side or snowshoeing there may be an option. Your favorite cabin may be near the mouth of a small stream, and the ice in front of the stream may be either thin or overflowed. The time to make these determinations is while you are still in the air, not after you are on the surface. The prevailing winter winds are often from a predictable direction, so you can almost guarantee a smooth landing surface on a given lake. It is likely to be on the leeward side of the lake, which is sheltered by the shoreline and trees.

Next, you will need to determine the wind direction. A wind circle is one means for determining wind direction and approximate velocity. At a relatively low height, initiate a constant rate turn over a selected point, fly a complete circle at a constant bank angle and speed, making no corrections, and the drift of the airplane will tell you the direction and approximate velocity of the wind. Using a GPS, you can simply fly the four cardinal directions and note the wind effects on your ground speed.

Once you determine the wind direction and find a likely landing area, start taking a closer look at your proposed landing zone, as there will be no white stripes indicating the centerline of the "runway." You must fix in your mind precisely where the runway is. It's best to do this using good landmarks, because once close to the surface, everything will look different. Find a point you can fly over, and line that point up with a tree well beyond the departure end; use these references to keep you where you intend to be. At the same time as this "high recon," you must consider the effect of obstacles in the area—such as terrain, turbulence, etc.—and how these may affect the landing and subsequent takeoff.

The next task is to determine if the surface is in fact suitable for landing. By flying very low, parallel to, and just slightly offset from the "runway," you can clearly inspect the surface. On this pass, you should be looking for obstacles of any kind: snow drifts, beaver houses, wet spots, etc. You can also time it during this pass to determine the length of the landing surface. At 60 knots (or about 70 mph) over the ground, you are moving at about 100 feet per second. As you pass the approach end, start counting: "One one thousand, two one thousand." If you counted twenty seconds, this means that your intended landing site is about 2,000 feet long.

Traffic patterns in the bush are flown differently, and 300–400 feet high might be enough, depending on terrain. Your downwind pass should be close to your proposed landing site so you can get a good look at it from different perspectives and sun angles. It's amazing how often some very large objects are nearly impossible to see from one angle but are quite obvious from another.

If you find no apparent obstacles, and the landing surface appears to be long enough during the first pass, your next pass will include a touch-and-go to start feeling out the surface. This first touchdown pass should include just a light touch of the skis on the surface; you will be looking for large anomalies—things that could break the airplane if you put more weight on the skis. This pass gives you the chance to investigate the snow conditions. If, in the middle of your proposed touchdown zone, you feel a solid bump, you will need to do a bit more investigating to determine exactly what that was. There may be a snow-covered log or a swale that is difficult to see, and you may have to realign your "airport" or give it up and go somewhere else.

If everything looks good, it's time to put more weight on the skis and test the snow more thoroughly. On downwind, look for any signs of free water from overflow and any irregularities at all in the tracks, and consider what that may mean. Evaluate your touchdown point and determine whether you should shift it forward or back, depending upon your needs and any obstacles in the approach path. On this pass, you will slow the airplane somewhat while on the surface. As you slow, you should be feeling for significant drag, bumps, and so forth as you put more weight on the skis. If the landing zone passes this test, and there are no real doubts remaining in your mind, the next pass may conclude in a landing. That is assuming you are comfortable with how deep the snow is and how safe the conditions are.

Suppose you're still a little suspicious. Maybe there has been a lot of overflow around recently, or perhaps the snow at home seems a lot deeper than it feels here. On your next pass, you may want to touch down and slow even more than on previous passes. In fact, you may slow down to nearly a walking pace, then power up and go again. You want to put sufficient weight on the skis in this pass to reveal whether the snow is very deep or if there is overflow. Keep the airplane moving even at a slow speed, as this may help to keep from getting stuck.

For snow more than about knee deep, you may want to put down several sets of tracks with the airplane, along the length of the "runway" you intend to use, to facilitate the subsequent takeoff. In below-freezing temperatures, tracks will "set up" over the next hour or so, and they will offer much less drag on your subsequent takeoff. Snow can "set up," as skis force much of the air out of the snow, compacting it. Cold temperatures also change the consistency of the snow to very hard and compacted. If you land in an area where multiple passes are not practical due to terrain, you can pack down an airstrip ahead of the airplane with snowshoes after you land. A few hours after this treatment, you'll be able to walk on the crust that is created, even in very deep snow. Be aware, though, that in warm temperatures, snow may not set up, so be careful of landing in deep snow in temperatures above the freezing point.

Rather than making one very precise set of tracks with the skis on multiple passes, it's preferable to make several sets of overlapping tracks. Once a single set of tracks sets up, they act almost like railroad tracks composed of compacted snow instead of steel. You may be able to land on those tracks, but as you slow, or during your takeoff attempt, your skis will tend to slide off the edge into the deeper snow surrounding them and get stuck. The overlapping tracks will decrease the likelihood of sliding off the tracks. The same logic applies to packing down a takeoff surface with snowshoes: Pack a runway, not a single track (Figure 7-12). This packed "runway" does not need to be a thousand feet long. Its primary purpose is to help the ski plane accelerate to a speed that will allow the skis to float until takeoff.

Figure 7-12. This runway was packed using snowshoes. Although powder is the most supple and soft form of snow, it can also be a lot of work if it has any depth. *(Photo by Michael Vivion)*

Touching Down

After completing your reconnaissance passes and deciding to land, you must first determine where to park. Is the landing zone long enough for you to land, stop, and then take off straight ahead? Or will you have to turn around at one end of the landing zone and either taxi back or take off in the opposite direction? Are there other airplanes accompanying you that also need to land?

Many incidents involving pilots becoming stuck on skis occur when the pilot attempts a turn. Turning puts significant side loads on the skis. The edges of the skis may tend to dig in and cut through the surface crust. In any case, as you turn around, you will put more weight on the outside ski than on the inside ski. If you must turn around, do so. But it is better to land, stop, and take off straight ahead in the same direction.

If you do need to turn around at the end of a landing, for whatever reason, it is always best to turn to the left in order to use the aircraft's left-turning tendency to help tighten the turn. Executing a 180-degree turn can be a difficult exercise, so practice the technique on an open lake or field with no nearby obstacles before trying it in a confined area.

The maneuver should be started as a gentle turn to the right, with controls neutral and power just sufficient to move the plane. Once the nose is about 20 degrees to the right of the initial heading, start the turn to the left, with full left rudder, and add some power. I generally push forward on the stick or yoke in an attempt to lighten the weight on the tail ski. The next problem to overcome is that if power is left on, the airplane will start to slide straight ahead rather than turning, because the airplane is accelerating. So, to prevent acceleration, quick bursts of power can bring the tail around. Keep the airplane turning, but minimize acceleration. The rudder needs to be held to the stop during the turn. Once headed back to your tracks, let the tail settle, reduce power, and slide into the tracks you just made, facing the opposite direction.

If you misjudge and end up pointed the wrong direction with your path blocked by an obstacle, it's time to shut down, get out, and prepare for some hard work. Turning the plane without power can be very difficult, and it is easy to do serious damage to the airplane's axles and landing gear if you're not careful. Before you go back to the tail to try to lift it and push it around, consider the torque those big long skis are going to apply to your airplane's axles as you try to turn the plane with the skis firmly stuck to the snow. This turning-around process must be done very slowly and deliberately, literally an inch or so at a time. Move the tail just slightly, and then go give each ski a gentle kick at the toe of the ski and/or shovel snow away from the sides of the skis. As the skis move sideways a bit, return to the tail and move it a bit. Continue the process until the airplane is headed in a safe direction. The importance of taking this process slowly and deliberately cannot be overemphasized.

Once you have come to a stop where you intend to park, wait for a few seconds with the engine at idle. Then power the airplane forward about one ski length and wait a bit longer. Power forward yet another ski length and shut down. Skis generate heat as they slide across the snow. By allowing the skis to cool off in contact with the snow prior to parking, and then moving them before you park, you will find that the tendency of the skis to freeze down is considerably reduced.

If you are here for a short visit—maybe for ice fishing, for a "biological" break, or just to take a few photos—throw the engine cover on to keep the engine warm while you conduct your business. If, on the other hand, you plan to spend the night, you may want to try to minimize the amount of ski bottom that remains in contact with the snow to prevent the skis from freezing down. This can be done by digging snow from under the skis and leaving just a "pillar" of snow under the axles and at the heels; by propping the skis up on spruce boughs; or by sliding plastic garbage bags over the toes of the skis and moving the aircraft forward until the bags cover the ski bottoms. Putting spruce boughs or a couple of two-by-fours under the skis can work as well. With retractable skis, it may be possible to cycle the skis to the "wheel" position, slightly elevating the skis off the snow. In morning, cycle back to "skis" and you will be ready to go. Whatever method you use, the idea is to prevent the ski bottoms from freezing down while parked.

Takeoff

Ski takeoffs require a little less preparation and evaluation than landings. You should have figured out the takeoff path and length before you landed. But takeoff can be a difficult process, sometimes requiring all the thrust your engine and propeller can develop and then some. Snow conditions can change considerably in a short period of time, often associated with changes in temperature. And, of course, snow happens, as in overnight arrival of the fluffy stuff while you were parked, changing the takeoff challenge considerably.

As with a wheel takeoff, the problem is using thrust to overcome the drag associated with the landing gear's contact with the surface in order to accelerate the wing to a speed at which it develops enough lift to fly. However, snow can create a tremendous amount of drag. As noted earlier, bigger is better here: Bigger ski bottoms, bigger engine, bigger propeller, and maybe even bigger wings can all help in getting underway. So, let's say you fire up your ski plane, after having removed the covers, pre-flighted as appropriate, and warmed up the engine, and now you are ready to depart. If the skis have now been in contact with the snow while your passengers boarded, a gentle kick (the emphasis on gentle) side to side on the toe of each ski should free up the skis just before you board (or make it obvious that the skis are frozen down).

Sometimes skis freeze down fairly quickly, and the airplane will not move. Assuming the area ahead of the plane is free of obstacles, you may be able to break it loose with power. With full power applied in a light airplane, raising the tail and banging it down on the snow may break the skis loose. In an airplane with a constant-speed propeller, at full power, pull that propeller pitch control all the way to coarse pitch, then right back to fine pitch. That surge of thrust may be enough to get you moving. Once the plane moves, it will quickly scrub this minimal frost from the skis.

Once lined up with the "runway" on skis, you are faced with what airplane manufacturers refer to as a "soft-field takeoff" scenario. Follow the guidance in your flight manual for a soft-field takeoff. Because a tail wheel acts as an anchor in snow, you need to get the tail up and out of the snow as soon as possible. Here is where a tail ski is truly a blessing, particularly with an airplane that has a heavy tail.

As the airplane accelerates, the challenge is to keep the tail wheel up out of the snow but to keep from coming up taut on the aft limit cables of the skis. When you force the tail up, the plane rotates on the main skis, and at some point, you'll encounter tension on the aft limit cables. Raising the tail any higher forces the toes of the skis down into the snow, which significantly increases drag. You must find the balance point where the skis are fairly level, the aft limit cables are just taut, and the tail wheel is up out of the snow. The sensations of acceleration versus drag are somewhat subtle, and it takes some practice to get the hang of it. With that fine balance point achieved, the airplane should accelerate to flying speed, and off you go.

Although tricycle-gear ski planes are not as common, they have some distinct advantages in the realms of turning around and taking off in deep snow. For one thing, they have three *large* skis instead of two large skis and one little bitty one on the tail. Second, you can pull back pretty hard on the yoke, apply some power, and if you have loaded the airplane right, you can lighten that nose ski up enough to help facilitate turning. The same application of nose up elevator helps reduce the drag for takeoff. A Cessna 206 on skis with a competent pilot at the controls can go just about anywhere a Cessna 185 ski plane can and maybe some places it can't.

Ski takeoffs from glaciers and in canyons can be tricky since these areas often involve downhill takeoffs. Afternoon winds are frequently down slope, creating a tailwind on takeoff. This adds to the challenge of achieving takeoff speed, and can extend the takeoff run significantly, even though you are taking off down a fairly steep slope. Paul Claus describes operating from glaciers in the next section.

Glacier Flying with Paul Claus

Glacier flying is unique and very specialized. Ski-equipped airplanes operate during all seasons of the year, including the long days of summer above the Arctic Circle, so pilots can encounter a wide variety of temperatures, weather, and conditions, all in a day's work. The middle to uppermost parts of glaciers are typically covered with a thick blanket of snow, or crust, that can hide deep cracks, called **crevasses** (Figure 7-13). In the warm summer months, the crust is weak and can give way under the weight of an airplane or even a person.

Figure 7-13. Crevasses on a glacier. Crevasses form in the top layers of a moving glacier because some parts move at a different rate than the rest. These large, deep cracks in the glacial ice are dangerous to people and airplanes. *(Photo courtesy Paul Claus)*

Other physical features, such as **moraines** composed of rock, gravel, and dirt, and **sastrugi** (parallel, wavelike ridges caused by winds on the surface of hard snow), form and shift constantly. The surface of any glacier is dynamic, making glacier flying some of the most hazardous and specialized type of flying in the world.

Terry (2000) recommends that no pilot should attempt to land on a glacier without getting flight instruction and that pilots should never land on a glacier unless they have recently landed there or done a thorough reconnaissance, including photo documentation of the glacier features.

Paul Claus is an Alaska native who learned to fly in his father's PA-18 before he was old enough to drive. There was an airstrip in his front yard, and he learned to fly skis on Lake Hood in Anchorage at the age of 14. His whole life has been devoted to aviation, and he is a widely respected legend throughout many parts of the world.

Figure 7-14. The Garret-powered de Havilland Single Otter takes skiers, climbers, and explorers into the remote Alaska wilderness. *(Photos courtesy Paul Claus)*

Claus owns the Ultima Thule Lodge (www.ultimathulelodge.com) with his wife and family and has lived there since 1978. He operates under an FAA Part 135 Operating Certificate and uses six Super Cubs, three de Havilland Beavers, a Cessna 180 and 185, and a Garret-powered de Havilland Single Otter (Figure 7-14).

Claus has more than 6,000 hours in the Otter alone, and his wife and three children are also pilots. His primary instructor was Alden Williams, a legendary Wein Alaska Airlines pilot with more than 35,000 hours of bush flying experience. One of his early memories during primary instruction was Alden telling him not to just look at things during the preflight, but to give everything a good hard shake, since things were going to get shaken in the backcountry anyway. Sure enough, he found a cracked cabane V (gear structures, forming a V shape, that hold the bungees and suspension system for the gear) during a vigorous preflight. Before the days of safety gear cables, this was an important find!

Claus starts his flying season by taking clients to photograph or watch the famous Iditarod dog sled race each March, which he has done for 34 years. After that, the spring skiing season begins, and he spends several weeks delivering backcountry skiers to pristine powder skiing with ski-equipped airplanes. Then comes mountain climbing season, and his business transporting and supporting climbers, as well as rescue operations, is combined with regular lodge business.

During an interview with Claus transcribed below, he contributed the following observations about glacier flying:

> There are four critical things I evaluate in a glacier landing. The first is the light conditions. Having good light is absolutely essential, and you cannot land in poor light without proper markers. The best markers are climbers on the ground spread out along the landing path, but spruce boughs or black garbage bags with a rock in them will work. One time I had dropped several garbage bags in flat light conditions, and after unloading, taxied down to retrieve them. The light was so flat that when I jumped out of the airplane to retrieve a bag, the passengers in the plane up above couldn't tell I was on the ground and thought I had jumped out of the airplane from the air! Other times I have simply had to turn around and go home when the climbers didn't understand I needed them to mark the surface, and fuel finally ran low.
>
> The second thing I look for is crevasses. I am a climber, which helps me a great deal when identifying dangerous areas. Glaciers are sloped, one way, and similar to a flowing river, so evaluating soft, covered crevasses is crucial. Open crevasses, of course, are obvious.
>
> Third, I evaluate the roughness of the surface. I am looking for the effects of wind ridges and the size and hardness of those ridges. If they look like high ridges, I will try to find a nearby place to land with smaller ridges and determine the snow softness. If they are both tall and hard, it is not safe to land and you will knock your gear off.

Fourth, you have to consider snow depth. In some conditions, you just don't know for sure until you are almost stopped and began to sink in. One time, a friend and I spent 3 days packing a landing area with snowshoes so my father could come and pick us up in a Cessna 185. It was backbreaking work, and then he ended up coming in a Super Cub, so we hadn't needed to pack it like that after all. I swore I would never pack an airstrip with snowshoes again, and now I use skis, which work better anyway. (Claus, 2018)

Claus stated that although landing on slopes is advantageous with respect to reduced ground roll landing uphill and improved takeoff performance downhill, there are disadvantages when turning around on the slope, and the reality is there is usually no go-around option. He described unimproved landing areas as either "go-aroundable" or "not go-aroundable" and stressed that pilots need to know in which category each landing area falls and what that means with respect to commitment and risk.

Regarding glacier flying in general, Terry (2000) noted that holes and crevasses are always present, and personnel should always use safety lines clipped or tied to the airplane while working in the vicinity. He also recommended tying up with other people when venturing away from the aircraft and having an ice axe ready to self-arrest. Taking off from glaciers introduces another set of challenges, a primary one being the downhill takeoff. Pilots will notice they become airborne even when the vertical speed indicator indicates a descent (Geeting & Woerner, 1988), and it is critical to monitor airspeed and not become fooled into pitching up and causing a dangerous decrease in airspeed.

Rocky Mountain Ski Flying with Mike Dorris

Although many ski operations in Alaska, Canada, the European Alps, and elsewhere do not use established airstrips, most in the Central Idaho Rocky Mountains do. Since the Idaho backcountry has become a popular destination for recreational pilots, even in winter, some specific notes regarding that area are worthwhile. Unless an Idaho backcountry airstrip and lodge have winter habitation and airstrip maintenance, deep powder will be the general rule, although fall and springtime snow conditions are variable. Density altitude, although lower during winter, is always a factor in the Rocky Mountain region. For example, International Standard Atmosphere (ISA) temperature at an airstrip at an elevation of 7,000 feet MSL is 34°F, and at 15°F the DA is approximately 5,700 feet. At -20°F, it is approximately 3,100 feet. This is important to remember when coming from lower elevations.

Mike Dorris, owner and operator of Sawtooth Flying Service (sawtoothflyingservice.com), learned ski operations from his father Bill, an Idaho Aviation Hall of Fame inductee who operated in the Idaho backcountry from the 1950s to the 1990s. Dorris has been flying the U.S. mail and supplying backcountry ranches and U.S. Forest Service stations during all seasons of the year for decades, and he has over 23,000 hours in the Idaho backcountry. He has flown ski-equipped aircraft ranging from Piper J-3 and PA-12 airplanes to Cessna 170s and 185s. Dorris operates on public airstrips as well as private, uncharted ones, some as high as 7,000 feet MSL. Many of the strips are only a few hundred feet long and a couple of wingspans wide between tall timber. Some are in narrow canyons, with blind approaches, and on slopes of 20% or more with no go-around possible. After landing on a steep strip, the airplane has to be turned around either on a hill or a small flat spot at the top. This highly specialized type of flying into and out of such airstrips is difficult even when operating on wheels, but on skis it presents an ultimate challenge. In an interview, Dorris (2018) shared some of his valuable experience with respect to ski flying, which is incorporated into this section.

Dorris flies his Cessna 185 with the Fluidyne Fli-Lite 4000 hydraulic wheel skis in the up position during cruise because they create less drag, have slightly higher cruise speed, and have increased climb performance. If he finds himself in bad weather where he might need to make a precautionary landing, he will lower the skis, since it takes more than 70 pumps on the hydraulic handle to pump the skis down. Otherwise, he generally flies en route with the skis up.

Taxi and Turn Around

As described by Vivion earlier in this chapter, the heavier the tail, the more important it is to have a tail ski. Using a tailwheel lock can help with directional control in icy or hard pack conditions. On narrow airstrips, the airplane should be turned around only at the ends, not in the middle, because turning disturbs the snow and creates a hole that can hinder the takeoff or the next landing.

Turning around in a small area at the end of a strip is challenging. Dorris has perfected a technique using hydraulic skis that can be individually raised and lowered one at a time. Trim the stabilizer full forward to lighten the tail, and make left turns, since engine torque helps pull the airplane to the left. You can start with a slight right turn while flipping the hydraulic switch to up, then hold the right brake and add left rudder to begin the left turn. Rapidly pump the hydraulic handle to raise the left ski so the airplane pivots around the left tire. Holding the right brake prevents the right ski from raising. As you complete the turn, reverse the process with switch down, pump, and right rudder to stop the turn. Use the throttle to blast the tail and oscillate the elevator to keep it light as you anticipate the airplane's movements to end up in your original tracks. Not all hydraulic retractable skis have the option of raising just one ski, and some have an electric pump that eliminates the manual hydraulic pumping. This procedure takes practice, and in deep powder it may be the only possible way to reverse direction in a loaded Cessna 185.

Takeoff

Takeoffs are highly variable and depend on snow depth and consistency, ice and surface condition, temperature, aircraft and load, ski type and bottoms, runway gradient, and pilot skill and experience. Full flaps might be needed during the takeoff to help break loose from the snow. Packing the snow is helpful, and you might be able to use the airplane by taxiing back and forth if the strip is relatively flat, but plan for fuel reserves and monitor engine temperatures.

Planning is critical. Dorris pointed out that after aborting a takeoff, the airplane has to be taxied to the end of the airstrip, turned around, taxied back to the departure end, and turned around again before another takeoff attempt can be made. This consumes both time and fuel and can be frustrating for the pilot and passengers, but Dorris has had to abort many ski takeoffs. Deep powder takeoffs may not be possible on very short or steep airstrips due to excessive drag. You may want to pack the snow manually or with a snow machine, if available, to ensure a rapid acceleration because you will not be able to abort the takeoff on very steep strips.

Dorris commented, "In the right snow consistency, I have had the 185 sitting on the belly pod thinking it is going to be stuck and a long day ahead. Then just by packing a small ramp in front of the skis and kicking them from side to side to loosen them, I powered back into the air."

One airstrip on Dorris's mail route is 5,888 feet MSL elevation and is surrounded by higher terrain on all sides. Snow conditions are variable depending on the season. Dorris said just one inch of sticky snow over an ideal surface can ruin his ability to get airborne. He has had many close calls and aborts at this location over the years, even though the airstrip is relatively long. After takeoff, he must pump the hydraulic skis up as quickly as possible to reduce drag and be able to maneuver or clear obstacles. That is a good job for someone in the right seat.

Landing

The recommendations of Vivion and Claus in this chapter are also valid for established airstrips. Ski plane landing distances in powder can be about half the distance of a normal landing on wheels at the same airstrip. On ice, the distances can be three to four times longer, and on hard-packed snow with temperatures below freezing, they average about 20% longer. Overflow is not typically an issue on a snow-covered airstrip, but many pilots in the Rocky Mountain region land on frozen lakes as well and should understand the phenomena.

Dorris said he often puts the wheels down on his hydraulic Fli-Lite skis when landing on hard snow at a short airstrip. He has developed a technique of landing with the skis only partially down and the wheel ram extended about six inches. This can give him better stopping and directional control in some conditions. The skis act to prevent nosing over. Dorris also believes that tail skis help for all but the lightest airplanes, and he uses them on both his Cessna 170 and 185.

Flat light conditions can also be a problem. One of the airstrips on Dorris's mail route gets a lot of snow, and in flat light it is difficult to tell where the airstrip is. The terrain to either side is uneven and can be treacherous, so Dorris tries to have the local townspeople place pine boughs along the edges of the strip to mark it. More pine boughs have to be placed after a new snowfall.

Ski landings on extremely steep slopes may require full power to get to the upper end of the airstrip. Sometimes it is not possible to make it all the way to the top. Ski operations are hazardous or almost impossible on some of the steepest strips. Once a turn is started on a slope, it is easy for the airplane to start tracking down or across the hill, and the pilot can lose control. On airstrips that have a good turn-around spot at the top, have someone pack the snow, if possible, before landing.

Dorris described a tough situation after landing on a very steep (approximately 22% gradient) airstrip (elevation 4,200 feet MSL and length approximately 600 feet), where he happened to have two passengers going into the ranch to rescue some heavy equipment that a tent had collapsed over:

> I landed about halfway up, not sure of the snow conditions, and had my wheels down, anticipating a snow crust which causes the skis to slide faster. Instead, we stopped almost immediately about halfway up the strip in 15 inches of new, heavy, wet snow. We unloaded everything we could to no avail. I held the airplane from sliding backwards with the engine running while my two passengers shoveled ahead of the airplane. Then they would slide the airplane back down the hill 25 feet or so, and with both passengers pushing we would make it an additional 15–20 feet before getting stuck again. We did this over and over again until we finally made the small flat spot on top where we could secure the airplane from sliding off the hill. This was hard on the engine and even harder on my passengers; they were thoroughly exhausted by the time we finally got to the top of the strip. The 4 × 4 tractor would not move in the sticky wet snow. We finally got a track Skid Steer to run and move some of the snow off the airstrip. The operator had left deeper snow and a snow berm at the bottom of the runway that I did not notice until using every inch of the strip to get off by myself [during a takeoff alone in the airplane] having to do a last-minute maneuver around it. Then, quite stupidly in hindsight, I landed again to tell my passengers they would have to spend the night and continue working the airstrip. That left me with another very marginal takeoff! (Dorris, 2018)

Another ski plane adventure involving the Dorris family turned into a rescue that continued for several days and nights, as described by Holm (2013).

Summary

In summary, ski flying, whether on lakes or meadows, glaciers, or established airstrips, can be an adventure. It is more variable than float or wheel flying and can be a fun way to enhance your mountain flying experience. However, as evidenced from the expert advice in this chapter, it requires an entirely new set of skills, preparation, practice, and sound judgment. As noted by Potts (1993) "...how well you think (and look ahead, anticipating potential problems) determines not only how successful you are in completing your assigned flight safely and economically, but also your very survival."

Accident Scenarios

Several accidents are presented here as examples of mishaps resulting from conditions described by guest authors.

The first accident (NTSB Accident GAA17CA294 on 05/28/2017) demonstrates the dangers of turning around in poor snow conditions:

> The pilot of the ski-equipped airplane reported that, as the tailwheel touched down on the glacier, the snow was deeper and softer than he had expected. He added that, during the uphill landing, he chose not to stop the airplane and risk getting stuck. Instead, he completed a turn at the top of the landing area but was unable to straighten the direction of travel enough for a takeoff. Subsequently, to straighten the airplane before the takeoff, he completed a left 360° turn.
>
> During the downhill takeoff, the airplane had poor acceleration and insufficient airspeed to fly, so he aborted the takeoff. As he reduced the engine power, the airplane slowed to what he felt to be a reasonable speed, and he initiated a left turn to taxi back to the top. Subsequently, the right ski dug into the snow, and the airplane came to rest inverted.
>
> The airplane sustained substantial damage to the empennage.
>
> The National Transportation Safety Board determines the probable cause(s) of this accident to be: The pilot's selection of unsuitable terrain for taxiing, which resulted in a nose-over. (NTSB, 2017b)

Next, NTSB Accident GAA17CA187 on 02/15/2017 exhibits hazards of landing in flat light conditions:

> The pilot of the tailwheel, ski-equipped airplane reported that, while landing off airport in flat light conditions, he was unable to maintain a good visual reference of the hard-packed snow-covered landing area. After touchdown, the airplane drifted off the hard-packed snow, and the left ski sunk in softer snow. He increased power and attempted to recover with "hard right control" to no avail. The airplane's left ski struck a snow-covered tank.

The airplane sustained substantial damage to the left-wing lift strut. The National Transportation Safety Board determines the probable cause(s) of this accident to be: The pilot's failure to maintain directional control while landing in flat light conditions on a hard-packed snow-covered landing area. (NTSB, 2017a)

Ridges and hard drifts present hazards, as shown in the third example from NTSB Accident ANC09CA027 on 04/02/2009:

The commercial pilot reported that he was landing on the frozen snow-covered lake in a ski-equipped airplane. During the landing roll the airplane's main landing gear skis encountered a snowdrift, which stripped the nuts that connect the skis to the main landing gear axle. Both skis separated and the airplane's left main landing gear leg collapsed. The left wing struck the snow-covered frozen lake. The airplane sustained substantial damage to the left wing and fuselage. The pilot said that there were no preaccident mechanical problems with the airplane, and noted in his report to the NTSB that he should have inspected the landing site before landing, then selected a better area to land on.

The National Transportation Safety Board determines the probable cause(s) of this accident to be: The pilot's selection of an unsuitable landing area. (NTSB, 2009b)

Finally, NTSB Accident CEN09CA210 on 03/15/2009 demonstrates the hazards of overflow:

The pilot landed the ski-equipped airplane on the snow-covered frozen lake earlier in the day. After several hours of ice fishing, he taxied the airplane to the east side of the lake for departure. The lake's longest axis (east/west) was approximately 2,000 feet long. The pilot reported that the lake's orientation, terrain gradient, shoreline trees, and prevailing winds favored a departure to the west. During the takeoff run, the airplane accelerated slower than normal due to a slush layer that had formed since the previous landing. The pilot reported that the tail became airborne about halfway across the lake, but he aborted the takeoff when the airplane had not attained flying airspeed after crossing 3/4 of the lake. The airplane was unable to stop before running aground and impacting several trees, substantially damaging the fuselage and both wings. (NTSB, 2009a)

As all of these accident scenarios reveal, operations with ski-equipped aircraft, whether on snowfields, frozen lakebeds, glaciers, or even mountain airstrips, can be fraught with hazards and certainly require planning, diligence, and specific training.

Review Questions and Exercises

Answers to review questions are provided in Appendix B.

Circle the correct answer:

1. Adverse effects of DA are not significant during winter operations because of the colder temperatures. (**True** / **False**)

2. Airframe icing cannot occur at temperatures below 0°F. (**True** / **False**)

3. Fog can linger for a longer time in the winter. (**True** / **False**)

4. In the United States and Canada, flying a ski-equipped plane requires a pilot logbook endorsement from a Certified Flight Instructor qualified to give ski instruction. (**True** / **False**)

5. Straight skis have the best overall performance on snow. (**True** / **False**)

6. Some languages have dozens of different words to describe differing snow conditions. (**True** / **False**)

7. (**False light** / **flat light**) is the primary weather phenomenon affecting a pilot's depth perception in winter conditions.

Short answer:

8. List some important additions to your survival gear for winter operations.

9. List four important factors to consider when evaluating a glacier landing.

SECTION III

Aircraft and Human Performance

(Photo by Amy Hoover)

8

HOW TO LIGHTEN UP:
DENSITY ALTITUDE, LOADING

and

AIRCRAFT PERFORMANCE

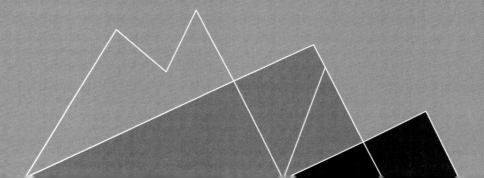

The majority of flights into mountain and canyon terrain will likely be during the hotter months of the year, since airstrips are bare and free from snow, and days are longer. However, as the air becomes less dense due to higher altitude and hotter temperatures, aircraft performance is diminished. Thinner air equates to reduced power because the engine takes in less oxygen. All the airfoils on an aircraft lose effectiveness as **density altitude (DA)** increases, and loss of propeller efficiency is significant, resulting in decreased takeoff and climb performance. **True airspeed (TAS)**, and therefore **ground speed (GS)**, increases with altitude, which also affects takeoff and landing distance. According to the FAA:

At airports in higher elevations, such as those in the western United States, high temperatures sometimes have such an effect on density altitude that safe operations are impossible. In such conditions, operations between midmorning and midafternoon can become extremely hazardous. Even at lower elevations, aircraft performance can become marginal and it may be necessary to reduce aircraft gross weight for safe operations. (FAA, 2008)

This chapter explores some ways pilots can mitigate risk by developing an awareness of how heat and elevation affect performance and how pilots can load and operate their airplane to increase safety. Factors such as gradient, surface conditions, and wind also affect performance (see Chapters 5 and 6). Descriptions and examples are adapted from Williams (1986) and Hoover (1999, 2001). All rules of thumb are cited from Porter (1986) unless otherwise specified and are based on the mathematical derivations used by Porter. The simple calculations and rules of thumb are presented to help pilots quickly estimate the effects of DA on aircraft performance and to stimulate critical thinking. If math is not your thing, it may still be helpful to look at the outcomes from the calculations as they relate to common sense applications. Rules of thumb are not a substitute for the aircraft owner's manual, flight operations manual, **pilot's operating handbook (POH)**, or common sense and good judgment.

What is Density Altitude?

As air temperature or altitude increase, the air becomes less dense. Since aircraft performance is referenced to standard temperature and pressure, variations must be accounted for to accurately predict the airplane's performance and ensure the

---

[1] National Transportation Safety Board (2015). *NTSB Safety Alert: Mastering Mountain Flying.* SA-039. https://www.ntsb.gov/safety/safety-alerts/Documents/SA_039.pdf

flight can be conducted safely. To predict performance, you must know the DA, which is a measure of the air density compared to a standard reference. Figure 8-1 shows the types of altitudes defined by the FAA. Whereas true, absolute, indicated, and pressure altitudes relate to height, DA is an indicator of aircraft performance in nonstandard conditions. As DA increases, engine horsepower, propeller thrust, and climb performance all decrease, while takeoff and landing distances increase. Density altitude is a "feels like" altitude for aircraft performance in a similar way that wind chill factor is a "feels like" temperature for humans. Both can have important ramifications on safety.

Types of Altitude

Pilots sometimes confuse the term "density altitude" with other definitions of altitude. To review, below are some types of altitude:

- **Indicated Altitude** is the altitude shown on the altimeter.
- **True Altitude** is height above mean sea level (MSL).
- **Absolute Altitude** is height above ground level (AGL).
- **Pressure Altitude** is the indicated altitude when an altimeter is set to 29.92 inHg (1013 hPA in other parts of the world). It is primarily used in aircraft performance calculations and in high-altitude flight.
- **Density Altitude** is formally defined as "pressure altitude corrected for nonstandard temperature variations."

Figure 8-1. The different types of altitude used in aviation. Density altitude is the value used to predict aircraft performance. *(From FAA [2008])*

Because high density altitude "has particular implications for takeoff/climb performance and landing distance, pilots must be sure to determine the reported density altitude and check the appropriate aircraft performance charts carefully during preflight preparation" (FAA, 2008). The FAA also states that humidity is not generally considered a major factor for DA computations because it is related to engine power rather than aerodynamic efficiency and notes that "high density altitude and high humidity do not always go hand in hand" (FAA, 2008). However, the FAA does recommend adding 10% to takeoff distance with high humidity and anticipating a reduced climb rate.

Since most aircraft performance charts take temperature and pressure into consideration, why is it important to know the DA? The reason is to alert pilots to exercise caution and ensure the airplane can perform adequately and safely. Generally, any time the DA is above 3,000 feet, loss of performance becomes noticeable.

Weather reporting services, such as AWOS or ASOS, often give the DA. However, at a remote mountain airstrip without weather reporting, you will have to estimate DA using your altimeter and the ambient air temperature. Ensure that the aircraft temperature gauge is not in direct sunlight, as it could give an erroneously high reading. Standard methods to figure DA include using a **Koch Chart** or **Denalt computer**. There are also several apps for mobile devices that will calculate DA based on data you input. Without a chart or computer, you can use one of two simple rules of thumb to quickly determine DA.

> *Each 1°C variation from standard temperature equals about 120 feet.*

> *Each 10°F variation from standard temperature equals about 600 feet.*

To use the rules of thumb, you must know the standard temperature at a given **pressure altitude (PA)** and add or subtract the variation. It helps to know the standard temperatures for the airports you intend to use (Table 8-1).

Table 8-1. Standard temperature for pressure altitudes (rounded to the nearest whole number). *Pilots should be familiar with the standard temperature for the airports they routinely use.*

Altitude (feet)	Temperature	
	(°C)	(°F)
0	15	59
1,000	13	55
2,000	11	52
3,000	9	48
4,000	7	45
5,000	5	41
6,000	3	38
7,000	1	34
8,000	-1	31
9,000	-3	27
10,000	-5	23

(Derived from FAA [2016])

Here is an example using a mountain airstrip and standard mathematical rounding (to make it easier):

Pressure altitude (PA)	= 5,000 feet
Temperature	= 30°C
Standard temp at 5,000 ft	= 5°C
Temp difference	= 25°C above standard
Rule of thumb:	
Density altitude (DA)	= 5,000 + (120 × 25)
	= 5,000 + (3,000)
	= *8,000 feet*

A typical summer DA at a mountain airstrip can be more than a mile and a half high before you even take off. For actual elevations ranging from over a mile to as high as 14,000 feet or more, aircraft performance will be drastically reduced.

For temperatures below standard, performance will increase. However, be cautious, as DA could still be well above sea level:

Pressure altitude (PA)	= 6,500 feet
Temperature	= −8°C
Standard temp at 5,000 ft	= 2°C
Temp difference	= 10°C below standard
Rule of thumb:	
Density altitude (DA)	= 6,500 − (120 × 10)
	= 6,500 − (1,200)
	= *5,300 feet*

A quick check of DA should be a starting point to consider how to maximize aircraft performance and minimize risk. For example, do you fly an airplane whose service ceiling is only a few hundred feet above the DA? What will your climb rate be? How long will your takeoff distance be at a certain aircraft weight? How much weight can you realistically carry? Should you plan to make more than one trip and take only a partial load? How will that affect your fuel planning? Knowing the DA can alert you to the hazards and the need to carefully consider lost performance.

Aircraft Performance

There are ways to compensate for loss of performance at high DA. STOL kits and other devices (Chapter 1) might be an option. Turbocharged piston engines and turbine engines increase airplane performance. However, airfoils are less effective at higher DA, even with more power, and loss of propeller efficiency has a drastic effect on performance (Smith, 1992). The engine, propeller, wings, and tail surfaces will all perform better when the air is cooler. That makes mornings or evenings the best time to fly in hottest weather.

The most important variable you can control is how you load your airplane (Figure 8-2). The question is: How much weight must you remove to compensate for lost performance? Your aircraft performance charts are a good place to start. However, many charts only give figures at one or two weights, and some POHs and owner's manuals do not include adequate charts or reference data. Also, you may not be flying a new airplane, and performance will probably not meet the expectations of the charts. Airplanes modified with STOL kits, vortex generators, or other devices will not perform according to the POH criteria for a stock airplane.

Figure 8-2. A load of river gear to be flown out of an approximately 1,200-foot-long airstrip at 2,800 feet elevation in the bottom of a canyon. Pilots must carefully determine how much weight can safely be loaded and decide how many trips will be required to carry all the cargo and passengers. This load was split up and ferried to a longer airstrip at lower elevation and then reloaded for the flight out. *(Photo courtesy George Dorris, G&S Aviation)*

A good way to estimate the effects of DA on performance is to build your own charts through experimentation. Load your airplane to different weight and **center of gravity (CG)** positions and record takeoff and landing distances and climb performance at different DAs for each weight/CG combination. This requires some time commitment but is worth the effort. For climb performance, note the rate of climb on the vertical speed indicator and use a GPS to calculate your angle of climb (altitude per distance traveled).

For takeoff and landing distances, use an airport where you have references, such as spacing of runway edge lights, to be as accurate as possible. You will need to account for variables such as gradient, surface conditions, aircraft weight, DA, and wind.

FAA Advisory Circular 90-89B, *Amateur-Built Aircraft and Ultralight Flight Testing Handbook* (FAA, 2015), offers procedures for flight testing homebuilt aircraft. These same procedures can be used to develop performance data for certificated airplanes, either ones without data or aircraft that have been significantly modified.

Lowry (1999) developed software you can use to input empirical data from test flights to compute various performance criteria. Links to Lowry's information for both fixed-pitch propeller aircraft and constant-speed propeller aircraft are available on the Reader Resources webpage at www.asa2fly.com/reader/mountain. You can also attend a density altitude clinic sponsored by the FAA or other organizations that collect real-time performance of your takeoffs and landings.

The following sections explore how changes in weight affect takeoff, landing, and climb performance. The rules of thumb are meant to provoke thoughtful planning but are not a substitute for the POH, aircraft performance charts, or actual experience.

Power versus Density Altitude

One of the first things you will notice at higher altitude is a reduction in the amount of horsepower produced by the engine. Table 8-2 shows terms used to describe aircraft engine power and measure of power output.

Table 8-2. Definitions of the different types of horsepower and how engine power is measured.

Indicated Horsepower (IHP)	The power developed within the engine combustion chambers without friction.
Brake Horsepower (BHP)	The amount of power delivered to the crankshaft of a reciprocating engine. Horsepower is a function of both torque and RPM.
Shaft Horsepower (SHP)	The horsepower delivered to the propeller. For a direct drive engine, BHP and SHP are the same. For propellers connected to the engine by reduction gears, some power is lost through friction of the gears.
Thrust Horsepower (THP)	The actual power output of the engine propeller combination. THP = BHP × Propeller Efficiency.
Rated Brake Horsepower (RBHP)	The power output of the engine at standard sea level pressure and temperature at maximum rated engine RPM.
Manifold Pressure (MP)	The average pressure of the air or fuel/air charge in the engine intake manifold measured in units of inches of Hg. MP is dependent on ambient air pressure, engine speed, throttle setting, and turbo/supercharging.

For most GA aircraft, **thrust horsepower (THP)** is the most important value, as it takes propeller efficiency into consideration. **Manifold pressure (MP)** is the most common method pilots can use to directly monitor power output. For fixed-pitch-propeller aircraft, engine RPM gives an indirect indication of THP.

This discussion and the rules of thumb presented refer to the rated brake horsepower (RBHP) of the engine, indicated throughout simply as horsepower (HP). You can approximate HP lost for a reciprocating engine using the following rule of thumb:

> A normally aspirated engine loses approximately 3% HP per 1,000-foot increase in density altitude (DA)

For example, a 160 HP Cessna 172 at 7,000 feet DA will lose approximately 21% power, thus producing approximately 126 HP.

Another way to determine loss of power is to note **manifold pressure (MP)** at full power on a sea-level standard day, and calculate power based on the lower MP at altitude. Normally aspirated reciprocating engines lose 1" MP per 1,000 feet DA. Following is an example.

Example: For a 300 HP Cessna 185 on a standard day that produces 30" MP:

$$\frac{HP}{MP} = \frac{300 \text{ HP}}{30" \text{ MP}} = \frac{10 \text{ HP}}{1" \text{ MP}}$$

At 8,000 feet DA, MP = 30" − 8" = 22" MP

and

22 × 10 HP = 220 HP

Knowing the HP produced by the engine does not give precise information about loss of total airplane performance, since thrust horsepower (THP) depends on propeller efficiency, which in turn depends on the amount of drag produced by the propeller. However, using the rule of thumb for HP lost should cause you to stop and consider how drastically performance will be affected, and take appropriate measures to mitigate risk. It should be a warning that you need to carefully consider your airplane's capabilities as the DA increases. By reducing aircraft weight, you can partially compensate for loss of engine power, as discussed next.

Power Loading and Weight Reduction

One way to estimate how much weight to remove is to use the power-to-weight ratio (power loading) at sea level and remove enough weight at the new DA to get the same power loading. Standard day power loading is defined as gross weight (GW) divided by HP. Many POHs list power loading, and it is easy to calculate. Below is an example from Williams (1986) using a 300 HP Cessna 185:

Example:

$$\text{Power loading} = \frac{3,000 \text{ lb}}{300 \text{ HP}} = 11 \text{ lb/HP}$$

The new GW needed to maintain the original power-to-weight ratio is:

Actual HP × power loading = new GW

At 8,000 feet DA:

220 HP × 11 lb/HP = 2,420 lb new GW to maintain the sea-level power loading

That means on a summer day at 8,000 feet DA, you would have to reduce the load by *580 pounds* to get the same power loading. Basically, it is not possible to obtain sea-level performance, no matter how much weight is removed from the airplane.

Approximating performance based on conditions you are familiar with is another way to use power loading. If you normally operate at a 3,000-foot elevation airport and think the performance there is adequate, simply calculate the power loading using 3,000-feet MSL PA and standard temperature and use that figure for comparison.

Power loading is only part of the equation, since the airfoils lose efficiency, and the real question is how much overall performance will be degraded. Specific values can be calculated from your POH or owner's manual, and there is a simple rule of thumb:

> *Reduce weight by the following percentages to recover lost performance.*
>
> *For each 1,000-foot variation from the reference altitude, reduce GW by:*
>
> 3.0%   *fixed-pitch propeller airplanes*
> 2.85%   *constant-speed propeller airplanes*
> 2.3%   *constant-speed/turbocharged propeller airplanes*

The rule gives figures very close to those in most GA aircraft performance charts and can be used to estimate takeoff and climb performance.

The CG should always remain within limits, but its position affects performance. With a forward CG, the airplane will be more stable and the stall speed (and therefore, approach speed) will be higher. Takeoff and landing rolls will be longer with a forward CG. Stall speed will be lower and the airplane will be less stable (more maneuverable) with a rearward CG. Takeoff and landing rolls will be shorter with a rearward CG because approaches can be flown at slower speeds.

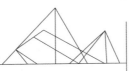

Amy's Axiom

Wait! Weight!
When DA goes up, wait for cooler weather or take the weight out. Relax, and make more than one trip.

In summary, you have control over how you load your airplane and the time of day you fly. Reducing weight and/or flying in cooler temperatures will increase performance. You may choose to fly with a given load and accept lost performance. The manufacturer's performance charts should always be your starting point. However, for older airplanes without detailed performance charts, or airplanes that have been modified, you can make your own charts by flying the airplane at different weights, CG positions, and altitudes and recording actual performance. Plan your flights during cooler mornings or evenings rather than the middle of the day, or make multiple trips with lighter loads.

Safety should always be the primary concern. As described by Claus (2018), the goal when choosing a high-performance aircraft is to keep it light. Claus quoted F. Atlee Dodge, the Alaskan aviation and modification guru: "It's not so much what mod you put on; it's what you take off." And anything that can add horsepower without gaining weight is also a big advantage.

Takeoff Performance

Takeoff and departure from high elevation and backcountry airstrips should be considered the most critical phases of the flight (Chapter 6). Many airplanes can easily be landed on a short mountain strip at high DA yet not be able to take off with the same weight under the same conditions. Hoover wrote:

> Typical summer afternoon Density Altitude (DA) can easily exceed 10,000 feet at many mountain strips, and the associated decrease in airplane performance is enormous. The takeoff ground roll at high DA is significantly increased due to reduced engine power, loss of propeller efficiency, and higher groundspeeds. Grass, dirt, sand, and gravel can greatly lengthen the takeoff roll. Climb performance is also drastically reduced. (Hoover, 2001)

Because TAS increases 2% per 1,000 feet increase in DA, ground speed also increases by the same amount—assuming wheel friction, gradient, wind, and other variables are held constant. As the airplane accelerates to the correct **indicated airspeed (IAS)** for takeoff, the faster ground speed equates to a longer ground roll. Additionally, it is accelerating with reduced power and thrust compared to sea level, as just discussed. Thus, you need to figure your takeoff performance before you decide to land. You might not be able to calculate takeoff performance ahead of time using the POH or charts, since you may not know the future temperature at your destination. One option is to estimate performance for several different temperatures.

There are some simple estimates to help you anticipate lost performance and whether or not you will be able to depart safely. You can use the rule of thumb in the previous section, or another simple rule of thumb.

> *Each 1% increase in GW will increase takeoff distance about 2%.*

Example: A Cessna 182 weighing 2,200 lb

Takeoff distance   = 1,250 ft

Add 10%   = 220 lb (equal to a 180-lb passenger + 40 lb of gear)

The takeoff distance must be increased by 20% (10 × 2)

New takeoff distance = 1,500 feet

This rule of thumb could be used to decide whether or not to take off with an extra passenger and gear. For example, on a 2,500-foot-long airstrip, a 1,250-foot takeoff roll would use up half the airstrip. You might consider that sufficient, depending on what obstacles you have to clear and the terrain past the departure end, given adequate distance to abort the takeoff. With a ground roll of 1,500 feet, how comfortable will you be using two-thirds of the airstrip before the airplane reaches flying speed? Will that still leave you with a safe abort plan? What other choices exist?

One option is to make more trips with partial loads. You can shuttle gear and passengers to a longer strip or one at a lower elevation and then take off with the full load from there. Although it will take more fuel and time, it can help eliminate the risk of departing with a full load and finding out too late you do not have adequate performance.

At a given aircraft weight, you can use the following rule of thumb to approximate the impact of increased DA on takeoff performance.

> *At a given gross weight, each 1,000-foot increase in DA will cause the following increase in takeoff distance:*
>
> | | |
> |---|---|
> | *Fixed-pitch propeller* | *8.5% increase* |
> | *Constant-speed propeller* | *8.0% increase* |
> | *Constant-speed/turbocharged propeller* | *7.0% increase* |

Example: A Cessna TU206 weighing 3,400 lb

Takeoff distance at 4,000 feet DA = 1,400 feet

Takeoff distance at 6,000 feet DA = 1,400 + (1,400 × 0.14)

$$= 1,400 + 196 = 1,596 \text{ feet}$$

Determining takeoff performance with all the variables involved can be a daunting task. Even after doing twenty minutes of calculations, the conditions can change, or that nasty tailwind gust can come out of nowhere at just the wrong time. Most professional mountain pilots I know, including me, have had more than one instance where things did not go as well as planned on departure. It may be because of not waiting that extra half hour for the wind to completely calm down, or due to that tailwind gust right at liftoff—it is a miscalculation, not enough conservatism for the unexpected, or just not quite enough experience or judgment for the situation.

Experienced backcountry pilots are often more concerned about the takeoff from an airstrip than the landing, particularly with a heavy load. For commercial operators, many flights consist of dropping off a load and returning empty, and the airplane's performance is dependable. But on departures with a heavy airplane, everything changes. A few degrees change in temperature, a wet spot on the surface, a little breeze, or a few extra pounds all change the liftoff point and the ensuing climb.

One such instance was a miscalculation on the part of my chief pilot (see Williams, 2015). Luckily, the airplane was a Twin Otter, with a certificated gross weight in the United States of 12,500 pounds. However, the Twin Otter is flown at heavier weights in other countries and has been ferried as heavy as 17,500 pounds. The

For those averse to calculations, a different method is to gather information empirically. Load your airplane the way you want to operate it, then do some takeoffs from an airstrip where you have known distance markers, such as trees or rocks you have paced off. Choose a marker a third or half-way down an airstrip, do some takeoffs, and record where the airplane lifted off relative to it. Even better, have a passenger or someone on the ground mark your spot. This will give you a realistic estimate based on the elevation, temperature, and surface as well as the piloting technique used.

The practice of doing takeoffs at lower altitudes with partial power to simulate high DA should be approached with caution because it does not accurately replicate performance at altitude. The technique only demonstrates performance with reduced power at a given elevation, ambient temperature, and pressure. It does not simulate the loss of aerodynamic lift or thrust on the airfoils (e.g., wings, tail surfaces, and propeller). Additionally, the higher TAS (and GS) is not simulated. On a sea level standard day, assuming little or no instrument errors, IAS = CAS = TAS, so an airplane that flies at 60 knots will be traveling roughly 60 knots over the ground, regardless of how much power is used. At 8,000 feet density altitude, the takeoff at 60 knots IAS would be roughly 70 knots TAS. The corresponding 70 knot ground speed means the airplane would need more distance for its takeoff

pilot was counting bags of cement to fly into the company lodge, and as we loaded, he lost count. It was my leg to fly, and he gave me some tips on the use of flaps as I climbed out, since he could tell we were heavy. I noticed a bit of a frown on his face. As we unloaded, I counted the sacks and realized we had been more than 1,000 pounds over gross weight!

Another story involved a takeoff from a backcountry ranch airstrip with a load of hunters, gear, and game. I had flown similar loads there before, but this one was probably heavier by several pounds (there were no scales available). My ground roll was longer than normal, and the airplane went through a wet bog just at liftoff, which lowered the climb out over the trees at the end and etched one of those "unforgettable" flight experiences into my brain.

These stories are not intended to demean the importance of calculations. Those are the pilot-in-command's duty and responsibility. These stories correlate to human factors, human error, and to the importance of judgment, experience, and the development of a critical "sixth sense" that should be a part of every takeoff calculation. If it doesn't feel right, it probably isn't. Err on the side of conservatism and learn from your own mistakes as well as other's.

roll. Visual cues could be simulated by taking off with a tailwind, but doing so introduces the hazards discussed in Chapter 6. The airplane at 60 knots would have to take off with a 10-knot tailwind to simulate the increased ground speed.

By knowing the effects of DA and weight on takeoff performance, you can better decide how to load (or unload) your airplane, when to fly (or not), and how to minimize potential risk to you and your passengers.

Climb Performance

Many backcountry airstrips in the mountains and canyons are surrounded by trees, obstacles, and rising terrain. It is often necessary to maneuver immediately after departure to avoid obstacles or to follow a river or canyon during climb-out. Since you may already be at a high DA, getting maximum climb performance is critical. Pilots new to high-altitude flying are often alarmed by the enormous reduction in climb performance. A common mistake is attempting to increase climb by pulling back on the yoke or stick to increase the pitch attitude. Pitching up will increase drag and reduce airspeed and possibly cause a departure stall. You will need to use the correct IAS for the altitude and operating conditions. See Chapter 6 for discussion of takeoff and climb techniques.

Effects of Weight and DA on Climb Performance

A heavier airplane must fly at a higher **angle of attack (AOA)** to maintain altitude and airspeed. Higher AOA increases induced drag. Therefore, more thrust is required, which means less excess thrust is available for climbing, and the plane will not be able to climb as steeply. The plane's increased drag also means more power is needed to provide the required thrust, which reduces available power and affects rate of climb. The increased weight not only reduces the maximum rate of climb, it increases the speed at which maximum climb is achieved.

With regards to the effects of DA on performance, "An increase in altitude also increases the power required and decreases the power available. Therefore, the climb performance of an aircraft diminishes with altitude" (FAA, 2016d).

Excess Thrust and Climb Performance

To understand the effects of weight and DA on climb performance, it may help to review the relationship of aerodynamic forces during a climb. An airplane does not climb because of excess lift (Figure 8-3). In a steady speed, unaccelerated climb, aerodynamic forces are in equilibrium; upward forces are equal and opposite to downward forces, and forward forces are equal and opposite to rearward forces. Lift produced by the wing (perpendicular to flight path) is less than the downward force of weight, since the vertical component of thrust helps counteract some of the weight. A component of weight acts rearward and contributes to total drag. That means at any given airspeed, the airplane climbs because it has excess thrust, produced by the engine and propeller. As the FAA stated:

> The thrust required for a stabilized climb equals drag plus a percentage of weight dependent on the angle of climb. For example, a 10° climb would require thrust to equal drag plus 17 percent of weight. To climb straight up would require thrust to equal all of weight and drag. Therefore, the angle of climb for climb performance is dependent on the amount of excess thrust available to overcome a portion of weight. Note that aircraft are able to sustain a climb due to excess thrust. When the excess thrust is gone, the aircraft is no longer able to climb. At this point, the aircraft has reached its "absolute ceiling." (FAA, 2016d)

The terms "power" and "thrust" are sometimes used interchangeably, but they are not the same. **Thrust** is a force exerted on an object and is independent of the amount of time it takes to exert that force. **Work** is the amount of distance the force can move the object, and **power** measures the rate at which work is done. Think of power as the motion the thrust force creates over a period of time. The distinction is important to understand the relationship between different climb speeds and how they are affected by changes in DA and weight, as discussed next. The FAA notes "Since weight, altitude and configuration changes affect excess thrust and power, they also affect climb performance. Climb performance is directly dependent upon the ability to produce either excess thrust or excess power" (FAA, 2016d).

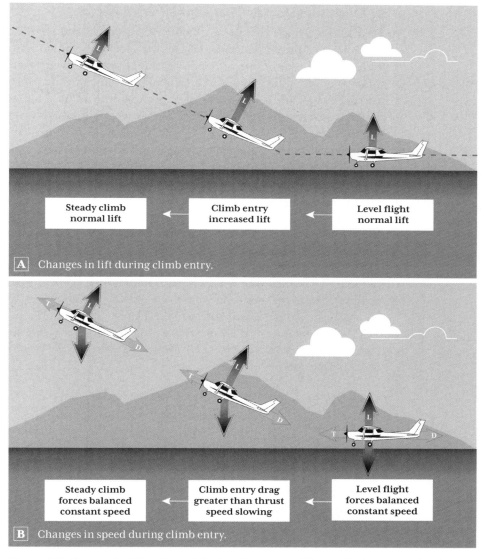

A. Changes in lift during climb entry.

| Steady climb normal lift | ← | Climb entry increased lift | ← | Level flight normal lift |

B. Changes in speed during climb entry.

| Steady climb forces balanced constant speed | ← | Climb entry drag greater than thrust speed slowing | ← | Level flight forces balanced constant speed |

Figure 8-3. Changes in lift and speed during climb entry. When a climb is entered without increasing power, raising the airplane's nose momentarily increases the angle of attack. Lift is then momentarily greater than weight and starts the aircraft climbing. After the flight path is stabilized in the climb, the angle of attack and lift revert to the level flight values. As the flight path is inclined upward, a component of weight acts in the same direction as total drag, thereby increasing the total effective drag. Thus, the rearward acting forces exceed forward forces, and the airspeed decreases. The reduced airspeed gradually results in a corresponding decrease in drag until the total drag (including the component of weight acting in the same direction) equals thrust, and forces are again balanced. *(FAA [2016d])*

Best Angle and Best Rate of Climb Performance

Angle of climb is measured as the amount of altitude gained relative to distance traveled. **Best angle of climb speed (V_X)** is the speed that provides maximum altitude gain with minimum horizontal distance traveled over the ground.

Rate of climb is the amount of time it takes to gain altitude, and **best rate of climb speed (V_Y)** is the speed that provides maximum altitude gain in a given time period. It is also the speed that corresponds to the maximum lift-to-drag ratio.

After takeoff, you will select a pitch attitude for the proper IAS to maximize your climb performance and also provide a safe margin of excess speed should you encounter downdrafts or wind shear (see Chapter 6). Whether you use V_X, V_Y, or a cruise climb will depend on the individual situation and conditions. The speeds for V_X and V_Y vary with altitude (Figure 6-2). As you fly at higher DA, V_X and V_Y may be almost the same speed, and your primary concerns will be determining whether you can clear an obstacle, how to maximize your rate of climb, and compensating for wind shear or turbulence.

The airplane manufacturer may not provide climb performance charts for higher altitudes, which should be a warning about high DA operations. Many charts give climb data at only one or two weights, so you will need to extrapolate based on the airplane's weight and the DA. The previous section showed how to find HP available for a given DA. Based on your airplane's sea level climb rate, you can calculate the amount of excess HP available at DA, and the resulting rate of climb, using the following formula.

$$\frac{Excess\ HP \times 33,000}{Aircraft\ weight} = Rate\ of\ climb\ in\ fpm$$

Example: A Cessna 182

GW	= 2,950 lb
Sea level rated HP	= 230 HP
Rate of climb at sea level	= 1,010 fpm (from POH)

First, solve the equation for excess HP:

$$\frac{Rate\ of\ climb \times aircraft\ weight}{33,000} = Excess\ HP$$

$$\frac{1,010 \times 2,950}{33,000} = 90\ HP\ (excess\ HP\ at\ sea\ level\ and\ V_Y\ airspeed)$$

The 90 HP (39% of total HP) is the excess power available for climb at sea level, which means it will take 230 HP − 90 HP = 140 HP for the plane to fly level at V_Y.

To find excess HP and resulting rate of climb for a given altitude, determine the HP lost using the following rule of thumb:

> A normally aspirated engine loses approximately 3% HP per 1,000-foot increase in density altitude (DA)

Example: the Cessna 182 at 8,000 feet DA:

HP lost = 230 × 0.24 = 55.2 HP

and

HP available = 230 − 55.2 = 174.8 HP

Since 140 HP is required to fly level at V_Y, then at 8,000 feet DA:

Excess HP for climb = HP available − HP required = 174.8 HP − 140 HP = 34.8 HP

and

$$\frac{34.8 \text{ HP} \times 33,000}{2,950 \text{ lb}} = 389 \text{ fpm at 8,000 feet DA}$$

That is more than a 60% reduction in climb rate, which is significant.

A slightly different method is presented by Imeson (2005) as shown in Figure 8-4.

To Calculate Rate of Climb at DA

Fixed-Pitch Propeller
Reduce the sea-level rate of climb 7 percent for each 1,000 feet density altitude up to 8,500 feet and 8 percent for each 1,000 feet above 8,500 feet.

Constant-Speed Propeller
Reduce the rate of climb 6 percent for each 1,000 feet density altitude up to 8,500 feet and 8 percent for each 1,000 feet above 8,500 feet.

Figure 8-4. Percentage decrease in rate of climb with increase in density altitude. *(Imeson, 2005)*

Example: Using the Cessna 182 at 8,000 feet DA:

Rate of climb at GW	= 1,010 fpm
Reduction (for constant-speed propeller)	= 8 × 0.06
	= 48% reduction = 525 fpm at 8,000 feet DA

Although the two methods give different results, the point is that climb rate is drastically reduced as DA increases. Rules of thumb are a way to help you think more critically about how weight and DA affect your airplane's performance but are not a substitute for thorough preflight planning and use of your aircraft performance charts.

On July 22, 1991, I lived in Salmon, Idaho, and had the day off, so I took my 90 HP Cessna 120 up the river to Stanley (elevation 6,403 feet MSL) for some hiking, swimming, and relaxing with friends. It was a hot summer day, and I waited until after 8:00 p.m. to depart from Stanley for the return trip. On the way home, I noticed a small forest fire up one of the canyons just south of Salmon, so I reported it to the Forest Service. The dispatcher said they knew about the fire because it had been started earlier that day by a plane crash. Tragically, all 4 occupants were killed after the airplane entered a box canyon south of the airport and could not out-climb the terrain (see figure at right).

The person from the fixed-base operator who refueled the accident airplane said there were four friends from the west coast on a pleasure trip, and this was a refueling stop before they headed on to Idaho Falls, 125 NM to the southeast. He said they topped off the fuel tanks. As shown in the accident report on the next page, the pilot attempted to turn back, but the airplane was still angled toward rising terrain when it crashed.

Several years later, I was playing around with Porter's (1986) rules of thumb calculations while writing the training manual for our company's mountain/canyon flying seminars, and I thought about the Salmon accident. I wondered how well the airplane might have been climbing on that fateful day. I researched the historical temperature data, which showed it was 92°F at noon in Salmon (the accident occurred at approximately 12:30 p.m.). Using a standard lapse rate, I calculated temperature at the altitude of the crash (5,600 feet) to be about 87°F. Based on that, the DA was approx-

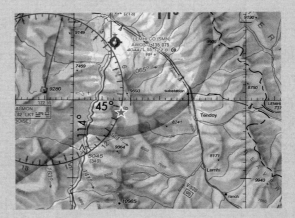

Location of the crash site (red star) in a box canyon south of the Salmon airport.

imately 8,600 feet. Applying Porter's rule of thumb for HP lost, the engine would have been producing about 70% of maximum power.

The Cardinal's IO-360 engine produces sea level rated 200 HP and a published rate of climb of 925 fpm. I calculated an excess of only about 18 HP available for climb at 8,600 feet DA, which corresponds to about a 200 fpm rate of climb. It is possible the pilot was not even getting that climb rate, since it assumes the mixture was leaned, the airplane was not over gross weight, the pilot maintained the correct airspeed, and there were no excess loads imposed during maneuvering.

As noted in the accident report, the mixture was full forward and the airplane was in a turn when it crashed, so it is possible the pilot had little or no climb performance.

In 1991 it was unlikely the pilot would have been using GPS, and although **LORAN** units were available, there were large gaps in coverage over the central Idaho area. It is unknown what type of navigation the pilot was using, but had he followed the highway to Idaho Falls, just one valley to the east (see the road through the town of Tendoy in the figure), they would probably have survived. The highest point on the highway is lower than the elevation of the accident site. Other options would have been to wait until the temperature dropped and depart later in the evening or to reduce the airplane's weight (possibly with a lighter fuel load).

The NTSB stated the probable cause to be "improper inflight planning and decision by the pilot..." but it also can be attributed to poor preflight planning. If the pilot questioned any of the local pilots or operators, they most assuredly would have advised following the highway to Idaho Falls.

National Transportation Safety Board
Aviation Accident Final Report

Location:	SALMON, ID	Accident Number:	SEA91FA183
Date & Time:	07/22/1991, 1230 MDT	Registration:	N1573H
Aircraft:	CESSNA 177RG	Aircraft Damage:	Destroyed
Defining Event:		Injuries:	4 Fatal
Flight Conducted Under:	Part 91: General Aviation - Personal		

Analysis

THE PILOT DEPARTED SOUTHBOUND FROM THE SALMON, IDAHO AIRPORT AFTER A REFUELING STOP. A WITNESS SAW THE AIRCRAFT ENTER A CANYON SOUTH OF THE AIRPORT AT LOW ALTITUDE. SUBSEQUENTLY, IT COLLIDED WITH THE EAST SIDE OF THE CANYON AFTER TURNING BACK TOWARD A NORTHERLY DIRECTION. DURING INITIAL IMPACT, THE RIGHT WINGTIP & NOSE OF THE AIRCRAFT COLLIDED WITH A 30 TO 35 DEG RISING SLOPE. THERE WAS EVIDENCE THE AIRCRAFT WAS STILL ANGLED TOWARD RISING TERRAIN WHEN THE ACCIDENT OCCURRED. THE ACCIDENT OCCURRED AT AN ELEVATION OF ABOUT 5600 FT, ABOUT 11 MI SOUTH OF THE AIRPORT. LEADING EDGE GOUGES & CHORDWISE SCRATCHES WERE NOTED ON THE PROPELLER BLADES. THE THROTTLE, MIXTURE & PROPELLER CONTROLS WERE FOUND IN THE FULL FORWARD POSITION.

Probable Cause and Findings

The National Transportation Safety Board determines the probable cause(s) of this accident to be: IMPROPER INFLIGHT PLANNING AND DECISION BY THE PILOT, AND HIS FAILURE TO MAINTAIN SUFFICIENT ALTITUDE AND CLEARANCE FROM MOUNTAINOUS/HILLY TERRAIN.

Findings

Occurrence #1: IN FLIGHT COLLISION WITH TERRAIN/WATER
Phase of Operation: MANEUVERING - TURN TO REVERSE DIRECTION

Findings
1. (C) IN-FLIGHT PLANNING/DECISION - IMPROPER - PILOT IN COMMAND
2. (F) TERRAIN CONDITION - MOUNTAINOUS/HILLY
3. (C) PROPER ALTITUDE - NOT MAINTAINED - PILOT IN COMMAND

NTSB report for the accident that occurred on July 22, 1991, near Salmon, Idaho, in which a Cessna 177RG Cardinal crashed in a box canyon.

Landing Performance

As discussed in Chapter 5, use the same IAS for landing with a given airplane weight, regardless of the DA. As your airplane gets heavier, the stall speed increases, and therefore the landing speed will increase. The effects of DA and weight on landing performance differ from takeoffs because reduced engine power and thrust are not factors. For landing, you only need to consider the distance it will take to stop the airplane traveling at a given speed in the landing configuration. Brake effectiveness does not change with density altitude and is the same whether your airplane is fixed-pitch, constant-speed, or turbocharged. However, when landing with a given IAS, the TAS and GS will be faster, so brakes will need to stop the same mass traveling at higher speed. Several rules of thumb below show how weight and DA affect the landing roll distance.

1. *Each 2% change in GW will cause about a 1% change in landing airspeed.*

2. *A 1% change in landing airspeed will cause about a 2% change in landing distance.*

3. *Each 1% change in GW will cause about a 1% change in landing distance.*

4. *A 1,000-foot change in DA will cause a 2% change in TAS (and therefore GS).*

Close inspection shows that reducing or increasing weight directly affects landing distance. Also, the increased GS at high DA causes a longer landing roll, although the approach and landing should be flown at the same IAS as at lower altitude.

To estimate change in landing distance with change in weight, all other factors held constant, use rule number 3 above.

> *Example:* Cessna 182 weighing 2,300 lb
> Landing distance = 1,200 feet
> Add 10% (230 lb) (a 180-lb passenger and 50 lb cargo)
> New landing distance (1,200 × 10%) = 1,320 feet

If you decide not to change your aircraft weight, the following rule of thumb shows how you can estimate the landing distance.

Each 1,000-foot increase in DA will increase landing distance about 4%.

In summary, how you load the airplane affects landing distance. Other factors, such as surface, gradient, wind, and the condition of your tires and brakes, are discussed in Chapters 1 and 5.

Leaning the Mixture

Always refer to the engine or aircraft operating manual regarding mixture settings. Most manuals recommend leaning normally aspirated engines above DA anywhere between 3,000 and 5,000 feet to obtain the proper fuel/air mixture for optimum power. You can use an **exhaust gas temperature (EGT)** gauge to lean the mixture during flight. The general recommendation is to find the peak EGT and enrich the mixture as specified by the manufacturer, which varies between 50–150 degrees rich of peak. Multi-cylinder engine monitors such as described in Chapter 1 usually have a "lean-find" feature you can use to lean to the hottest cylinder. Lean of peak operations are not discussed here.

If you have no EGT, lean the mixture until the engine begins to run rough, then set it slightly richer. On many GA planes, you can use the "calibrated finger method"—lean the mixture until the engine runs rough, then push the mixture control in about one to two finger widths. Remember to enrichen the mixture slightly every 1,000 feet or so as you descend. Before final approach, make sure the mixture is leaned for the DA at your destination to ensure the engine functions properly during power changes on approach, or in case you need to abort the landing and execute an immediate climb. There have been accidents at high-altitude airports because the pilot attempted a go-around with the mixture set at full rich for landing, so add this to your pre-landing checklist, as discussed in Chapter 5.

The DA can be more than 5,000 feet on the ground at higher altitude airstrips. That means you will have to lean the mixture for taxi as well as takeoff, climb, cruise, approach and landing. Lean the mixture immediately after engine start at high DA to avoid running a too-rich mixture during ground operations. A mixture that is too rich for the conditions can foul spark plugs, cause valves to stick, and increase valve guide wear. According to Pope:

> The way to prevent fouling during taxi is to aggressively lean your engine while on the ground by following the specific procedure in your POH or, failing that, by pulling the mixture control slowly back until the engine begins running rough and then enriching it slightly. (Pope, 2015)

Leaning for Takeoff

The most common mistake pilots new to high-altitude operations make is improperly setting the mixture during takeoff and climb. You must lean the mixture to obtain maximum takeoff power. The mixture will need to be continuously adjusted during climb and set for cruise once you have leveled off. In hot weather, or during long climbs, you may need to richen the mixture to keep the cylinder heads from overheating or perform a "step-climb" by leveling off periodically to keep the cylinders cooled.

Machado (2017) described why you must lean for takeoff at altitudes above approximately 4,000 feet elevation. From sea level up to approximately 4,000 feet, most airplane engines can produce 75% or more of their maximum rated power. According to Machado, engines produce a lot of heat with power settings at or above 75%, and the fuel enrichment valve opens during the last 1/5 of the throttle travel as full throttle is applied, such as during takeoff and climb. This adds approximately 15% more fuel than is needed for combustion to help cool the engine. However, at higher DA, the engine will not be able to produce more than 75% power, so fuel enrichment is not only unnecessary but will produce an excessively rich mixture at full throttle and drastically decrease engine performance.

The purpose of leaning the mixture for takeoff is to obtain the maximum power output for the engine without producing detonation. Since detonation is not likely if the engine is producing less than 75% power, you should generally lean at DA above 4,000 feet. Machado gives the following rule of thumb for knowing how to lean.

> **Rod's Rule:**
> *Don't lean the mixture when the engine will develop 75% or more power.*

You can reference the operating manual to determine what the power output of the engine should be for a given DA, or you can estimate it based on the rule of thumb for loss of power with DA increase.

You may be able to do a full-power run-up to lean the mixture, but it is not recommended at unimproved strips where there is the hazard of sucking dirt and debris into the propeller or throwing it onto the airplane's fuselage and tail surfaces. Since the engine will not produce full power during a static run-up, you might need to make small adjustments during the takeoff roll to obtain the correct mixture for maximum power. However, if doing so produces distractions that could cause loss of control on a narrow or short airstrip, it is best to leave the mixture control alone during the takeoff roll.

For fixed-pitch propeller airplanes, lean the mixture until the engine begins to run rough, then enrich it slightly for best power. For constant-speed propeller aircraft, Machado (2017) gives four different methods:

1. Least precise: Do a full throttle run-up and lean the mixture based on sound and make small adjustments during climb-out to produce maximum power by the sound of the engine.

2. Lean for maximum EGT on the hottest cylinder on a multi-cylinder engine monitor, then increase the mixture by 75–125 degrees rich for best power.

3. If the engine has a fuel flow gauge, lean to the specified fuel flow for the DA.

4. Least favorite: Lean for takeoff during takeoff (for the reasons just described).

For turbocharged engines, set the mixture for recommended takeoff fuel flow and monitor during takeoff to avoid over-boosting. This usually happens on the first takeoff of the day as the turbocharger is spooling up. Set the fuel flow to the manufacturer's recommendations during climb and cruise.

Many high-altitude accident reports indicate the aircraft mixture control was not leaned for maximum power, and often it is found in the "full forward" position. Engine temperatures, fuel flow, and mixture settings should be constantly monitored and adjusted to increase engine performance and preserve the life of your engine. Multi-cylinder engine monitors and fuel flow meters are a good investment to help with proper engine and fuel management, but even a simple analog EGT gauge is sufficient to help develop proper leaning techniques.

Accident Scenario

On a hot summer afternoon in 2012, a Stinson 108 departed from Bruce Meadows airstrip, elevation 6,370 feet, and crashed about a mile and a half off the departure end of the airstrip (Figure 8-5).

National Transportation Safety Board
Aviation Accident Final Report

Location:	Stanley, ID	Accident Number:	WPR12LA283
Date & Time:	06/30/2012, 1415 MDT	Registration:	N773C
Aircraft:	STINSON 108	Aircraft Damage:	Substantial
Defining Event:	Loss of lift	Injuries:	1 Serious, 3 Minor
Flight Conducted Under:	Part 91: General Aviation - Personal		

Analysis

Before taking off from the 5,000-foot turf-dirt airstrip located at an altitude of 6,370 feet mean sea level, the pilot checked his performance charts and calculated that the density altitude was about 9,200 feet; this was 3,200 feet above the 6,000-foot maximum altitude listed in the takeoff performance charts. He also noted that at the time of departure, the wind was from 30 degrees at 10 knots, with gusts to 20 knots, which was close to a nearly direct tailwind for the takeoff from runway 23. The pilot indicated that the airplane was within 86 pounds of its maximum gross takeoff weight. When the airplane was about three-quarters of the way down the runway during the takeoff roll and not yet airborne, the pilot was about to abort the takeoff, but a gust of wind lifted the airplane in the air. The pilot thought the airplane would remain airborne, but when he could not get the airplane to climb as expected, he attempted to locate an open field to land in. However, the airplane subsequently encountered a downdraft, collided with a stand of trees, and came to rest inverted about 1.64 nautical miles from the departure end of the runway. A postaccident examination of the airplane and engine revealed no mechanical malfunctions or failures that would have precluded normal operation.

Probable Cause and Findings

The National Transportation Safety Board determines the probable cause(s) of this accident to be:
The pilot's inadequate preflight planning and decision to takeoff at a density altitude outside of the airplane's takeoff performance envelope, with a tailwind, and near the airplane's maximum gross weight, which resulted in the airplane's inability to climb and clear trees.

Findings

Aircraft	Climb capability - Capability exceeded (Cause)
Personnel Issues	Decision making/judgment - Pilot (Cause)
	Performance calculations - Pilot (Cause)
Environmental Issues	High density altitude - Effect on operation (Cause)
	Tailwind - Effect on operation
	Gusts - Effect on operation
	Tree(s) - Not specified

Figure 8-5. NTSB analysis and findings for an aircraft accident related to high DA operations. *(NTSB, 2013)*

Two separate videos were recorded during the accident flight by passengers and were made public on the website YouTube (see link at www.asa2fly.com/reader/mountain).

The NTSB cited several causes, including pilot judgment and decision making, performance calculations, climb capability exceeded, and high DA (Figure 8-5). Closer analysis of the accident videos reveals several interesting findings related to the aircraft, the environment, and the pilot's decision-making.

Analysis of the video taken by the right front seat passenger shows the following sequence (airstrip locations are shown in Figure 8-6):

Video time stamp	Event
0:13	Mixture control full forward
0:22	Throttle full forward and takeoff roll begins
0:49	Plane lifted off into ground effect
0:53	Plane passed the 1/3 distance marker
0:56 to 1:01	Windsock visible showing a half-sock left quartering headwind
1:02	Plane touched down again
1:13	Plane pitched up and lifted off again (just past the 2/3 distance marker)
1:31	Plane passed the end of the airstrip
2:31	Plane crossed tree-line from open meadow to forest (pitch increased)
2:35	Plane began to sink
2:56	Plane impacted trees in a nose-high attitude

Based on the position of the airplane at various locations during the takeoff roll, it would have been possible to abort the takeoff. When the plane touched down on the ground again at approximately midfield, that would have been the appropriate time to abort. However, after the second time it lifted off just past the 2/3 distance marker (with approximately 1,650 feet remaining), there was still room to land again. Extrapolating for a DA of 9,200 feet from the Stinson operating manual, it should have been able to land and stop in approximately 1,400 feet. This scenario exemplifies the importance of having an abort plan, including an identifiable abort point for every takeoff (Chapter 6).

The pilot stated in the NTSB report that there was a tailwind for takeoff. However, the windsock is visible in the video for approximately 20 seconds, and for at least 5 seconds shows a steady left-quartering headwind. It is possible the wind could have been gusting from several directions, so that a tailwind at the beginning of the takeoff roll would have sheared to a headwind later during the takeoff. Any time there are gusting conditions, it is important to study the wind several minutes prior to takeoff to observe the wind patterns and figure out how

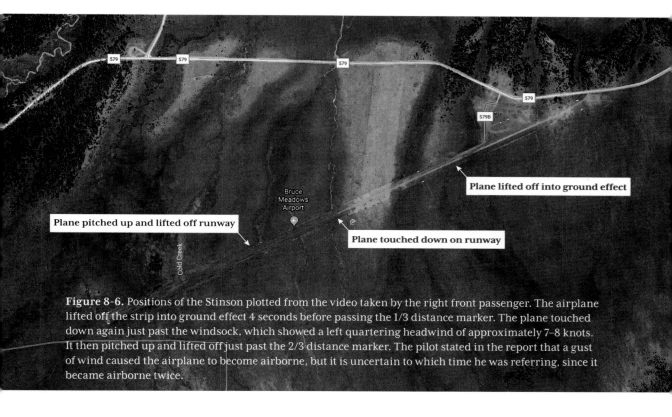

Figure 8-6. Positions of the Stinson plotted from the video taken by the right front passenger. The airplane lifted off the strip into ground effect 4 seconds before passing the 1/3 distance marker. The plane touched down again just past the windsock, which showed a left quartering headwind of approximately 7–8 knots. It then pitched up and lifted off just past the 2/3 distance marker. The pilot stated in the report that a gust of wind caused the airplane to become airborne, but it is uncertain to which time he was referring, since it became airborne twice.

the wind gusts might affect your takeoff. Also, pilots should monitor the windsock during the takeoff roll.

Video from the right rear seat passenger shows the wing at high angles of attack during the last 28 seconds before the plane impacted trees. The angle between a line drawn perpendicular to the trees (assuming the trees stand vertically) and the bottom of the wing is approximately 20° in the video at a point 28 seconds before the airplane struck trees. During those 28 seconds, the pitch attitude changed several times and the right wing dipped down and to the right three times before the plane hit the trees. During the last few seconds before impact the wing angle increased.

Stinson 108-3 POH charts do not list performance figures for the DA reported by the pilot (9,200 feet). However, extrapolating from the charts, the takeoff distance on a hard surface with no wind would have been between 3,250 and 3,575 feet, depending on the flap setting and the liftoff speed. The video shows the airplane lifting off (for the second time) at the 2/3 marker of the 5,000-foot long airstrip, 12 seconds after passing the windsock. The windsock showed a left quartering headwind at half sock, which would equate to approximately 7–8 knots on a standard 15 knot windsock. When the airplane lifted off the second time, there was approximately 1/3 of the 5,000 feet remaining.

The Stinson operating manual for the aircraft does not list rate of climb for the DA reported by the pilot, but extrapolating from the charts gives figures between 115–140 fpm, depending on the position of flaps and the airspeed maintained by the pilot.

Performance figures from the Stinson operating manual indicate that during the approximately 1.5 minutes from the time the airplane departed until it impacted trees, it should have been able to climb about 175 feet. The terrain elevation rises gradually toward the southwest in the direction the airplane was climbing.

At the beginning of the video the panel is visible, showing the mixture control in the full forward position. The NTSB final report notes that the on-site inspector "provided the IIC with documentation relative to the airplane's Franklin, model 6A4-165-B3 engine, which was equipped with a Marvel Schebler, model MA-4-5 carburetor. With respect to USE OF MIXTURE CONTROL IN FLIGHT, the information revealed, 'When adjusting the mixture control for altitudes higher than 3,000 feet, move the [mixture] control in and out slowly, with the throttle at cruising position until the highest RPM is attained'" (NTSB, 2013).

Based on the inspector's findings, the engine may not have been operating with the optimum mixture setting, which would have reduced performance, thus contributing to further loss of climb capability.

The ultimate cause, as stated by the NTSB, was the pilot's decision to takeoff at a high DA. However, even after the takeoff commenced, there were opportunities to abort and stop the airplane. It was almost a minute from the time the takeoff started until the airplane finally lifted off, even after settling back to the ground before doing so. The example from this accident enforces the importance of making and following through with a plan for every takeoff. Pilots should choose an abort point ahead of time, preferably by walking the airstrip, and then resolve to stop the takeoff if not airborne by the abort point.

Review Questions and Exercises

Answers to review questions are provided in Appendix B.

Circle the correct answer:

1. In any flight condition, a heavier airplane must fly at a lower angle of attack (AOA) to maintain altitude and airspeed. (**True / False**)

2. The purpose of leaning the mixture for takeoff is to obtain the maximum power output for the engine without producing detonation. (**True / False**)

3. Loss of propeller efficiency has a drastic effect on performance as density altitude increases. (**True / False**)

4. The takeoff roll will be shorter with the airplane loaded to a forward CG. (**True / False**)

hypoxia." **Hypoxia** and its associated signs and symptoms are a major risk factor in the physiological deficient zone (Figure 9-1).

Signs	Symptoms
Rapid breathing	Fatigue
Cyanosis (blue skin)	Nausea
Poor coordination	Headache
Decreased reaction time	Euphoria
Lethargy	Impaired vision
Impaired judgment	Disorientation or confusion
Loss of consciousness	Lightheaded or dizzy sensation
	Tingling in fingers and toes
	Numbness
	Limp muscles
	Tunnel vision

Figure 9-1. Signs and symptoms of hypoxia. These can vary from minor to life-threatening. Pilots should vigilantly watch for signs in their passengers and symptoms in themselves and use supplemental oxygen to avoid the hazards associated with hypoxia.

Signs of hypoxia can be detected by an observer but are usually not an effective tool for recognizing it in oneself. According to the FAA:

Personal symptoms of hypoxia are as individual as the person experiencing them. A group of people who are hypoxic will, a majority of the time, get the same symptoms. But, the symptoms will appear in a different order and in varying intensities. The greatest benefit in hypoxia symptoms is that the order and the intensity of the symptoms will usually remain constant over the years. This is a great gift, because a pilot will always know what to look for to keep hypoxia in check. (FAA, 2018)

The best way to understand how hypoxia will affect you is to experience it in an **altitude chamber**, which is a safe and controlled environment that allows you to become familiar with your symptoms.

Unprepared or unwary pilots can be caught off guard. For example, you may be tempted to fly during **visual meteorological conditions (VMC)** over an undercast cloud layer. However, the cloud layer will rise as temperature increases (see Chapter 2) and you can quickly become "trapped" at a high altitude and risk becoming hypoxic. Also, as stated by Garrison (2011), "It is important to note that when hypoxia is discussed in terms of altitude, it is pressure altitude, not density altitude that matters. There is always plenty of oxygen around—a whole atmosphere of it—but what controls the amount that reaches the brain is pressure differences across various membranes in the body."

Because supplemental oxygen systems (either built into the aircraft or portable) can be expensive, many pilots do not use them. The FAA recommends, "For optimum protection, pilots are encouraged to use supplemental oxygen above 10,000 feet during the day, and above 5,000 feet at night" (FAA, 2018). Consider using supplemental oxygen at altitudes above 10,000 feet for more than short periods of time.

Although not directly related to high altitudes, when people become anxious or have other health issues, **hyperventilation** can result from rapid breathing and excessive oxygen intake. Breathing into and out of a paper bag, holding your breath repeatedly for 10–15 seconds, or relaxed breathing from a rebreather type mask (which most GA O_2 masks are), can relieve hyperventilation by rebalancing the oxygen/carbon dioxide ratio. If you or your passengers experience hypoxia, hyperventilation, or other health issues, you may need to divert or make a precautionary landing, as discussed later in this chapter.

Since the beginning of aviation, human error has been recognized as a major factor in accidents and incidents. Indeed, one of aviation's biggest challenges has been—and will continue to be—human error avoidance and control. 🙶

International Civil Aviation Organization [2]

Human Factors

When humans took to the skies, they brought all their attitudes, behaviors, talents, and limitations (physical, mental, and emotional) with them. It seems to be human nature to push for greater achievements, and with that comes increased risk. The International Civil Aviation Organization (ICAO) published the first comprehensive manual that explored many of the human factors affecting pilots and others (ICAO, 1989). Pilot-related causes consistently account for about 75% of non-commercial fixed-wing accidents and 72% of helicopter accidents in the United States (Aircraft Owners and Pilots Association, 2017). Managing risk is not only about ensuring that your airplane is mechanically safe or that weather and other environmental factors are favorable; it is about reducing errors and approaching every flight from a perspective of safety. Following are some suggestions about how to evaluate your skill and knowledge.

Previous Flight Time and Experience

It is critical to evaluate your own experience and skill before attempting flight into any new regime. Since it is sometimes hard to objectively evaluate oneself, seek help from a qualified backcountry pilot or instructor who can help you assess your level of proficiency in your airplane and your limitations. Create a set of guidelines for your mountain and canyon flying, including personal limits with

---

[2] International Civil Aviation Organization (1989). *Human Factors Digest No. 1: Fundamental Human Factors Concepts, Circular 216-AN/131.* Montreal, Canada: International Civil Aviation Organization.

respect to weather and wind, airstrip lengths, density altitude, aircraft loading, and other considerations before you start flying in a particular area. As you gain experience, you can revise your personal limits, which may become more or less conservative based on the knowledge you gain and as your skills develop or you fly a different aircraft.

Evaluate your previous flight experience to set personal limits. Consider not only your total time, but the type of flight time; you may have thousands of hours in transport-category airplanes (or flying at the flight levels with the autopilot on) but those hours are not relevant to backcountry flying. Hours logged in make and model are important, and the best experience includes a lot of takeoff and landing practice, at many different types of airports, and with wind. Although flying with wind can be dangerous in the backcountry (see previous chapters), any experience you gain by practicing takeoffs and landings with gusting winds and crosswinds will give you a better feel for the airplane and more precise aircraft control. Time and instruction in gliders (sailplanes) may be invaluable if you intend to fly powered planes in the backcountry. That time will help you understand how to read wind, thermals, and the effects of terrain on updrafts and downdrafts. Tailwheel experience is helpful, as it can help you gain a more precise feel for the subtleties of aircraft control.

In the life of every airman there comes a turning point when, having experienced the sublimity of great altitudes, he either seeks to become worthy of the vision which has been granted to him, or else turns to boastful arrogance casting aside all restraint or respect.

Hanna Reitsch[3]

Aeronautical Decision Making, Attitude, and Judgment

Aeronautical decision making (ADM) is the systematic approach to the mental process used by pilots to consistently determine the best course of action in response to a given set of circumstances (FAA, 2018). Making safe and appropriate decisions depends on having the proper **attitude** and exercising good pilot judgment.

Regardless of your previous flight time, your experience, and your level of skill, you need to honestly evaluate your own personal attitude, as there are some that are potentially hazardous and even deadly, especially in the mountain and canyon environment. Safe operations "rely on good decision-making, not performance. That is, use your brains and common sense to keep out of trouble rather than rely on aircraft performance to get you out" (Civil Aviation Authority of New Zealand, 2012).

---

[3] Reitsch, Hanna (1955). *The Sky My Kingdom*. London, UK: Green hill Books.

The FAA defined five hazardous attitudes as **anti-authority**, **impulsivity**, **invulnerability**, **macho**, and **resignation**, and identified behavioral antidotes to mitigate risks associated with each attitude (FAA, 2001). Those attitudes are directly applicable to increased risk. For example, the invulnerable backcountry pilot might say, "I can land at that difficult airstrip without a checkout; nothing will happen to me." And the macho pilot may want to show off by flying lower than anyone else in a tight canyon. The pilot with an anti-authority attitude might land at private or closed airstrips without permission or break other rules knowing it is a long way to "civilization" where they might be observed. An impulsive pilot could decide to do something dangerous on a whim, like landing downhill on a steeply sloped airstrip or not consider the consequences of abnormal operations. Bob Johnson, of the famed Johnson Flying Service in Missoula, Montana, gave a great antidote for the attitude of resignation, "If you can't fly the biggest piece back, then ride it down. Fly what you have left to the ground and land the damn thing. Even in the trees, land it and walk away..." (Smith, 1979).

Amy's
Axiom

Curtail complacency.

One of the most hazardous, and insidious, attitudes pilots face is complacency. Factors such as fatigue, boredom, mental overload, or repetition can all lead to complacency (Tolleson, 2007). Although you may have taken off and landed at the same canyon airstrip hundreds of times, it does not warrant taking the environment or the operation for granted. Wind, weather, local conditions, and other hazards as well as your mental, emotional, and physical condition are always changing. As Clark (1991) stated, "Even if you just landed at the same airstrip 20 minutes ago, check it out again, because everything could have changed since then." Complacency can cause pilots to misjudge the conditions or be caught off guard by a sudden gust of wind, an animal on the airstrip, or slow reflexes. Vigilance at all times is the best antidote for complacency.

Evaluation of your own hazardous attitudes is important so that you can act and avoid the consequences of risky behavior. One way to mitigate risk is to develop sound judgment, along with skill and knowledge. Pilot judgment is defined by the *Judgment Training Manual for Student Pilots*:

> Pilot judgment is the process of recognizing and analyzing all available information about oneself, the aircraft and the flying environment, followed by the rational evaluation of alternatives to implement a timely decision which maximizes safety. Pilot judgment thus involves one's attitudes toward risk-taking and one's ability to evaluate risks and make decisions based upon one's knowledge, skills and experience. A judgment decision always involves a problem or choice, an unknown element, usually a time constraint, and stress. (FAA/Transport Canada/GAMA, 1986)

Machismo, impulsivity, and invulnerability all hit me at the same time back in the 1970s in a Super Cub. I was returning from a hunting trip in the western part of Idaho, following the Salmon River back to the town of Salmon, when I spotted three huge bull elk just below a fire lookout. I was close to the primitive area but not inside it. As I circled the elk to admire them, I was tempted to land and shoot one (not illegal to do in Idaho at the time). It was steep (over 17%) and grassy terrain, with some large boulders in the area, not all of them visible due to long grass. The bulls seemed to watch casually waiting for the probable crash landing. I made about 15 approaches to various potential landing areas. Some small grain of sanity remained and kept me from touching down, and eventually I realized an attempted landing was incredibly foolish and risky. I still shudder and shake my head today at the foolishness of my thinking. I have never heard a better definition of "bull fever" and falling victim to several hazardous attitudes at once. As I think back, I believe suddenly considering the consequences of my potential actions was the mitigating factor.

To develop good pilot judgment, you must constantly and objectively evaluate yourself, the environment, and potential risks. You need to understand your limitations, recognize new and unknown factors, and use your experience and knowledge to make sound decisions. A study conducted by Hunter (2006) evaluated the level of risk perception of 630 general aviation pilots and determined that the best indicator of involvement in hazardous aviation events was inaccurate risk perception. In other words, pilots considered situations to be less risky than they actually were.

When tempted to do something risky, think about the consequences of your actions; you could crash the airplane, be injured, and be stranded a long way from help. Take a moment and ask yourself whether what you are about to do is worth the risk; think backwards from consequences to causes. Is it wise to gamble the rest of your life in one dangerous, possibly disastrous flying hour? By thinking about what follows from poor judgment and bad decisions, you can develop better judgment and heighten your understanding of how attitudes are related to risk aversion. Sometimes continuing a flight might be the riskiest option. Pilots who are too embarrassed to turn around or afraid to damage the airplane in a precautionary landing increase the potential severity and probability of risk. It might be better to break the airplane, bruise the ego, or violate regulations if the alternative is injury or death. Make up your mind that you will take life-saving action, regardless of other consequences.

Amy's Axiom

Eschew the ego.

Idaho Aviation Hall-of-Fame inductee, WWII Marine Corps pilot, and highly experienced backcountry pilot Bill Dorris once taught me an unforgettable lesson in judgment. I was taking a ride with him into an Idaho back-country airstrip with paying passengers, on a clear beautiful day. But when he detected a slight wind at ground level coming in from a side canyon, he aborted the flight, explaining to the passengers that they just had a nice sightseeing trip on the house. He knew how to say no and exercise superior judgment, even though it cost him time and money. Witnessing that has stayed with me for decades. With my lesser experience, skill, and judgment, I would have continued the approach.

Developing sound judgment includes conducting a post-flight critique after every flight. The realization of "never again" means there is a lesson to be learned, and it will help you evaluate and improve your personal attitude and ability to assess future risks. Possibly the most difficult judgment to develop is intuitive—the ability to use subliminal cues, such as weather trends or the sound and feel of your airplane. Although time and experience may sharpen intuitive judgment, you can begin now by practicing one good principle: pay attention to warning signs, and if it doesn't feel good, it probably isn't.

R.K.'s
Rule

Always do a post-flight review.

In addition to identifying potential risks and eliminating hazardous attitudes, it is important to identify and cultivate positive attitudes and practices that enhance safety. Hunter (2004) investigated a number of various attitude and risk assessment tools that can be used to evaluate the contribution of pilots' attitudes to accident involvement and to assess of the impact of training. Some of those tools evaluate attitudes such as **self-confidence**, **risk orientation**, and **safety orientation**. You can take quizzes to assess your own attitudes toward safety risk at www.avhf.com/html/Evaluation/HazardAttitude/Hazard_Attitude_Intro.htm

Good pilot judgment can be taught and learned (FAA, 2001; ICAO, 1993; Diehl & Lester, 1986). Educational psychologists generally concur that the most effective way to learn judgment is through modeling appropriate behavior (Schunk, 2015).

R.K.'s
Rule

Learn to say NO.

Contrary to popular belief, experience and judgment are not directly related (FAA, 2018), which is borne out by the accident statistics. Many highly experienced pilots have exercised bad judgment that resulted in incidents and accidents. Less experienced pilots can develop and exercise sound judgment by modeling behaviors that lead to proper attitudes and safe practices. By emulating pilots who practice good judgment and decision-making, you can enhance your ability to assess and mitigate risk.

Aarons (1991) presented a list of characteristics that make a good pilot, based on observations conducted by psychologist Robert O. Besco (Figure 9-2).

Characteristics of a Good Pilot

- Good pilots detect mistakes immediately after they are made—first their own errors, then their fellow crewmembers', then the errors of others.
- Good pilots cope, correct and compensate for these errors gracefully and uneventfully.
- They communicate their assessment of these errors immediately to crewmembers as well as to supporting personnel.
- They accept that errors will occur and know they can compensate for them.
- Good pilots do not let the threat of past, current or future errors increase their own error rates or ability to cope.
- They develop and maintain an attitude of awareness and anticipation of errors.
- Good pilots have the character to say *no* to marginal conditions and to resist pressures to "press on."
- They exert a stabilizing influence on others when the system is degenerating and goal conflicts develop.
- And, good pilots adapt quickly to changes in the demands and environmental conditions of their profession.

Figure 9-2. Characteristics of a good pilot, from Aarons (1991), based on psychologist, military, and airline pilot Dr. Robert O. Besco's 33 years of observing pilot behavior.

One way to practice good judgment is to develop your own **standard operating procedures** (SOPs) to refer to when faced with potentially risky decisions. For example, given lots of fuel and daylight, you might choose to circumnavigate a thunderstorm or other adverse weather. But if you are also running low on daylight, your options and odds drop dramatically. Faced with thunderstorms in the mountains, and low on both daylight and fuel, you have virtually no options. Other factors may play into your decision, such as your familiarity with the territory and your training, but since a superior pilot uses superior judgment to avoid having to use superior skills, your best option is to establish conservative SOPs and adhere to them.

R.K.'s Rule

Follow the Flying Rule of 3s: Weather, Daylight, and Fuel.

At the start of your mountain, canyon, or backcountry flying, your SOPs will provide the primary margin of safety. By setting your own limitations and standards and updating them as you learn from experience, you can develop sound judgment and make safe decisions. Survival ultimately requires preparation, practice, conservatism, caution, and a bit of good luck; by developing and practicing all of the former, you will not have to rely as much on the latter.

Situational Awareness and Task Management

"**Situational awareness** is the accurate perception and understanding of all the factors and conditions within the five fundamental risk elements (flight, pilot, aircraft, environment, and type of operation that comprise any given aviation situation) that affect safety before, during, and after the flight" (FAA, 2016d). Many factors can either enhance or degrade your situational awareness, including physical, physiological, emotional, and psychological stress.

The mountain and canyon environment itself can cause stress and lead to a loss of situational awareness. Your understanding of your situation is easily reduced by adverse wind and weather, visual illusions, taking off and landing at a one-way backcountry airstrip in a canyon, poor airplane performance due to high DA, and situations with limited options. It is important to practice maneuvers as described in Chapter 1 and prepare yourself as thoroughly as possible before you go so that you can focus on the environment instead of trying to figure out the airplane.

Physiological stress, such as fatigue, hunger, cold, heat, hypoxia, dehydration, or illness, can contribute to a loss of situational awareness. General life stress, such as preoccupation, worry, or emotional stress, as well as stress caused by a desire to complete a flight or please passengers can compound the lost situational awareness. Conversely, a well-rested, well-nourished, hydrated, comfortable pilot will be able to better assess a situation, perceive risks as they develop, and make the right decisions to maintain a safe flight. By thoroughly preparing yourself and your airplane before each flight—including a plan for alternatives, weather conditions, and other flight parameters—you will be able to reduce your workload and enhance your situational awareness. Develop and maintain an attitude of awareness. Anticipate errors and practice saying *no* to marginal conditions and resist pressures to "press on."

One factor contributing to loss of situational awareness is called **groupthink**, a term coined by Irving (1972). Irving noted groupthink "occurs when a group makes faulty decisions because group pressures lead to a deterioration of mental efficiency, reality testing, and judgment." Those affected by groupthink ignore alternatives and tend to take irrational actions (Irving, 1972). An example of groupthink is when a group of pilots decides something is okay to do, even though one or more individuals do not. Many professional pilot training programs stipulate that during a disagreement, the crew must follow the **most conservative response**.

By developing your own set of limitations and SOPs, you can use them to make a most conservative response to the group. For example, you can say, "Go ahead and try that. I will circle overhead," or "I will wait until the storm passes before I takeoff, but you make your own choice." By sticking to your own predetermined set of rules, you choose your level of acceptable risk and break from the influence of groupthink. Unacceptable risk is then easy to define. For example, you might wear your survival vest or helmet although your flying buddies tease you and do not wear theirs. This is one of your SOPs, one of your risk management tools, and you won't break your own rules.

Another proven method to enhance situational awareness is to reduce your workload at any given time by limiting distractions and prioritizing tasks (Chou, Madhaven, and Funk, 1996; Wickens, 2002; Hoover & Russ-Eft, 2005). Adherence to SOPs, and using the simple prioritization scheme **Aviate, Navigate, Communicate (ANC)**, has proven highly effective to prioritize cockpit tasks, reduce workload, and enhance situational awareness (Funk, et.al, 2003; Hoover & Russ-Eft, 2005). Task prioritization can be learned through training, but unless practiced on an ongoing basis it is typically not retained over the long-term (Hoover, 2008). Since the ANC scheme works and is taught by most pilot training programs, it is recommended for both normal and emergency situations. In short, fly the airplane first; figure out where you are and where you are going. Then make necessary communications to passengers, other pilots, or external resources, such as air traffic control or Flight Service.

Human factors play an important safety role in aviation, and mountain, canyon, and backcountry flying is no exception. Be willing to honestly evaluate your own level of skill and knowledge, adopt an "always mitigate risk" attitude, learn from your own and others' experience, practice good judgment, avoid pressure and stressors, manage your workload, maintain situational awareness, and you will be well on your way to a low-risk, high-enjoyment experience.

Backcountry Flight Safety and Etiquette with Jeanne MacPherson

Jeanne MacPherson is a retired Chief of Safety and Education for Montana Department of Transportation Aeronautics Division. While employed by the state of Montana, she coordinated air search operations, promoted aviation education, and taught mountain flying for more than 15 years. Prior to that, Jeanne was a freight pilot and flight instructor. She is a commercial pilot and CFII with SEL, MEL, and SES ratings. Jeanne is a member of the Society of Aviation and Flight Educators (SAFE) as well as the FAA Safety Team. She operates her own flight school, Mountain Air Dance (mountainairdancellc.com), and gives backcountry instruction. She also uses her American Champion Super Decathlon to teach the Emergency Maneuver Training Program developed by Master Instructor Rich Stowell.

In this section, Jeanne shares insights about flying responsibly and courteously in the backcountry.

Etiquette is basically following the Golden Rule. We all have our personal expectations of what a recreational experience is, and we want to respect each other's rights and consider how our own actions affect other users. We want to adopt a practice to do our part to protect, preserve, and improve future airstrip recreational opportunities. Our goal is to promote a good impression for aviation. It's important to remember that we share the wild country with a variety of users, many of whom are out there for quiet and solitude. There are ways to fly quietly and respect other users. Safety is always the first concern.

If you use action cameras, mounted outside or inside the airplane, don't become distracted by the technology. Preoccupation with cameras, tablets, and remote controls while flying can cause loss of situational awareness. Even worse, you could become distracted and lose control of the airplane. Photography should not take priority over flying the airplane.

En route

- Power back, slow down, and enjoy the scenery. Aircraft noise can be disturbing because sound is intensified in the canyons and mountains.
- Maintain a respectful altitude. 2,000 feet is recommended over wilderness areas en route, and try to maintain at least 1,000 feet above river level in canyons until you are ready to land.
- Do not make low flights over noise-sensitive areas.
- Practice quieter engine RPM management when able.
- Fly the recommended altitudes.
- No formation flying or low passes.
- Minimize radio talk. Keep your communications to what is necessary for aviation safety. If you use a discreet frequency for personal communication, monitor the common traffic frequency at the same time.

Arrival

- Be courteous and minimize the number of takeoffs and landings.
- No touch-and-goes.
- Fly standard or recommended patterns.
- Make surveillance passes at appropriate altitude and speed; no high-speed flyovers.
- Taxi slowly and avoid high-RPM turns or blasting other aircraft or people.

Repeated approaches and high-speed flyovers are a pet peeve of non-flying backcountry users. Avoid touch-and-goes in the backcountry. Flying a stabilized approach at the exact target airspeed to a predetermined spot is the best way to ensure a successful landing and reduce the likelihood of a go-around.

You can—and should—perfect your short-field/soft-field technique before you head to the mountains. Do most of your practice close to home. Review your performance charts. Higher temperatures, elevations, and aircraft weights will decrease performance...a lot! Just like good instrument pilots learn to "fly by the numbers," nail down what power settings and configurations you will use for each phase of flight.

Minimize radio chatter and don't fly in formation, especially in narrow canyons. If flying together, keep some separation and pre-arrange a frequency that will not interfere with other traffic or nearby airports. Stay on the common frequency in the traffic area at backcountry strips. Maintain adequate altitude clearance above the traffic patter when flying over airstrips. If you intend to land, it is best to arrive at pattern altitude.

Taxiing and parking require courtesy as well. Taxi in such a way that your prop wash will not throw debris on your neighbor's aircraft or campsite. If there is no way to turn into your parking spot without blowing dirt on a neighbor, stop short, turn your plane by hand, and push it back into place. If there are other aircraft present, there is usually plenty of help available. The same goes for run-ups—be aware of what's behind you.

While There

Practice "leave no trace" outdoor ethics. Use designated campsites and fire grates. In fact, carry garbage bags and leave the place nicer than you found it.

- Leave the airstrip better than you found it. This might mean picking up after someone else.
- Travel and camp on durable surfaces or sites that are planned campsites.
- Store food correctly and out of reach of wildlife.
- Be considerate of other visitors.
- Respect wildlife.
- Be careful with fire.
- Leave what you find there.
- Minimize camp areas and campfire impacts.
- Dispose of waste properly.
- Fly it in, fly it out.

Departure

- Check propeller area for people, pets, and livestock.
- Taxi slowly and don't make high-RPM turns.
- Fly recommended departures.
- Practice quiet engine RPM management whenever appropriate.

Preserving Backcountry Airstrips

- Volunteer to help with airstrip maintenance.
- Participate in wilderness, backcountry, and recreational airstrip planning.
- Practice and promote good flying etiquette.
- Fly safely.

Prepare for the unknown, unexpected and inconceivable...after 50 years of flying I'm still learning every time I fly.

Eugene Cernan, last man to walk on the moon [4]

Emergencies

The ability to effectively react and handle emergencies is a major part of managing risk. Preparation begins long before you depart on any flight and should be integral to everything you do; always be on the alert for the unexpected and inconceivable as best you can and be current with respect to emergency procedures for your particular airplane and equipment. Routinely practice the procedures and always ask yourself "what if" during every phase of flight. Attending seminars, workshops, or online courses can help you stay current and plan for how you will deal with an emergency. One of the most comprehensive online resources is Rod Machado's Handling In-flight Emergencies eLearning Course (see link in the online Reader Resources at www.asa2fly.com/reader/mountain).

This chapter assumes pilots have a basic level of emergency training and provides a review of general practices with focus on situations unique to mountainous and backcountry areas, including diversions, precautionary and forced landings, and post-crash survival.

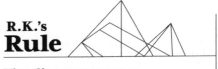

R.K.'s Rule

Visualize consequences.

Always educate passengers as to possible emergency situations and how to prepare for them. You do not want to alarm people unnecessarily but let them know that your primary concern is their safety and that you may not be able to adhere to a schedule. Someone who thinks they cannot tolerate delays may want to excuse themselves from a trip. Advise passengers how to dress for flying over and into remote mountain areas. Everyone should wear practical clothing and footwear and bring extra warm layers in case you have to make a precautionary or emergency landing. Nighttime temperatures at high altitudes can be below freezing, even during summer. Alert passengers to the possibility of hypoxia or other physical symptoms they might experience at high altitudes, and make sure they understand how to alert you if they are not feeling well.

---

[4] Davis, Donald A. and Cernan, Eugene. (1999). *The Last Man on the Moon: Astronaut Eugene Cernan and America's Race in Space.* New York, NY: St. Martin's Press.

Augment your normal preflight briefing (items such as how to operate seatbelts, doors, windows, fire extinguishers, etc.) by advising passengers as to the location of survival gear and first aid kits. Ask them to help you scan for and point out other airplane traffic and identify landmarks en route. Demonstrate how to operate or activate any emergency devices such as emergency locator transmitters (ELT), personal locator beacons (PLB), satellite phones, or other emergency signaling devices. Involving your passengers in emergency preparedness can help mitigate risk and enhance your chances of a successful outcome during an emergency, diversion, or forced landing.

R.K.'s Rule

Visualize an emergency a day.

Diversions

There is always the chance of the unexpected, no matter how well you planned. Unforecast or rapidly changing weather, mechanical problems, or passenger or pilot illness are all reasons to divert or make a precautionary landing.

Weather

Mountain thunderstorms form and move rapidly. Fog can form almost instantly, and winds increase and change direction radically over short periods of time and distance. Attempted VFR flight in **instrument meteorological conditions (IMC)** is one of the most consistently lethal mistakes in all of aviation. Since 2002, more than 86% of all fixed-wing VFR-into-IMC accidents have been fatal (AOPA, 2017). Although you and your aircraft may be instrument-capable, mountainous areas have high **minimum en route altitudes (MEAs)**, and icing and embedded thunderstorms are common. Attempting to transition to IMC in a canyon, or below the mountain tops, can be deadly.

At the first realization that you are facing weather you had not planned for, such as wind, fog, thunderstorms, or a rapidly advancing frontal system, turn around or divert to an alternate destination. Ideally, your preflight preparation included at least one alternative plan of action or you may have to make a precautionary landing. If you are fortunate enough to have more than one option, promptly select the best one. Options might be a backcountry ranch airstrip with satellite communication to the outside world for flight plan updates as well as shelter, a nearby town with an airport, or a mountain airstrip (albeit with no facilities whatsoever). The important thing is to divert before you get disoriented, become lost, or have to make a precautionary off-airport landing as the only alternative to attempting flight into IMC.

Physical Illness

If a passenger becomes airsick, provide ventilation and ask the person to monitor and update you on their condition. Hypoxia is the most common illness; provide oxygen if available. If the problem is potentially life-threatening, such as a heart attack, stroke, or allergic or diabetic reaction, declare a medical emergency to air traffic control (ATC) or anyone on the radio frequency. You or one of your passengers can call for help on a satellite or cell phone. Many headsets have Bluetooth capability for use with a cell phone, and satellite phones are worth the investment. You may need to climb to get radio or phone reception and should use supplemental oxygen. Head to the nearest medical facility if you can do so safely. Over remote areas, you might be hours from a fully-equipped hospital and may have to rely on a village nurse or EMT.

Concentrate on flying the airplane and direct other passengers to deal with the emergency. When alone with a passenger during a medical emergency, you may have to make some tough decisions. Do not become distracted while helping the passenger, lest you create an even greater emergency. Landing at the nearest possible airstrip and administering medical aid might be your only option. Never compromise the safety of the flight by trying to deal with a medical emergency and losing control of the airplane or flying into a hazardous situation.

If you become ill while flying, try to land as soon as practical at a nearby airport or airstrip. With no suitable place to land, use oxygen and declare an emergency to ATC, or make a call to the nearest 911 facility over the cell or satellite phone.

Mechanical Problems

Partial power loss, alternator or electrical systems failure, loss of cabin pressurization, landing gear malfunctions, and other instrument or equipment malfunctions are more common than total engine failure. Often, a situation that is not an emergency is exacerbated by a pilot who panics and takes inappropriate action, making the situation worse.

Check for carburetor or induction ice immediately if your engine loses power. Intake icing is more common in carbureted than fuel-injected engines. Ideal temperatures for the formation of carburetor ice vary with conditions (Figure 9-3). Apply full carburetor heat for conditions likely to form ice. Preventing carburetor icing is easier and more effective than curing it once it has formed.

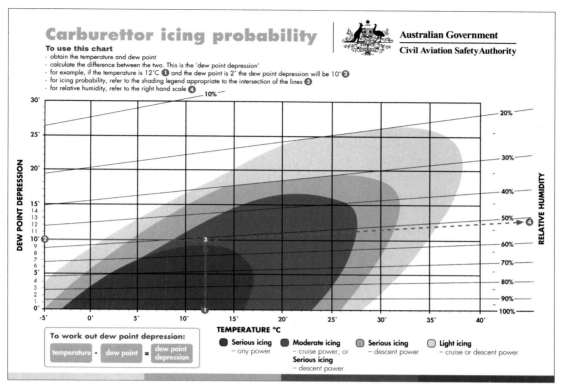

Figure 9-3. The likelihood of formation of carburetor ice at varying temperature, dew point, and power settings. Carburetor icing is more likely at partial power settings due to the cooling effect of a partially closed throttle butterfly. *(Reprinted with permission from the Civil Aviation Safety Authority of Australia)*

Visible moisture is not necessary for carburetor ice to form; sufficiently humid air, particularly at lower power settings, is often enough. Application of carburetor heat will enrich the mixture and require more leaning for best power. Even experienced pilots confronted with incipient carburetor ice for the first time may not think to apply carburetor heat unless they have practiced for it. This is particularly true for pilots used to flying in dry environments where induction ice is not common. For example, over a remote area such as along the coast of British Columbia, with only mountains, trees, and water underneath, a pilot might react to partial power loss by immediately selecting a place to make an emergency landing without thinking about using carburetor heat or other engine troubleshooting measures. Mitigate such risk by memorizing the proper procedures and reviewing them regularly. A good practice is to emulate the professionals: sit in the pilot's seat and physically review your emergency checklist until you develop muscle memory as well as a conscious recall of items. This practice could save your life during a time-critical emergency.

I satisfied a life-long passion for antique airplanes when my wife and I bought a 1937 Fairchild 24. Following an exhaustive search, I found our Fairchild near Augusta, Georgia. She was beautifully restored in original factory yellow and green with matching green interior and powered by a Warner 145 radial engine, the sound of which reminded one of a well-tuned Harley motorcycle.

I clearly recall that first engine start during my inspection flight. The procedure was to move mixture rich, push the starter button, count three blades, then turn on the magnetos and listen to the seven cylinders roar to life. A bit of smoke and a lot of rumble tells the pilot the engine is running as the oil and cylinder head temperatures move up into the green, and the entire airplane shakes with anticipation.

Another surprise with the old Fairchild 24 was the roll-up-and-down windows. "How cool is this?" I thought, sitting with an elbow out the window listening to that little 145 horsepower radial purr and smelling the exhaust fumes. Ahhh, where is my leather helmet and white scarf?

By now you might be getting a feel for what draws some pilots toward antique airplanes. What it must have been like to be a barn-stormer back in the day. My paper sectionals are stacked beside airport directories for several regions east to west, all in my flight bag in the back seat. This really is a different way of flying and perhaps not all that appealing to those who are drawn more to the new age of technology. There is no iPAD, no GPS, only one communications radio, and an old ADF for navigation.

My wife and I flew the old Fairchild west from Georgia through Missouri, Kansas, and Colorado in a two-day cross-country. The May weather brought the expected diversions around thunderstorms and a couple of memorable crosswind landings, but nothing the Fairchild couldn't handle. Then an unexpected cylinder problem resulted in an off-airport landing on a ranch near Kemmerer, Wyoming. With the help of the friendly ranch owner and a few parts from our friends at home, we finally flew her to Nampa, Idaho, with a little more than 25 hours of flying time in the old logbook.

Not to sound contrite, but eight years of prior experience flying in Alaska had provided me with some similar experiences in the bush. Aviators there learn to be fairly self-reliant and need to be prepared for problems (or survival) in the backcountry. My experience operating de Havilland Beavers in Alaska was no exception, and that turned out to be good training for what I was later required to put into practice as the new owner/operator of the Fairchild.

The next three months passed without incident as the old yellow Fairchild and I got to know each other better. The Warner requires more attention than flat engines, such as a routine 25-hour lubrication of the rocker arms and the addition of oil after each flight. However, she seemed to leak as much oil as she burned internally, and much time was spent tightening things and replacing gaskets to improve the mess on the fuselage. A post-flight wipe-down became a normal routine as well as a good preventive measure.

By August, we were ready to venture farther away from home base and decided to attend the Evergreen antique fly-in near Portland, Oregon. Two other pilots were joining in the excursion with a Stinson and another Fairchild. The weather forecast for the weekend was good, but included westerly winds gusting to 25 knots. En route the winds proved to be consistently nearer the higher number, so we elected to stop for fuel at Pendleton, Oregon. That would ensure a safe flight for the last leg into Evergreen, or so we thought.

Other than some significant bumps caused by turbulence, the only change in the plan was when we found fairly low ceilings and drizzle through the pass at Cascade Locks (KCZK) on the Columbia River. Fortunately, there is a nice paved runway there and a convenient place to take a break for lunch, so that became the revised plan. The group landed there and took a nice two-hour lunch while we waited for the weather to improve.

By the time we returned to our planes, the pass had lifted and Evergreen was reporting good VFR weather. We were anxious to make the final leg of our journey. Each plane started in turn, taxied, and completed run-ups and takeoff checklists. All thumbs were up and the other Fairchild departed first, then the Stinson. As the Stinson lifted off, I noticed a fine mist coming off around the propeller. That was an observed clue, but not connected to anything that would normally indicate a threat.

We were last in the lineup, and power came up smoothly for takeoff. As we passed the end of the runway, I heard the other Fairchild call for a frequency change and the Stinson in front of me was answering when I felt a slight vibration, followed by a loss of power. I immediately checked the engine gauges, but did not find anything in the red. I started the emergency checklist from memory at about 200 feet over the river. The mixture, throttle, magnetos, master—all in their correct settings with no improvement in power. Temperatures and pressure were good, but the engine was getting rougher and airspeed was beginning to drop. I lowered the nose for best glide about the same time the engine quit altogether.

A quick look over my left shoulder told me the runway was not an option, and I made the decision, and a mayday call on the radio, to ditch straight ahead in the river. Nothing left to do but trim, move the mixture to idle cutoff, magnetos off, and note the airspeed down to 55 knots. I remember not wanting to point the nose toward the water, but I forced it over in order to maintain airspeed until the landing flare. Oddly, I remember thinking I was float rated, but the airplane is not equipped with floats. Time to focus on ditching.

It all happened in a matter of seconds. The impact was flat and surprisingly soft at first. Then as the drag of the water overcame inertia, the airplane rolled nose-low into the current and the front left window failed under the pressure. Water fumed into the cockpit for a second, reminding me of diving into a pool from a high board. That was one of those unusual moments when prior training tended to kick in from some distant recess of the brain, and in my case, I suddenly remembered my Navy training in the **Dempsey Dumpster** for simulated ditching. I waited for 10 counts as the bubbles cleared and I got my bearings under water. By now the airplane had settled wings level with the cabin entirely submerged.

Continued...

Holding my breath, I moved into egress mode by unlatching my seatbelt then lifting my nose into a small air pocket near the ceiling of the cabin. Then I realized my wife was still underwater and struggling to get free of her belt. I helped her release the buckle and lifted her up to the air pocket. Once she confirmed she was OK, I told her to hang on and we would exit out my door. I had failed to open my door before impact, so rolled the window down to help equalize pressure, and opened it with my left arm as she put a strangle-hold on my right arm and never let go. We swam under the wing and floated to the left wing-tip with nothing more than a few bruises.

To our good fortune, the Fairchild wings floated the plane for a few minutes rather than sinking immediately. People from the Cascade Locks marina were kind enough to come to our rescue and picked us up with a boat. One gentleman dashed to our rescue on his surf-board! All were very welcome and much appreciated for their efforts. Someone sent us a picture taken from the docks as the tail gradually submerged under 35 feet of water.

We were anxious to know what caused the sudden engine failure. Was it a fuel problem, mechanical failure (again), or something else? The FAA arrived for the investigation later that same afternoon and interviewed us. Together we established that we had added fuel and oil only an hour prior to the mishap, so the investigator focused on other indications as clues. Then I remembered the water vapor gener-

Notwithstanding total engine failure, which is an immediate emergency, other mechanical problems mean you need to divert to a maintenance facility. If possible, climb to increase your ability to call for help over the radio or a satellite or cell phone. If you cannot restore lost power, a precautionary landing may be the only option. Do not pass by an acceptable landing area unless you are within gliding distance of an even better one (i.e., one with better facilities and repair). Landing with some power is always a better option than landing with none.

Other problems, such as an electrical failure, might not warrant an immediate precautionary landing. For example, after landing at a remote strip with a dead battery due to a bad alternator, you could be stuck there with only the option of jump-starting or hand-propping the airplane, which can lead to a further incident or accident. Consider as many scenarios ahead of time as you can and have a plan for how you might deal with each. Understand that the plan will change with the conditions, such as daylight, weather, and fuel reserves.

Precautionary Landings

Determine whether or not the situation warrants a precautionary landing. Visualize possible outcomes and practice the most conservative response. If you think lives are in immediate danger and a landing will make a difference, then it is warranted. If you are losing engine power with inhospitable terrain ahead, it is warranted. If weather is closing in and you cannot proceed either ahead

ated by the high RPM prop on the Stinson and mentioned it to the FAA investigator.

Later teardown of the engine revealed no internal failures and the accessories all appeared to be functioning normally. Induction icing was determined to be the most probable cause. We learned that, although rare, conditions were in the range for carburetor icing to occur even during takeoff power. We also learned that the pre-1940 Warner induction system was highly susceptible to carburetor icing, which had caused several accidents and led to a carburetor design change in later years. In fact, the version on my engine had no carburetor heat assembly installed.

While there may be several lessons learned from this story, I wanted to share this one obscure and misunderstood fact about carburetor icing with my fellow aviators. Even with modern engines, if using a carbureted fuel system (as opposed to fuel injected) it may be vulnerable to carburetor icing. Ice can form during high power settings, such as on takeoff. Take time to review the temperature ranges where icing may occur and be aware of the conditions when flying in them. Use your carburetor heat and accept a slight loss of performance when operating within those temperature ranges. You may also be motivated to reflect on how you would react in an emergency situation. Being well prepared and well trained significantly increases your chances of survival!

or behind, it is warranted. You divert or land at another airstrip short of your destination to wait out the weather or take care of a sick passenger.

A precautionary landing can be more difficult than a true emergency landing because you often have more options and must make more decisions. For an engine rapidly losing power, you may choose to land off-airport rather than to proceed into a true emergency landing situation. Most important, decide on a plan of action, follow your emergency procedures, and reduce distractions. Have passengers prepare as best they can, and above all, fly the airplane first.

Forced Landings

By flying over areas with more emergency options, you can greatly increase your chances of survival should you have to make an emergency off-airport landing. Study the area as you fly over it and identify potential landing sites.

The primary reasons to make a forced landing are total loss of power in a single-engine airplane, structural failure, or onboard fire. Study and practice for emergency operations is the best preparation. Memory aids, such as the ANC scheme previously discussed, can help you prioritize tasks during a time of high stress. With total power loss, set the airplane up for best glide speed and select an emergency landing spot. Below a thousand feet **above ground level (AGL)**, pick your landing spot and stick with it. Indecision usually wastes time and altitude.

Given enough time and altitude, scan the area for a best location. It might be behind you. If you just passed an airstrip and have enough altitude, the best option may be to reverse course rather than land straight ahead. Follow recommended procedures for troubleshooting or attempting to restart or shut down the engine. Professional pilots use **flow checks**, which are simple movements that "flow" down or across the panels for the purpose of accomplishing critical checks without having to use a checklist. You can develop your own emergency flow check for your airplane and memorize it.

During an inflight fire, follow the recommendations for your airplane and get on the ground as quickly as possible. Time is of the essence, and you will need to act fast and land at the best location you can find.

Study your route when flying over remote areas, even if you fly there often. Look for potential landing areas such as open fields and straight stretches of roads or jeep trails. Make "mental notes" and constantly update your options as you proceed. Sand or gravel bars next to lakes or rivers can be good choices for an emergency landing, as can the top of a desert mesa or a bench above the river. Observe where the straight and wider stretches are along rivers and review ditching procedures for your airplane. Large, slow-moving rivers might be a better choice than adjacent rocky areas or forests, but steep-gradient, whitewater rivers usually have swiftly moving currents with rocky terrain underneath and can be hazardous. Land downstream on moving water, as the relative speed will be slower. Whether in a lake or river, try to ditch close to shore, since it is highly likely you and your passengers could be injured. You don't want to risk hypothermia trying to get to land. If you routinely fly over large bodies of water, train for emergency water landings, including ditching procedures and post-crash water survival techniques.

The most important aspect of making an emergency off-airport landing without power is to fly the airplane until it stops moving. You want to land as slowly as possible under control, without stalling. A stall usually results in a nose-down uncontrolled crash into terrain; stalling 100 feet above the ground can be fatal. A common misconception is that it takes hundreds of feet of obstacle-free ground to make a survivable crash landing, but accident studies show it does not (Moran, 2015). It is not the speed itself but how it is dissipated that causes injury. Maneuver to allow the airplane wings to take the brunt of the impact on trees or other obstacles and keep the cabin and occupants intact. Your primary goal is to maintain the integrity of the aircraft cabin so its occupants can survive. Intentionally hitting smaller trees with the airplane wing may be better than striking large ones because the smaller trees will flex with impact and absorb more energy. The largest trees are generally closer to water at the bottom of canyons, and a better choice might be to land on a ridge near the top of a canyon where the trees are smallest and where you will be more visible to rescue aircraft (Parfit, 1977).

Controlled crash landings are survivable, and your main concern is to reduce injury, not to save the airplane. This can be counterintuitive, as the initial reaction might be to extend the glide for as long as possible. According to Moran (2015), a crash is deemed survivable if:

- Cockpit and cabin structure remain relatively intact providing sufficient living space for occupants.
- Deceleration forces experienced by the occupant do not or should not exceed the survivable limits of human "G" tolerance.
- Post-accident environmental factors allow egress or rescue before conditions become intolerable.

Furthermore, survivability depends on several factors, including the magnitude and direction of forces, the angle of impact, the duration of deceleration (how long it takes to stop), how rapidly the deceleration is applied, and most critically, the position of the occupants and how well they are restrained (Shanahan, 2005). Young (1966) tested various restraint systems and concluded that inadequate or incomplete body restraint was a major factor in the trend of increasing numbers of fatal injuries reported from general aviation accidents at the time, which led to current FAA regulations requiring flight crew to wear both lap and shoulder restraints during flight.

Cullen (2005) analyzed several well-documented aviation accidents, and his findings "suggested that the fatality rate could be drastically reduced by the incorporation of efficient upper torso restraint particularly if this was coupled with the use of adequate head protection." A large body of research and tests concluded a 5-point harness is the most protective, and the wider the restraint the better, as it spreads the force over a wider area—ideally 4 inches for lap belts and 2 inches for shoulder straps (Moran, 2015). In summary, you can increase your chance of surviving a controlled crash landing by using the highest quality restraint system available, including both lap belts and torso restraints, and preferably a crotch strap or 5-point harness.

Finally, do not expect **emergency locator transmitter (ELT)** devices to activate automatically or even survive a crash. Studies conducted at NASA Langley Research Center, including historical data from countries around the world as well as results from crash tests, have shown that ELTs can be unreliable, with failures to activate or survive crash forces as high as 70% (Stinson, Littell, Mazzuca, Foster, and Theodorakos, 2017). Given time, activate your ELT or **personal locator beacon (PLB)** device before you land to ensure it is working. Make a "mayday" call over the aircraft radio; use any common traffic or ATC frequency for your area, or the emergency guard frequency 121.5 in the United States. You must fly your airplane first, but have a passenger establish communication over a cell or satellite phone or do so yourself if you have a connection through your headset and can do so safely. Remember the ANC scheme; communication is the last-priority item.

As with any emergency procedure, the more you contemplate possible outcomes ahead of time, prepare, practice, and maintain a positive attitude, the better your chances of making and surviving an off-airport emergency landing.

Post-Crash Survival

The purpose of survival is to remain alive so you can be found and rescued. Remaining with the aircraft, especially when injured, is almost always the best plan. Carry several different signaling devices, such as PLB, cell phone, satellite phone, signal mirrors, and others as described in the next section, to increase your chances of being found. After a crash landing, even a controlled one, you will probably face one or more life-threatening factors, including physical injury, cold, heat, fatigue, sleep deprivation, thirst, hunger, fear, anxiety, panic, boredom, hopelessness, and depression (Civil Aerospace Medical Institute [CAMI], 2011). One of the greatest immediate hazards is post-crash shock. As noted:

> Being suddenly introduced to a new and threatening environment can be a very traumatic experience. Your ability to handle this change will depend heavily on your mental state. A person who thinks randomly and/ or irrationally will act in the same manner. After evacuating the aircraft and treating for injuries, you should sit down and take an objective look at your situation. If you have any water, drink it, it will help you to think rationally and minimize the risk of shock. (CAMI, 2011)

In any survival situation, there are priorities established based on how long a human can survive without each item. The list below, from CAMI (2011), is based on the "rule of threes":

- Air (3 minutes)
- Shelter (3 hours)
- Rest (30 hours)
- Water (3 days)
- Food (30 days)

Chances for survival are greatly diminished without the "will to survive," which includes determination, hope, goals, and/or a positive mental attitude (U.S. Air Force, 2008; CAMI, 2011). Survival training is the best way to prepare for success after a crash landing. There are many courses available to general aviation pilots, including those conducted by the military, search and rescue groups, private organizations, and aviation safety and education branches of government. General aviation pilots in the United States can register for an on-site survival training course through the Federal Aviation Administration. See www.asa2fly. com/reader/mountain for more information, resources, and links to educational documents and survival courses.

After surviving an emergency landing, your first responsibility is to yourself and your passengers. You must assess and deal with life-threatening injuries. Consider taking at least basic first aid training and carry an emergency first aid or basic trauma kit on board your aircraft. With serious or life-threatening injuries, you and your passengers will need to evaluate your situation and decide on a course of action. Medical triage is the highest priority, followed by communicating your position and activating search and rescue operations. Uninjured people can coordinate responsibilities and tasks to maximize their efforts.

Signal for help as soon as possible after dealing with medical trauma. Someone may have heard your Mayday call in the air; call again over the aircraft radio or a handheld radio. Activate the aircraft ELT or your PLB if they are not already operating. Send an emergency text or signal over your tracking device and make a cell or satellite phone call.

Next, attend to other needs as dictated by the rule of threes—shelter, rest, water, food, etc. Injuries are not always immediately evident. Adrenaline shock can mask symptoms, so continue to monitor yourself and your passengers. Survival training emphasizes staying mentally alert and occupied. One way to do that is to document what you remember about your situation, including your memory of what happened, actions you took, and your current situation on the ground. It may help to make notes or voice memos and take photos. However, never prioritize those tasks before essential survival items, such as trauma, injury, or shelter.

Survival Vest

You may have only what you are wearing on your person to survive after escaping from a burning or sinking airplane. The best option is to wear a survival vest equipped with items that you can use to signal for help, start a fire, transport water, and administer basic first aid or repairs. A simple fishing vest stocked with survival items works well, or you can purchase a survival vest. Items in your vest are essential to your immediate need to signal for help, provide basic first aid, start a fire, and secure water.

Tailor equipment to meet your specific needs and the type of terrain and climate over which you are flying. It is a good idea to unpack, check, and repack your vest periodically and replace worn, used, or expired items, especially batteries. Below are listed items to include as a minimum list for your survival vest.

Minimum Survival Items for Vest:

- PLB or tracking/communication signaling device attached to vest (Figure 9-4)
- small signal mirror with sight hole and lanyard
- glow sticks with lanyard (these can be used in low light or at night to signal search and rescue aircraft, as well as a light source)
- brightly colored tape or cloth
- whistle with neck string
- laser flare

- emergency strobe attached to vest (Figure 9-5)
- more than one means to light a fire, such as butane lighter, waterproof matches, flint and steel, striker (e.g., Blastmatch fire starter), Alaska Paracord bracelet (Figure 9-6)
- knife
- multipurpose or Leatherman tool
- parachute cord
- insect repellent and sunscreen
- basic first aid items (Band-Aids, sterile pads, pain medication)
- any prescription medications you need to survive
- condoms (to use for water receptacles)

Survival Kits

Besides your survival vest or items in your pockets, it is highly recommended to have a survival kit. As pointed out by Vivion in Chapter 7, this can more realistically be considered camping gear, and it could be critical to your survival if you are stuck out overnight (or longer) in cold or inclement weather. You can build your own or purchase prepackaged kits that range from compact to larger kits with enough food and gear for several people to survive comfortably

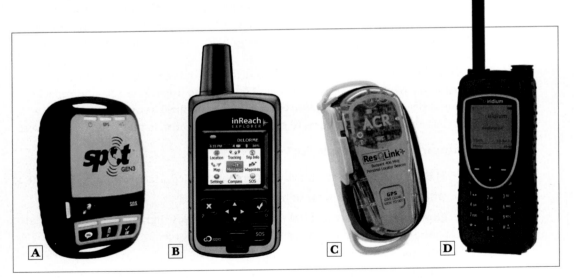

Figure 9-4. Communication and tracking devices: **(A)** SPOT, **(B)** Garmin inReach, **(C)** ResQLink ACR, and **(D)** Iridium satellite phone. They can be used to send location and text messages or make voice calls via satellite.

for a week or more. Your choice of what to include will depend on your needs, experience, the terrain, climate, and time of year. Chapter 7 outlined some additional items for winter and ski flying. You can pack your survival items in a backpack or other type of waterproof bag or box or distribute them throughout the cargo area as needed. The hardest decision may be what *not* to take, especially when limited by weight or space available. Training and experience will help with that decision. Following is a sample list of items you can use to build a survival kit:

Signaling Devices (in addition to vest items):

- large 5 × 3-inch signal mirror with sight hole and lanyard
- conventional or laser flare, or flare gun
- additional strobe light or beacon
- more glow sticks with lanyards
- brightly colored clothing (emergency vest, hat)
- additional fire starters (e.g., butane lighter, waterproof matches, flint and steel or magnesium striker)

Figure 9-5. Coast Guard-approved emergency strobe light.

Figure 9-6. This bracelet is made from 17 feet of military-spec 550 paracord and contains military grade firesteel, a ceramic knife scraper, and waterproof waxed jute tinder. The buckle is a whistle. (*Courtesy Grayson Davey, Alaska Paracord; alaskaparacord.com*)

Survival Items:

- bags—30-gallon plastic garbage bags
- blanket, 84 × 56-inch survival/signal blanket (orange/silver)
- compass with instructions
- large knife
- basic tool kit
- saw
- candles
- yellow or orange surveyor's tape (200 feet × 1 inch)
- water bottle with water (1 liter per person) wrapped in plastic bag
- flashlight or headlamp
- solar lights (such as Luci Light)
- mosquito netting
- tube tent/poncho/tarp for shelter
- aluminum foil
- bandana or Buff headwear
- parachute cord or nylon rope
- fish hooks
- water filter or purification tablets
- insect head net
- insect repellent
- sunscreen
- warm (wool or pile) gloves and stocking hat
- wool, pile, or other warm, waterproof jacket or coat
- extra socks (wool is best)

Personal Items:

- toothbrush and toothpaste
- small comb
- moisturizer
- castile soap

Food:

Pack food in plastic bags; you can use the bags as water containers or for other purposes. Food with high calorie content is good. For example:

- beef, salmon, or another jerky
- energy or protein bars
- dried fruit and nuts
- trail mix
- electrolyte drink mix
- MRE or other survival food

Cooking Utensils:

- cooking pot with lid and handle for boiling water
- drinking cup

Basic First Aid Kit:

- antiseptic wipes
- aspirin/ibuprofen/pain medication
- Ace athletic bandage
- knuckle bandage
- sterile pads (2 × 2, 4 × 4)
- sanitary pads
- triangular bandage
- blood stopper pack
- Band-Aids
- first aid guide
- antibiotic cream (usable in eyes)
- dental floss
- gauze wrap
- Moleskin for blisters
- needle and thread
- aluminum "SAM" Splint
- scissors
- waterproof adhesive tape
- tweezers
- burn ointment

Accident Analysis—Amy Hoover's Story

Several pilot friends were having dinner on a summer Sunday evening and decided to fly out and meet at a nearby backcountry ranch for breakfast the next morning. It would be a mix of airplanes, including a Scout, a Found Bush Hawk, my Citabria, and a friend visiting from Colorado with his Cessna Hawk XP. We all had different times planned. The Colorado friend had been visiting for the past week or so, flying around the backcountry camping with some other pilots, and said he wanted to leave around 6:30 a.m. so he could visit the folks at Sulphur Creek Ranch before heading home. The rest of us planned to arrive between 7:30 and 8:00 a.m. for breakfast.

The next morning, July 7, 2014, was clear and sunny with not a cloud in the sky. It was a beautiful day to fly. I drove to the McCall, Idaho, airport (KMYL, Figure 9-7), pre-flighted my airplane, a 2009 American Champion Citabria, and pushed her out of the hangar. It was 7:00 a.m. and I did not see the Scout or the Bush Hawk. Our friend with the Cessna had spent the night with his airplane at a nearby private airstrip and was probably already on his way, so it was just me. I taxied out and readied for departure.

I took off about 7:15 a.m. from the 5,024-foot elevation runway, and the air was as smooth as silk. After departure, I turned southeast toward the backcountry and set up for a cruise climb in the cool morning air. I was following a direct route from KMYL to Sulphur Creek Ranch (Figure 9-7), which would take me just south of the Landmark USFS airstrip.

As I climbed through approximately 7,000 feet, I looked down and to my right toward the Flying A Ranch (Figure 9-7) and saw a white Cessna taking off to the south. It was about 45 minutes later than the Hawk SP pilot had planned to depart, but I guessed it was him. I called on the published frequency of 122.8 but got no answer, so I switched to 122.9 and called again. I got an answer that time and he confirmed it was the Hawk XP, call sign 90K. By then I was at the position marked on Figure 9-7 as the red dot #1, and 90K was turning southeast after departure approximately 2,000 feet below me at my 5 o'clock position, indicated by the blue dot position #1. I made a position report and told him I was at the south end of Jug Handle Mountain, approximately 4 miles northeast of him, and that I had him in sight. He responded, saying "I have you in sight." I knew the airplane since I had done some mountain flying instruction with the pilot more than 10 years before and flew with him several times in the backcountry. The 210 HP airplane had good climb performance and was faster than the stock C172, and he flew it to Idaho every few years to do some backcountry flying and camping with friends.

Having established he had a visual on me, I continued climbing and leveled off just as I crossed the ridge and made a position report at 8,000 feet en route to Sulphur Creek over a visual landmark called the Needles, which is a common reporting point in the area (red dot #2 on Figure 9-7). 90K responded over the radio and again reported he had me in sight. When I was at the position just north of Warm Lake (red dot #3 in Figure 9-7), I heard the pilot of a de Havilland Beaver

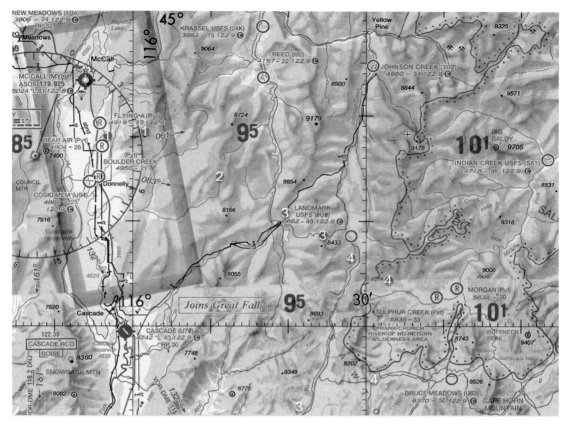

Figure 9-7. The reported position of three aircraft at different points in time. The red numbered dots represent the Citabria, the blue numbered dots are the Cessna, and the green numbered dots indicate the Beaver. At a fixed point in time (for example, #3), each airplane was reporting the position corresponding to their color and numbered dot.

report his position south of me, over a place called Bear Valley (green dot #3 position) and also headed toward Sulphur Creek Ranch. Immediately after the Beaver reported, 90K came on the radio and said he was over Warm Lake Summit at 8,000 feet (indicated by the blue dot #3).

I was confused when 90K made the call, since Warm Lake Summit was approximately 3–4 miles in front of me, and I had not seen him pass me; he was reporting the same altitude, so I should have seen him. I reported my position over the radio and asked if he had passed me. He replied, "Yeah, I passed you. You're slow." I then asked him his ground speed, which he replied was 129 knots. I reported mine as 101 knots, and he again said, "You're slow."

A snapshot in time of the red, blue, and green dots labeled #3 shows the three reported positions (Figure 9-7). I scanned the horizon in front of me, but I could not see the Cessna. I did a little mental math: based on his reported ground speed, he was about 25 knots faster than me. That would be a relative speed of about a mile every two minutes. So, he could have gone from a couple miles behind me to 3–4 miles in front of me during the approximately 10–12 minutes since I had seen him behind and below me. I had no reason to doubt the accuracy of his position report because I had flown with him over the same route in his airplane the week before. We had identified various reporting points from the air, including Warm Lake Summit, where the road peaks the ridge, and we had also looked at it on the chart.

About now you may be asking, "How can she remember the events so accurately?" which is an important question, and the forthcoming answer is relevant to the human factors of my story.

After I crossed Warm Lake Summit, I heard the Beaver report over Bear Valley Creek (green dot #4 in Figure 9-7), so I made a position report. I usually state a location as well as GPS distance from an airstrip, and I said "2CG is over the south end of Landmark Meadows, 10 miles from Sulphur Creek, 7,800 feet for Sulphur Creek." My friend in 90K came on the radio immediately, within a couple of seconds, and reported his position as 5 miles west of Sulphur Creek at 6,800 feet descending for Sulphur Creek. I made a mental note that his reported position placed him approximately 4–5 miles ahead of me and 1,000 feet lower. I figured he must have already crossed the ridge (known as Whisky Creek Summit and depicted as the wilderness boundary on the aeronautical chart in Figure 9-7) into the Sulphur Creek drainage, since he said he was descending. My mental snapshot of the three airplanes converging toward Sulphur Creek is depicted by the red, blue, and green dots labeled #4 on Figure 9-7. Figure 9-8 shows flight path data from my Citabria's GPS overlaid on a terrain map. The reported positions of the Cessna and Citabria are shown in relation to major terrain features.

The view out the front and to the side of my airplane looked like that shown in figure 9-9 just after the position reports were made. The Landmark airstrip was to my left, and I was about a half mile past the south end of the meadow where I had reported my position.

I happened to be scanning toward the left when something caught my attention. I turned my head further to look and saw a white, high-wing airplane fly under me; it appeared under my left wing, overtaking me from behind and below, and flew by very fast. I barely had time to register what I had just seen when the plane climbed from left to right across my flight path at about a 30–40° angle. It all happened so suddenly I had no time to react, as it was only about two seconds from the time I saw it until it hit me. I was still trying to make visual sense of what was happening one moment, and the next moment all I saw was the top of the fuselage and left wing. I heard a loud sound like someone pounding on sheet metal with a hammer, and felt my airplane being pushed up. The whole incident took only a few seconds, and it is hard to describe in words the level of shock I experienced; it was as if my brain could not comprehend what my eyes, ears, and other senses were recording. It literally felt like my heart leapt into my throat, I gasped, and I heard myself say, "It hit me!"

Figure 9-8. Flight path data from the GPS in the Citabria's panel overlaid on a terrain representation. The Citabria's flight path is shown by the red track. The reported positions of the Citabria (red dot #4) and the Cessna (blue dot #4) at a point in time are indicated. The red dot #5 shows the Citabria's position just before being overtaken; the view from the Citabria at that position is depicted in Figure 9-9.

Figure 9-9. The view forward (**A**) and to the left (**B**) at the position indicated by the red dot #5 in Figure 9-8. The photos were taken July 8, 2015, approximately one year after the accident, at approximately the same time, altitude, and flight path as on the day of the accident. *(Photos by Amy Hoover)*

Then…there was complete silence.

My engine had quit, the propeller was at a dead standstill, and the blades were bent. The other airplane just disappeared. My heart was racing, I was completely and momentarily confused for several seconds, and then I felt the adrenaline. It was the oddest sensation. I became acutely aware of every detail of my surroundings and it felt like time was magnified, like every second lasted for an hour. And that is when all the training, practice, experience, study, preparation, and luck over the previous 26 years of flying kicked in. I have a vividly clear and detailed memory of the next two minutes of my life, until just before my wheels touched solid ground.

Even as I was trying to make sense of the situation consciously, my subconscious reflexes were already at work, and I set the airplane up for best glide speed. Besides the engine stopping, I had no idea how much damage my airplane had sustained. It was still flying, but I feared the flight controls might be damaged or could jam, so I very gently began to test the stick for elevator and aileron movement, as well as the rudder pedals. Everything seemed OK. As evidenced by the GPS track from my airplane (Figure 9-8), I had been flying a straight path, then my plane was hit and pushed up and to the right. I automatically started a turn toward the left (north) since I knew the Landmark airstrip was to the left. Although there was unforested terrain to the right (south) of the airplane, turning north toward the nearest airstrip was an immediate reaction.

It is very easy to do a lot of second-guessing through hindsight, sitting calmly without the immediate shock and stress of the situation. One might go crazy trying to think of all the what-ifs. What if I had turned the other way; would there have been a better landing spot? What if there had been time to maneuver before the airplane struck me? What if? The reality is, all the what-ifs are irrelevant.

Here is what is relevant. A situation can happen over which you have no control, but you must take control as soon as possible, and that is what I did. The surge of adrenaline was immediate, which I knew was sending me into a high stress situation. Studies in the literature show that a certain level of stress in survival situations (such as combat) can improve visual and cognitive reaction times as well as increase strength and improve motor skills. However, a higher level of stress can cause loss of situational awareness, hearing impairment, loss of motor skills, possibly a "freeze" reaction, and loss of bodily function (Christensen, Grossman, & Asken, 2010). Based on that, I knew it was imperative to be able to automatically revert to what I had trained and practiced for in order to "push through" the shock and do what I needed to do to survive.

When something sudden and unexpected happens, there are a lot of variables, which you must either use to your advantage or dismiss. There will be distractions. There could be indecision. However, you must be able to act quickly, evaluate the situation, prioritize tasks, and fly the airplane all the way until it stops. I had about two minutes to make everything work out.

In order to take control of the situation, I had to be prepared—mentally, procedurally, and emotionally. For me that meant relying on my previous training, on my years of classroom teaching and in-flight instruction, and on advance planning and practice for emergencies. Ironically, the focus of my research on concurrent task management was a key element; for several years I had conducted experiments, designed and tested training courses, and published papers on single pilot task prioritization. All that paid off, because I had done a lot of mental preparation and deep thinking about the subject, as well as actual in-flight practice.

I have identified four things that stand out as strategies that worked for me that day:

1. **Training**—I did what I had trained for. My research and experience had showed me time after time that simple is better. I pushed through the shock and purposefully focused on the immediate situation. I used the *Aviate, Navigate, Communicate* prioritization scheme I had studied and written about, and it worked.

   - *Aviate*—First and foremost, I pitched for best glide speed, tested the flight controls, and took positive control of the airplane.

   - *Navigate*—Next, I chose a landing site, set up the airplane for the approach, and used the aim point technique as I had practiced for power-off glides.

   - *Communicate*—Only after making sure the airplane was set up and pointed at the right spot did I think about using the radio. I made two Mayday calls in the air. I still remember my exact words: *"Mayday, Mayday—162CG—I've been in a mid-air collision and am making an emergency landing southeast of Landmark airstrip."*

2. **Procedures**—I went through an emergency flow by memory. The Citabria is a simple airplane, but there were still decisions I had to make. Here are some things that went rapidly through my thought process:

   - *Should I release the door?* The Citabria only has one door on the right side. The pilot can remove a safety ring and then pull an emergency release handle that allows the door hinge to be quickly removed and the door ejected in flight should the pilots need to bail out. I decided it was too much of a distraction, would take time, and I had no idea how cleanly the door would fall away, so I only unlatched the door, but did not release the emergency lever.

   - *Should I use the flaps?* I had no idea if the flap cables were damaged. I knew if there were a split flap situation—if one deployed and one did not—it would create differential lift and would destabilize everything, as well as being another distraction, so I left the flaps alone.

- *Should I transmit my Mayday call again on 121.5?* Since I had already transmitted on the multicom frequency of 122.9, and I had just been talking to other pilots, I decided that trying to switch frequencies was too much of a distraction and immediately shed the thought. What about my ELT or PLB? The ELT did not have a panel remote switch, and my ACR PLB was attached to the left side of my vest. Activating it required unfastening the release mechanism and turning a lever. *Distraction*—I decided to shed that action until I had more time.
- *My seatbelt!*—I had a five-point aerobatic harness, and I cinched it down so tight I could barely breathe. I knew the tough little aerobatic airframe was stressed to take a lot of G-forces, and I wanted to make sure I was as tightly belted in as possible.
- *There were procedures I failed to do.* After I was on the ground and safe, I realized that although I had pulled the fuel mixture out and shut off the electrical switches, I had not reached down and turned off the fuel shutoff lever, which is positioned low by the pilot's left leg. I also did not unlatch the left side window, which in an emergency could also be used to egress.

3. **Practice**—The best procedures and training in the world are useless if you don't practice. As a CFI, I spend flight time training with students. When I fly my own airplane, I try to make every flight a training opportunity. I practice emergency landings and plan for emergencies all the time. And that all paid off. I had built a muscle memory of what to do as well as a mental state of knowing I could land the plane where I wanted. Because of that, a lot of stress was removed during those two minutes, which allowed me to focus my attention on other tasks.

4. **Attitude**—I never gave up. There was no doubt in my mind. I was going to have a successful outcome. Indecision was not a factor. Even as I made an automatic turn toward Landmark Airstrip, I realized I could not glide to the strip. I scanned the area and chose a clearing in the trees long enough and within gliding distance. After I chose the spot, *I did not change my plan.* I have given so many flight reviews and student check flights where pilots kept changing their mind and their plan during a simulated emergency, and invariably put themselves in a situation that would have ended badly. The literally hundreds of hours I had spent observing, discussing, and demonstrating that indecision simply removed it from the situation.

And then, after the two most intense minutes of my life, I set up for a landing in a marshy area beside the creek. The main thought I had coming over the trees was that I wanted to stay upright; I hoped the airplane did not flip over on the rough, soft ground.

Figure 9-10. Terrain overlay of GPS data from my Citabria showing speeds in the final recorded data points.

The airplane bounced but remained upright, and the left wing struck a dead tree that spun it about 180 degrees around the vertical axis. However, I have no memory of those things. My memory is blank from just before I touched down until I "woke up" sitting in the airplane, pointed in the opposite direction from which I landed. The GPS data from my airplane shows I flew over the trees at 52 knots ground speed, and touched down at about 43 knots ground speed, which is pretty much spot on for the minimum speeds of the airplane at that density altitude (Figure 9-10).

I have read it is not uncommon to have a blank memory under such high stress conditions, and it is possible I blacked out from the G-forces. My G-meter (accelerometer) indicated forces from +5 to -2.5 G, but the instrument only records vertical acceleration, so lateral G-forces could have been much greater as the airplane did a pirouette after striking the dead tree. The 26-inch, oversize Goodyear tires, which I kept inflated to 12 psi, probably helped cushion the impact and kept the wheels from digging into the wet ground.

After I regained consciousness, my first thought was "how badly am I injured?" and at the same time, "is the airplane on fire?" I checked myself; my whole body felt like it had just been run over by a truck, but I was not bleeding, my limbs worked, and I did not think anything was broken. I unbuckled, opened the door, and got out. The plane was upright, and the door functioned normally (Figure 9-11). I did not see or smell fuel, and there was no fire.

Figure 9-11. The Citabria immediately after the emergency landing. The door functioned normally. *(Photo by Amy Hoover)*

Then more of my training kicked in. I had taken several wilderness and post-crash survival courses with Air Force and Army instructors over the years and taught post-crash survival in my mountain/canyon flying courses at the university, so I did first things first. Check for injuries and take care of immediate physiological needs. I knew shock was going to be a factor (the Air Force instructor had called it post-ejection shock) and I drank water from my supply to help flush the adrenaline from my system and stay hydrated. There were a lot of mosquitos. I did not need insect bites on top of everything else, so I used some insect repellent from my survival vest I was wearing. I took out my bright orange sweater from my survival pack, then got back into the airplane to see if my ELT had activated. It had not. I also wondered if I should activate the personal locator beacon (PLB) I wear on my survival vest, since it was registered with NOAA and would send out a GPS signal to Air Force Search and Rescue. However, I knew I had been talking to other airplanes, so decided to first check and see if anyone had heard my call. I wished I had already bought the satellite phone I had been meaning to get.

I got back in the airplane, turned the master switch and radio on, and made another Mayday call, using both 122.9 and 121.5. The de Havilland Beaver that had reported to the south (the green dot) was circling the area and we made radio contact on 122.9. The pilot said he had responded to my first Mayday call and that he saw a downed airplane on fire at the tree line to the south. I saw a column of smoke in that direction at about the location of the collision. As we were talking, another airplane came on the frequency, a Cessna 206 that was en route to a private airstrip further east. I gave both pilots my GPS bearing and distance relative to Landmark airstrip and the phone numbers of the friends in McCall with whom I had dispatched my flight, and I asked them to tell everyone I was OK. I decided I did not need to activate my PLB as it might just cause another layer of confusion, since I had already made contact with the two airplanes.

The Beaver continued on to Sulphur Creek and I later learned the pilot made a call out on the satellite phone to my friend in McCall. The Cessna 206 pilot had to leave because it was getting warm enough he did not want to land at his destination airstrip too late due to high DA. He was able to reach Salt Lake City Center on their frequency, gave them my tail number and position, and reported I was OK.

After I made sure someone knew where I was, I continued to assess my condition and situation. I had no idea how long I might be waiting, but I knew to stay with the airplane. I could also feel myself going more into shock and I needed to stay occupied. I thought of all the times in my classes when we studied the need to accurately document events as much as possible after an accident. We also discussed how people's memories can become contaminated after talking to others or can change over time or with more input. So, I set about documenting as best I could what had happened while it was fresh in my memory, and to keep myself busy.

I took my smartphone out and walked around the airplane taking photos of the damage (Figure 9-12). The propeller blades were bent forward, and the left wing had struck a dead tree on landing, which is visible in front of the airplane. When the wing hit the tree, it caused the airplane to do a pirouette around the vertical axis and come to a stop almost 180 degrees from the direction it had landed. Incredibly, the wing hit the tree outboard of the fuel tank, and directly on the wing spar, which absorbed the kinetic energy and spun the airplane around. I could not see the airplane's belly since it had stopped in thick brush. The ground was marshy, and water came up to my ankles in places (Figure 9-12).

I got back in the airplane, continued drinking water, and turned the radio back on. I realized I could give a more precise position by centering the GPS to get exact coordinates rather than the bearing/distance to Landmark airstrip, so I called on 121.5 in the blind and a corporate jet aircraft overhead responded. I explained I had been in a midair collision, made an emergency landing, had already contacted two GA pilots, and wanted to report my position and status more accurately. I gave the pilot the location both in GPS coordinates and bearing/distance from the

Figure 9-12. Photos of the Citabria taken a few minutes after the emergency landing. *(Photos by Amy Hoover)*

Landmark airstrip and reported that I was still OK. I figured the more people who knew where I was, the better. I shut down the GPS, engine monitors, and other electrical equipment except the radio to conserve battery life.

I remembered telling students in class to write down what they could recall as soon as possible after an accident, which I realized was ludicrous; I was shaking so badly I could not have written anything down! So, I started making voice memos on my smartphone. I told my phone what had happened—what I had seen and heard. I noted all the radio communications and position reports made by me and by the other pilots. I recalled my altitudes, positions, heading, the timing and sequence of events. I made several of those recordings over the next hour, going over all the events leading up to the collision and emergency landing. That was invaluable when I wrote my report to the National Transportation Safety Board (NTSB), as I was able to review the recordings to make sure my memory was accurate. I discovered later (almost two years later) that what I reported matched the GPS and radar data, which helped the NTSB with their analysis.

In between making voice memos, I listened on the radio for status updates on 121.5 guard frequency. I heard a helicopter overhead at one time, but it was north of me by the Landmark airstrip and could not hear my radio calls. I stayed in contact with several aircraft high overhead, including an Alaska Airlines jet, which relayed information both to Salt Lake Center and to Boise Flight Service Station. As I went more into shock, I cannot convey how comforting it was to talk with those pilots. They were incredibly kind, and I think they could tell from my voice that just making contact was helpful. The Alaska Airlines pilots told me two Life Flight helicopters had been dispatched from Boise and were en route to my location, and the pilots passed me off to another Alaska flight when they went out of range.

After a while, my voice memos became more about my physical and emotional symptoms as my system went deeper into shock. I knew from my survival training that I needed to stay focused and alert. I realized that, silly as it sounded, talking into my phone helped me stay calm. It was a kind of triage; I knew I was in shock and could feel my system starting to go into super-overdrive, and I needed to stay occupied. I was uncertain what kind of internal injuries I might have sustained, but I knew the adrenaline was probably masking some of my pain and symptoms. I also knew I needed to stay conscious in case I had suffered a head injury.

These are the things I focused on:

· Continuing to assess my injuries
· Updating my status with aircraft overhead
· Staying focused and mentally alert
· Monitoring myself and documenting my progress

And then I heard the Life Flight helicopter. I got out of the airplane and waved, and they landed close by (Figure 9-13).

Figure 9-13. St. Alphonsus Life Flight helicopter making a rescue landing next to my Citabria. *(Photo by Amy Hoover)*

The flight nurse walked over and asked if I would be able to direct them to where the other airplane went down. I said I could and asked if they had more water. He gave me an electrolyte drink. I was still wearing my survival vest, so I grabbed my headset and my purse from the back seat and boarded the helicopter. We lifted off and flew south toward where the collision had occurred, and I snapped a quick shot of my little Citabria; that was the last time I ever saw it (Figure 9-14). Pilots may anthropomorphize their airplanes in the same way sailors do their boats, but on that day, I knew that tough little airplane had done the job of keeping me alive.

I was sitting in the back seat on the right side of the helicopter facing forward, and the flight nurse and I were scanning the ground as the pilots circled the area where my airplane had been struck. I remember it vividly; as we circled to the right I saw the other airplane first. It was in a burned-out area of trees, and when I saw it, I suddenly felt like I had been kicked in the stomach. It had to be 90K! Everything just came together at once; it was a white, high-wing airplane, and it had been an hour and a half since the collision, but my friend had not returned to look for me.

Figure 9-14. The Citabria facing south in the marshy meadow. The landing was toward the north, and the airplane came to rest facing the opposite direction. *(Photo by Amy Hoover)*

The helicopter pilot landed in a small clearing, and the crew walked over to the crash site while I stayed behind. I remained by myself for about half an hour, sitting in the helicopter. I could tell I was going deeper into shock and started feeling lightheaded and disoriented. When the flight nurse returned, he said, "There were no survivors. And you don't look good." He then put a cervical collar on me, secured me on the gurney, and hooked up blood pressure and O_2 monitors. When the pilots returned, I was flown to McCall Airport and taken by ambulance to the hospital emergency room.

It is amazing how clear my memory is of some things, like how nauseating the diesel fumes were during the ambulance ride and what it was like to be wheeled into the ER under the bright lights. The ER doctor did a lot of scans and tests and was about to put an IV in my arm when she exclaimed, "You're already hydrated!" I had been drinking my own water, the helicopter crew's water, and electrolyte drinks since the emergency landing, which had kept me from dehydrating. I had soft tissue injuries, including bruised organs, but no broken ribs, bones, or apparent head injury. My friends were on the way to the hospital.

Oddly, as I lay on the table with a neck brace on and all kinds of monitors stuck to me, the deputy sheriff showed up, handed me a piece of paper, and said he wanted me to fill out an accident report. The doctor shooed him away and conducted some more tests. She said she had not wanted to alarm me, but when I first came in my blood pressure was incredibly high, and I was in a pretty advanced state of shock. After a few hours in the ER, I was released with a bunch of pain medication to go home and rest.

Although that might seem like some kind of ending, everything up to that point was really just the beginning. My friend that picked me up at the hospital said, "Don't talk to anyone, and call AOPA right now." Both of us knew that when there has been any kind of airplane accident, it is best to use the "duct tape" rule: keep your mouth shut and get help. I have belonged to the AOPA legal services plan for years, and even through the haze of the pain medications and the shock, I knew he was right. I called AOPA, and the first thing the consultant said was, "Don't speculate about anything, and don't talk to anyone except the NTSB." She then gave me a list of resources to help with what I was to discover would be a long road ahead.

I did not sleep for two days. When I finally did, it was fitful, and I had nightmares of the moment the airplane hit me. Even when I was awake, I kept seeing it over and over again in my mind; I could not shake the image and the shock that accompanied it. My injuries hurt more, and everyone was trying to contact me. I checked in with immediate family but put everyone else on hold except to let them know I was OK. I just could not deal with the emotional "noise."

By then it was confirmed that the other airplane was 90K and that the pilot was killed in the crash. Then all the questions started. What had happened? How? Why? I had met his wife once, years before, when they were airplane camping in Idaho, but I did not know his other family members or friends, and he had no children.

The media was crazy. Newspaper and television reporters relentlessly tried to contact me for many days. Within hours of the crash, my sister-in-law in Oregon received a call from a major New York City news network, and my mother saw it on a Florida news channel. I followed the advice from AOPA and did not speak to anyone. Social media and online chat forums were abuzz with speculation about what might have happened. I saw none of that; I had to ignore that "flak" and focus on what I needed to do, which was to work with the NTSB, make a written report within 10 days, and take care of my own health.

Months later I looked through more than 30 articles and news stories about the accident, and at least half the information was speculative or just plain fabricated. The social media and forums were full of stories about what the other pilot and I were supposed to have done. Some said we had taken off in formation from Landmark Airstrip and collided, and others speculated it was a "photo mission gone wrong" or that we were "dogfighting" with our airplanes. One said it was a head-on collision. But during the immediate aftermath, I thankfully knew none of that.

What I knew was I needed to focus on the task at hand, and unfortunately my pilot logbooks were 300 miles away in another state. My airplane had been recovered by a salvage operation, and my personal belongings and the rest of my emergency and survival gear were still in it. It was all I could do to collect my records, gather up the information I needed, and talk to the NTSB and the FAA (the FAA assists the NTSB with certain items in such an investigation). I was thankful to have my friends and support around me. I had a lot of help, both physically and emotionally, and I needed it.

Here are some things I learned:

- *Use the duct tape rule*—Talk only to the people and organizations that need to know. Especially important, *do not speculate*. Relate the facts as best you can remember, but do not try to second guess the circumstances.

- *Don't ignore stress*—Have a strong support network. Within hours after I was released from the ER, my aircraft insurance company contacted me. I was still reeling from the shock and injuries and was glad to have someone assisting me with the paperwork and reports that needed to be filed. Others helped by keeping the media at bay and recovering my property from the airplane. Many friends came by to check in on my emotional health and offer support, and they knew to give me breathing room as I processed what had happened and what was next.

- *Ignore the flak*—Some people seem to have a need to spread rumors, and I could not control that. However, there were occasions when a rumor needed to be quashed. For example, the insurance adjuster who was investigating the accident called me and speculated about the circumstances, and was spreading falsehoods to whomever might listen. I told the insurance company that if the individual did anything that compromised the accident investigation, I would hold the company responsible, and they put a stop to it. Months after the accident, the local newspaper wanted to interview me. When I asked why, the reporter said she was told I was being forced to resign from my job because I had been in a plane crash and someone died. I overheard someone telling others I should have my pilot's license revoked. I was accosted by a total stranger at the airport who accused me of all kinds of crazy things. It seemed I was being condemned simply for having survived. It takes courage and patience, but ultimately it must all be ignored.

- *Have patience*—An investigation takes time, a lot of time. The NTSB and FAA gather a lot of data, then disappear for a long time before anything is made public. It took them almost two years to complete the investigation.

Just because I was learning those things does not mean it was easy or that I always got it right. I was good at the duct tape rule; if people asked, I told the truth—that I was hit by another airplane in flight, I survived an emergency landing, and I did not know exactly why it happened.

It turns out I was not so good at managing stress. I think most people want to do the best they can, and as pilots we think we can handle whatever is thrown at us. After all, that is what we train for. But it was insidious. First, there was the physical and physiological response to stimuli; for more than a year afterward, I would flinch or jump unexpectedly when I saw sudden movement in my peripheral vison, particularly to my left. It did not happen so much when I was flying, but when I drove through an intersection I would suddenly panic, thinking I was about to be hit by something I could not see. The nightmares continued for many months, and gradually became less frequent and less intense. There was also a high level of stress due to circumstances at work that were unrelated but that compounded my situation. I had read and talked about post-traumatic stress, but I was not prepared for what it really entailed. Over time, and with a lot of compassion for myself and understanding from my loved ones, I got better, but it was not an easy road.

About a year and a half after the accident, I was asked to share my story publicly. I did not want to at first, but I agreed to speak at an FAA Wings Seminar, and people told me they valued the talk. Other pilots came forward and told their own stories of having been involved in airplane accidents. The FAA employee who had done the field investigation was at the presentation and told me afterward he wanted to send me some photos (Figure 9-15). It was the first I saw of the damage to the underside of my airplane and the hole showing where the impact had almost severed my elevator cable. I realized how incredibly lucky I had been that day, by a matter of inches.

Talking about the accident and telling my story helped others, and it helped me as well. Yet there was still a nagging question of just what had happened that day, and why. That is where I had to practice the fourth bulleted item above and be patient. Finally, the accident report came out after almost two years of waiting. The report and public docket, which includes photos as well as GPS and radar data, can be seen on the NTSB's website. The accident final reports are available by searching the Aviation Accident Database (www.ntsb.gov/_layouts/ntsb.aviation/index.aspx) using the accident numbers:

Citabria—Accident Number: WPR14FA283A
Cessna—Accident Number: WPR14FA283B

The public docket is available through the NTSB Docket Management System (www.ntsb.gov/investigations/SitePages/dms.aspx) by entering the NTSB Accident ID: WPR14FA283AB.

Additionally, direct links to the reports and public docket are available on the Reader Resources page for this book at www.asa2fly.com/reader/mountain.

Figure 9-15. The Citabria the day after the emergency landing. Note the marks on the belly of the airplane; the elevator cable is about an inch above the hole in the metal skin. *(Photos courtesy Cliff Smart, Boise FAA Flight Standards District Office)*

The NTSB used a commercial product called Exelis OpsVue that provides replays of FAA radar data and ADS-B (Automatic Dependent Surveillance-Broadcast) reports to create a visual replay of the combined data, which is available on the public docket site. Figures 9-16 through 9-20 show sequential screen shots taken from the NTSB video (NTSB, 2016c). My Citabria is the lead target, and Cessna 90K is the trailing target. Neither airplane was equipped with ADS-B. Note the altitudes for the Citabria on the radar do not exactly correspond with altitude data from the GPS, presumably due to transponder reporting error. There was no GPS data for the Cessna.

Figure 9-16. Screen shot of NTSB radar data video showing the lead target (Citabria) over the Needles at 8,200 feet, which corresponds to the red dot #2 position in Figure 9-7. The Cessna was behind at 8,775 feet. *(NTSB, 2016c)*

Figure 9-17. When the Citabria was north of Warm Lake at 8,200 feet (red dot #3 in Figure 9-7), the Cessna was still behind, showing 8,675 feet. That corresponds to the time when the Cessna pilot reported a position of 8,000 feet altitude over Warm Lake Summit (blue dot #3 in Figure 9-7) and stated he had passed the Citabria. *(NTSB, 2016c)*

Figure 9-18. Before the Citabria target was lost due to terrain interference, it was still showing 8,200 feet and the Cessna had closed to less than a mile in trail showing 8,600 feet. *(NTSB, 2016c)*

Figure 9-19. Just after the Citabria dropped off the radar, the Cessna showed 8,575 feet and 117 knots. *(NTSB, 2016c)*

Figure 9-20. Immediately before the Cessna dropped off radar, it was 11 miles from Sulphur Creek at 8,350 feet and 197 knots. This was about the same time the pilot reported his position at 5 miles from Sulphur Creek at 6,800 feet. *(NTSB, 2016c)*

The NTSB composite video sequence shows the Cessna never passed my Citabria. When the pilot reported positions in front of me, he was actually behind me. When he reported his speed as 129 knots, the data shows his plane was traveling at 115 knots. The NTSB report noted, "the trailing target is at 8,600 feet MSL, 119 knots ground speed, and has closed to about 1 mile from the lead target, which was still at 8,200 feet MSL and 103 knots. Both targets had just passed the north edge of Warm Lake" (NTSB, 2016a). The video shows the Cessna then closed on my Citabria until it was about a mile in trail, then went into a descent. The Cessna was at 8,500 feet and 117 knots when my airplane dropped off the radar, presumably due to terrain interference. Five seconds later the Cessna showed 8,350 feet and 197 knots before it also vanished from the radar display, presumably because of data loss due to mountainous terrain. The collision occurred roughly 2 miles to the southeast along the same trajectory the targets were traveling.

The NTSB report states, with regards to the Cessna: "The engine control knobs were pushed IN...The engine control cables remained attached to the mixture control lever, the throttle body, and the propeller governor" (NTSB, 2016b). As just described, the Cessna overtook me from behind, then climbed into and struck my plane from below. My airplane's propeller cut through the top of the fuselage on the Cessna and also damaged the right horizontal stabilizer (Figure 9-21).

Figure 9-21. The right horizontal stabilizer from the Cessna. *(Photo courtesy Cliff Smart, Boise FAA Flight Standards District Office)*

The National Transportation Safety Board "determines the probable cause(s) of this accident to be: The failure of the overtaking airplane's pilot to maintain visual contact and separation from the airplane being overtaken" (NTSB, 2016a).

At the time of this publication, it has been almost five years since the accident, and I have shared my story with students in classes at the university and with groups of pilots around the northwest and Alaska. I was reluctant at first but have come to realize that it is important to tell the story. When people hear my tale, invariably all the "why" questions emerge. Why was the other pilot not where he said he was? Why was his altitude so different from what he reported? Why had he said he passed me when he was behind me? Why did he descend and then climb? Did he see me? What was he thinking? What was he trying to do? The only answer I have is…I don't know. Any other answer would be speculation, and that is an important part of the tale. The data shows what happened, but not why. Ultimately, the only person who knows why is not here to tell us.

I did not originally intend to write about the accident in this book. My co-author urged me to consider it, but I was reluctant. What changed my mind was an email I received from a former student (Figure 9-22).

And I realized why I had to write my story; if something good can come from that tragic event, if the telling of it can help save even one person, then it needs to be told.

In summary, if I can send the reader off with any takeaway, it would be this: The unexpected can happen, anytime and anywhere. As pilots, we must be prepared, not just through talking but through doing. Treat every pre-flight inspection, every takeoff, every flight, every landing, and every debrief as if you were preparing for that day when something will come "out of the blue" without warning. To survive, you must be ready, and hopefully lucky. Follow procedures, stay current with your training, have a positive attitude, don't ever give up, and practice, practice, practice.

If you ever have the misfortune to have an incident or accident, take care of people first—yourself and your passengers. Treat shock and injuries and be prepared for a potential survival situation. Invest in emergency signaling devices, or just get the darn satellite phone. Remember to document the situation as best you can. After the fact, seek support; you will need it. Take care of yourself; don't ignore the stress, but do ignore the flak. One of the most important things I do every day is practice gratitude. Each day of my life is a gift to be treasured, whatever it may bring.

Thank you for Teaching

████████████████

Sat 12/16/2017 7:53 PM

To: Amy Hoover <Amy.Hoover@cwu.edu>;

Hello Dr. Hoover,

My name is ████████████████ I'm not sure if you remember me but I took your mountain flying course at Moses Lake this year and I wanted to say thank you. About two weeks ago I was involved in an airplane crash, and if it wasn't for you and what you taught me, I'm not sure if I would be sending you this email.

Hearing about your experience and what you did is something I will forever be grateful for. As you know I'm not allowed to talk about any details while the investigation is ongoing, and I don't want to speculate, but I have a voice recording from right after the accident talking about what happened, I didn't give up, I flew the plane into the crash, and if you have a chance to look at the pictures and see where the airplane landed, I remembered what you said about losing momentum by hitting the wings on other objects.

I again wanted to say thank you for giving me the knowledge to not only make me a better pilot, but giving me the ability to better handle the situation I was given, and in turn be able to save not only my life, but my student's life as well. Below is the link to the article and pictures.

http://komonews.com/news/local/small-plane-crash-at-paine-field

Best Regards,

████████████████

Figure 9-22. Email from a former student outlining an accident.

Review Questions and Exercises

Answers to review questions are provided in Appendix B.

Circle the correct answer:

1. Blood oxygen saturation decreases as altitude increases and is about 90% at 10,000 feet MSL. **(True / False)**

2. For optimum protection, pilots are encouraged to use supplemental oxygen above 12,000 feet during the day, and above 8,000 feet at night. **(True / False)**

3. Experience and judgment are directly related. **(True / False)**

4. Groupthink occurs when everyone in the group collaborates to make the best decision possible, after weighing all the risks. **(True / False)**

5. It is best not to tell passengers about emergency procedures or equipment since that could cause them to be unduly alarmed. **(True / False)**

6. Partial power loss is much more common than total power loss. **(True / False)**

7. Mitigating risk is accomplished through preparation, planning, and practice. **(True / False)**

8. In an emergency, the order of priority for items is (1) **(alliterate / aviate)**; (2) **(navigate / nominate)**; and (3) **(correlate / communicate)**.

Answer the following:

9. Name the survival rule of 3s.

10. List at least five emergency signaling devices.

APPENDIX

A

—

AXIOMS, RULES

and

SUGGESTIONS

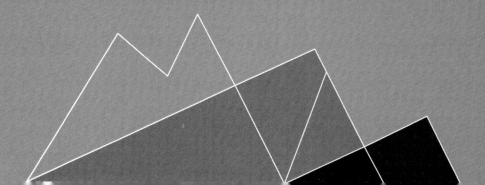

Amy's Axioms

Protect your gear; take your pants off!

Wheel pants (fairings) are not for rough airstrips. Remove them so you can see the wheels and brakes and so they do not collect dirt, rocks, and debris. They can break apart on rough strips and jam your wheels, brakes, or brake lines and cause an accident.

Do not try to out-climb a downdraft! Turn and fly away, to live again another day.

Single-engine GA airplanes lack the performance to outclimb most downdrafts. If you try to climb (say at V_Y), all you will do is spend more time in the downdraft! Take a lesson from glider pilots; put the nose down and turn away immediately.

What goes up must come down—be alert for downdrafts near thermals.

If you learn how to "read" wind, similar to running whitewater, you can spend most of your time going up. But the air has to go down somewhere, so always look for the downdrafts and avoid them. If you do get caught, see the previous axiom.

Lift is where you find it; stay clear of downdrafts, always be wary of turbulence, and if the winds aloft over the mountains and canyons exceed 25 knots, consider not flying.

When flying close to terrain, the cardinal rule is: Don't hit anything!

Well, duh. Although it may seem intuitive, obstacles may be hard to see in low-angle sun or low-light conditions. Dead trees (snags) are particularly hard to spot. Learn to visualize exactly where your landing gear and wingtips are and maintain adequate clearance over obstacles.

If the rocks and trees are your enemies, keep them close!

And then, after not hitting anything, stay as close as you can (without turbulence) so you can catch the lift, maneuver in a canyon, and have enough space to turn back in a tight spot.

As you cross a ridge, have a back door and keep your hand on the doorknob.

This is true in about any situation. Always know what is behind you and cross at an angle that lets you turn back immediately if you are not going to clear a ridge.

Always fly your approach at the same IAS for a given weight, regardless of DA.

The pitot tube measures the same airflow that is producing lift and drag over the wing and other airfoils. Do not add "extra" speed at high altitudes—the airplane does not need it. The TAS will already be higher, and so will the GS, so adding indicated speed creates an even greater hazard.

Faster and lower beats higher and slower.

There is an old bush pilot saying that "it is better to be 50 feet over the trees at 80 knots than 80 feet at 50 knots." Once you know you will clear an obstacle, it is better to lower the nose and gain speed rather than altitude, because unexpected turbulence, wind shear, and possible downdrafts are common. In that case, speed is your friend.

Wait! Weight! When DA goes up, wait for cooler weather or take the weight out. Relax, and make more than one trip.

You do not have to take it all in one trip. Keep the airplane light and plan your fuel so you can shuttle people or gear back and forth rather than risking an accident with a heavy airplane taking off from a backcountry airstrip at high altitude.

Curtail Complacency.

Pilots can let their guard down when they do the same thing many times over and lose the vigilance needed to stay alert to potential hazards. Even if you have made the same flight or been into the same airstrip many times, the next time may be different. Always plan for the unexpected and anticipate what could go wrong.

Eschew the Ego.

If you have something to prove, either to yourself or others, this type of flying (or any type, really) is not for you. Think that there will always be someone better than you, and there will always be a situation that exceeds your skills and abilities. The old saying "there are old pilots and bold pilots, but no old bold pilots" fits—leave your ego at home and think about the consequences of every action. I learn something every time I fly and make it a point to do so.

R.K.'s Risk Reduction Rules

Practice, practice, practice!

Bob Hoover, often referred to as the best stick and rudder pilot ever, practiced rolls thousands of times before going before a crowd. Bob Hannah, ex-Reno air racer, aerobatic pilot, off-field landing expert, and one of the most professional pilots I know, is constantly practicing his off-field landings, aerobatics, and instrument flying to keep his skills razor sharp. If the best are always practicing, we should be, too.

Use the right equipment.

Use the right airplane for the mission. Don't use a 172 for a Super Cub task. Get the best maintenance you possibly can to avoid mechanical issues in the wilderness. Use appropriate survival equipment for the area and the season.

Carry enough fuel to make a complete round trip plus 50%, or plan a fuel stop. The 30-minute rule is for flat land!

The wind doesn't blow, it sucks!

Every pilot has a wind story. If you are lucky, yours was a close call and you survived, but you don't want to experience it again. You can't accurately control approaches with speed and altitude in the wind, and that makes mountain and canyon flying much riskier and less fun.

Be able to do spot landings on speed.

This is the crux of short airstrip flying, and it takes constant practice. Look at the rules of thumb and the actual calculations. Even small variances in speed and altitude can have radical consequences.

Set personal limits and re-evaluate them daily.

In mountain and canyon flying, your limits will generally pertain to the airstrips you feel comfortable with and the weather you feel okay flying in. But it might even be something like flying through a "Star Wars canyon" (what we call one unique little remote place). It is very narrow at the bottom, with only a few wingspans of width, and has a ninety-degree turn at one point. I have flown it a few times, and it is definitely an adrenaline rush. But most of the time, and every time in the last few years, I have opted to fly it a couple of hundred feet higher where there is a little more room. I may never feel comfortable flying it at less than 100 feet AGL again. And that's okay.

I used to water ski occasionally, putting my tires on the water. That is another thing I haven't felt comfortable doing in some time.

When it comes to off-field landings or a very short or challenging airstrip landing, I may opt to do it one day but not another. This is not because of the flying conditions, but because I don't feel that I am up on my game at that particular time. It is a constant evaluation of what is happening and how I am doing at any particular time.

When I flew the mountains for a living, I knew the country I flew in well and often pushed the weather. But that changes, too. Now I don't remember the country as well, and I certainly don't want to use those old weather limitations in areas I am not as familiar with.

I think a successful mountain pilot must constantly be evaluating their personal limits. Remember, you do not have anything to prove. In his book *Forever Flying: Fifty Years of High-flying Adventures, From Barnstorming in Prop Planes to*

Dogfighting Germans to Testing Supersonic Jets, An Autobiography (1997), Bob Hoover said, "Know your airplane, know it well, know its limitations, and above all—know your own limitations."

Always do a post-flight review.

Review your flight on the drive home, and with other crewmembers, and don't kid yourself. Think about what went right, what went wrong, and what you should never do again.

Follow the Flying Rule of 3s: Weather, Daylight, and Fuel.

You can probably manage the risk of running low on any one of the 3, but accepting 2 out of 3 makes it unacceptable. Envision running low on fuel but having good weather and plenty of daylight. You can easily divert for fuel or make a precautionary stop. If the weather is deteriorating but you have plenty of fuel and daylight, you can easily divert around or turn back. If it is getting dark, but you have fuel and good weather, your concerns are definitely less. Now imagine those scenarios with two of the three elements against you, and your comfort level will change!

Visualize consequences.

This is the "what if" game. You can play it during any phase of flight. It is not necessarily meant to keep you from doing anything, but it does help you manage risk.

Visualize an emergency a day.

Every day you fly, visualize an emergency. It can be an engine failure, total or partial, a fire, a medical issue, or something else. Then go through the procedure in your mind. For total engine failure, go to best glide, carb heat if you have it, and locate a place to land, all simultaneously within the first 5 seconds. Then attempt a restart and shutdown if time permits. A partial power failure might be much more complex.

Learn to say NO.

This can be one of the most difficult things to do. Pressure from a boss, a friend, family, or yourself can be immeasurable. Saying no could mean loss of a job, harassment, and ego damage. But saying yes could mean loss of equipment and life. The experienced pilot learns to rely on intuition in the final "go, no-go" decision. Learning to gather and listen to these subliminal cues is a mark of experience and superb judgment.

Axioms, Rules, and Suggestions **329**

Stockhill's Sage Suggestions

Michael L. Stockhill was a test pilot in experimental airplanes, aviation magazine editor and contributing editor, airmail pilot, FAA Inspector, FBO owner, and NTSB Investigator. He has three type ratings, including the B727. He is a licensed A&P mechanic with Inspection Authorization. He is now content flying gliders: He claims he can get his flying fix without going far from home, and he hardly has to talk to anyone on the radio.

He shares the following suggestions.

For aircraft accident investigators, as long as man wants to fly in mountains, there will be job security.

During my career as an FAA inspector and NTSB investigator, mostly in the northwestern states, I spent altogether too many beautiful summer and autumn mornings picking through crushed wing panels, fuselages, and sooty puddles of melted aluminum alloys. Oddly, confronted with carnage and sad catastrophes, the investigators I knew and worked with found satisfaction—and occasional pleasure—in the challenge of determining why the accident had happened.

Inventive as pilots can be, only rarely now do they invent new ways of wrecking airplanes. But they are pretty adept at replaying old standbys. With that in mind, I long ago distilled my advice to mountain flyers into three points. Following them would have a significant effect on the accident rate.

First, if there is any concern about takeoff performance due to high density altitude, temperature, runway length, or any other salient parameters, make another trip. Leave a passenger or two or a quarter of that trophy elk. Fly to a longer airstrip. Then go back for the rest of your load.

Second, make a normal takeoff. Altogether too many airplanes are bent by premature liftoff at high-altitude airstrips and/or at high density altitude. This book delves in depth into the reasons why. My notion of a normal takeoff—especially with Cessnas—is a bit tail low, an attitude held until the airplane is ready to lift off at normal flying speed. Don't try to force the airplane into the air before it is ready to fly.

Third—and this gets altogether too personal—don't attempt to outclimb a mountain in an airplane. You can't shift down into low gear like an off-road vehicle. Even if you are climbing up a canyon or upslope and maintaining ground clearance, odds are that the slope will eventually steepen while your aircraft performance is deteriorating as altitude is gained. Literally, as I am composing this sidebar, it is the anniversary date of the loss of my young brother, who flew upslope with three other persons in a Cessna 182. His maneuver did not end well. Nor is it likely to work any better for you.

APPENDIX

B

ANSWERS

to

REVIEW

QUESTIONS

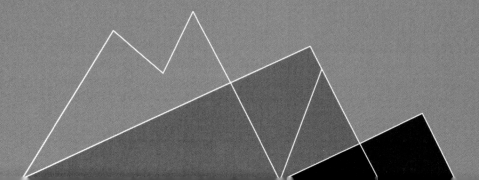

Chapter 1

1. False
2. True
3. False
4. False
5. True
6. False
7. More; higher; higher
8. More; lower; slower
9. Some important aircraft preflight items include:
   - Look your airplane over from a short distance to get an overview of potential damage, leaks, top of wing, tail surfaces, etc.
   - Confirm fuel amount with manual check, and confirm that fuel is clean of contaminants.
   - Remove tow bars and tie downs.
   - Double check fuel and oil caps and dipsticks.
   - Check firewall fuel strainer for leaks.
   - Check brake pads for wear limits.
   - Test magneto switch for a hot mag or worn key.
   - Check tires for wear, checking, and inflation.
   - Ensure pitot tube is clear.
   - Clean the belly.
   - Ensure windscreen is clean and free of crazing and scratches.

Chapter 2

1. True
2. False
3. True
4. False
5. upslope; morning
6. downslope; evening
7. downdrafts; updrafts

Chapter 3

1. True
2. False
3. True
4. False
5. False
6. False
7. Pilotage
8. dead reckoning; pilotage

Chapter 4

1. False
2. True
3. False
4. False
5. center of gravity
6. heavier; forward
7. turn-around point
8. To decrease the turn radius at a given angle of bank.

   Visual illusions/disorientation; Increase in stall speed; Increase in load factor.

Chapter 5

1. True
2. False
3. False
4. True
5. below; slower
6. pitch; power
7. Lift, sink, gusts, turbulence
8. One-inch; 100 fpm

9. The aim point is the spot on the ground toward which you will descend at a constant angle for landing; it is the point where your visual approach path intersects the runway surface.

10. Confining terrain, one-way airstrips, obstacles, and high DA are all hazards of go-arounds. The airplane must transition from a descent (or bounce) to a climb and may not be able to out-climb terrain past the end of the airstrip or maneuver in a canyon.

11. IAS for V_{S0} at 40 degrees flaps   = 48 knots (Table 5-1)
    = 55 knots CAS (Figure 5-3).
    1.2×55 knots CAS   = 63 knots IAS (Figure 5-3).

Chapter 6

1. False

2. True

3. True

4. False

5. False

6. False

7. True

8. shortest horizontal distance; increases

9. shortest amount of time; decreases

10. decreases; lower

Chapter 7

1. False

2. False

3. True

4. False

5. True

6. True

7. flat light

8. Engine and wing covers, engine preheater, snowshoes or skis, sleeping bag, snow shovel, fire-making equipment, garbage bags, rope and/or come along

9. Light conditions, crevasses, roughness of the surface, snow depth

Chapter 8

1. False

2. True

3. True

4. False

5. True

6. increases; increase

Chapter 9

1. True

2. False

3. False

4. False

5. False

6. True

7. True

8. (1) aviate, (2) navigate, (3) communicate

9. Air—3 minutes
   Shelter—3 hours
   Rest—30 hours
   Water—3 days
   Food—30 days

10. GPS tracker, personal locator beacon, signal mirror, laser flare, strobe light, glow sticks, bright clothing, fire starters, whistle.

APPENDIX

C

GLOSSARY

of

TERMS

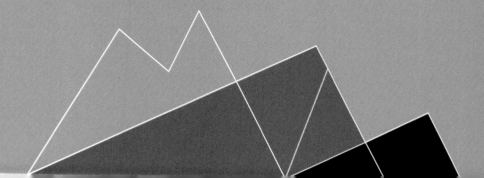

advisory circular (AC). A publication offered by the FAA to provide guidance for compliance with airworthiness, pilot certification, operational standards, training standards, and any other rules with the 14 CFR Aeronautics and Space title.

aeronautical decision making (ADM). A systematic approach to the mental process used by pilots to consistently determine the best course of action in response to a given set of circumstances.

Aeronautical Information Manual (AIM). Formerly *Airman's Information Manual.* In United States and Canada, the *AIM* is the respective nation's official guide to basic flight information and air traffic control procedures.

AeroWeather Pro 2.0. A weather app that provides current and precise weather conditions (METAR), forecasts (TAF), Airport NOTAMs, and more. www.lakehorn.com/products/aeroweather-pro

air traffic control (ATC). A service provided by ground-based air traffic controllers who direct aircraft on the ground and through controlled airspace and can provide advisory services to aircraft in non-controlled airspace. The primary purpose of ATC worldwide is to prevent collisions, organize and expedite the flow of air traffic, and provide information and other support for pilots. In some countries, ATC plays a security or defensive role or is operated by the military.

Aircraft Owners and Pilots Association (AOPA) (www.aopa.org). A Maryland-based American non-profit political organization that advocates for general aviation.

airframe icing. Formation of ice on aircraft surfaces. Certain atmospheric conditions can lead to the formation of ice on the surfaces of an aircraft.

airworthiness directive (AD). A regulatory notice sent out by the FAA to the registered owner of an aircraft informing the owner of a condition that prevents the aircraft from continuing to meet its conditions for airworthiness. Airworthiness directives (AD notes) must be complied with within the required time limit, and the fact of compliance, the date of compliance, and the method of compliance must be recorded in the aircraft's maintenance records.

altitude chamber. Also called a hypobaric chamber; a chamber used to simulate the effects of high altitude on the human body, especially hypoxia (low oxygen) and hypobaria (low ambient air pressure).

anabatic lift. Lift created by anabatic wind (or anabatic flow) when the sun heats the surface of a mountain or canyon wall and causes a warm upslope flow.

angle of attack (AOA). The angle at which relative wind meets an airfoil. It is the angle that is formed by the chord of the airfoil and the direction of the relative wind or between the chord line and the flight path. The angle of attack changes during a flight as the pilot changes the direction of the aircraft and is related to the amount of lift being produced.

anti-authority. One who resents supervision, does not like to be bound by schedules or habits, and has a need for complete freedom. Identified by the FAA as a potentially hazardous attitude for pilots.

ASOS/AWOS. The Automated Surface Observing Systems (ASOS) program is a joint effort of the National Weather Service (NWS), the Federal Aviation Administration (FAA), and the Department of Defense (DOD). The ASOS systems serves as the primary surface weather observing network in the United States. Types include Automated Weather Observing System (AWOS) and the Automated Surface Observing System (ASOS).

attitude (psychology). A settled way of thinking or feeling about someone or something, typically reflected in a person's behavior.

Automated Flight Service Station (AFSS). Air traffic facilities that communicate directly with pilots to conduct preflight briefings, flight plan processing, inflight advisory services, search and rescue initiation, and assistance to aircraft in emergencies.

Automatic Dependent Surveillance Radar–Broadcast (ADS-B). A satellite-based system in which properly equipped aircraft broadcast their identification, position, altitude, and velocity to other aircraft and to air traffic control (ATC). Broadcasting this information is called ADS-B Out, and receiving it is known as ADS-B In.

> **ADS-B Out.** All U.S. airspace designated in 14 CFR§91.225 must be equipped with ADS-B Out avionics that meet the performance requirements of 14 CFR §91.227. Aircraft not complying with the requirements may be denied access to this airspace. Other countries around the world have different requirements for ADS-B.

> **ADS-B In.** ADS-B In pilot cockpit advisory services consist of **Flight Information Service-Broadcast (FIS-B)** and **Traffic Information Service-Broadcast (TIS-B)**. These are free services transmitted automatically to aircraft equipped to receive ADS-B In.

Automatic Direction Finder (ADF)/Non-Directional Beacon (NDB). A low/medium frequency or UHF radio beacon transmitting non-directional signals whereby the pilot of an aircraft equipped with direction finding equipment can determine bearing to or from the radio beacon and "home" in on or track to or from the station. When the radio beacon is installed in conjunction with the ILS marker, it is normally called a compass locator.

Aviate, Navigate, Communicate (ANC). A memory aid to help pilots prioritize tasks during normal and during emergency situations. In order of importance, they are:

> *Aviate*—Maintain control of the aircraft.
> *Navigate*—Know where you are and where you intend to go.
> *Communicate*—Let someone know your plans and needs.

calibrated airspeed. Indicated airspeed corrected for instrument and position error.

Canada VFR Navigation Chart (VNC). The VNC is used by VFR pilots on short to extended cross-country flights at low to medium altitudes and at low to medium airspeeds.

canard. A horizontal surface mounted ahead of the main wing to provide longitudinal stability and control. It may be a fixed, movable, or variable geometry surface, with or without control surfaces.

canyon speed (V_{CANYON}). *See* V_{CANYON}.

cap cloud. A stratiform, orographic cloud that hovers above or over an isolated mountain peak, formed by the cooling and condensation of moist air forced up and over the peak and lenticular-shaped by horizontal upper level winds.

center of gravity (CG). The point at which an airplane would balance if it were possible to suspend it at that point. It is the mass center of the airplane, or the theoretical point at which the entire weight of the airplane is assumed to be concentrated. It may be expressed in inches from the reference datum or in percent of mean aerodynamic chord (MAC). The location depends on the distribution of weight in the airplane.

Chart Supplements U.S. Formerly *Airport/Facility Directory*; provides comprehensive information on airports, large and small, and other aviation facilities and procedures.

cirrus clouds. Clouds composed of ice crystals that originate from the freezing of supercooled water droplets in regions where air temperature is lower than -20° or -30°C.

Civil Aerospace Medical Institute (CAMI). The medical certification, research, education, and occupational health wing of the FAA's Office of Aerospace Medicine. The goal of the office is to enhance aviation safety.

controlled flight into terrain (CFIT). A situation when an airworthy aircraft under the control of the flight crew is flown unintentionally into terrain, obstacles, or water, usually with no prior awareness by the crew.

convergence effect. The phenomenon observed where two wind flow patterns meet and interact, such as at the confluence of two river drainages. Both horizontal and vertical wind shear and turbulence may result.

crevasse. A deep crack, or fracture, found in an ice sheet or glacier.

cruise climb. A gradual climb at higher airspeed than V_Y that enables increased visibility and engine cooling.

cumulonimbus cloud. From the Latin cumulus ("heaped") and nimbus ("rainstorm"). A dense, towering, vertical cloud formed from water vapor carried by powerful upward air currents. If observed during a storm, these clouds may be referred to as thunderheads.

dead reckoning. Navigation solely by means of computations based on airspeed, course, heading, wind direction and speed, ground speed, and elapsed time.

Dempsey Dumpster. Nickname used by U.S. Navy pilots for an underwater escape training device that simulates an aircraft cockpit and that is submersed while being rotated in one or more direction. Pilots practice situational awareness and learn techniques to escape the sinking aircraft.

Denalt computer. A handheld mechanical computer used to determine density altitude and aircraft performance.

density altitude (DA). Pressure altitude corrected for nonstandard temperature. Density altitude is used to compute the performance of an aircraft and its engines.

descent rate. Also called rate of descent. Amount of altitude loss per unit of time, typically defined in feet per minute (fpm).

diurnal wind. Local winds recurring on a daily basis along the axis of a valley, blowing upslope by day and downslope by night. They occur mostly in calm, clear weather.

Doppler weather radar. A type of radar used to locate precipitation, calculate its motion, and estimate its type (rain, snow, hail, etc.). Modern weather radars are mostly pulse-Doppler radars, capable of detecting the motion of rain droplets in addition to the intensity of the precipitation.

Drooping ailerons and wingtips. STOL devices added to the wing to lower stall speed and increase controllability in slow flight.

Dutch roll coordination exercise. An exercise used to develop control touch, as described in Chapter 1 of this book. Not to be confused with the FAA definition of Dutch roll.

electronic flight instrument system (EFIS). A flight deck instrument display system in which the display technology used is electronic rather than electromechanical. Also called glass cockpit.

emergency landing. A landing made in a distress or urgent situation. Precautionary landings and forced landings are types of emergency landings.

emergency locator transmitter (ELT). Equipment that broadcasts distinctive signals on designated frequencies and may be automatically activated by impact or can be manually activated.

exhaust gas temperature (EGT). A meter used to monitor the exhaust gas temperature of an internal combustion engine in conjunction with a thermocouple-type pyrometer. This gives the pilot an idea of the engine's air-fuel ratio.

Federal Aviation Administration (FAA). The Federal Aviation Administration is an operating mode of the U.S. Department of Transportation with the authority and powers to regulate all aspects of civil aviation in the United States.

fixed-base operator (FBO). An airport-based company serving aviation with fuel sales and other aircraft services.

Flight Information Service-Broadcast (FIS-B). FIS-B provides a broad range of textual/graphical weather products and other flight information to the general aviation community. It is only available on the 978 MHz Universal Access Transceiver (UAT) equipment, and includes:

- Aviation Routine Weather Reports (METARs)
- Non-Routine Aviation Weather Reports (SPECIs)
- Terminal Area Forecasts (TAFs) and their amendments
- NEXRAD (regional and CONUS) precipitation maps
- Notice to Airmen (NOTAM) Distant and Flight Data Center
- Airmen's Meteorological Conditions (AIRMET)
- Significant Meteorological Conditions (SIGMET) and Convective SIGMET
- Status of Special Use Airspace (SUA)
- Temporary Flight Restrictions (TFRs)
- Winds and Temperatures Aloft
- Pilot Reports (PIREPS)

See also universal access transceiver (UAT).

flow check. A basic method for running through system checks and setup of the aircraft in varying phases of flight. It follows a logical "flow" around the cockpit instruments and switches, generally followed by a written checklist.

FltPlan Go. A commercial app for flight planning and weather.

fog. A thick cloud of tiny water droplets suspended in the atmosphere at or near the earth's surface that obscures or restricts visibility (to a greater extent than mist; strictly, reducing visibility to below 1 km).

Foreflight. A commercial app that provides flight planning, flight support, weather, and electronic flight bag (EFB) for pilots.

fuel strainers. Devices designed to strain aviation fuel for impurities. They are mounted in the engine compartment and are accessible for the pilot to drain and inspect fuel samples before flight.

Gs. Load factor; in aviation, typically the ratio of an airplane's lift to its weight. In straight-and-level flight, for example, lift equals weight and the load factor is 1G. In a coordinated, level turn at 60 degrees of bank, the load factor would be 2Gs.

gap seals. STOL devices that fill the various gaps between flight controls (i.e., flaps, ailerons, rudders, and elevators) to streamline airflow, increase control, and lower stall speeds.

Garmin InReach. A commercial personal locator device using satellite technology.

Garmin Pilot. A commercial app designed for flight planning purposes.

general aviation (GA). All civil aviation operations other than scheduled air services and non-scheduled air transport operations for remuneration or hire. General aviation flights range from gliders and powered parachutes to corporate business jet flights.

Global Positioning System (GPS). Worldwide positioning, navigation, and timing determination capability available from the U.S. satellite constellation. The service provided by GPS for civil use is defined in the GPS Standard Positioning System Performance Standard. GPS is composed of space, control, and user elements.

ground-based transmitters (GBT). For ADS-B, GBTs receive broadcasts and relay information to ATC and other aircraft.

ground loop. A sharp, uncontrolled change of direction of an airplane on the ground.

ground speed (GS). The actual speed of the airplane over the ground. It is true airspeed adjusted for wind and density altitude (DA). Ground speed decreases with a headwind and increases with a tailwind. It increases with increased DA.

groupthink. The practice of thinking or making decisions as a group in a way that discourages creativity or individual responsibility.

hazardous attitudes. The Federal Aviation Administration's literature defines five hazardous attitudes that can undermine a pilot's aeronautical decision making. They are anti-authority, impulsivity, invulnerability, macho, and resignation.

hyperventilation. Occurs when the rate or tidal volume of breathing eliminates more carbon dioxide than the body can produce. This lowers the concentration of carbon dioxide dissolved in the blood, leading to hypercapnia.

hypoxia. A state of oxygen deficiency in the blood, tissues, and cells sufficient to cause an impairment of body functions.

IFR chart. Charts used for flying under instrument flight conditions and rules.

impulsivity. The tendency to act on a whim, displaying behavior characterized by little or no forethought, reflection, or consideration of the consequences. The FAA has identified this attitude as potentially hazardous for pilots.

indicated airspeed (IAS). The direct instrument reading obtained from the airspeed indicator, uncorrected for variations in atmospheric density, installation error, or instrument error. Manufacturers use IAS as the basis for determining airplane performance. Takeoff, landing, and stall speeds listed in the AFM or POH are indicated airspeeds and do not normally vary with altitude or temperature.

instrument meteorological conditions (IMC). Meteorological conditions expressed in terms of visibility, distance from clouds, and ceiling less than the minimums specified for visual meteorological conditions, requiring operations to be conducted under instrument flight rules (IFR).

International Civil Aviation Organization (ICAO). A specialized agency of the United Nations. It codifies the principles and techniques of international air navigation and fosters the planning and development of international air transport to ensure safe and orderly growth.

invulnerability. The attitude that one is incapable of being wounded, injured, or harmed. The FAA has identified this attitude as potentially hazardous for pilots.

judgment. The mental process of recognizing and analyzing all pertinent information in a particular situation, a rational evaluation of alternative actions in response to it, and a timely decision on which action to take.

knowledge. Facts, information, and skills acquired by a person through experience or education; the theoretical or practical understanding of a subject.

Koch chart. Chart used to determine the effects of altitude and temperature on airplane performance.

leading-edge wing cuffs (devices). High-lift devices on the leading edge of an airfoil. The most common types are fixed slots, movable slats, and leading-edge flaps.

lenticular clouds. Technically known as altocumulus standing lenticularis, these are stationary lens-shaped clouds that form at high altitudes, normally aligned at right angles to the wind direction.

LORAN. An electronic navigational system used before 2010, after which the U.S. Coast Guard terminated all U.S. LORAN-C transmissions.

macho. Attitude of showing aggressive pride in one's masculinity. Identified by the FAA as a potentially dangerous pilot attitude.

mammatus clouds. Associated with anvil clouds and severe thunderstorms. They often extend from the base of a cumulonimbus, but may also be found under altocumulus, altostratus, stratocumulus, and cirrus clouds, as well as volcanic ash clouds.

maneuvering speed (V_A). The speed calculated by the manufacturer at which the aircraft will stall before exceeding the design limit G-loading, thus preventing damage to the airframe. V_A (CAS) is determined by multiplying the flaps-up, power-off stall speed, V_{S1} (CAS), by the square root of the design limit. Thus, in the normal category with a positive design limit of 3.8G, $V_A = \sqrt{3.8} \times V_{S1} = 1.95 V_{S1}$.

manifold pressure (MP). The absolute pressure of the fuel/air mixture within the intake manifold, usually indicated in inches of mercury.

maximum performance takeoff. A takeoff using all of the maximum performance numbers available for the aircraft, at the lowest possible operating weight.

mean aerodynamic chord (MAC). The average distance from the leading edge to the trailing edge of the wing.

microburst. A strong downdraft which normally occurs over horizontal distances of 1 NM or less and vertical distances of less than 1,000 feet. Despite its small horizontal scale, an intense microburst could induce wind speeds greater than 100 knots and downdrafts as strong as 6,000 feet per minute.

minimum controllable airspeed (MCA). An airspeed at which any further increase in angle of attack, increase in load factor, or reduction in power would result in an immediate stall.

minimum en route altitude (MEA). The lowest published altitude between radio fixes that ensures acceptable navigational signal coverage and meets obstacle clearance requirements between those fixes.

Mode S transponder-based 1090 extended squitter ES. By definition, the word "squitter" refers to a periodic burst or broadcast of aircraft-tracking data that is transmitted periodically by a Mode S transponder to provide position, velocity, and time. Consequently, pilots who want to fly outside the United States—or operate at or above FL180—will need the 1090 ES transponder for ADS-B Out.

moose stall. A common stall/spin scenario close to the ground, originally named from a low-level stall/spin caused by an uncoordinated turn around a moose on the ground in Alaska. Commonly used to describe any circling, low-level stall scenario.

moraine. Unconsolidated glacial debris (rocks, dirt, gravel) formed from debris previously carried along by a glacier. Debris consists of somewhat rounded particles ranging in size from large boulders to minute glacial flour. Lateral moraines are formed at the side of the ice flow and terminal moraines at the foot.

most conservative response. In the event of a disagreement, the parties involved agree in advance to take the most conservative action until additional information is available.

National Oceanic and Atmospheric Administration (NOAA). An American scientific agency within the United States Department of Commerce that focuses on the conditions of the oceans and the atmosphere. NOAA warns of dangerous weather, charts seas, guides the use and protection of ocean and coastal resources, and conducts research to provide understanding and improve stewardship of the environment.

National Transportation Safety Board (NTSB). An independent U.S. government investigative agency responsible for civil transportation accident investigation. In this role, the NTSB investigates and reports on aviation accidents and incidents, certain types of highway crashes, ship and marine accidents, pipeline incidents, and railroad accidents. When requested, the NTSB will assist the military and foreign governments with accident investigation. The NTSB is also in charge of investigating cases of hazardous materials releases that occur during transportation.

NDB. *See* Automatic Direction Finder (ADF)/Non-Directional Beacon (NDB).

New Zealand Civil Aviation Authority. The government agency tasked with establishing civil aviation safety and security standards in New Zealand.

nimbostratus clouds. Mid- or low-level, rain-bearing layer cloud, generally covering the whole sky and thick enough to hide the sun.

Notice to Airmen (NOTAM). A notice filed with an aviation authority to alert aircraft pilots of potential hazards along a flight route or at a location that could affect the safety of the flight. NOTAMs are unclassified notices or advisories distributed by means of telecommunication that contain information concerning the establishment, conditions or change in any aeronautical facility, service, procedure or hazard, the timely knowledge of which is essential to personnel and systems concerned with flight operations.

obscurations to visibility. Any phenomenon in the atmosphere, other than precipitation, that reduces the horizontal visibility, including mist, fog, smoke, volcanic ash, dust, sand, haze, or spray.

offset navigation. Strategic lateral offset procedure (SLOP) is a solution to a byproduct of increased navigation accuracy in aircraft. Because most aircraft now use GPS, they track flight routes with extremely high accuracy. As a result, if an error in height occurs, there is a much higher chance of collision. SLOP allows aircraft to offset the centerline of an airway or flight route by a small amount, normally to the right, so that collision with opposite direction aircraft becomes unlikely.

orographic lift. Occurs when an air mass is forced from a low elevation to a higher elevation as it moves over rising terrain. As the air mass gains altitude, it quickly cools down adiabatically, which can raise the relative humidity to 100% and create clouds and, under the right conditions, precipitation.

overflow. Also described as "slush," a condition where unfrozen liquid water is lying on top of ice and snow.

personal locator beacon (PLB). Transmits personalized distress signals in the 406 MHz spectrum range and aids in search and rescue missions.

physiological deficient zone. The atmospheric zone above an altitude threshold at which a person begins to experience symptoms of hypoxia. Some sources define the threshold at 10,000 feet MSL and some define it at 12,500 feet MSL.

physiological efficient zone. The atmospheric zone in which human physiology is evolutionarily adapted to be efficient, from sea level up to the altitude threshold at which a person begins to experience symptoms of hypoxia.

pilot judgment. The ability to perceive and select alternatives. Judgment is based on experience, training, intuition, and the particular circumstance at hand. It includes identifying problems, specifying alternative courses of action, assessing risks associated with each alternative, and choosing the best action within the available time.

pilot report (PIREP). A report of actual weather conditions encountered by an aircraft in flight. This information is usually relayed by radio to the nearest ground station, but other options (e.g., electronic submission) also exist in some regions. The message is then encoded and relayed to other weather offices and air traffic service units.

pilot's operating handbook (POH). Replaced by the aircraft flight manual (AFM) after 1978. The AFM is serial number specific, and the POH is model specific. Both provide information required to safely operate the aircraft.

pilotage. Navigation using fixed points of reference on an aeronautical chart.

pitch attitude. The angle between the airplane's longitudinal axis and the horizon. This angle is displayed on the attitude indicator or artificial horizon. Should not be confused with angle of attack (AOA).

pitot tube. A pressure measurement instrument used to measure fluid flow velocity. The pitot tube was invented by the French engineer Henri Pitot in the early 18th century and was modified to its modern form in the mid-19th century by French scientist Henry Darcy.

power. The rate of doing work; the amount of energy transferred per unit time.

power-off glide. A glide is a basic maneuver in which the airplane loses altitude in a controlled descent with little or no engine power; forward motion is maintained by gravity pulling the airplane along an inclined path and the descent rate is controlled by the pilot balancing the forces of gravity and lift.

pressure altitude (PA). The altitude indicated when the altimeter setting window (barometric scale) is adjusted to 29.92. This is the altitude above the standard datum plane, which is a theoretical plane where air pressure (corrected to 15°C) equals 29.92" Hg. Pressure altitude is used to compute density altitude, true altitude, true airspeed, and other performance data.

pretend VFR. Defined by Vivion (2000): A situation in which the meteorological conditions meet the definition of "basic VFR" but conditions are such that there are too few visual references within the range of the prevailing visibility to keep the airplane upright by reference to a visual horizon, and to safely navigate.

resignation. The acceptance of something undesirable but inevitable. Identified by the FAA as a hazardous attitude for pilots.

retractable wheel skis. Aircraft skis added to existing wheels and brakes with the ability to retract and extend either by controls in the cockpit or manually on the ground.

reverse-direction winds. Winds blowing in the opposite direction from the prevailing upper winds. These winds are usually within 1000 feet of ground level.

risk management. The part of the decision-making process that relies on situational awareness, problem recognition, and good judgment to reduce risks associated with each flight.

risk orientation. A person's attitude toward risk and risk decisions.

rotor cloud. A closed, vertical circulation that develops in the lee of high mountain barriers or in the valley between two mountain ranges. Rotors are often associated with extreme turbulence and are often marked by a rotor cloud. Rotor clouds belong to the altocumulus lenticularis family.

safety orientation. A person's or company's attitude and training towards the safety environment.

sastrugi. Parallel wavelike ridges caused by winds on the surface of hard snow, especially in polar regions.

Sectional Aeronautical Chart. The primary navigational reference medium used by VFR pilots in the United States. The 1:500,000 scale Sectional Aeronautical Chart Series is designed for visual navigation of slow- to medium-speed aircraft.

self-confidence. A feeling of trust in one's abilities, qualities, and judgment.

service bulletin (SB). A notice to an aircraft operator from a manufacturer informing of a product improvement.

short takeoff and landing (STOL). STOL is an acronym for a short takeoff and landing aircraft. Many STOL-designed aircraft also feature various arrangements for use on runways with harsh conditions (such as high altitude or ice).

short-field operations. Procedures including short-field takeoff, maximum performance climb, and rejected takeoff procedures, as described in the FAA Airman Certification Standards.

situational altitude. Described by Baldwin (2010): the altitude above the ground level that permits maneuvering to a suitable landing site in the event of complete power loss.

situational awareness (SA). An accurate perception by pilots of the factors and conditions currently affecting the safe operation of the aircraft and the crew.

skeg (or wear strip). A device attached to the bottom of an airplane ski surface to prevent side slippage and wear. May be constructed of metal or UHMW.

skill. The ability to carry out a task with determined results often within a given amount of time, energy, or both.

slow flight. A portion of an airplane's performance envelope above the speed at which the airplane will stall, but below the aircraft's endurance speed.

soft-field takeoff. Used to obtain maximum performance when departing from a soft or rough runway surface. Also the best technique for high density altitude operations.

Spidertracks. A commercial satellite aircraft tracking device.

SPOT Satellite Messenger. A commercial personal locator device using GPS satellite and Globalstar networks to transmit messages and GPS coordinates to others, including an international rescue coordination center.

stabilized approach. A landing approach in which the pilot establishes and maintains a constant angle and airspeed that permits the airplane to reach the desired touchdown point at an airspeed that results in minimum floating just before touchdown. It is based on the pilot's judgment of certain visual cues and requires minimal changes to pitch and power.

stall fences. Small, chordwise plates that protrude from the upper wing surface and leading edge. Their purpose is to disrupt spanwise flow, shielding the outboard wing section from stalled airflow migrating outward from the inboard part of the wing.

standing lenticular clouds. *See* lenticular clouds.

standard operating procedures (SOPs). A set of step-by-step instructions compiled to help carry out complex, routine operations.

straight skis. Aircraft skis that replace the existing landing gear (wheels or floats). Also known as wheel replacement skis.

stratus cloud. From the Latin prefix "strato," meaning layer. May produce a light drizzle or a small amount of snow. These clouds are essentially above-ground fog formed either through the lifting of morning fog or through cold air moving at low altitudes over a region.

supplemental type certificate (STC). A national aviation authority-approved major modification or repair to an existing type certified aircraft, engine or propeller. Because it adds to the existing original type certificate for an aircraft, engine, or propeller, it is deemed "supplemental."

synthetic vision. An aircraft installation that combines three-dimensional data into intuitive displays to provide improved situational awareness by using terrain, obstacle, geo-political, hydrological and other databases. Typically uses databases stored on board the aircraft, an image generator computer, and a display. Navigation solutions are obtained through the use of GPS and inertial reference systems.

Temporary Flight Restrictions (TFRs). Specified areas of airspace where air travel is limited because of a temporary hazardous condition, such as a wildfire or chemical spill; a security-related event, such as the United Nations General Assembly; or other special situations. The text of the actual TFR contains the details about the restriction, including the size, altitude, time period that it is in effect, and what types of operations are restricted and permitted.

thermal lift. Columns of rising air that are formed on the ground through the warming of the surface by sunlight. Often used by raptors, vultures and storks, as well as sailplanes.

thrust. The force that moves an aircraft through the air. Thrust opposes drag.

thunderstorms. A storm with thunder and lightning and typically also heavy rain or hail. Associated with cumulonimbus clouds.

TIS-B. Traffic Information Services–Broadcast. Provides traffic information for aircraft with ADS-B In and ADS-B Out. TIS-B is an advisory-only service available to both 1090ES and UAT equipment users. TIS-B increases pilots' situational awareness by providing traffic information on all transponder-based aircraft within the vicinity of the ADS-B In equipped aircraft receiving the data.

Transport Canada. The department within the government of Canada that is responsible for developing regulations, policies, and services of transportation in Canada.

true airspeed (TAS). In low-speed flight typical of light airplanes, calibrated airspeed corrected for altitude and nonstandard temperature. Because air density decreases with an increase in altitude, an airplane has to be flown faster at higher altitudes to cause the same pressure difference between pitot impact pressure and static pressure. Therefore, for a given calibrated airspeed, true airspeed increases as altitude increases; or for a given true airspeed, calibrated airspeed decreases as altitude increases.

tundra tires. A large, low-pressure tire used on light aircraft to allow operations on rough terrain. A common variant of a tundra tire is the bushwheel. These tires include an integral inner tube with the valve manufactured into the sidewall, allowing the tire to operate at very low pressures without risking shearing-off the valve stem and causing a flat tire. Low-pressure tires provide greater cushioning and enable aircraft to land on rough surfaces unsuitable for normal tires. Bushwheels are a common modification for backcountry aircraft.

type certificate. Signifies the airworthiness of a particular category of aircraft, according to its manufacturing design (type).

ultra-high molecular weight (UHMW) plastic. Originally developed for the food industry, this product is now used on many aircraft ski bottoms because of its strength and slick surface.

universal access transceiver (UAT). A data link intended to serve the majority of the general aviation community. The data link is approved in the Federal Aviation Administration's "final rule" for use in all airspace except class A (above 18,000 feet MSL). UAT is intended to support not only ADS-B, but also flight information service–broadcast (FIS-B), traffic information service–broadcast (TIS-B), and, if required in the future, supplementary ranging and positioning capabilities.

venturi effect. The increase in air velocity through a constriction due to the pressure rise on the upwind side of the constriction and the pressure drop on the downwind side as the air diverges when leaving the constriction; also called the Bernoulli effect.

V_A. The calibrated design maneuvering airspeed. This is the maximum speed at which the limit load can be imposed (either by gusts or full deflection of the control surfaces) without causing structural damage. Operating at or below maneuvering speed does not provide structural protection against multiple full control inputs in one axis or full control inputs in more than one axis at the same time. It is important to consider weight when referencing this speed. For example, V_A may be 100 knots when an airplane is heavily loaded but only 90 knots when the load is light.

V_{CANYON}. Canyon speed. A speed determined by performing specific maneuvers as described in this text, usually in a gear down and partial flap configuration. V_{CANYON} is used to slow the aircraft for safe and easy maneuvering in confined areas.

V_{FE}. The highest speed permissible with the wing flaps in a prescribed extended position. This is because of the air loads imposed on the structure of the flaps. The upper limit of the white arc.

VFR Sectional Aeronautical Chart. Aeronautical chart used for visual navigation.

virga. An observable streak or shaft of precipitation falling from a cloud that evaporates or sublimates before reaching the ground.

visual flight rules (VFR). Rules that govern the procedures for conducting flight under visual conditions. The term "VFR" is also used in the United States to indicate weather conditions that are equal to or greater than minimum VFR requirements. In addition, it is used by pilots and controllers to indicate the type of flight plan.

visual meteorological conditions (VMC). An aviation flight category in which visual flight rules (VFR) flight is permitted—that is, conditions in which pilots have sufficient visibility to fly the aircraft maintaining visual separation from terrain and other aircraft. They are the opposite of instrument meteorological conditions (IMC). The boundary criteria between IMC and VMC are known as the VMC minima and are defined by visibility, cloud ceilings (for takeoffs and landings), and cloud clearances.

V_{LE}. The maximum speed at which the aircraft can be safely flown with the landing gear extended. This is a problem involving stability and controllability.

Vortac (VOR). A navigation aid providing VOR azimuth, TACAN azimuth, and TACAN distance measuring equipment (DME) at one site.

vortex generators (VGs). Small aluminum blades placed in a spanwise line aft of the leading edge of the wing and tail surfaces. VGs control airflow over the upper surface of the wing by creating vortices that energize the boundary layer. This results in improved performance and control authority at low airspeeds and high angles of attack.

V_{S0}. The calibrated power-off stalling speed or the minimum steady flight speed at which the aircraft is controllable in the landing configuration. The lower limit of the white arc.

V_X. Best angle of climb speed. The speed at which the aircraft obtains the highest altitude in a given horizontal distance. This best AOC speed normally increases slightly with altitude.

V_Y. Best rate of climb speed. The speed at which the aircraft obtains the maximum increase in altitude per unit of time. This best rate of climb speed normally decreases slightly with altitude.

wheel penetration skis. Aircraft skis that are added to standard landing gear (wheels, tires, and brakes).

Wide Area Augmentation System (WAAS). A method of navigation based on GPS. Ground correction stations transmit position corrections that enhance system accuracy and add vertical navigation (VNAV) features.

wind shear. Sometimes referred to as wind gradient; a difference in wind speed and/or direction over a relatively short distance in the atmosphere. Usually described as vertical or horizontal.

work. Done when a force that is applied to an object moves that object. The work is calculated by multiplying the force by the amount of movement of an object (W = F × distance).

XM Satellite Weather. Sirius XM Weather & Emergency was a free satellite radio channel dedicated to providing critical, updated information before, during and after natural disasters, weather emergencies and other hazardous incidents as well as amber alerts to listeners across North America. It was discontinued during November 2010. It is currently a commercial product that provides real-time weather to the cockpit for a paid subscription.

Glossary Sources:

Federal Aviation Administration (2019). *Aeronautical Information Manual.* Oklahoma City, OK: FAA.

Federal Aviation Administration (2016). *Airplane Flying Handbook*, FAA-H-8083-3B. Oklahoma City, OK: FAA.

Federal Aviation Administration (2016). *Pilot's Handbook of Aeronautical Knowledge*, FAA-H-8083-25B. Oklahoma City, OK: FAA.

Federal Aviation Administration (2019). *Pilot Controller Glossary.* Oklahoma City, OK: FAA.

Federal Aviation Regulations (2019). 14 CFR Part 1, Definitions and Abbreviations. Oklahoma City, OK: FAA.

Federal Aviation Administration (2008b). *On Landings Part II*. FAA-P-8740-12. AFS-8. Oklahoma City, OK. U.S. Federal Aviation Administration.

Garrison, P. (1979). The V-Speeds. *Flying Magazine*, 104(5), 50, May 1979. New York, NY, Fawcett Publications.

Hanselman, Galen (2015). *Fly Idaho*, Third edition. Hailey, ID: QEI Publishing.

Hoover, A. (1999). Flying a constricted approach. *Pilot Getaways*, 2(2), 54. Glendale, CA: Airventure Publishing.

Hoover, A. (2000). Go-arounds: making the decision. *Pilot Getaways*, 3(2), 54. Glendale, CA: Airventure Publishing.

Hoover, A. (2002) Uphill, downhill; airstrips with a gradient. *Pilot Getaways*, 5(2), 58. Glendale, CA: Airventure Publishing.

Imeson, S. (2005). *Mountain Flying Bible Revised*. Long Beach, CA: Airguide Publications, Inc.

Lester, P.F. (2013). *Aviation Weather*, 4th Edition. Englewood, CO: Jeppesen

National Transportation Safety Board (1999). NTSB Aviation Accident Final Report, Accident SEA00LA017. Seattle, WA: National Transportation Safety Board.

Porter, Jim (1986). *Flight Planning Simplified*. Azle, TX: Library of Congress No. TXu 258 893.

Potts, F.E. (1993). *Guide to Bush Flying*. Tucson, AZ: ACS Publishing.

Terry, Hal (2000). *Fly the Wild and Stay Alive*. Tucson, AZ: Terry Aviation Enterprises. Tucson, AZ.

Williams, R.K. (1986). *The Mountains to Canyons Flying Manual*. Boise, Idaho: Library of Congress No. TXu 301 630

Chapter 6

Federal Aviation Administration (2016). *Pilot's Handbook of Aeronautical Knowledge*, FAA-H-8083-25B. Oklahoma City, OK: FAA.

Garrison, Peter (2015). Tabulating Takeoff. *Flying Magazine*, February 25, 2015. Winter Park, FL: Bonnier Corporation. Accessed 2/14/2019 https://www.flyingmag.com/technique/proficiency/tabulating-takeoff

Hanselman, Galen (2015). *Fly Idaho*, Third edition. Hailey, ID: QEI Publishing.

Hoover, A. L. (2001). Soft, hot, & high takeoffs: It's a different game at high density altitude. *Pilot Getaways*, 4(2), 58. Glendale, CA: Airventure Publishing.

Hoover, A. (2002). Uphill, downhill; airstrips with a gradient. *Pilot Getaways*, 5(2), 58. Glendale, CA: Airventure Publishing.

Imeson, Sparky (2005). *Mountain Flying Bible Revised*. Long Beach, CA: Airguide Publications, Inc.

Porter, Jim (1986). *Flight Planning Simplified*. Azle, TX: Library of Congress No. TXu 258 893.

Potts, F.E. (1993). *Guide to Bush Flying*. Tucson, AZ: ACS Publishing.

Chapter 7

Claus, Paul (2018). Personal communication, via Skype, 2/7/2018.

Dorris, Mike (2018). Personal communication, live interviews, 3/14/2018; 4/12/2018.

Geeting, Doug & Woerner, Steve (1988). *Mountain Flying*. Blue Ridge Summit, PA: Tab Books.

Holm, Richard H. Jr. (2013). *Bound for the Backcountry: A History of Idaho's Remote Airstrips*. McCall, ID: Cold Mountain Press.

National Transportation Safety Board (2009a). NTSB Aviation Accident Final Report, Accident CEN09CA210. Denver, CO: National Transportation Safety Board.

National Transportation Safety Board (2009b). NTSB Aviation Accident Final Report, Accident ANC09CA027. Anchorage, AK: National Transportation Safety Board.

National Transportation Safety Board (2017a). NTSB Aviation Accident Final Report, Accident GAA17CA187. Anchorage, AK: National Transportation Safety Board.

National Transportation Safety Board (2017b). NTSB Aviation Accident Final Report, Accident GAA17CA294. Anchorage, AK: National Transportation Safety Board.

Potts, F.E. (1993). *Guide to Bush Flying*. Tucson, AZ: ACS Publishing.

Terry, Hal (2000). *Fly the Wild and Stay Alive*. Tucson, AZ: Terry Aviation Enterprises. Tucson, AZ.

Chapter 8

Claus, P. (2018). Personal communication, via Skype, 2/7/2018.

Federal Aviation Administration (2008). *Density Altitude*. FAA Safety Team publication FAA–P–8740–2, AFS–8. Accessed 2/14/2019 at www.faasafety. gov/files/gslac/library/documents/2011/Aug/56396/FAA%20P-8740-02%20 DensityAltitude%5Bhi-res%5D%20branded.pdf

Federal Aviation Administration (2015). *Amateur-Built Aircraft and Ultralight Flight Testing Handbook*. Advisory Circular 90-89B. Accessed 2/14/2019 at www.faa. gov/documentLibrary/media/Advisory_Circular/AC_90-89B.pdf

Federal Aviation Administration (2016d). *Pilot's Handbook of Aeronautical Knowledge*. FAA-H-8083-25B. Oklahoma City, OK: FAA.

Hoover, A. (1999). How to lighten up: understanding density altitude. *Pilot Getaways*, 2(3), 45–46. Glendale, CA: Airventure Publishing.

Hoover, A. L. (2001). Soft, hot, & high takeoffs: it's a different game at high density altitude. *Pilot Getaways*, 4(2), 58. Glendale, CA: Airventure Publishing.

Imeson, Sparky (2005). *Mountain Flying Bible Revised*. Long Beach, CA: Airguide Publications, Inc.

Lowry, John T. (1999). *Computing Airplane Performance with The Bootstrap Approach: A Field Guide*. Missoula, MT: M Press.

Machado, Rod (2017). *Leaning the Mixture for a High Density Altitude Takeoff*. Rod Machado's eLearning center. Accessed 2/14/2019 at https://www.youtube.com/watch?v=eBUfWI4C6sE

National Transportation Safety Board (2013). NTSB Aviation Accident Final Report, Accident WPR12LA283. Seattle, WA: NTSB.

Pope, Stephen (2015). Leaning While Taxiing: How to prevent spark plug fouling during taxi. *Flying Magazine*, April 28, 2015. Winter Park, FL: Bonnier Corporation. Accessed 2/12/2019 at www.flyingmag.com/technique/tip-week/leaning-while-taxiing

Porter, Jim (1986). *Flight Planning Simplified*. Azle, TX: Library of Congress No. TXu 258 893.

Smith, H.C. (1992) *The Illustrated Guide to Aerodynamics*, 2nd Edition. Blue Ridge Summit, PA: Tab Books McGraw-Hill.

Williams, R.K. (1986). *The Mountains to Canyons Flying Manual*. Boise, Idaho: TXu 301 630

Williams, R.K. (2015). *Notes from the Cockpit: A Mountain Pilot's Perspective*. Salmon, ID: Williams Summit Publishers.

Chapter 9

Aarons, R.N. (1991). Egomaniacal Pilots. *Business and Commercial Aviation*, December 1991, 112. Washington, D.C.: Aviation Week and Space Technology.

Aircraft Owners and Pilots Association Air Safety Institute (2017). *26th Joseph T. Nall Report*. Frederick, Maryland: Aircraft Owners and Pilots Association Air Safety Institute.

Chou, C.D., Madhavan, D., & Funk, K.H. (1996). Studies of cockpit task management errors. *International Journal of Aviation Psychology*, 6(4), 307–320.

Christensen, Loren W., Grossman, Dave, & Asken, Michael J. (2010). *Warrior Mindset: Mental Toughness Skills for a Nation's Peacekeepers*. Jonesboro, AR: Warrior Science Group.

Civil Aviation Authority of New Zealand (2012). *Mountain Flying*. Wellington, New Zealand.

Civil Aviation Medical Institute (2011). *Basic Survival Skills for Aviation*. Oklahoma City, OK: Federal Aviation Administration Office of Aerospace Medicine. Accessed 2/14/2019 at www.faa.gov/pilots/training/airman_education/media/CAMISurvivalManual.pdf

Clark, I.E. (1991). *Backcountry Flying Instructional Video*. McCall, ID: Lyn's Flight Instruction, Inc.

Cullen, S.A. (2005). *Mechanisms of Injury in Aircraft Accidents*. Buckingham, UK: North Atlantic Treaty Organization Report RTO-EN-HFM-113.

Diehl, Alan E. & Lester, Lewis F. (1987). *Private Pilot Judgment Training in Fight School Settings*. Report DOT/FAA/AM-87/6. Washington D.C.: U.S. Government Printing Office.

Federal Aviation Administration (n.d.). *Introduction to Aviation Physiology*. Oklahoma City, OK: Aeromedical Education Division. Accessed 2/14/2019 at www.faa.gov/pilots/training/airman_education/media/IntroAviationPhys.pdf

Federal Aviation Administration (2001). *Aeronautical Decision Making*, Advisory Circular 60-22. Washington D.C.: U.S. Government Printing Office.

Federal Aviation Administration (2009). *Risk Management Handbook*, FAA-H-8083-2. Washington D.C.: U.S. Government Printing Office.

Federal Aviation Administration (2016d). *Pilot's Handbook of Aeronautical Knowledge*, Chapter 2: Aeronautical Decision Making. FAA-H-8083. Washington D.C.: U.S. Government Printing Office.

Federal Aviation Administration (2018). *Aeronautical Information Manual, section 8-1-4 Fitness for Flight*. Washington D.C.: U.S. Government Printing Office.

Federal Aviation Administration, Transport Canada, General Aviation Manufacturer's Association (1986). *Judgment Training Manual for Student Pilots*. Accessed 2/14/2019 at www.avhf.com/html/Library/Judgment_Training_Manual_for_Student_Pilots.pdf

Funk, K. H., Colvin, K., Bishara, S., Nicolalde, J., Shakeri, S., Chen, J. Y., & Braune, R. (2003). Training pilots to prioritize tasks: Theoretical foundations and preliminary experiments. NASA Grant NAG 2-1287 Final Report. Corvallis, Oregon.

Garrison, Peter (2011). Technicalities: Hypoxia at Your Fingertips. *Flying Magazine*, Winter Park, FL: Bonnier Corporation. Accessed 2/14/2019 at www.flyingmag.com/technique/proficiency/technicalities-hypoxia-your-fingertips

Hoover, A.L. (2008). Long Term Effect of Concurrent Task Management Training on Single Pilot Task Prioritization Performance. *International Journal of Applied Aviation Studies, 8*(1), 12–19. Oklahoma City: FAA.

Hoover, A.L. & Russ-Eft, D.F. (2005). Effect of Concurrent Task Management Training on Single Pilot Task Prioritization Performance. *International Journal of Applied Aviation Studies, 5*(2), 233–252. Oklahoma City: FAA.

Hunter, David R. (2004). Measurement of Hazardous Attitudes Among Pilots. *The International Journal of Aviation Psychology, 15*(1), 23–43. Hillsdale, NJ: Lawrence Erlbaum Associates, Inc.

Hunter, David R. (2006). Risk Perception Among General Aviation Pilots. *The International Journal of Aviation Psychology, 16*(2), 135–144. Hillsdale, NJ: Lawrence Erlbaum Associates, Inc.

International Civil Aviation Organization (1989). Fundamental Human Factors Concepts. *Human Factors Digest No. 1*, Circular 216-AN/131. Montreal, Canada: International Civil Aviation Organization.

International Civil Aviation Organization (1993). Human Factors, Management and Organization. *Human Factors Digest No. 10*, Circular 247-AN/148. Montreal, Canada: International Civil Aviation Organization.

Irving, Janis L. (1972). *Victims of Groupthink*. New York: Houghton Mifflin.

Littel, Justin D. (2015). Crash Tests of Three Cessna 172 Aircraft at NASA Langley Research Center's Landing and Impact Research Facility. NASA/TM–2015-218987. Hampton, Virginia: Langley Research Center.

Moran, Katherine (2015). Aircraft Accident Investigation Massive Open Online Course (MOOC). Embry Riddle Aeronautical University. Accessed 2/14/2019 at https://learn.canvas.net/courses/549

National Transportation Safety Board (2016a). Aviation Accident Final Report: American Champion Aircraft 7GCBC Midair Collision on 07/07/2014. Accessed 2/14/2019 at https://app.ntsb.gov/pdfgenerator/ReportGeneratorFile. ashx?EventID=20140707X70004&AKey=1&RType=Final&IType=FA

National Transportation Safety Board (2016b). Aviation Accident Final Report: Cessna R172K Midair Collision on 07/07/2014. Accessed 2/14/2019 at https://app.ntsb.gov/pdfgenerator/ReportGeneratorFile. ashx?EventID=20140707X70004&AKey=2&RType=Final&IType=FA

National Transportation Safety Board (2016c). Aviation Accident Public Docket, Accident WPR14FA283A on Date July 7, 2014. Accessed 2/14/2019 at http://dms. ntsb.gov/pubdms/search/dockList.cfm?mKey=89618

Parfit, Michael (1977). Flying Idaho's Back Country. *Private Pilot Magazine*, November 1977.

Schunk, Dale H. (2015). *Learning Theories: An Educational Perspective* (7th Edition). London, United Kingdom: Pearson Publishing.

Shanahan, Dennis F. (2005). Human Tolerance and Crash Survivability. North Atlantic Treaty Organization Science and Technology Organization, Open Access Forum. Accessed 2/14/2019 at https://www.sto.nato.int/publications

Smith, Steve (1979). *Fly the Biggest Piece Back*. Missoula, MT: Mountain Press.

Stinson, Chad M., Littell, Justin D., Mazzuca, Lisa M., Foster, Anthony W., & Theodorakos, George J. (2017). Emergency Locator Transmitter Survivability and Reliability Study. NASA/TM–2017-219584. Hampton, Virginia: Langley Research Center, National Aeronautics and Space Administration.

Tolleson, Terry (2007). The Curse of Complacency. *Aviation Maintenance Technology Magazine*, 9/19/2007. Fort Atkinson, WI: Aviation Pros.

United States Air Force (2008). *US Air Force Survival Manual*. Spokane, WA: Skyhorse Publishing.

Wickens, C. D. (2002). Situation awareness and workload in aviation. *Current Directions in Psychological Science*, 11(4), 128–133.

Wilson, Dale, & Binnema, Gerald (2014). *Managing Risk: Best Practices for Pilots*. Newcastle, WA: Aviation Supplies and Academics.

Young, J.W. (1966). Recommendations for restraint installation in general aviation aircraft. Report AM 66-33. Federal Aviation Agency, Oklahoma City, Oklahoma.

INDEX

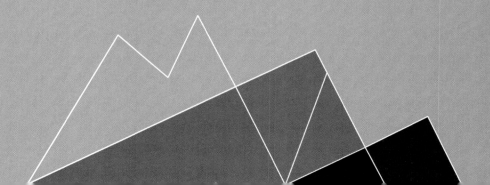

A

abort planning, *137, 140, 141–146, 178–179, 181–182, 193, 194, 197, 253, 266, 268*
absolute altitude, *245*
ADS-B In, *74–75, 77*
ADS-B Out, *74–75*
advisory circular (AC), *30, 249*
aeronautical decision making (ADM), *272, 275–281*
Aeronautical Information Manual (AIM), *56*
AeroWeather, *31*
Aircraft Owners and Pilots Association (AOPA), *4, 314*
airframe icing, *206*
Airframes Alaska, *18*
airport environment, *136–141*
airspeeds, *8, 97*
airstrips
  evaluating, *18, 34, 118, 136–141, 147–153*
  landing surface, *147–149*
  one-way, *53, 120, 141, 144, 146, 148, 150, 155, 158, 159, 169, 175, 190*
  shape and width, *150–152*
  sloped, *158–169, 192–199*
air traffic control (ATC), *74–76*
airworthiness directive (AD), *17*
Alaska, *31, 44, 75, 76, 109, 128, 205, 207, 215, 221, 224, 232, 234, 288*
Alaska Paracord bracelet, *296–297*
Alaska Range, *34, 44*
Alaska Tundra Tires, *17, 18*
altimeter settings, *50, 86*
altitude chamber, *273*
American Champion, *12, 13, 209, 281, 300*
anabatic lift, *40–42*
Anderson, Fletcher, *xix, 30, 32, 44, 88, 103*
angle of attack (AOA), *18, 256*
  during approach and landing, *127, 128*
  during climb, *257*
  during go-arounds, *145*
  during takeoffs, *180*
  effects of aircraft loading on, *11*
anti-authority, *276*
approach and landing, *117–175. See also* go-arounds; abort planning; precautionary landings; forced landings
  aim point technique, *130–133, 305*
  airspeed, *122–125, 127*

  descent angle, *120–122, 125–130, 164*
  descent rate, *129–130, 157*
  in ski flying, *225–229*
  on sloped airstrips, *158–169*
  power, *122–125, 127*
  stabilized approach, *120–136*
  touchdown and rollout, *140, 170, 226*
  with wind, *152–158*
Arnold, Ray, *78*
attitude (psychology), *272, 275–279, 294, 306*
Automated Flight Service Station (AFSS), *31*
Automated Surface Observing System (ASOS), *37, 245*
Automated Weather Observing System (AWOS), *37, 245*
Automatic Dependent Surveillance–Broadcast (ADS-B), *32, 74–75, 205. See also* ADS-B In, ADS-B Out
automatic direction finder (ADF), *71*
Aviate, Navigate, Communicate (ANC), *281, 291, 293, 305*
Aviat Husky, *12, 104, 113, 209, 214*

B

Baldwin, C.J., *xix, 87, 91, 104, 108*
bank angle, *94–109*
Bellanca, *209*
best angle of climb speed. *See* V_X
best rate of climb speed. *See* V_Y
Boone, Daniel, *86*
box canyon, *68, 78–79, 102, 260*
brakes, *17–19, 170, 173, 212*
British Columbia, *287*
Britten-Norman, *11, 12*

C

calibrated airspeed (CAS), *123*
California, *41, 269*
Canada, *75, 234. See also* Transport Canada; Transportation Safety Board of Canada; Natural Resources Canada
Canada VFR Navigation Chart, *61*
canards, *12*
canyons, flying in, *92–94*
canyon speed. *See* V_{CANYON}
cap clouds, *35, 41*
carburetor icing, *286–287, 291*
Cascade Mountains, *32, 34, 35, 41, 46–47, 51–52*

Index **367**

center of gravity (CG), *5, 8–9, 11, 97, 123–125, 134, 248, 251–252*

Cernan, Eugene, *284*

Cessna, *11, 26, 170, 190, 197, 207, 209*
 120, *260*
 170, *209, 236*
 172, *250*
 177, *261*
 180, *22, 46, 113, 233*
 182, *8, 10, 12, 17, 62, 124–125, 129, 253, 258–259, 262*
 185, *17, 76, 90, 109, 145, 198, 212, 213, 221, 230, 233, 234, 235, 236, 250*
 206, *12, 112–113, 148, 186–187, 198–199, 208, 230, 253*
 210, *12, 184*
 337, *25*
 Hawk XP, *300*

Champion, *209*

Chart Supplement U.S., *55*

checklist, *14*
 emergency, *287*
 preflight, *23*
 pre-landing, *137, 263*
 pre-takeoff, *178–179*

cirrus clouds, *35*

Citabria, *300–322*

Civil Aviation Authority of New Zealand, *4, 38, 61, 89, 275*

Claus, Paul, *xii, 18, 122, 128, 204, 230–234, 236, 252*

cloud types, *36*

Colorado, *32, 44*

Columbia River Gorge, *51–52, 289*

confluences, *48–49, 53*

controlled flight into terrain (CFIT), *74*

convergence effects, *48, 153, 188*

crevasses, *230–231, 233–234*

crosswind, *12, 101, 158, 170, 191*

cruise climbs, *67, 86, 112–113, 183, 258*

cumulonimbus clouds, *36*

Curtiss, Glenn, *40, 178*

D

dead reckoning, *64, 66, 71*

de Havilland, *ix, 11, 12, 113, 192, 207, 209, 232, 233, 288, 300, 309*

Dempsey Dumpster, *289*

Denalt computer, *246*

density altitude (DA), *5, 272, 275*
 effects of, on aircraft performance, *8, 67, 101, 205, 244–270*
 effects on engine power, *249–252*
 effects on landing, *120*
 effects on takeoff, *178–179*
 in cold weather, *205, 234*

descent rate, *129, 156–157, 169*

dispatching, *75–77*

diurnal winds, *46–48*

diversions, *70, 285–290*

Doppler weather radar, *31, 206*

Dorris, Bill, *278*

Dorris, Mike, *xii, 204, 234*

drag, *10, 11, 90, 104, 122, 126–128, 148, 161, 175, 184, 192, 236, 250, 255–258*
 in snow, *208–209, 213, 227, 229–230*

drag-and-drop approach, *128*

drooping ailerons or wingtips, *12*

Dutch roll coordination exercise, *6–7, 134*

E

electronic flight instrument system (EFIS), *64*

emergencies, *15, 284–322*

emergency landing, *8, 92, 140, 182, 184, 287–294, 306–315, 317*

emergency locator transmitter (ELT), *20, 285, 293, 295, 306, 308*

emergency turns, *102–104*

engine failure, *15, 140, 183, 286, 290*

engine maintenance and inspection, *15*

engine preheat, *204, 218*

excess thrust, *256–257*

exhaust gas temperature (EGT), *263*

F

F. Atlee Dodge, *215, 252*

Federal Aviation Administration (FAA), *4, 31, 249, 294, 315*

first aid kit, *294, 296, 299*

fixed-base operator (FBO), *76*

flat light, *220–221, 233, 237, 238*

flight etiquette, *281–284*

flight following, *75–77*

flight plan, *64, 76*

flight planning, *60–80*

flight safety, *281–284*

flow check, *292*

FltPlan Go, *64, 65*

Fluidyne, *213, 215, 235*
fog, *30, 31, 37, 41, 206, 223, 285*
forced landings, *291–293*
ForeFlight Mobile, *31, 64, 65, 73, 76*
Found Bush Hawk, *300*
fuel planning and management, *14, 66, 70, 173, 212, 264–265, 279*
fuel strainer, *16*

G
Gann, Ernest, *61*
gap seals, *12*
Garmin InReach, *77, 296*
Garmin Pilot, *31, 64*
Geeting, Doug, *xix, 103, 222, 234*
general aviation accidents, *30, 293*
general aviation (GA) aircraft, *10, 11, 97*
glacier flying, *230–234*
G-load, *54, 98, 102–103*
Global Positioning System (GPS), *64, 70–74, 78, 129, 160. See also* GPS trackers
go-arounds, *51, 137, 141–146, 168, 169, 170, 175, 234*
Goodyear, *18, 179, 307*
GPS trackers, *77*
Grand Tetons, *90*
ground-based transmitters (GBTs), *74*
ground loop, *12, 145, 170*
ground operations, *171–173*
ground speed (GS), *101, 103, 129, 157, 178, 244, 252*
groupthink, *280*

H
Hanks, Ron, *xii, 288*
Hannah, Bob, *327*
Hanselman, Galen, *158, 159, 162, 186, 193*
hazardous attitudes, *272, 276–278*
haze, *39, 44*
headwind, *101, 153–156, 169, 188–190, 197, 198, 199, 266–267*
Holm, Richard H., Jr., *xii, 237*
Hoover, Bob, *327, 329*
human factors, *274–281, 302*
hyperventilation, *274*
hypoxia, *273–274, 280, 284, 286*

I
Idaho, *14, 22, 24, 33, 41, 62, 72, 78, 90, 186–187, 192, 198–201, 234, 260–261, 277, 278, 288, 300*
IFR chart, *31, 64*

Imeson, Sparky, *xix, 88, 91–92, 102, 103, 113–116, 125, 181, 182, 259*
impulsivity, *276, 277*
indicated airspeed (IAS), *5, 8, 10, 123, 178, 252*
indicated altitude, *245*
instrument meteorological conditions (IMC), *36, 285*
International Civil Aviation Organization (ICAO), *272, 274*
invulnerability, *18, 276, 277*

J
Jarvis, Carol, *5, 72–73, 101*

K
Kantorowicz, J.C., *113–116*
Katmai, *12, 17*
Kern, Tony, *60*
Koch Chart, *246*
Kounis, John, *198–199*

L
Landes Airglas, *215*
landing. *See* approach and landing
landing gear, *10, 17–19, 171, 173, 204–205, 210–214, 228. See also* skis
landing surface, *137, 147–149, 226*
Langewiesche, Wolfgang, *11*
Larkin, James, *viii*
leading-edge wing cuffs, *12*
leaning fuel/air mixture, *263–265*
lenticular clouds, *35*
limit load factor, *10, 36, 97, 104*
Lindbergh, Charles A., *70*
load factor, *94–96, 98*
loading, aircraft, *5, 8, 11, 124, 248–255*
LORAN, *62, 260*
low-level maneuvering, *104–111*

M
Machado, Rod, *x–xi, 5–6, 30, 264, 284*
macho, *276*
MacPherson, Jeanne, *xii, 281–284*
mammatus clouds, *36*
maneuvering. *See* low-level maneuvering
maneuvering speed. *See* V_A
maneuvers, practicing, *5*
manifold pressure (MP), *130, 249, 250*
Maule, *12, 209*

maximum flap extended speed. *See* V_{FE}
maximum gear extended speed. *See* V_{LE}
maximum performance takeoffs, *8, 181*
meteorology, *30–56*
microbursts, *36, 48, 50*
minimum controllable airspeed (MCA), *5, 125, 127*
minimum en route altitude (MEA), *64, 285*
Mode S transponder-based 1090 extended squitter (ES), *74*
Montana, *41, 113, 205, 276, 281*
moose stall, *104, 109–111*
moraines, *231*
most conservative response, *280, 290*
mountain waves, *31, 32, 34–36, 54–56*
mountain winds, *33–36*

N

National Oceanic and Atmospheric Administration (NOAA), *31, 308*
National Transportation Safety Board (NTSB), *25, 54–56, 78, 113–115, 145, 174–175, 201, 238–239, 261, 265–266, 268, 314–322*
Natural Resources Canada, *62*
navigation, *60–80*
    software and apps, *64–65*
New Mexico, *54*
New Zealand, *34*
nimbostratus clouds, *36*
non-directional beacon (NDB), *64, 71*
Northern Companion, *218*
Notice to Airmen (NOTAM), *31*

O

obscurations to visibility, *205, 206*
offset navigation, *66*
Oregon, *51, 145, 173–174, 289*
orographic downdrafts, *188–189*
orographic lift, *40, 41–43, 53, 91, 113, 138, 183*
overflow, *222–224, 225, 226, 236, 239*

P

performance, aircraft, *244–270*
    climb, *255–261*
    landing, *262*
    takeoff, *252–255*
personal locator beacon (PLB), *20, 285, 293, 294, 295, 306, 308, 309*

physiological deficient zone, *272*
physiological efficient zone, *272*
pilotage, *64, 66, 71, 72–74, 79*
pilot judgment, *115, 238, 255, 266, 272, 275–279, 281*
pilot report (PIREP), *31–32*
pilot's operating handbook (POH), *123–125, 136, 180, 244*
Piper Cub, *204, 209, 235*
Piper Super Cub, *11, 13, 124, 142, 210, 214*
PIREP. *See* pilot report
pitch attitude, *8–9, 87, 134–135, 146, 153, 170, 175, 180–181, 184, 255, 258*
pitot tube, *19*
point of no return, *92, 183*
Porter, Jim, *112, 153, 160, 170, 190, 244, 260*
post-flight inspection, *20, 22–24, 173*
Potts, F.E., *xix, 30, 118, 121, 140, 180, 181, 182–183, 238*
power, *256*
power loading, *250–252*
power-off glides, *8, 305*
power settings, *5, 8, 97, 121–122, 127, 130, 134, 283, 287*
precautionary landing, *235, 285, 290–291*
preflight inspection, *15–20, 22–24*
preflight planning, *17, 30, 60, 141, 163, 259*
pressure altitude (PA), *245, 246–247, 273*
pretend VFR (PVFR), *39*

R

Reed, John, *xii, 112–113*
region of reversed command, *127–128*
Reitsch, Hanna, *275*
resignation, *276*
reverse-direction winds, *44–45*
ridges, crossing, *34, 88–90*
risk management, *272–299*
risk orientation, *278*
Rocky Mountains, *32, 34, 41, 44, 234–237*
Rosen, *21*
rotor clouds, *35*
route selection, *66–70*

S

safety orientation, *278*
sastrugi, *231*
satellite phone, *32, 77, 285, 286, 294, 295, 296, 308*
Scout, *13, 300*

self-confidence, *278*

service bulletins, *17*

Seuss, Dr., *30*

short-field operations, *8, 12, 124, 179–180, 282*

short takeoff and landing (STOL), *124, 128*
  components, *12, 180, 247–248*

Sierra Nevada, *32, 34, 41*

signaling devices, *294, 295, 297*

situational altitude, *91*

situational awareness (SA), *4–5, 60, 63, 64, 71, 91, 104, 136, 272, 280, 282, 304*

skeg, *216*

ski-equipped airplanes, *207–219*

ski flying, *204–240. See also* glacier flying
  equipment, *217–218*
  in Rocky Mountains, *234–237*
  landing, *225–229, 236–237*
  site evaluation, *220, 225–227*
  takeoff, *229–230, 236*
  taxiing, *224–225, 235*
  touching down, *228–229*
  turning around, *235*
  weather considerations, *205–207*

skis
  manufacturing materials, *215–216*
  nose wheel, *217*
  retractable wheel, *209, 213–214, 215, 229, 235*
  straight, *209, 215*
  tail, *216–217*
  wheel penetration, *209, 212–213, 215*

Skunberg, Lenny, *xiii, 14–23*

slips, *136*

slow flight, *5*

smoke, *33, 39*

soft-field operations, *8, 170, 179–180, 230, 282*

solar lift, *40*

Spidertracks, *77*

SPOT Satellite Messenger, *77, 296*

stabilized approach. *See* approach and landing

stall fences, *12*

standard operating procedures (SOPs), *279–281*

standing lenticular clouds, *35, 55*

Stinson, *265–268, 289*

Stockhill, Michael L., *xiii, 26, 33, 330*

Stowell, Rich, *6–7, 107, 281*

stratus clouds, *36*

supplemental type certificate (STC), *208*

survival kit, *217, 296–299*

survival, post-crash, *115, 292, 294–295, 308*

survival vest, *115, 218, 281, 295–296, 308, 312*

Switzerland, *219*

synthetic vision displays, *64–65, 74*

T

tailwind, *46–47, 50, 101, 141, 153, 156–157, 169, 175, 188, 190, 192–193, 197, 198–199, 230*

takeoff and departure, *178–202*
  abort planning, *181–182*
  effect of surface conditions on, *182–183*
  on sloped airstrips, *192–199*
  with wind, *188–193, 197–199*

taxiing, *171–173, 179, 263, 282–283*
  in ski planes, *224–225, 235, 236, 238*

Taylorcraft, *209*

Temporary Flight Restriction (TFR), *64*

terrain flying, *90–92*

Terry, Hal, *xix, 15, 122–123, 125, 128, 231, 234*

thermal lift, *33, 40–42, 45, 53, 62, 91, 113, 114, 142, 183*

thrust, *245, 256*
  in approach and landing, *126, 161, 170*
  in ski flying, *208, 229–230*

thrust horsepower (THP), *249, 250*

thunderstorms, *31, 36, 50, 60, 205, 279, 285*

tires, *17–19, 21, 173, 212–214*

tool kit, *21*

tracking devices, *77, 295, 296*

Traffic Information Services-Broadcast (TIS-B), *74*

Transportation Safety Board of Canada, *86, 102, 104*

Transport Canada, *4, 276*

Tremblay, Ray, *217–218*

tricycle-gear aircraft, *12, 18, 170, 172, 180, 207, 217, 230*

true airspeed (TAS), *101, 129, 178, 244*

true altitude, *245*

tundra tires, *17, 18*

turbulence, *32–35, 36, 41, 42–44, 48–50, 52, 53–54, 66–67, 73, 92, 113, 206*
  during approach and landing, *121, 122, 124, 128, 153–154, 169, 226*
  during takeoff and departure, *183, 184, 186, 197*

turn-around point, *91–92, 102*

turn radius, *5, 94–98, 97–102*
turns
    airspeed in, *97–102*
    emergency, *102–104*
    medium-bank, *94–96*
type certificate, *208, 209*

U

ultra-high molecular weight (UHMW) plastic, *216*
United States, *36, 75, 91, 104, 159, 207, 214, 244, 274, 293, 294*
universal access transceiver (UAT), *74*
U.S. Geological Survey, *62*

V

V_A (maneuvering speed), *5–10, 36, 90, 97, 103, 184*
Vantage Plane Plastics, *21*
V_{CANYON} (canyon speed), *9, 10, 97, 134–135, 136*
venturi effect, *46, 51–56, 153*
V_{FE} (maximum flap extended speed), *5, 9, 10, 97, 103*
VFR sectional aeronautical chart, *54, 60, 62, 68, 78, 199, 269*
virga, *36, 45*
visibility, *30, 32, 36, 37, 39, 206. See also* obscurations to visibility
    in approaches, *121, 125–126, 128*
    in cruise climbs, *112, 183*
    in ski flying, *220–221*
visual flight rules (VFR), *64, 72–73, 91*
visual illusions, *86, 104–108, 112, 164, 166, 168*
visual meteorological conditions (VMC), *36–37, 39, 273*
Vivion, Michael, *xiii, 12, 32, 39, 76, 104, 109–111, 204–234, 236*

V_{LE} (maximum gear extended speed), *5, 10*
Vortac (VOR), *64, 71*
vortex generators (VGs), *12–13, 248*
V_{SO} (calibrated power-off stall speed), *123–125, 129*
V_X (best angle of climb speed), *146, 175, 181, 183–185, 258–259*
V_Y (best rate of climb speed), *36, 103, 112, 146, 183–185, 258–259*

W

Washington, *35, 46, 51*
wear strip. *See* skeg
weather, *29. See also* fog; mountain winds; cloud types; smoke; haze
    for ski flying, *205–207*
    information sources, *31–32*
wheel replacement skis. *See* skis, straight
Wide Area Augmentation System (WAAS), *74*
Williams, Alden, *233*
windscreen, *20, 139*
wind shear, *31, 41, 43, 48, 50–53, 55, 90, 92, 258*
    on approach and landing, *121, 125, 126, 128, 132, 138, 153, 154, 168, 169*
    on takeoff and departure, *183, 184, 188–189, 191, 197*
Woerner, Steve, *xix, 103, 222, 234*
work, *256*
Wright, Wilbur, *4, 272*
Wyoming, *90, 288*

X

XM Satellite Weather, *32, 206, 207*